Utopia and Its Discontents

Utopia and Its Discontents

Plato to Atwood

Sebastian Mitchell

BLOOMSBURY ACADEMIC
LONDON • NEW YORK • OXFORD • NEW DELHI • SYDNEY

BLOOMSBURY ACADEMIC
Bloomsbury Publishing Plc
50 Bedford Square, London, WC1B 3DP, UK
1385 Broadway, New York, NY 10018, USA
29 Earlsfort Terrace, Dublin 2, Ireland

BLOOMSBURY, BLOOMSBURY ACADEMIC and the Diana logo are trademarks of Bloomsbury Publishing Plc

First published in Great Britain 2020
This paperback edition published 2022

Copyright © Sebastian Mitchell, 2020

Sebastian Mitchell has asserted his right under the Copyright, Designs and Patents Act, 1988, to be identified as Author of this work.

The quotation from Wallace Stevens in Chapter Seven is used with permission: 'The Poems of Our Climate', from *The Collected Poems of Wallace Stevens*, copyright © 1954 by Wallace Stevens and copyright renewed 1982 by Holly Stevens. Used by permission of Alfred A. Knopf, an imprint of Knopf Doubleday Publishing Group, a division of Penguin Random House LLC. All rights reserved.

Cover design by Jason Anscomb | Rawshock Design
Illustration © Cristophe Dessaigne

All rights reserved. No part of this publication may be reproduced or transmitted in any form or by any means, electronic or mechanical, including photocopying, recording, or any information storage or retrieval system, without prior permission in writing from the publishers.

Bloomsbury Publishing Plc does not have any control over, or responsibility for, any third-party websites referred to or in this book. All internet addresses given in this book were correct at the time of going to press. The author and publisher regret any inconvenience caused if addresses have changed or sites have ceased to exist, but can accept no responsibility for any such changes.

A catalogue record for this book is available from the British Library.

A catalog record for this book is available from the Library of Congress.

ISBN: HB: 978-1-4411-9525-8
       PB: 978-1-4411-0963-7
     ePDF: 978-1-4411-3633-6
    eBook: 978-1-4411-7218-1

Typeset by RefineCatch Limited, Bungay, Suffolk

To find out more about our authors and books visit www.bloomsbury.com and sign up for our newsletters.

For Rachel, Alasdair, Phoebe and Connie

Contents

List of Illustrations	viii
Acknowledgements	ix
Introduction	1
1 Plato versus Plato: Art and Idealism	11
2 Oxymorus: Thomas More and Utopia	37
3 Hippophilia: Swift, Kant, and Eighteenth-Century Utopia	63
4 The Machine Age: Carlyle to Morris	93
5 English Triptych: Wells, Huxley, Orwell	123
6 Post-Utopia: America in the 1970s	157
7 Atwood's Scar; or, the Origins of Ustopia	185
Conclusion: The Utopian Prospect	217
Bibliography	229
Index	245

Illustrations

2.1 Hans Holbein the Younger, *Portrait of Sir Thomas More*, 1527, oil on oak, 74.2 cm x 59 cm, The Frick Collection, New York, Copyright The Frick Collection.   39

2.2 Hans Holbein the Younger, *Preparatory Drawing for the Family Portrait of Thomas More,* 1527, pen and brush over chalk outline on Japanese paper, 38.9 cm x 52.4 cm, Kunstmuseum, Basel.   43

7.1 Johannes Vermeer, *The Milkmaid, c.* 1660, oil on canvas, 45.5 cm x 41 cm, Rijksmuseum, Amsterdam.   193

7.2 Kelly McGillis as Rachel Haas, *Witness*, 1985, film still, film directed by Peter Weir, © Paramount Pictures, All Rights Reserved.   194

also been interested in how such idealistic considerations suffuse works by the same authors which are not usually considered to be part of their utopian corpus. And utopianism in this study is about artistic expressiveness, subjective perspective and historical exemplification, rather than having set social and political ends in view.

Utopia and Its Discontents is a trans-historical study, ranging from antiquity to the twenty-first century. In its scope, the book follows in the tradition of the accounts of utopia by, among others, Frank and Fritzie Manuel, Krishan Kumar and Gregory Claeys.[18] And while I consider the views and finding of these authors, my approach here is different to theirs. I do not attempt to produce a comprehensive account and classification of utopian types within a given epoch (even if elements of survey have been retained in the interests of providing sufficient context). I have examined the selected works using the methods standardly associated with literary criticism rather than those of intellectual and social history. This approach has involved analysing the chosen texts, both in terms of their formal properties and their subject matter, and being alert to their registers, allusions, fissures, contradictions, and in a good number of cases, their use of a finely gradated irony. I hold in this study with the general opinion that the aesthetic sits both inside and outside the dominant currents of an age (of the defining ideologies, but not identical with them); and that the literary is at its most effective and revealing when exemplifying personal and cultural circumstances, including hopes and desires, rather than as a direct means of social transformation. I have employed conceptual models when it seems appropriate for illuminating a particular text or constellation of works: and I have drawn on recent period scholarship and undertaken some archival research and journalistic interviewing for the same purpose.

This book's title, *Utopia and Its Discontents* is, of course, an allusion to Freud's late treatise *Civilisation and Its Discontents* (1930); and while there is an implicit understanding that utopianism almost always embraces constructive and destructive tendencies, I should also emphasise that the book's principal concern is with the utopian rather than the dystopian and anti-utopian; though it becomes increasingly difficult to disentangle such conceptions in the modern era, and one might suggest that it had become virtually impossible to do so by the beginning of this century. Within this historical framework, I have selected individual works and clusters of works by authors; and treated them as nodal points of utopian expressiveness. One might object that the selection is canonical, non-canonical, arbitrary and self-evidently subjective. Another critic would no doubt have come up with a different and quite possibly more stimulating list. Nevertheless, it remains my contention that all the works considered here are exemplary of the utopian spirt of the age in which they were composed, even if they cannot be said to be exclusively so. All the authors from Thomas More onwards write self-consciously within a tradition of literary utopianism, often with an explicit attempt to overwrite and transform the schemes and styles of their predecessors. As

---

[18] Frank E. Manuel and Fritzie P. Manuel, *Utopian Thought in the Western World* (Cambridge, MA: Belknap Press, 1979), Krishan Kumar, *Utopia and Anti-Utopia in Modern Times* (Oxford: Blackwell, 1987), Krishan Kumar, *Utopianism* (Milton Keynes: Open University Press, 1991), and Gregory Claeys, *Searching for Utopia: The History of an Idea* (London: Thames & Hudson, 2011).

such, the study has a vertical axis. We can trace, for example, the vertical thread of satirical utopianism connecting More, Jonathan Swift, Thomas Carlyle, George Orwell and Margaret Atwood. But it is also the case that utopian writings have a horizontal axis and, as such, should be understood as responding in an imaginative fashion to the anxieties and preoccupations of their own period.

The study commences with an account of Plato's *Republic* and other projections of ideal states in Socratic dialogue. The opening chapter draws, in particular, on the writings of Iris Murdoch and Alasdair MacIntyre on the relation of artists to the ideal dispensation. I consider the rival accounts of Socratic dialogue and Attic tragedy to describe the fundamental circumstances of humankind, and the extent to which one can plausibly conceive of a perfect commonwealth. Plato provides a foundational account of the ideal state in the *Republic* which rejects the truth claims of epic poetry and dramatic performance; yet the opposition of art and idealism is compromised by the means in which this argument is formulated. The most lyrical and involuted of Plato's dialogues, the *Symposium* offers a vision of an alternative social settlement with its celebration of Eros, and a putative reconciliation of artistic expressiveness and philosophical reflection. A modern complaint about the reception of Sir Thomas More is that his historical significance as Humanist author, court official, Lord Chancellor and defender of the Catholic faith has become increasingly obscured by his various fictional guises. However, as the second chapter suggests, the depiction of More in one prominent modern novelistic account is notable insofar as it utilises a range of ironic devices and perspectives which More himself deploys to such startling effect in his *Utopia*. Indeed, that approach is dependent on an imaginative modern utilisation of portraiture (an artistic genre in which More shared a keen interest with Erasmus). The chapter considers, in particular, the meta-utopian consequences of More's literary style both for himself and the tradition for which he is of central significance. It concludes by arguing against the prevalent view that no significant connection can be made between *Utopia*'s depictions and arguments and More's subsequent public career and writings.

There are two parallel strands to the third chapter. As already mentioned, Jürgen Habermas has suggested that the modern doctrine of human rights has a Kantian core, and that those rights in their legal codification constitute 'a realistic utopia'. The chapter considers this Enlightenment inheritance in comparison to Jonathan Swift's anatomy of social and political idealism in satire. The chapter draws upon the extensive body of recent textual scholarship on Swift, which has revealed a much greater debt to More's *Utopia* than previously acknowledged. One can now consider *Gulliver's Travels* (1726) as being central to the utopian imagination in the eighteenth century, rather than peripheral to it. The chapter considers the extent to which Swift's satire tests the limitations of idealistic projection. In this discussion, Swift becomes the improbable companion to Kant, with the latter providing an influential version of the doctrine of universal rights rooted in the conception of human dignity, and the former producing a compelling narrative on the limitations of universal reason as a means of achieving the perfect commonwealth. A seminal modern discussion of Swift's cultural inheritance concluded with an account of mid-twentieth-century genocide as the absolute denial of human rights and dignity. And it was out of that genocidal moment, the chapter suggests, that the 'realistic utopia', the modern international order with its Kantian rational basis, came into being.

Among the many authors who have written on social idealism and have been influenced by Swift, Thomas Carlyle does not usually feature. However, Carlyle was known as 'Jonathan' by his fellow students at the University of Edinburgh in recognition of his enthusiasm for the satirist; and Carlyle extended Swift's savage projections into the machine age. The fourth chapter argues Carlyle's social writing did much to define the central themes of utopian examination in the nineteenth century. In the era's most prominent and idiosyncratic body of social criticism, Carlyle effectively defined the categories through which the modern times should be comprehended. His key tropes, recurring in various combinations throughout his writings, were temporal specificity, history, industry and heroism. For William Morris, who would produce the most influential of utopian romances out of an amalgamation of Chaucerian dream vision, utopian-socialist communitarianism, anarchist and Marxist doctrines and a pre-Raphaelite aesthetic sensibility, Carlyle still remained a champion, in his analysis of contemporary social difficulty, in his unstinting opposition to mechanisation, and in the utilisation of a holistic medieval community as an alternative to the industrial age. The chapter suggests one way to interpret Morris's utopianism is as an attempt to produce concrete responses to the questions on personal and social idealism which Carlyle's opaque and vatic writings insistently posed, but never quite answered.

The fifth chapter conceives of three of the most influential utopian and anti-utopian writers of the first half of the twentieth century, H.G. Wells, Aldous Huxley and George Orwell, as an English Triptych (with Wells at its centre). The chapter examines the range of their various fictional and non-fictional accounts of ideal state. It considers the intersections of their writings (and indeed their personal relations); but also the extent to which one can detect utopian motifs, ideas, undercurrents in their works which were not ostensibly attempts to describe the perfect state or its opposite. For these authors, the chapter suggests, utopia and its discontents was a matter of shaping the possibilities of that project in response to the political and social upheavals of the first half of the twentieth century. That undertaking required the active rejection of much of what had gone before when it came to idealistic projection, on the grounds of irrelevance and misguided thinking. For all these authors, utopianism and even its negation was ultimately a matter of reconciling public policy with a subjective perspective, a determinedly personal vision of how the perfect state should be constituted.

The penultimate chapter considers American utopian fiction in the 1970s. It focuses on the works of Ernest Callenbach, Ursula K. Le Guin and Marge Piercy (with some consideration of Tom Wolfe's New Journalism). The chapter argues that the decade should be characterised as being 'post-utopian', that there was an original sense across the political spectrum in the USA that utopia had been within the collective grasp; but because of a range of the social, political, economic difficulties, the opportunity to construct the good society had been squandered. The 1970s post-utopian context is apparent in Ernest Callenbach's secessionist environmentalism, Ursula K. Le Guin's exploration of an 'ambiguous utopia', and Marge Piercy's intertwined account of a radically free future society with a current psychiatric confinement. Margaret Atwood coined the term 'Ustopian' to encapsulate her view that the utopian must always contain an element of the dystopian and vice versa. The final chapter examines a range of her fiction, both realist and speculative, from the 1970s to the second decade of the twenty-first century, in light of this suggestion. Atwood believes 'Ustopia' is a universal circumstance, whereas as this chapter argues, it is better understood as a historically contingent category, peculiarly appropriate for the current age (a consequence of postmodern artifice and impending environmental calamity). Moreover, the chapter suggests 'Ustopia' is not so much a matter of the utopian and dystopian being latent aspects of one another, but rather as having converged to such an extent that they now effectively constitute the same thing.

I conclude the study with a utopian prospect, in the course of which I discuss both how imaginative writers bring their own projections of an ideal state to a close, as well as the terminal positions of prominent modern utopian commentators. This final section considers the ongoing relation of the utopian to the ustopian, and the ways in which such idealistic tendencies have become especially apparent in contemporary fiction which is minimally speculative. Such writing often features a first-person narrator with an 'authentic' voice, and without a trace of qualifying irony. The conclusion argues against the popular view that the utopian is destined to remain a subset of dystopian expressiveness. There is a closing set piece, as a means of exemplifying the study's central themes: social idealism in art, and importance of the subjective perspective in ideal projection. But we should begin now in ancient Athens, or rather in the city's port district, and probably sometime during the Peace of Nicias (421–414 BCE). In the *Republic*'s dramatic, even novelistic style, Plato envisages a group of Athenian citizens and residents informally meeting just after a festival and procession in honour of a goddess. They decide to retire to the house of one of the party who lives locally; and there, in this hiatus in Greek hostilities, Socrates sets out his vision of the ideal polis.

1

Plato versus Plato: Art and Idealism

In their landmark study, *Utopian Thought in the Western World* (1979), Frank and Fritzie Manuel made it clear that they did not think Plato's dialogues were utopian. Those kinds of writings did not emerge until the sixteenth century. Any works demonstrating idealistic impulses before the Renaissance should be regarded as a foreshadowing of utopia without actually embodying the genre's essential characteristics. And even then, there was a delicate balance to be struck. One could easily identify a point of origin in Thomas More's *Concerning the Best State of a Commonwealth and the New Island of Utopia* (1516); but one still had to keep in mind the 'shadowy' nature of the whole utopian enterprise, the extensive range of books and ideas drawn into its orbit, and the rapid multiplication of the various forms in which the utopian was manifest.[1] There was Jewish and Christian apocalyptic thought, sabbatical millenarianism and monasticism, all synthesised with the regulatory frameworks to be found in Plato, Aristotle and Cicero. The Manuels believed the resultant genre had multiple aspects: 'geographical, historical, psychological, sociological, as a form of belles-lettres; as philosophico-moral treatises; as a new mythology'.[2] Despite the proliferation of forms and approaches, it was still just about possible to detect an animating utopian spirit, a 'propensity', until the twentieth century that is.[3] By the 1930s, utopianism 'was a corpse', the Manuels claimed, 'the nails were hammered into the coffin with resounding blows struck by Marxists at one end and Fascist theorists at the other'.[4] If Plato's thought could not be seen to provide an origin for utopia, then it could easily be taken as a blueprint for authoritarian regimes which speciously insist on absolute obedience to the state. The best-known example of that argument was Karl Popper's *Open Society and its Enemies* (1945), which traced the origin of totalitarianism to Plato's examination of the principles of effective political society (while also condemning the philosopher for misrepresenting the liberal views of his former teacher, that 'great individualist', Socrates).[5] Writing in the same epoch, but from a very different political perspective, Ernst Bloch came to a similarly sceptical conclusion about the apparent idealistic aims of this schema. With Bloch's more capacious application of the term, the utopian could readily be applied to Plato, but still

[1] Frank E. Manuel and Fritzie P. Manuel, *Utopian Thought in the Western World* (Cambridge MA: Belknap Press, 1979), p. 5.
[2] Manuel and Manuel, *Utopian Thought*, p. 21.
[3] Manuel and Manuel, *Utopian Thought*, p. 1.
[4] Manuel and Manuel, *Utopian Thought*, p. 10.
[5] See Karl Popper, *The Open Society and its Enemies*, 8th edn (London: Routledge, 2002), p. 119.

not in a complimentary fashion. Bloch describes the *Republic* 'as a work well thought out as it is reactionary', a 'splendid-utopian ship', which 'transposes the land from which the ship is destined and replaces the Golden Age with that of black soup'.[6]

Bloch's vivid observations are open to the objection that they diminish nuanced Socratic argument for the purposes of aphoristic effect. These interpretations also depend on an almost exclusive focus on the *Republic* as the central source of Plato's political ideas; and they provide a selective reading of the dialogue at that. Yet such attacks are also a tacit acknowledgement of the long-standing influence of the *Republic* as a source of compelling political ideas. And then there are wider considerations, even if one rejects the organisational model Socrates advances in the course of the dialogue. Popper conceded the point, at least in part. As aberrant as he found the *Republic*'s political vision, Popper still believed Plato was a fine sociologist, who constructed 'an astonishingly realistic theory of society'.[7] Plato's dialogues raise questions of the relationship of private and public virtue, of freedom and authority, of the relationship between a universal claim for political organisation and the appropriate arrangement for a historically specific set of circumstances; and especially pertinent to this study, they raise the question of the relationship of art to the ideal state. Plato's projection of a perfect constitution is not limited to the *Republic*. He offers other models in the *Statesman* and the *Laws*. And then there are more impressionistic, mythological accounts of ideal societies in *Timaeus* and the incomplete *Critias* (a vision of ancient Athens). However, one might also pose in this context the more unusual question as to whether it is possible to detect a different kind of foreshadowing of the ideal state, or at least the general circumstances of the ideal state, in the ostensibly poetic dialogue of the *Symposium*. And that would be to place an emphasis on the literary and the dramatic in the dialogue as a form of anticipatory consciousness, rather than attempting to trace out or construct the general lines of continuity within a coherent body of philosophical analysis.

Nevertheless, we should begin with the *Republic*, the longest and most sustained example of Plato's constitutional thought. There has been some debate as to whether it is possible to assign a date for the events described in the dialogue (the matter of composition now being beyond exact determination), but the modern consensus is that it takes place sometime during the Peace of Nicias (421–414 BCE). The discussants have attended a festival and procession in honour of the Thracian goddess Bendis in Piraeus, the port area of Athens. After the celebrations, the group retires to Polemarchus' nearby house. With his brother, Polemarchus ran a successful armament workshop; and he was aligned politically with the city's democratic faction (the harbour district was a hotbed of radical opinion). Socrates converses in the dialogue with a variety of fictionalised versions of Athenian citizens, including Plato's older brothers, Glaucon and Adeimantus, Polemarchus' father, Cephalus, and a Sophist, Thrasymachus. The dialogue's circumstances and exchanges are informed by its dramatic irony. Contemporary readers would almost certainly have been aware of Athens' traumatic

---

[6] Ernst Bloch, *The Principle of Hope*, trans. by Neville Plaice, Stephen Plaice and Paul Knight, 3 vols (Cambridge, MA: MIT Press, 1986), I, p. 485.
[7] See Popper, *Open Society*, p. 39.

of the psychological consequences of dispensing with the family as a fundamental means of social organisation. Aristotle may misremember that the prohibition on the family is supposed to apply to the elite rather than to the ordinary citizenry, but the general point remains persuasive in spite of the interpretative error. This society, he suggests, would both be beset by a fear of incest, and a desperate yearning as the citizens desperately searched for signs of the kinship, institutionally denied to them, in the face of every stranger they meet.

It is similarly possible to regard the formalist analysis of Aristotle's *Poetics* as a response to what he regards as the faulty psychological modelling one encounters in Plato's dialogues. For Aristotle, of course, tragedy is to be understood in terms of its emotional and psychological effect on the audience, with its insistency on the unities of time and space, the anagnorisis as the moment of revelation of the protagonist's true circumstances, the peripeteia as the sudden reversal in his or her fortune (and the exquisite coincidence of both in Sophocles' *Oedipus Tyrannos*), and the katharsis as the audience's moment of release, the purification of the soul at the play's dénouement. Tragedy for Aristotle does not cause a critical imbalance in the soul in the way in which Plato suggests in the *Republic*. The nub of Bloch's jibe at the 'Black Soup' of Plato's ideal political vision is that it establishes the convention of the incompatibility of the ideal state with aesthetic practice, even if this notion requires some qualification. Socrates lists the erroneous and ethically defective descriptions that one can find in epic verse in Book Four of the *Republic*. He considers Homer's account of both Achilles' actions and his essential being in the *Iliad*. It is not true, Socrates says, that Achilles 'dragged the dead Hector around the tomb of Patroclus, or massacred the captives on his pyre' (391b). He goes on 'nor will we allow our people to believe that Achilles, who was the son of the Goddess and of Peleus [...] and who was brought up by the most wise Chiron, was so full of inner turmoil as to have two diseases in his soul – slavishness accompanied by the love of money, on the one hand, and arrogance towards gods and humans, on the other' (391b-c). One might well ask on what authority Socrates can question the veracity of Homer's narrative given there are no more authoritative sources on which he can draw. The grounds on which such passages are to be rejected are because poetry is a discursively imitative activity which cannot offer any proper comprehension of the events it describes; and as a matter of logical inference, such events cannot be true, because the divine for Socrates must be aligned with the good, as he suggests to Adeimantus, 'for surely we won't say that a god is deficient in either beauty or virtue' (381c).

Despite the allusion to the general populace in the account of misrepresentation of Achilles, the emphasis in this section is on poetry's educational purpose; that poetic expression of all kinds should be subordinated to the control and selection of guardian officials. They will construct a syllabus of instructive and morally improving verse for the city's youth (it remains a moot point whether the educational provision is intended as a citywide measure or merely for its elite). At this stage, Socrates is not prepared to commit to outright prohibition: and on the question as to whether tragedy and comedy should be permitted under an ideal constitution, he says that he does not know yet, 'but whatever direction the argument blows us, that's where we must go' (394d). But there is an intimation of what is to come in the ambivalent treatment of someone who in many respects is conceived as an excellent reciter of verse. This skilful performer is conceived as a foreigner, who should be lauded, crowned with wreaths for his expert and moving delivery; but he should also be courteously escorted beyond the city's walls, as the polis requires for its own wellbeing, 'a more austere and less pleasure-giving poet and storyteller' (398b).

Socrates' position hardens by Book Ten where the close control and oversight of performance is now replaced with outright prohibition. Comedy is summarily dismissed as being no more than cheapening ridicule. The three overlapping arguments which then lead Socrates to reject representative art are as follows: first; all depictions are dependent on external perception, which do not encourage us to question how such images come to us (such as when we see a straight stick apparently bend when submerged in water, because of the different refractive index of air and liquid); second, when the mimetic principles are transferred to the work of art, the result is an image being twice removed from its immutable form, such that a picture of a couch can only convey the external appearance of an actual couch, rather than the couch in its ideal and immutable form; the image is also technically deficient on the grounds that it is experientially restricted (unable to convey the presence of the object in space and time). Painters possess the skills of their profession as manufacturers of images, rather than those of carpenters. The latter must know how to design and make furniture while the former do not; and third, and most importantly, dramatic performance appeals to the non-rational components of our souls. We enjoy 'one of the heroes sorrowing and making a long lamenting speech, [...] give ourselves up to following it' (605d). Such presentations provoke an emotional response in the audience, and appear to legitimate irrational behaviour beyond the auditorium. In Plato's late dialogue, *Philebus*, drama is denigrated because it promotes a self-indulgent pleasure incommensurate with the public good. The *Republic*'s argument is more flatly pragmatic – exposure to performance disturbs the balance of the individual soul, and consequently poses a threat to the state's order. Socrates concludes in the *Republic* that 'the ancient quarrel between [poetry] and philosophy' (607b) should be resolved in the ideal state by the banishment of the former. The argument's immediate significance lies in the suggestion that a central feature of contemporary Athenian cultural life is incompatible with the practice of civic virtue. Expelling dramatic poets is not just a means of preventing the public rendition of epic verse, but also a de facto means of banning Athenian theatre festivals. These biannual events attracted audiences in excess of 30,000 citizens, with day-long performances of three tragedies, a comedy and a farce.[19] Tragedy explored the place of humankind situated between human and divine law, often with an oblique allusion to current affairs (such as in the working out of the tension between domestic and foreign policy in Sophocles' *Antigone*); comedy often provided a savage commentary on contemporary politics, addressing the apparent failings of the city's leaders and other prominent citizens (including Socrates as portrayed in Aristophanes' *Clouds*), and a farce, intended as a burlesque on the serious drama.

---

[19] See J.R. Green, *Theatre in Ancient Greek Society* (London: Routledge, 1994), pp. 8–12, and Peter D. Arnott, *Public and Performance in the Greek Theatre* (London: Routledge, 1991), pp. 5–11.

The twentieth-century philosopher and novelist Iris Murdoch paradoxically styled Plato as a puritan with artistic inclinations. In her account of Plato's objections, she adopts an explicitly religious register: 'art', she says, 'prevents the salvation of the whole man by offering pseudo-spirituality and a plausible imitation of direct intuitive knowledge (vision, presence), a defeat of the discursive intelligence at the bottom of the scale of being, not at the top. Art is a false presence and a false present. As a pseudo-spiritual activity, it can still attract when coarser goals are seen as worthless. We seek eternal possession of the good, but art offers spurious worthless immortality. It thus obscures the nature of true *catharsis* (purgation)'.[20] However, Murdoch also provides an unusual assessment as to why one might agree that art *should* be banished from the ideal state, or at a minimum subjected to heavy censure in terms of its modern reference. She is in partial agreement with the suggestion that 'art delights in the endless profusion of senseless images' (television for her, streaming services for us); and she also has some sympathy for Plato's low opinion of comedy, an anxiety about a genre which encourages 'the cheapening and brutalising effect of an atmosphere where everything can be ridiculed'.[21] The shadow of Plato's condemnation of aesthetic social function can be detected in those cultural theories which set their own idealism against art, which suggest contemporary aesthetic practice vapidly and endlessly repeats and mirrors the structures of the current economic order. We can detect that Platonic inheritance in Fredric Jameson's scepticism over postmodern culture (explicitly likened to being in the delusional state of Plato's cave), and in Boris Groys' suggestion that for all its apparent brashness and defiance of the standards of conventional taste, the avant-garde functions as propaganda for the status quo.[22]

There is also the question as to whether the *Republic*'s absolute prohibition of poets should be taken at face value, and that, in turn, is related to the matter of the status of the text as whole. Put bluntly – did Plato intend the text as a set of real-world practical measures, or as a thought experiment to highlight the deficiencies of all extant forms of political society? Modern commentators such as M.F. Burnyeat have argued that the 'non-existence of the ideal city is a fact of history, not of metaphysics', while W.K.C. Guthrie is convinced that the dialogue is an exclusively theoretical undertaking. That view is shared by Trevor Saunders, who states that the dialogue is 'an extreme statement [which is] designed to shock, in fact the application of certain political principles – in fact, an *un*attainable ideal'.[23] For Saunders, such idealism is to be contrasted with the pragmatic social vision of the *Laws*. The suggestion that the text does mean exactly what it seems to state was taken a stage further by Leo Strauss, who understood Socratic

---

[20] Iris Murdoch, *The Fire and the Sun: Why Plato Banished the Artists* (Oxford: Oxford University Press, 1977), p. 26.
[21] Murdoch, *The Fire and the Sun*, p. 25, p. 14.
[22] See Fredric Jameson, *Postmodernism; or, The Cultural Logic of Late Capitalism* (London: Verso, 1991), p. 25; and Boris Groys 'On the New', in his *Art Power* (Cambridge, MA: MIT Press, 2013), pp. 23–32.
[23] M.F. Burnyeat, 'Utopia and Fantasy: The Practicability of Plato's Ideally Just City', in *Psychoanalysis, Mind and Art: Perspectives on Richard Wollheim*, ed. by Jim Hopkins and Anthony Savile (Oxford: Blackwell, 1992), pp. 175–87 (p. 176); See Guthrie, *Plato*, p. 470; and Plato, *Laws*, ed. and trans. by Trevor J. Saunders (Harmondsworth: Penguin, 1975), p. 28.

irony not as an ingenious way of modifying or qualifying the central arguments, but as a means of decisively reshaping them, such that the whole work turns out to be an ironic edifice, a 'noble dissimulation' designed to demonstrate the impossibility, or even the undesirability of the political order it ostensibly proposes. In this reading the *Republic*, then, ends up providing an odd back-to-front endorsement of the arts, rather than a condemnation of them.[24]

The notion that the dialogue's argument is being deliberately compromised by its own approach has some evidential support in the sheer weight of literary allusion in Plato's oeuvre. As Susan Levin suggests, 'Plato's writings give eloquent testimony to the tremendous influence of the traditional literary education'.[25] This utilisation of the materials of a standard Greek cultural education is apparent in the *Republic*. At one stage Socrates utilises a Homeric quotation as a means of underwriting his point when the same passage had been proscribed earlier in the dialogue for its misleading depiction of the gods' behaviour. A similar point can be made about the use of visual culture. In order to address the relationship between ideal and real states, Socrates uses a painterly analogy which assumes that art *can* represent the ideal. He asks Glaucon in Book Five, 'do you think that someone is a worse painter if, having painted a model of the finest and most beautiful human [...] and having rendered every detail of his picture adequately, he could not prove that such a man could come into being' (472d). Glaucon responds, 'No, by god, I don't' (472d). The example seems to run counter to the *Republic*'s central argument and general aesthetic scepticism. For it suggests that painters *are* capable of grasping the form of beauty without any immediate physical example before them, and accordingly, that it is legitimate to propose a comparison of beautiful art with the beautiful city in order to clinch the point.

One might, however, wish to challenge the overall persuasiveness of such counter arguments to the *Republic*'s ostensible hostility to art in general and to epic and dramatic poetry in particular. Irony may modify and encourage a range of perspectives on the ostensible argument, but there is no consistent attempt to overturn the central thesis. There is also the question of probability. Given that Plato considers versions of the ideal state in *Critias*, *Timaeus* and the *Laws*; one might ask why this text should be read against the grain of its thesis. The biographical evidence of Plato's *Seventh Letter*, if it can be relied upon, suggests that the principles espoused in this work informed his tutoring of Dionysius II, the ruler of Syracuse. And there is sufficient coherence in the proposal to offer a credible means of addressing the political and social problems which bedevilled Athens. The argument that the *Laws* is a realistic projection of the ideal state whereas the *Republic* is a form of unqualified idealism seems contradictory. For it suggests there can be more than one kind of ideal (while Plato repeatedly stresses its singularity). Even if we accept the case that the doctrine of forms does not conceive of the polis as a realisation of a single ideal entity, but rather the exemplification of individual forms (i.e. justice, the beautiful, the good), which are then combined in

---

[24] Leo Strauss, *The City and Man* (Chicago: University of Chicago Press, 1978), p. 51.
[25] Susan B. Levin, *The Ancient Quarrel between Philosophy and Poetry Revisited: Plato and the Greek Literary Tradition* (Oxford: Oxford University Press, 2001), p. 8.

optimal fashion, this still does not overcome the difficulty that the conception of the ideal is of primary significance in the *Republic*; and then we have to accept the *Laws* can be differently ideal *and* pragmatic at one and the same time.

Saunders' proposal that the *Laws* is an attempt to resolve the *Republic*'s constitutional difficulties runs up against the same problem insofar as it suggests an incremental or progressive improvement on the ideal. It is, perhaps, more credible to argue that the projections operate on the basis of distinct premises. In the case of the *Republic*, the starting point is rational governance, and the recommended measures are those that preserve the state's integrity and stability. There is almost no discussion of law in the *Republic*, as either statute or precedence, or indeed, the processes by which criminal cases and civil disputes should be tried and settled. The lack of detail in this respect gives the impression that such cases would be judged by guardians on the basis of fundamental judicial principles, rather than relying on an extensive body of codified law for their determinations. In the case of the *Laws*, the central position is that one should start from the assumption that civilised society arises from and is sustained by its customs and laws. Hence, the dialogue's main purpose is to provide the context and codification of the rules by which that society should operate. The shift from rational standards to explicit codification means that the organisation of the state is transferred from the *Republic*'s elite cohort, which reaches its decisions on the basis of abstract principles, to a body of legal and social code in Magnesia, the ideal Cretan state in the *Laws*, where the key task of the governors is to interpret and apply these standards. The argument on the problematic use of the analogy of the painter to encapsulate beauty in the *Republic* is addressed by Christopher Janaway. He argues that Socrates' comparison does not in itself imply endorsement.[26] Janaway draws on Wittgenstein's observation that the value of such a comparative observation is in its subjective revelatory capacity, its ability to bring forth various components into an illuminating and convincing relationship, rather than seeking to validate the comparative example with reference to internal coherence or empirical accuracy.[27]

Indeed, there are other convincing reasons as to why one should treat the suggestion in the *Republic* to banish poets and dramatists from the ideal state as having been made in earnest. One can view the measure as part of an ongoing tussle which has epistemological and personal aspects to it, and subject to motivations not fully acknowledged in the dialogues themselves. As already mentioned, comedy is dismissed in the *Republic* as being scurrilous. Raucous laughter deprives its subjects of dignity, 'the part of you that wanted to tell the jokes and that was held back by your reason, for fear of being thought a buffoon, you then release, not realising that, by making it strong in this way, you will be led into becoming a figure of fun where your own affairs are concerned' (606c). That was Socrates' own experience. Plato has Socrates say in his own defence in the *Apology* that being ridiculed in Aristophanes' comedy, the

---

[26] See Christopher Janaway, *Images of Excellence: Plato's Critique of the Arts* (Oxford: Oxford University Press, 1995), p. 117, n. 33.

[27] Wittgenstein's main observations on art are contained in his *Lectures and Conversations on Aesthetics, Psychology and Religious Belief*, ed. by Cyril Barrett (Oxford: Blackwell, 1970), see pp. 19–36. For a persuasive overview, see Frank Cioffi's 'Aesthetic Explanation and Perplexity', in his *Wittgenstein on Freud and Frazer* (Cambridge: Cambridge University Press, 1998), pp. 47–79.

Clouds (produced at the City Dionysia in 423 BCE) established the widely-held view that philosophers were devious and self-serving (though it was not the only play to depict him in this way). Plato's Socrates claims the popular opinion of him was as someone who 'busies himself studying things in the sky and below the earth; he makes the worse into the stronger argument, and he teaches the same thing to others'.[28] Aristophanes certainly did characterise him as the leading proponent of new knowledge. It seems unlikely that Socrates in reality had a sustained interest in astronomy and the physical sciences (Plato's grandest and most extended example of cosmic theorising is delivered by Timaeus in the eponymous dialogue, rather than by Socrates). Aristotle's most damaging claim in the *Clouds*, however, was that Socrates was an exponent of mendacious rhetoric, rather than its fiercest opponent. The *Clouds'* plot features a middle-aged farmer, Strepsiades, who enrols in Socrates' academy in an attempt to learn how he might outsmart his creditors (he is on the verge of bankruptcy because of his son's prolificacy). Strepsiades is a hopeless student, too old and inflexible in his thinking, but his son, Pheidippides, turns out to be much more pliant and astute. Pheidippides rewards his father's investment in his fashionable education, not by deploying his new-found rhetorical skill to defeat his father's creditors, but in arguing convincingly that it is entirely legitimate to beat one's own parents (a heinous offence for the play's original audience). The play ends with the spectre of the enraged common man revenging himself on condescending intellectual elitism and fatuous argument, as Strepsiades assaults Socrates and then burns down his academy.

The excessiveness of Aristophonic comedy with its scatological jokes and crude if ingenious line of punning self-evidently could not be accommodated within an idealistic Platonic schema. In a long sequence in *The Acharnians*, for example, the old Athenian famer Dikaiopolis (a part possibly taken by Aristophanes himself) negotiates with a half-starved Megarian over the sale of two piglets (in fact, his daughters in porcine disguise). This episode's 'humour' hinges on the double meaning of 'choîros' as piglet and female genitalia.[29] And one might suppose that the philosopher's slanderous portrayal would in itself be sufficient reason for Socrates and his best-known student's hostility toward comedians. Aristophanes' plays also provide a mode of representation at odds with any attempt to conceptualise the cosmos in idealistic terms. It may well be, as Kenneth Dover has argued, that the principal aim of Aristophonic comedy was to bring about a joyous release of pent-up frustration at one's rulers through the stark depiction of a disobedience and disdain which would not be tolerated outside the theatre. 'It is a stock joke in Aristophanes', Dover points out, 'that *rhétores*, "speakers", i.e. those who are influential in the assembly, because they spoke cogently, were prostituted as boys'.[30] Comedy could also provide a semblance of revenge on the divine by showing ordinary Athenians for once getting the better of their demanding and vengeful gods. Iris, Zeus's daughter, for example, is sent as a spy to the avian city in Aristotle's *Birds*, only to be humiliated by the bumptious low-born Athenian, Pisthetaerus. The *Birds*

---

[28] *Apology*, in *Plato: Complete Works*, trans. by G.M.A. Grube, pp. 17–36 (p. 20).
[29] See Henry J. Liddell and Robert Scott, *Greek-English Lexicon*, 7th edn (Oxford: Clarendon Press, 1883), p. 1732.
[30] K.J. Dover, *Aristophanic Comedy* (London: Batsford, 1972), p. 35.

also offers an oblique and not very flattering commentary on the ideal city. The birds construct a fantastical edifice in the sky, a challenge to divine authority. But the rational and systematic approach to the construction of the perfect city is also treated with disdain. The distinguished architect and engineer, Meton, announces himself in bird city as being 'famous throughout the Hellenic world' for his 'hydraulic clock at Colonus'.[31] He offers to design the bird city as a radial conurbation on an astronomical model. 'In the centre you have the market place; straight streets leading into it, from here, from here, from here', he declares, 'very much the same principle as the rays of a star'.[32] Pisthetaerus backed up by the avian chorus responds menacingly. He suggests that in this airborne world suspended between men and gods, 'there's going to be a purge of pretentious humbugs; they're all going to get beaten up, you know what I mean'.[33]

A related scepticism as to the value of idealistic thinking can also be detected in Attic tragedy. Alasdair MacIntyre argues that drama and philosophy offer rival and incompatible versions of morality and epistemology. If the aim of philosophy is to arrive at clear judgements as to what constitutes the good society with appropriate standards of justice and the principles of virtue, then the function of tragedy seems to lie in the opposite direction, in the suggestion that all such cogent determinations are ultimately fruitless. Hence in the dénouement of Sophocles' *Antigone*, the apparent resolution between filial duty and piety is achieved by the intervention of the deity, with the abrupt termination to rival claims, rather than by either party finding a means of mediation or justifying one set of principles over another. Such conclusions, MacIntyre believes, 'leave unbridged the gap between the acknowledgement of authority, of a cosmic order and of the claims to truth involved in the recognition of virtue on the one hand, and our particular perceptions and judgements in particular situations on the other'.[34] For MacIntyre, the significance of the opposition of dramatists and Plato is that it prefigured rival accounts of morality in the twentieth century. Classical dramatists provide a striking precursor to the decontextualised modern traditions of morality from both liberalist and Marxian perspectives. Traditions, MacIntyre says, which hold that 'the variety and heterogeneity of human good is such that their pursuit cannot be reconciled in any single moral order, and that any social order, which *either* attempts a reconciliation *or* which enforces the hegemony of one set of goods over all others is bound to turn into a straightjacket, and very probably a totalitarian straightjacket for the human condition'.[35]

However, one might wish to qualify this argument by suggesting that not all Greek tragedies end up by nullifying or cancelling their existential dilemmas with divine intervention. The concluding play, *Eumenides* of Aeschylus' trilogy *Oresteia*, for example, certainly works through of the tensions of the divine and the human. The vortex of

---

[31] Aristophanes, *The Birds and Other Plays*, trans. by David Barrett and Alan Sommerstein (London: Penguin, 1978), p. 187.
[32] Aristophanes, *Birds*, p. 188.
[33] Aristophanes, *Birds*, p. 188.
[34] Alasdair MacIntyre, *After Virtue: A Study in Moral Theory*, 2nd edn (London: Duckworth, 1985), p. 143.
[35] MacIntyre, *After Virtue*, pp. 142–43.

Acknowledgements

It has taken me some time to complete this book, and I have accumulated a good number of debts along the way. I have been fortunate to have worked over the last few years with a group of stimulating and supportive colleagues in the Department of English Literature at the University of Birmingham. They have read drafts and proposals and commented on these with a suitable combination of candour and circumspection. I have also benefited from the enthusiasm and support from librarians, archivists, keepers and curators in the United Kingdom, North America and continental Europe, who have guided me through their collections. Gerald Bär and Peter Hanenberg were good enough to invite me to speak on utopian themes to staff and students at the Universidade Aberta and the Universidade Católica, Portuguesa in Lisbon in 2017; and they gave the project some much needed impetus as a consequence. And I have accumulated debts of a more incidental, but no less significant kind, such as to the long-standing friends who invited me to stay on their own tropical island paradise in order to complete a portion of this study.

I am grateful to the following, though this is hardly an exhaustive list: Hugh Adlington, Judy Gumbo Albert, Dorothy Butchard, Paul and Maria Chamberlain, Diletta de Cristofaro, Louise Curran, Ken Dowden, Ian Duncan, Rex Ferguson, Marjory and Allen Flynn, Claude Fretz (for being the most steadfast and encouraging of research assistants), Andrzej Gasiorek, Howard Gaskill, Stuart Gillespie, David Griffith, Dave Gunning, Matt Hayler, Kate Heard, Andrew Hodgson, John Holmes, Nikolai Jeffs, Luke Kennard, Tom Lockwood, Deborah Longworth, Larry McCallister, Rebecca Mitchell, Rowan and Hope Mitchell, Dan Moore, Elizabeth and Duncan Murray, Adam Rounce, Kate Rumbold, Valarie Rumbold, Wendy Scase, Sue Schweik, Dan Vyleta, Nathan Waddell, Peter Wiley and Gillian Wright.

The research for *Utopia and Its Discontents* was conducted at the following libraries, galleries and museums: British Library, National Library of Scotland, Library of Birmingham, University of Birmingham Library, Thomas Fisher Rare Book Library, University of Toronto, Berkeley Public Library, Oakland Museum of California, National Portrait Gallery, Royal Collections, Windsor, Frick Collection, New York and Kunstmuseum, Basel. I was fortunate to receive an award from the Research and Knowledge Transfer Fund in the College of Arts and Law, University of Birmingham. The grant allowed me to visit the Margaret Atwood archive at the University of Toronto. I have benefited as well from periods of institutional study leave. My editors at Bloomsbury, David Avital and Lucy Brown, have been unfailingly supportive of this project, and David has shown the patience of Job. And I must also thank Bridget Pugh, who first gave me the idea to write a book about literary utopianism (and its downside). But my final and most heartfelt thanks go to the lively dedicatees of this volume for creating a domestic utopia, even if, like most families, we only glimpse that blissful state intermittently.

Introduction

As a topic of study Utopia recedes further from view the closer one approaches it, like granules of sand slipping through one's fingers. As soon as one arrives at a workable definition, then all other possible categories and interpretations seem to be on the verge of overwhelming that particular position. Of course, one might argue that such difficulties were apparent pretty much from the outset. Thomas More's coinage of 'Utopia' fused the notion of a good place with no place. 'Ou' means no in ancient Greek; and there's a homophonic play with 'eu' meaning good; 'topos' means place. Because *Utopia* (1516) was written in Latin, More then added a Latin suffix 'ia'. As a Greek scholar, More would also have been aware of the shifting and contradictory significance of the authentic Greek terms behind his neologism: the noun 'atopia' suggests strangeness, oddness, absurdity, eccentricity; and the associated term 'atopos' can refer to a paradoxical state of affairs.[1] A literalist interpretation of 'utopia' would, then, commit us to the notion that the good place must perforce be a place which does not exist; and the term obliquely alludes to its own contradictory nature. The word continues to have a significant presence in modern English. The Ngram chart of the frequency of occurrence of 'utopia' in books shows a sharp increase in its use from the 1950s until the turn of this century with some trailing off thereafter.[2] Anecdotal evidence suggests that 'utopia' remains in common parlance either as a wished-for state, or the suggestion of a superlative in a given institution, service or object, though sometimes the term's very familiarity means it is little more than a vaguely attractive label. Hence 'utopia' can be found on such fond things as a seaside villa and a lovingly restored campervan, but it is also the name of a range of bathroom furniture, a garden-design firm, a hairdressing salon, the title for a collection of electronic music, and a standard model of fluted wine glass (with the word 'Utopia' etched onto the foot).

'Utopia' also has a long-standing negative sense, especially when the abstract noun has been derived from its adjective. 'Utopianism' often suggests a hopelessly impractical scheme or set of measures. Idealism blinds the projector to the shortcomings of whatever he or she is proposing, and the damage such a scheme would cause if it were ever implemented. The *OED*'s earliest example of such depreciative usage is from a

---

[1] H.G. Liddell and R. Scott, *Greek-English Lexicon*, 7th edn (Oxford: Clarendon Press, 1883), p. 244.
[2] See https://books.google.com/ngrams/graph?content=utopia&year_start=1800&year_end=2008&corpus=15&smoothing=3&share=&direct_url=t1%3B%2Cutopia%3B%2Cc0#t1%3B%2Cutopia%3B%2Cc0, accessed 8 May 2019.

1649 political tract justifying the trial and regicide of Charles I.[3] The general sense of the folly of idealistic thinking without recourse to practical considerations was well illustrated by Samuel Johnson in his philosophical tale, *The History of Rasselas, Prince of Abissinia* (1759). The prince confesses to his tutor Imlac that he has entertained visionary schemes for the beneficial reorganisation of society, only to be horrified at the way in which he casually accepted the deaths of his siblings as a necessity for the establishment of the new harmonious state. In the early nineteenth century, Friedrich Schopenhauer attacked the idea of utopia as being inimical to our constitutions. '*Work worry, toil, and trouble* are certainly the lot of almost all through their lives', Schopenhauer writes, 'but if all desires were fulfilled as soon as they arose, how then would people occupy their lives and spend their time? Suppose the human race were removed to Utopia where everything grew automatically and pigeons flew about ready-roasted; [...] then people would die of boredom or hang themselves'.[4] Such objections may be long-standing; but came to be treated in a more systematic fashion by the middle of the twentieth century. Utopianism for Karl Popper was a common strand of German National Socialism and Soviet Communism in the imposition of arbitrary and authoritarian social forms that extinguished any sense of individual freedom. And the same scepticism on political idealism informed F.A. Hayek's neo-liberalism. He launched a scathing attack on socialism in *The Road to Serfdom* (1943) in a chapter entitled 'The Great Utopia'. He makes his point with the chapter's epigraph, translated from the German of Friedrich Hölderlin's novel, *Hyperion* (1797–1799): 'what has always made the state a hell on earth has been precisely that man has tried to make it his heaven'.[5]

Utopia became a byword for the kind of regulated and interventionist tendencies of the socialist state to be rebuffed by neo-liberalism. David Harvey was evidently aware of the irony when he disparaged the animating principles of Hayek, Milton Friedman and the Chicago School. This full-throated advocacy for market forces as a key determinant of global economic performance was nothing more, Harvey declared, than 'a utopian project'.[6] Yet the term could be still be used in a positive sense in political discourse last century. John Rawls proposed in his canonical *Theory of Justice* (1971) a model of social contract with the doctrine of 'justice as fairness' at its centre.[7] Rawls was initially sceptical of both utopian and realist denominators, but he subsequently defined his position as one of 'Realistic utopianism', which did not 'settle for compromise between power and political right and justice, but set limits to the reasonable exercise

---

[3] The *OED*'s earliest example of usage is from John Goodwin's *Hybristodikai: the Obstructours of Justice* (1649). The tract justifies the trial and execution of Charles I. See 'Utopianism', *OED*, http://www.oed.com/view/Entry/220786?redirectedFrom=utopianism#eid, accessed 8 May 2019.

[4] Arthur Schopenhauer, 'Additional Remarks on the Doctrine of Suffering in the World', in his *Pararega and Paralipomena*, trans. by E.F.J. Payne, 2 vols (Oxford: Clarendon Press, 1974), II, pp. 291–311 (p. 293).

[5] F.A. Hayek, *The Road to Serfdom* (London: Routledge, 2000), p. 18, Hayek's translation. The young Hyperion is discussing the French Revolution, see Friedrich Hölderlin, *Hyperion; or, The Hermit in Greece*, trans. by Howard Gaskill (Cambridge: Open Book, 2019) p. 27.

[6] David Harvey, 'Neoliberalism as Creative Destruction', *The Annals of the American Academy of Political and Social Science*, 610 (2007), 22–44 (28).

[7] John Rawls, *A Theory of Justice*, rev. edn (Cambridge, MA: Belknap Press, 1999), p. 10.

of power'.⁸ Robert Nozick challenged Rawls's principles in his *Anarchy, State, and Utopia* (1974), and offered a very different version of positive utopianism. Nozick points out that no set of standard goods, such as justice, security, freedom and happiness, can all be realised simultaneously and reconciled with one another. However, that conundrum did not excuse political philosophers from conjecturing as to the circumstances of the best possible world. Nozick argued for establishing the fundamental requirements of the good society, rather than for the good society per se. This turned out to be the minimal state where the polis made no claim on its citizens, and did not attempt to determine and enforce standards of rights. When Jürgen Habermas examined Kantian conceptions of dignity this century as a significant component of Human Rights legislation, he did so under the heading of a 'Real Utopia'; and the title of Erik Olin Wright's *Envisioning Real Utopias* (2008) announces his central claim for continued importance of the perfect society, 'to provide empirical and theoretical grounding for radical and democratic visions of an alternative social world'.⁹ Wright's thesis has a revisionist Marxian complexion; and he concedes there is a paradoxical aspect to this undertaking, not least because Marx was wary of the fantastical forms of social and economic projection which the term 'utopia' could connote.

It is still possible to use the term 'utopia' and the notion of utopianism within the fields of political theory and economics in a positive sense. David M. Bell's *Rethinking Utopia: Place, Power, Affect* (2017), for example, attempts to identify what might constitute an ideal society from what looks like a post-anarchist position; and he utilises an improvisational, associative style of presentation to make his case. Yet the works which have enjoyed extensive public interest have tended to link 'utopia' to concrete economic and fiscal measures. In *Capital in the Twenty-First Century* (2014), for example, Thomas Piketty describes his study's central measure of a global progressive tax on wealth as a 'useful utopia', in which the universal charge would 'serve as a worthwhile reference point, as standard against which alternative proposals can be measured'.¹⁰ Rutger Bregman draws upon the standard negative connotations of utopianism in his *Utopia for Realists: And How We Can Get There* (2014 in Dutch and 2017 in English). Bregman is a prominent proponent of a universal basic income, with the eye-catching suggestion that everyone should receive 'free money' as a matter of state policy.¹¹ 'Utopia' is used in this context as an idea which seems implausible, even bizarre, on first inspection; and then the book's intention is to build a convincing case that the scheme is both a readily attainable and sensible measure. We might note at this

---

⁸ John Rawls, *The Laws of Peoples* (Cambridge, MA: Harvard University Press, 1999), p. 6n, quoted in David Boucher, 'Uniting What Right Permits with What Interest Prescribes', in *Rawls's Laws of Peoples: A Realistic Utopia?*, ed. by Rex Martin and David A. Reidy (Malden, MA: Blackwell, 2006), pp. 19–37 (pp. 20–21).
⁹ See Jürgen Habermas, 'The Concept of Human Dignity and the Realistic Utopia of Human Rights', *Metaphilosphy*, 41 (2010), 464–80; and Erik Olin Wright, *Envisioning Real Utopias* (London: Verso, 2010), p. 6.
¹⁰ Thomas Piketty, *Capital in the Twenty-First Century* trans. by Arthur Goldman (Cambridge, MA: Belknap Press, 2014), p. 512.
¹¹ Rutger Bregman, *Utopia for Realists: And How We Can Get There*, trans. by Elizabeth Manton (London: Bloomsbury, 2017), p. 25.

stage, however, that unlike many of the grand utopian schemes of the late Victorian era, utopianism, as a matter of public economic discourse in the twenty-first century, has become largely a matter of advocating a single measure, intended to improve upon the available social and economic models, without necessarily sweeping away the current order to achieve this end.

As an article of faith or even theory, one might suggest that it is never entirely possible to separate the political and social from their means of expression; but this study's central focus is on the utopian in its literary context, even as that entails examining its social and political components. This analysis necessitates tracing those rhetorical aspects already apparent in More's beguiling and playful coinage, that the very state which is being evoked is being subjected to various kinds of aesthetic pressures in the moment of its articulation. Even if one wished to do so, one could not overlook Ernst Bloch's *The Principle of Hope* (1953, 1954, and 1959) when it comes to considering utopias as artistic phenomena. Bloch explored many different types of ideal projections: fairy tales, social utopias, technological utopias, Eldorado, Eden, geographical utopias. It was just from his perspective that such explicit articulations of easy and harmonious states were not always that utopian. Bloch wrote *The Principle of Hope* between 1937 and 1947 while in exile in the USA from his native Germany. He was impecunious. Unable to secure an academic post (his English was rudimentary), he was dependent on his wife's salary as a secretary in a Boston architectural firm. He was also treated warily by his fellow emigres of the Frankfurt School, because they feared his support for Stalin's Soviet Union could jeopardise their own positions.

Given his wearisome circumstances, it was perhaps not surprising that Bloch took a dim view of his hosts. Capitalist America was tawdry, glitzy and banal. The *Principle of Hope* is full of complaints of the trivialities of detective fiction, jazz and Hollywood musicals. Yet there is an irony to the work being written in the USA. Bloch evidently adopted a free-wheeling deregulated enterprising approach to the notion of utopia, such that all writing, all thought, all artefacts could potentially be the bearer of the transformative spirit. He is sceptical about the existence of the Freudian unconscious, but even so, the original psychoanalyst is to be applauded for the discovery 'that dreams are not just foam; and naturally not prophetic oracles either, but they lie half-way between the two as it were; precisely as hallucinated wish-fulfilments'; components 'in the vast field of utopian consciousness'.[12] Kantian idealism is praised for its capacity to produce an image of a 'beautiful world'.[13] Modern drama is compared and contrasted: Ibsen deprecated for dismal symbolic naturalism, and Brecht lauded for engaging and provoking his audience to heightened understanding through his optimistic anti-realistic theatre.[14] The hieroglyphics of the 'Egyptian Book of the Dead' are scrutinised for 'hopeful images against death': and that optimistic spirit could also be divined in

---

[12] Ernst Bloch, *The Principle of Hope*, trans. by Neville Plaice, Stephen Plaice and Paul Knight, 3 vols (Cambridge, MA: MIT Press, 1986), I, pp. 78–79.
[13] Bloch, *The Principle of Hope*, II, p. 844.
[14] On the similarities of Bloch and Brecht, see Keith A. Dickson, *Towards Utopia: A Study of Brecht* (Oxford: Clarendon Press, 1974), pp. 123–24.

the interiors of French gothic cathedrals, with their extraordinary sense of uplift, of light, air, space and glass.[15]

The transformative spirit was essentially progressive, and could reconfigure the world with different possibilities and conceptual horizons. The aesthetic is always conceived in Bloch's book in terms of its material earth-bound consideration: a cathedral's gravity-defying architecture may be wondrous; but the encounter with it had to be rendered distinct from any religious function, to be detached from conventional faith and the prospect of a happier world in the hereafter. Bloch writes throughout of this transformative effect as the not-yet conscious, a capacity for anticipatory illumination (*Vor-Shein*). He searches for such attributes in a bewildering array of artefacts, but he returns repeatedly, as a kind of textual leitmotiv, to German Romantic writings and music: Goethe's prose, Schiller's poetry, Beethoven's triumphant Ninth Symphony, his opera of Enlightenment emancipation *Fidelio*, and Brahms' grand and austere *German Requiem*. The celebration of these works indicates a degree of personal cultural inheritance and received value; but they also act as a symbolic declaration of the centrality of the aesthetic to his enterprise; that it is art where the utopian spirit is readily apparent; and that it is in the creative work that the transformative possibilities of the self and the social order can be felt most keenly. One can read the *Principle of Hope* as an attempt to render the aims of Marxian theory in aestheticised form; and in such a way as to elide the critical distance between the expressive object and the means of its analysis. If everything is potentially utopian, then it can, of course, be difficult to detect what principle is being applied when determining which works manifest anticipatory conscious and which do not, beyond the application of personal preference. Bloch has also been criticised for envisaging the end point of his leviathan-like analysis as being the concrete manifestation of Stalinism in the middle of the last century (though it is certainly possible to regard the teleological aspects of his writings as being significantly more hedged on the benefits of Soviet Communism than is often suggested).

Bloch, of course, has exerted a significant influence on utopian studies in the anglophone world since *The Principle of Hope*'s translation into English in the 1980s. Ruth Levitas, for example, is eloquently Blochian in her accounts of utopianism from a sociological perspective in which she advocates a phenomenological impulse toward a 'possible world', predicated on the twin internal categories of 'hope and desire'.[16] And Caroline Edwards has recently shown how contemporary British Fiction can be collectively understood as the bearer of Blochian hopefulness.[17] In this endeavour, I have followed Bloch to the extent of assuming it is axiomatic that the aesthetic is the central means of utopian expression, and that however difficult it may be to define it, one still might entertain the idea of a utopian spirit. The classification of the utopian is narrower than that considered by Bloch, in that I have in the main selected texts which are standardly classified as literary and have demonstrable utopian themes; but I have

---

[15] Bloch, *The Principle of Hope*, III, p. 1121.
[16] Ruth Levitas, *The Concept of Utopia* (New York: Philip Allan, 1990), p. 190.
[17] See Caroline Edwards, *Utopia and the Contemporary British Novel* (Cambridge: Cambridge University Press, 2019), pp. 18–19.

history between the periods of the dialogue's setting and its composition, probably about 375 BCE.[8]

Prior to the signing of the peace treaty in 421 BCE, Athens' attempt to dominate Greece had resulted in notable victories and territorial gains in the first stage of the Peloponnesian War. However, following the collapse of the peace, the state suffered a series of military reversals. Despicable acts were also committed in the name of the state, such as the massacre of all adult men and the selling into slavery of women and children after the capture of the Aegean island of Melos in 416 BCE. The following year, Athens embarked on a disastrous colonial campaign against Syracuse in Sicily. The intention was to subjugate the island for the purposes of securing a lucrative source of funding for the war with Sparta. The final Sicilian campaign resulted in the loss of 40,000 troops and the destruction of the Athenian fleet. There were further foreign policy debacles. In 410 BCE, the Athenians unnecessarily antagonised their long-standing Persian foes, and had to open up another front to the east. By 405 BCE (when Plato was twenty-two), Athens' imperial ambitions had collapsed, and the city was besieged by the rival Greek powers. Athens surrendered, and Sparta had to resist calls from its allies that the city should be rased to the ground. The terms of the Athenian surrender treaty of 404 BCE included the imposition of a ruling regime sympathetic to Sparta's interests. Athens was forced to surrender nearly all her ships to the victors, and the Piraeus as well as the city's defensive wall were demolished.[9]

The *Republic*, then, is set in the Athenian district which would be destroyed in the final act of the Peloponnesian War; and the account of the ideal state takes place in what could be retrospectively judged as a brief hiatus in an era of catastrophic military adventurism. Contemporary Athenian readers of the *Republic* would almost certainly have been aware of the individual fates of Socrates' interlocutors. Polemarchus, Socrates' host for the discussion, for instance, perished in the initial purge when the oligarchy backed by the Spartans came to power after the city's defeat (with Plato's uncle appointed as an oligarch). If the *Republic* was intended as a universal projection of the ideal state constructed on immutable principles of justice (the title in Greek, possibly Plato's own, suggests 'The State, or on Justice'), then it also seems to be a work which was intended to throw into sharp relief the chronic structural difficulties of contemporary Athenian politics – the inter-connectedness of disastrous military adventurism abroad and defective decision-making at home.[10] Athenian political culture was factional; it promoted personal and familial interest above those of the state; it depended, in Plato's view, on a partisan leadership which lacked the necessary expertise to be able to

---

[8] On the standard periodisation of Socratic Dialogues, see Richard Kraut, 'Introduction to the Study of Plato', in *The Cambridge Companion to Plato*, ed. by Richard Kraut (Cambridge: Cambridge University Press, 1992), pp. 1–51 (pp. 4–5). For an alternative perspective see Catherine H. Zuckert, *Plato's Philosophers: The Coherence of the Dialogues* (Chicago: University of Chicago Press, 2009). Robert Kraynak sifts the evidence in his 'A Revolution in Plato Scholarship', *Perspectives on Political Science*, 40 (2011), 188–91.

[9] See Claude Orrieux and Pauline Schmitt Pantel, *A History of Ancient Greece*, trans. by Janet Lloyd (Oxford: Blackwell, 1999), pp. 145–65.

[10] On the interpretation of the dialogue's title, see W.K.C. Guthrie, *A History of Greek Philosophy: IV Plato: The Man and his Dialogues: Earlier Period* (Cambridge: Cambridge University Press, 1975), p. 434.

undertake a sufficiently thorough diagnosis on any given political and social problem. There was an absurd over-reliance on eloquent public speaking, where the effectiveness of many public addresses bore scant relation to the truth, to the underlying facts of any case under review.

Then there was the difficulties of the extensive role of the citizenry in both legal judgements and governance, whereby both verdicts in trials and major political policy were to be determined by the votes of the demos, those ordinary Athenians, who were ill-equipped, according to Plato, to assess the merits of the affairs brought before them. Democracy, the prevalent political system in fourth-century and fifth-century Athens, was particularly susceptible to the winds of self-destructive populism. Plato's *Letters* may or may not be authentic, but the autobiographical claim in the seventh epistle is certainly plausible.[11] Plato claims in the epistle that it was Socrates' prosecution and subsequent execution which confirmed the younger philosopher's opinions on the state's structural defects. If democratic politics had been calamitous for Athens by the end of the Peloponnesian campaign, then it was the trial, sentencing and execution of Socrates for impiety and corrupting the young in 399 BCE (as recounted in *Euthyphro*, *Apology*, and *Phaedo*) which revealed in a stark fashion the malaise of Athenian public life – a system of back-to-front principles and personal manoeuvrings which condemned to death the city's most upright citizen, 'the justest man of that time', on trumped-up charges.[12]

The practical difficulty was that manifest defects of the Athenian state could not be appreciably improved upon by adopting any of the other extant political systems in the Hellenic world. As the Plato of the *Letters* reflects, 'I came to the conclusion that all existing states are badly governed and the condition of their laws practically incurable, without some miraculous remedy and the assistance of fortune; and I was forced to say, in praise of true philosophy, that from her height alone was it possible to discern what the nature of justice is, either in the state or the individual'.[13] And it would be the central intention of the *Republic* to demonstrate, as a contemporary diagnostic, the notion of right in the individual *and* the state, and to examine the inter-dependence of both. The *Republic*'s dialogue starts with a needling exchange on the nature of justice between Socrates and the Sophist, Thrasymachus. The latter insists that what is just is merely an expression of what is good for the strongest member of any social body, 'justice is nothing other than the advantage of the stronger' (338c), he claims.[14] Socrates argues as a preliminary to his imaginative social vision that Thrasymachus' view is profoundly mistaken. He insists that good rulers do not crave power, do not see it as a matter of personal advantage. Justice must be understood as an internal principle, not as an empty synonym for arbitrary authority.

---

[11] Charles H. Kahn considers the evidence for the letter's authenticity in his review 'Myles Burnyeat and Michael Freder, The Pseudo-Platonic Seventh Letter', *Notre Dame Philosophical Reviews*, 9 November 2015 [https://ndpr.nd.edu/news/the-pseudo-platonic-seventh-letter/, accessed 23 July 2019].

[12] Plato, *Letter VII*, trans. by Glen R. Morrow, in *Plato: Complete Works*, ed. by John M. Cooper (Indianapolis: Hackett, 1997), pp. 1646–67 (p. 1647).

[13] Plato, *Letter VII*, p. 1648.

[14] *Republic*, trans. by G.M.A Grube rev. by C.D.C Reeve, in *Plato: Complete Works*, pp. 971–1223 (p. 983). Further in-text references are to this edition and are given as Stephanus numbers.

Before Socrates initiates the discussion on the just state, termed Kallipolis [beauteous city], he outlines the differences between the polis which one might *think* would be ideal, and one which truly deserves the epithet. In conversation with Glaucon, Socrates itemises the necessary occupations: famers, merchants, shopkeepers and sailors. In this early model, the city is a place of exceptional comfort and civility. The easy and sensible denizens will 'put their honest cakes and loaves on reeds or clean leaves, and, reclining on beds strewn with yew and myrtle, they'll feast with their children, drink their wine, and crowned with wreaths, hymn the gods. They'll enjoy sex with one another but bear no more children than their resources allow, lest they follow into either poverty or war' (372b-c). This prospect looks like a version of Bloch's 'splendid-utopian ship' headed as a thought experiment toward a 'Golden Age'. But then the restful contented vision suddenly and unexpectedly becomes over-luxurious and odious. Glaucon suggests in a blunt simile that the rich diet and easy living makes it sound as though Socrates is on a mission to found 'a city of pigs' (372d). Luxury will encourage cupidity and exotic tastes, such as 'perfumed oils, incense, prostitutes, and pastries' (373a), and as a further indication of wastefulness, artists, actors and choral dancers will arrive to offer those types of entertainment 'that go beyond what is necessary for a city' (373b). However, the outcome of this thought experiment is not the spectre of moral collapse one might expect. Instead, Socrates shifts the dialogue's focus to consider the external pressures which shape the state's constitution. As the city expands, it will inevitably come into conflict over resources with its neighbours. As a consequence, the most important class of citizens are those with the responsibility for defending the polis. And this identification of an essential role, leads in turn to a consideration of the importance of specialisms in the city.

The aetiological account of the good city's origin and early development reveals the necessity of having an elite military cadre for the defence of the polis. As governance should be regarded as a singular and necessary activity, then this elite class should be sub-divided into the guardians who will govern the city, and those auxiliaries who will defend it (as well as providing internal security). Beneath those ranks which command public authority, there is everyone else, the demos. And then there seems to be a startling shift in the imaginary city's central character (Bloch's moment of transference from 'Golden Age' to 'Black Soup'). Socrates suggests while the luxurious city may or may not have embraced a principle of justice, this now becomes the central aspect of Kallipolis. The constitution is so designed to enshrine justice both on the level of the individual and the state. It is a top-down vision of the good society. Much of the dialogue's early and middle parts are given over to a consideration of the appropriate education for the governing elite to ensure that a just society is maintained. Effective and disciplined leadership is as much a consequence of the right kind of training as ability. Indeed, Socrates suggests that the opposite is also true. The most personally and social destructive behaviour is exhibited by able men who have been corrupted, as though they have been nurtured in the wrong kind of soil. Education is to be a thorough disciplining of the mind and body, with philosophy being the central element, complemented with instruction in mathematics, music (of a restrained and conservative kind) and gymnastics. Socrates argues in the third book of the *Republic* that poetry, a key component of actual contemporary Greek education, will be retained, but in a diminished role, and it will now be subject to rigorous philosophical oversight and censorship. As Socrates points out, poetry in general and epic poetry, in particular, often shows the gods acting in a decadent and destructive fashion. To portray the gods behaving poorly is illogical – gods are divine, precisely because they embody goodness, and they cannot then be plausibly represented as being otherwise. The young, in particular, should not be exposed to such pernicious examples of supernatural conduct.

In the *Republic*'s pyramidal structure, the guardians are the dominant class and the smallest in number. They live in conditions of Spartan asperity where private interest has been entirely subordinated to public service. Housed in military-style camps; they cannot own property; 'cannot drink from gold or silver goblets' (417), cannot even be in the same room where precious metals are kept. They live off modest stipends generated by taxes on the ordinary citizenry. There is no possibility of guardians having a family, or entering into enduring affective relationships. They can neither express nor act on an impulse of erotic love for another person. The philosopher ruler, a man of wisdom, courage and experience, will always sit at the apex of this political and social hierarchy. However, the most radical aspect of the *Republic*'s proposals is not that a group of marginalised Athenian intellectuals should outlandishly insist that they are better qualified to govern the polis than conventional experienced politicians. It is rather that the city's elite women are expected to play a full and active role in the state's governance and administration. If this was a barely comprehensible measure in patriarchal Athens, where women had no say in the state's affairs (and indeed were often treated as chattel), then there was some precedence for such a settlement in Sparta, where women were afforded a modest public role. Socrates agrees with a sceptical Glaucon that the best man will always be more capable than the best woman in any endeavour of consequence. But this is little more than a short-term tactical concession. It allows Socrates to make his main point in this section of the dialogue, that the best women will perform almost any intellectual and physical task better than the overwhelming majority of men. Not having active women in the highest echelons of society, the *Republic* suggests, is a waste of resource and ability. But the same expectation as to public service apply to guardian women as well as to the men. And that means all guardian women have to surrender their children at birth to the state's collective care.

The *Republic* represents the most striking synthesis in Plato's oeuvre of the doctrine of ideal forms with political and constitutional analysis. Philosophers, both men and women, because of their intellectual aptitude, disposition and training are the best equipped of all citizens to grasp the essential forms of things, and what constitutes ethical action. The philosopher's ability to examine the truth in ethical and metaphysical spheres is tellingly complemented with the claim that accurate knowledge of such fundamental aspects qualify them as expert practitioners of statecraft. Socrates responds to the obvious objections as to why anyone in the lower social echelons would tolerate having this philosophical cohort as their rulers by emphasising the disinterested nature of their public service. Everyone can be assured that the guardians will do their level best to take decisions in the general interest, rather than for the benefit of family, party or themselves. Public office is no longer a route to power and enrichment. This is now a society in which many of the ostensible causes of internal strife and discontent have been eliminated, or at least mitigated. All citizens are assessed from birth as to their fundamental aptitude and capabilities; and they are then allotted the social role to which they are best suited. Those possessing manual dextrousness, but only modest intellect, will accordingly be satisfied with their lot as shoemakers or carpenters, rather than aspiring to some higher office for which they are palpably unsuited, such as being a doctor or a ship's captain. One occupation will not be muddled with another. Socrates insists on the necessity of a single career for each citizen; and there will no longer be either the incentive or the possibility for ordinary citizens to enter politics.

Justice in the *Republic* on the individual level is not so much a matter of considering the deontological context or teleological consequences of a given action, but rather looking at the personal circumstances which result in moral conduct. The just individual will achieve an appropriate balance between the three constituent elements of the soul: the spirited, the appetitive and the rational. The last of these should be the dominant element. And the individual who strikes this balance of constituent parts will not only be justified in himself or herself, but should also be in a state of personal felicity. Even if the analogy is not drawn out in an exact fashion, the overall sense of systematic integration across the individual and the state is clear; that the soul's tripartite division with the rational element in a pre-eminent position reflects the hierarchical model of the state with the guardians in charge, and the auxiliaries and the demos in their subordinate positions. The material demands of public office will oblige these reflective rulers to set aside the higher realms of philosophical speculation. The famous analogy of the cave in Book Seven of the *Republic* begins as an account of deluded ontology. Humans are portrayed as chained beings, mesmerised by the shadows of synthetic objects cast onto the cave's walls. However, some of these captives crane their necks, work themselves free from their shackles, and eventually make their way, albeit painfully and reluctantly, out of the cave and into sunlight, and see the world for what it is. The analogy equates the liberated prisoners' recognition of the world around them with the philosophers' hard-won apprehension of the abstractions of pure knowledge and eternal verities. However, the second half of the analogy suggests the same philosophers are also under a social obligation to return to the cave – not so as to liberate their fellow citizens in an act of civic enlightenment, but rather to provide effective and knowledgeable leadership to those who lack the wherewithal to cast off their chains, and see beyond the material appearance of things.

The *Republic*, then, holds out the prospect of a strong and stable society, where all citizens have an allotted role according to their capabilities; where the virtues of courage, self-discipline are embedded in the state's social structure; and where the polis is governed in the public interest by an elevated cadre of public-spirited philosophers. Of course, as Popper and other commentators have observed, there are the significant difficulties with the society's authoritarian tendencies, where the interest of the individual is apparently subordinated to the state's requirements.[15] Socrates argues that felicity is a consequence of being a psychologically-balanced individual;

---

[15] In addition to Popper, *Open Society*, see, for example, Warner Fite's discussion of the inevitable collapse of democracy into tyranny in the *Republic* in his *The Platonic Legend* (New York: Scribner's Sons, 1934), pp. 74–81.

and he insists when challenged as to the probable happiness of the family-less, property-less guardians, that he is confident they will be more than content with their lot; but he then goes on to suggest that even if they are dispirited, that cannot be a significant concern of the polis as a whole. A key aim of the ideal state is to produce the happiness of the social body, and not to be overly worried about the emotional state of a single member of the state, however prominent.

Popper regarded the *Republic* as offering a blueprint for the National Socialism of the 1930s. However, it is possible to interpret the text in terms of less harsh and rigid formulations. The *Republic*'s emphasis on approved wisdom, public dedication and managerial efficiency, for example, is reminiscent of the appeal to technocratic administrations when Western democratic systems become incapable of resolving their political and economic difficulties (such as Mario Monti's administration in Italy, 2011–13, and Lucas Papardemos' in Greece, 2011–12). And indeed, it is possible to see, in theory at least, a broad justification of the general compact of the Chinese communist party from the 1990s onwards as a separation of a cadre charged with governing the state, with an apparatus for ensuring internal and external security, and an extensive degree of economic liberalism for the rest of the populace, so long as they do not challenge the ruling party's authority. However, the technocratic analogy can only be taken so far, because of Socrates' curious insistence that the political settlement in Kallipolis requires an element of systematic deception. He tentatively advances in the later stages of Book Four the idea of 'a noble falsehood', an autochthonic myth, that the citizens emerged directly from the soil of their homeland, and that the god had put a proportion of metal into each class, 'mixed some gold into those who are adequately equipped to rule [...]. He put silver in those who are used as auxiliaries, and iron and bronze in the farmers and other craftsmen' (415a). And it then becomes beholden on the polis as whole to maintain the appropriate mixture of metal for each class.

It is just about possible to mount a defence of such a falsehood on the basis of national cohesion. Patriotism does not require one to believe a foundational myth as being literally true (in the same way one can appreciate the patriotic appeal of the Arthurian cycle, Sagas of Icelanders, and Portuguese Sebastianism), so long as one accepts that the 'grand falsehood' is not a matter of direct imposition or strategic manipulation by the guardians. However, it is much harder to offer a plausible justification for the other practices of delusion, deception and coercion for purposes of effective social control which Socrates advocates elsewhere in the dialogue. These include the use of drugs as a means of deception, the eugenic disposal of defective infants, and selective breeding of the guardian class, where an apparently free selection of sexual partners is in fact the result of a rigged lottery. As Malcolm Schofield suggests, one should perhaps retain a sense of cultural relativism in the evaluation of such dissembling and duplicity. The notion that political legitimacy requires an exclusive appeal to the reason of the populace is a modern Western conception which emerges in the work of John Locke, Schofield argues, and the absolutist position on the immorality of lying is an ethical invention of St Augustine.[16] One might justify an

---

[16] See Malcolm Schofield, 'The Noble Lie', in *The Cambridge Companion to Plato's Republic*, ed. by G.R.F Ferrari (Cambridge: Cambridge University Press, 2007), pp. 138–64 (p. 146).

isolated deception on the grounds of principle and consequences, and that is not inconsistent with a state in which political goods have been maximised. But it is much harder to reconcile the advocacy of deception within a dialogue which is critical elsewhere of dishonesty. And then there is the question as to why anyone would think it necessary to resort to such subterfuge. This strand of the dialogue implies that social cohesion cannot be entirely guaranteed by an appeal to widespread rational judgement and the apparent contentment of citizens being allocated tasks to which they are best suited. If such deceptions are intended to introduce a pragmatic element into the nature of the ideal state, then they also raise the question as to the psychological implications of inhabiting this orderly and hierarchical society.

In the *Politics*, Plato's former student, Aristotle, considers the projection of ideal state in the *Republic* and the *Laws* alongside other theoretical constitutions by Phaleus and Hippodemus. It has been argued that in key respects Aristotle should be approached as endeavouring to complete the moral-political project which his erstwhile tutor had begun. Plato's conceptions of justice and virtue are complemented by a notion of practical intelligence, which is an essential component for all individuals to arrive at an appropriate comprehension of right action.[17] And in terms of his analysis of the political society, Aristotle agrees with Plato that cities need to be of a manageable size (Aristotle argues that a man should be able to circumnavigate its boundaries in a single day). He shares with his former teacher a faith in inherent virtues of location and temperament, a pan-Hellenism, which assumes the best forms of governance will be developed by ethnic Greeks. And there are other points of comparison, such as in Aristotle's belief that the constitution is not identical with its citizenry. The population may change without the state's fundamental principles being affected. However, there are significant differences as well. Aristotle affords theoretical constitutions no more inherent credibility or even desirability than those which have already been put into practice. Indeed, the stress upon observable phenomena and induction in Aristotle's philosophy gives rise to a certain scepticism as to the value of any such exercises in political abstraction. When Aristotle considers the overall purpose of political society, it is also clear that he radically departs from Plato's precepts. For Aristotle, political society is a natural occurrence for human beings, and the state's central purpose is to ensure the citizens' overall happiness, rather than regarding such an outcome as an incidental benefit of the stable and well-governed city. However, it is on the grounds of practical consequences that the student mounts the most searching examination of his erstwhile tutor. When contemplating the optimal size of the state's population, Aristotle suggests one needs to account for resident foreigners and slaves in the city as well as its main populace (which the *Republic* does not). Aristotle complains that Plato's guardians are no longer proper citizens; they act instead as an 'occupying garrison' in Kallipolis.[18] But the most striking criticism of the *Republic*'s programme is

---

[17] See Alasdair MacIntyre's argument on Aristotle's political philosophy as an extension of Plato's views rather than a repudiation of them in his *Whose Justice? Which Rationality?* (London: Duckworth, 1988), pp. 88–102.

[18] Aristotle, *The Politics and the Constitution of Athens*, ed. by Stephen Everson (Cambridge: Cambridge University Press, 1996), p. 38.

destruction in the house of Agamemnon has seen Clytemnestra defy patriarchal authority by murdering her husband after his return from the Trojan War in the first play, *Agamemnon*. This is followed by Clytemnestra and her lover being slayed by her son, Orestes; and then Orestes' descent into madness, his pursuit by the Furies in the second play, the *Libation Bearers*. The final play, *Eumenides*, takes place in front of the Athenian Acropolis, where the Furies, who seek by ancient right the son's destruction, are overruled by Pallas Athene. She insists that Orestes stand trial in front of a jury of Athenian citizens. The cases having been made, the jurors' votes are cast equally for Orestes' exculpation and his destruction. Pallas Athene then has the casting vote; and she chooses to dismiss the charge against Agamemnon's son. In acting in this way, Pallas Athene does not so much indicate the limitations of strictly human determinations as exemplify both the spirit and the mechanisms of Athenian justice and the central principles of the polis. It is only through the application of the modern state and modern law that the ancient destructive cycle can finally be broken; and it is only in the meshing of the divine and the human that such matters can be satisfactorily resolved.

There are substantial grounds, then, for Plato's arguments for the exclusion of such dramatic representation from Kallipolis, not just on the basis that poets and playwrights lack a proper understanding of what they claim to write about, not just because the mimetic principles of their art must leave them by necessity doubly removed from the truth they claim to reveal, and not just because poetry and performance destabilise the soul to such an extent that the spirited and appetitive aspects gain ascendancy over the rational portion; but also because tragedy offers an understanding of human beings and their place within the cosmos which rejects the notion that there are absolute goods which human beings can observe for any protracted period. Yet, the even more troubling possibility is that tragedy, at least in the form of the *Oresteia*, offers a rival version of how one might approach the construction of the state, that the means of achieving this aim cannot be on the basis of the imposition of rational appreciation of humankind, but in the all-consuming demonstration of blood, fury and revenge, which through a kind of social and psychological route map eventually leads to the merging of divine and human justice in the standards and protocols of modern Athens. Murdoch thinks Plato's animosity was at its keenest in the allusions to Aeschylus; and she wonders whether his disdain was motivated by envy at the playwright's capacity for dramatic and insightful revelation.[36] And as we will see in the later stage of this study that tension between the tragedy and the ideal settlement is revisited and revised in the works of Aldous Huxley, Ursula K. Le Guin and Margaret Atwood.

If we do concede the strength of the case against art in the rational hierarchical projection of the ideal state in the *Republic*, then this still leaves the argument that the significance of the aesthetic in relation to ideal social forms is subject to implicit commendation. The sense of internal qualification and objection to such arguments is evident in many dialogues. One could point to the dramatic components, and indeed the dramatic irony frequently employed in these pieces. In the opening stages of *Meno*, for instance, the politician Anytus is enraged when Socrates remarks that Athenian

---

[36] See Murdoch, *Fire and the Sun*, p. 82.

leaders fail to pass on their virtues to their sons; and on taking his leave, Anytus mutters dark threats against the philosopher (which would come to pass as he was one of the chief prosecutor's at Socrates' trial). In *Crito*, Plato considers the trial's aftermath. The dialogue starts with the student, Crito, sitting beside the philosopher's bed in his cell, waiting for his tutor to awaken. The purpose of Crito's visit is to inform Socrates that the Athenian state galley is about to return from its annual religious mission to the island of Delos. Its arrival signals the philosopher's execution is imminent. Socrates expostulates on learning that Crito has been sitting there for quite some time, 'then why did you not wake me right away but sit there in silence' (Crito suggests that sleep provides a brief respite from the tormented thoughts of impending catastrophe).[37]

In the course of the dialogue, Crito reveals that he has a plan to enable his tutor to escape and flee into exile. Socrates rejects the scheme. His principal reason for doing so is that he has a reciprocal obligation to the state in which he was raised. As a citizen, he is obliged to abide by judicial rulings even if he believes the court's reasoning to be flawed and his sentence unjust. Socrates argument is questionable, because it advocates passive obedience as a legitimate response to a gross injustice; and it also runs counter to the case he made in the *Apology*. Socrates had argued at his trial that he was not bound by the faulty application of Athenian law. A more plausible explanation for Socrates' reluctance to agree to Crito's scheme is implied rather than stated. Socrates, just about, suggests that his escape and evasion of Athenian justice would be to hand a political victory to his opponents. His foes would use his flight as further evidence of his intrinsically corrupt and self-serving nature. But there is also the suggestion that the life of the philosopher in exile would be not be much of a life at all. Socrates would be an elderly outcast, weary, penurious, stateless and beyond rehabilitation. In other words, it is the dialogue's psychological context rather than its logical coherence which gives the episode its dramatic force and appeal. In this respect, *Crito* encourages a reading against the grain; that it is not so much a case of the setting providing an impetus and context for philosophical disquisition, but rather philosophy providing a justification for inaction, which is a consequence of weary resignation.

When the Manuels wrote of Plato as being exemplary of the 'anticipations, forerunners, and prefigurations of utopian ideals', they were justified in suggesting that the projection of Thomas More and other early-modern Utopians were 'inconceivable without Plato', though this narrative requires the necessary shift from the imaginative contemplation of the ideal state to what they term the 'speaking-picture utopias'.[38] The transformation is achieved by More in his blending of Greek rationality and Christian narrative. More produces his enduring and influential portrait of an ironically inflected and perfected version of England, in 'the mythos and logos of the ideal city'.[39] Of course, reflections on Plato's political ideals have a long history. Cicero used Socratic dialogue as his literary model for *On the Commonwealth* and *On the Laws* (both 54–51 BCE), while emulating Aristotle's procedural example to question the projection of the ideal as a means of political analysis. Cicero also attacked Plato's political principles as being

---

[37] *Crito*, trans. by G.M.A Grube in *Plato: Complete Works*, pp. 37–48 (p. 38).
[38] Manuel and Manuel, *Utopian Thought*, p. 13, p. 216.
[39] Manuel and Manuel, *Utopian Thought*, p. 14.

both ineffectual and severe. In the Christian reading of Plato from early theologians through the Church Fathers to the medieval period, the central concern was the extent to which Plato's philosophy could be reconciled with Christian orthodoxy. Hence, the first-century Christian apologist, Justin, believed those aspects of Plato's thought which could be aligned with scripture were a consequence of being founded on the wisdom of Moses and the other Old Testament prophets (Plato, apparently, having been a disciple of Jewish elders).[40]

For Gregory of Nazianzus in the fourth century, Plato's idea of the philosopher king was a legitimation of royal power above the claims of the divine, and, as such, should be resisted at all costs.[41] And St Augustine, while examining the points of contact and similarities between Christian doctrine and Plato and Platonism, expressed similar reservations. One should meditate on the heavenly city rather than its terrestrial counterpart. However, the poets' expulsion from the Republic is still a comprehensible measure. We cannot condone the philosopher's polytheism, but we should still acknowledge the necessary alignment of the divine with the good in his writings. 'Plato', Augustine says, 'refused to have the souls of the citizens tainted and corrupted by falsehood'.[42] Despite his involvement in the composition of More's *Utopia*, Erasmus remained sceptical as to Plato's influence. He regarded Kallipolis as a strictly imaginary place, whose utility in terms of effecting a political transformation was not readily apparent. Indeed, he suggests that 'no prince plagued a state more than when the sceptre fell into the hands of some pseudo-philosopher, or devotee of literature'.[43] Seventeenth-century secular rationalism was similarly dubious as to the veracity and utility of Attic thought. Spinoza denied that his rationalism was indebted to Socrates, Plato and Aristotle. He contrasted his notion of democracy with the *Republic*'s elitism; and he favoured an appreciation of political reality over speculative projection.[44] As we might expect, Plato certainly provided a foreshadowing of utopianism for communists, but this was often negatively inflected. For Marx, it was the social utopianism of Saint-Simon, Fourier and Owen which the *Republic* anticipated; and these were superficial revolutionary programmes which had left the fundamentals of bourgeois ideology and practice intact.[45]

Yet, there has also been the comparative tradition, which treats Plato as a figure divided against himself when it came to his views on the poets. Milton, for example, configured his attack on Presbyterian censorship in *Areopagitica* (1644) with a conflation of the positions of the *Republic* and the *Laws*, such that Plato stood condemned 'as a lawgiver but a transgressor, to be expelled by his own magistrates both for the wanton

---

[40] See František Novotný *The Posthumous Life of Plato* (The Hague: Martinus Nijhoff, 1977), p. 131.
[41] See Novotný, *Posthumous Life of Plato*, p. 183.
[42] Augustine, *The City of God Against the Pagans*, ed. and trans. by R.W. Dyson (Cambridge: Cambridge University Press, 1998), p. 66.
[43] Desiderius Erasmus, *The Praise of Folly*, trans. by Clarence H. Miller, 2nd edn (New Haven: Yale University Press, 2003), pp. 37–38.
[44] See *A Critique of Theology and Politics*, in *The Collected Works of Spinoza*, ed. and trans. by Edwin Curley, 2 vols (Princeton, NJ: University of Princeton Press, 2016), II, pp. 45–356 (pp. 284–91), and 'Letter (NS) to [Mr Hugo Boxel] from B.D.S.', in *Collected Works of Spinoza*, II, pp. 420–24 (p. 423).
[45] See *Manifesto of the Communist Party*, in Karl Marx, *Later Political Writings*, ed. and trans. by Terrell Carver (Cambridge: Cambridge University Press, 1996), pp. 1–30 (pp. 27–29).

epigrams and dialogues which he made'.[46] This sense of mirrored division was also apparent in Sir Philip Sidney's *Defence of Poesy* (written 1579–80, published 1595). Sidney's essay offers an ostensible defence of the expressive and veridical qualities of verse. It adopts a Neoplatonic conception of art to suggest that the finest paintings do not stop at the accurate representation of external appearances; they exemplify universal moral qualities as well. The *Defence of Poesy* also playfully shadow's Plato's strictures in its disdain for modern drama and verse. Percy Shelley's revision of Sidney's treatise, 'A Defence of Poetry' (written 1821, published 1840) was intended as a humorous, semi-serious rebuttal of early nineteenth-century utilitarianism. Shelley included Plato in its pageant of poets as archetypal legislators and imaginative provocateurs. And in the later part of the century, Walter Pater produced an influential set of essays in which he emphasised the formal exquisiteness of Plato's dialogues, 'his wonderful savour of literary freshness'.[47] For all of the 'certain anticipations of the modern world', Pater suggests, 'we are also quite obviously among the relics of an older, a poetic, half-visionary world'.[48] For the youthful Nietzsche in the *Birth of Tragedy* (1872), Plato's dialogues certainly anticipated the modern world, but this was not so much in terms of the ideas they advocated; but in their heteroglossic presentation. Nietzsche thought Plato's multifarious style ended up hovering 'somewhere midway between narrative, lyric and drama, between poetry and drama'; and he proposed that we should in the final analysis regard Plato as a literary innovator, bequeathing 'the model of a new art form to all prosperity, the model of the *novel*'.[49]

Nietzsche did not intend this observation as an unalloyed compliment. He was arguing that the pre-eminent revelatory and transformative art form for the modern era with its perfect fusion of Dionysian and Apollonian impulses was Wagnerian opera, rather than prose fiction. Yet the notion that the novel is a genre we should consider for a comprehension of the particular combination of narrative and thematic components is not without its attractions; and one might further consider the uses of such a literary type when it is associated with the projection of the ideal. Those expressive elements appear to be most pronounced in the *Symposium*, the dialogue long considered to be Plato's literary masterpiece, 'the most beautiful and perfect of all works by Plato', according to Shelley.[50] And if there is a certain formal exquisiteness to the work, then it is also the dialogue's principal topic of Eros which is of significance here, given the extent to which the idea of love would become a fundamental principle of many projections of the good society from the nineteenth century onwards. The dialogue's action begins *in medias res*, as Apollodorus, the young student of the very elderly Socrates, answers an unreported question from whom we eventually learn is Glaucon, Plato's older brother. The question, Apollodorus says, 'does not find me unprepared' (172a), as he goes on to explain that he had been asked essentially the same thing by

---

[46] John Milton, *Areopagitica and Other Writings*, ed. by Edward Poole (London: Penguin, 2014), p. 115.
[47] Walter Pater, *Plato and Platonism* (London: Macmillan, 1893), p. 3.
[48] Pater, *Plato and Platonism*, p. 3.
[49] Friedrich Nietzsche, *The Birth of Tragedy and Other Writings*, ed. by Raymond Geuss, trans. by Ronald Speirs (Cambridge: Cambridge University Press, 1999), p. 69.
[50] 'Preface to the Banquet of Plato', in *Shelley's Prose; or, The Trumpet of a Prophecy*, ed. by David Lee Clark (London: Fourth Estate, 1988), pp. 335–36 (pp. 335–36).

another acquaintance who recently hailed him in the street. In this earlier exchange, there was some jocular, if sharp, interplay between Apollodorus and his friend on the not unfamiliar Socratic topic of the relationship of philosophy to worldly affairs.[51]

Apollodorus asserts that he loves to discuss philosophy and the conversation of a successful merchant (like his friend) is vacuous by comparison. The concentration on commercial matters rather than the life of the mind should be treated as a personal failure. The friend takes this joshing in good part, and indeed, he points out there is something very un-analytical in Apollodorus' passion for philosophical disquisition. He reminds Apollodorus that he goes by the soubriquet of 'the maniac' in their circle; and that he is 'always furious with everyone, but not with Socrates' (173d). It eventually emerges that the acquaintance, Glaucon, and indeed the reader by interpolation are all interested in the same question, which is what does Apollodorus know about a renowned 'symposium', a formal drinking party held many years before to celebrate the tragedian Agathon's first victory at an Athenian drama festival. The celebration was distinguished by Socrates' attendance. The involutions in this narrative multiply when Apollodorus reveals that he was not even present at the event (it took place when he was child); and that he has the story second-hand from someone who was there, Aristodemus from Cydatheneum, whom he describes unflatteringly as 'a runt of a man, who always went barefoot' (173a).

At the prompting of the rhetorician Phaedrus, the symposium's participants each agree to deliver a speech on the topic of love, Eros. Phaedrus complains that 'our poets have composed hymns in honour of just about any god you can think of; but has a single one of them given a moment's thought to the god of love, ancient and powerful as he is' (177a-b)? The dialogue then recounts the speeches on this topic by six participants (with Aristodemus via Apollodorus cautioning that he could not exactly recall what everyone said). Phaedrus gives the first address followed by Pausanias (the lover of Agathon), the doctor Eryximachus, the comic playwright Aristophanes, the victorious Agathon, and Socrates (who chooses to relate the views of another figure, an old wise woman, Diotima, possibly intended to be read as a contrivance for Plato's own opinions). And there is a final contribution from Alcibiades, a military commander, and sometime passionate adherent of Socrates, who arrives late at the celebration in an inebriated state. The dialogue is remarkable for its incidental detail, often comic, and its dramatic shifts. Socrates slips on his best sandals as a cursory attempt to smarten up for this event. He arrives at the party, or rather does not arrive. Everyone turns around wondering where on earth he is, only to be informed that he is inexplicably standing motionless in a neighbour's porch. Aristophanes suffers from a fit of hiccoughs, and is unable to give his address (eventually cleared by the 'sneeze treatment' [189a]); there are the walk-on parts for the flute girls, who never get to play their instruments, and the spectacular clattering entrance of the commander Alcibiades and his entourage (interrupting Aristophanes as he is just about to respond to Socrates' speech). The intoxicated former soldier is incongruously garnered with

---

[51] *Symposium*, trans. by Alexander Nehamas and Paul Woodruff, in *Plato: Complete Works*, pp. 455–505 (p. 459). Further in-text references are to this edition and are given as Stephanus numbers.

'a beautiful wreath of violets and ivy and ribbons in his hair' (212e), intended for Agathon's prize-winning head.

The *Symposium* operates within the standard expectations of Athenian drinking culture. The social consumption of wine enabled frankness, loquaciousness and congeniality. There is nothing in the discussion which can be readily construed as criticism of the sybaritic conduct of the participants. The dialogue offers a range of different perspectives of Eros; and while it is clear that Socrates' views are intended to be a repudiation of the arguments from earlier in the evening, it still remains the case that no opinion is fully endorsed or refuted in the course of the narrative. Often a speech contains a plausible idea only to run into an internal contradiction, or it flounders on the intricacies of the mythos it advances. Phaedrus begins by securing the agreement of the whole company that 'love is one of the most ancient of gods', and goes on to contemplate an idealised society predicated on Eros. 'A city or an army made up of lovers and boys', he suggests, 'would be the best possible system of society, for they would hold back from all that is shameful' (179a). If the avoidance of shame constitutes a negative impulse, the prospect of the loss is a means to acquire individual honour. He cites the example of Achilles' sacrifice for Patroclus as a noble instance of love (while disputing Aeschylus' claim that there was a sexual component to their relationship). Phaedrus concludes that 'in truth, the gods honour virtue most highly when it belongs to Love' (180b).

The homoerotic context of Phaedrus address in particular and the dialogue in general is a standard feature of Greek upper-class culture (and contains a significant expectation of instruction and mentoring of an adolescent by an older man). An objection to Phaedrus' idealism following the example of the *Republic* is that it confuses martial virtue with what is required for the orderly governance of the modern civilised state. And one might also question the identification of Eros as a principal impulse for Achilles rather than the all-consuming rage, usually taken to be his defining trait. Pausanias offers in contrast to Phaedrus' vision of the society of the loved, a form of affective relativism coupled to robust Greek nationalism. He declares that 'customs regarding love in most cities are simple and easy to understand, here in Athens (and Sparta as well) they are remarkably complex. In places where the people are inarticulate, like Elis or Boeotia, tradition straightforwardly approves of taking a lover in every case' (182b). Yet such fruitful relationships can only be contemplated between Greek people, and that, in itself, provides a definitional explanation of barbarianism. 'The Persian empire is absolute', Pausanias avers, 'and that is why it condemns love as well as philosophy and sport' (182b-c).

Deputising for the spluttering Aristophanes, the doctor, Eryximachus, proposes an anatomy of love. He offers an analogy with the taxonomy of his own profession. The effects of Eros can be readily mapped onto the opposing states of the 'healthy and diseased constitutions' (186b); and he notes that while such notions might be conceptually opposed, there is always the danger of the higher form degrading into the lower, a collapse of noble romance into debauchery. Just as one must be wary of the distressing after-effects of a sumptuous meal, one should remain alert to the possibility of fine music being corrupted. 'The honourable, heavenly species of love, produced by the melodies of Urania, the Heavenly muse' may be tainted by Polyhymnia, the muse of many songs, demeaned here as 'common and vulgar' (186d-e). Yet Eryximachus' closing oration returns to the transcendent adhesiveness which characterised Phaedrus' opening address. He suggests that when love is properly directed it results 'in temperance and justice, towards the good, whether in heaven or on earth; happiness and good fortune, the bonds of human society, concord with the gods above – all of these things are among his gifts' (188d).

Aristophanes is evidently intended as a comic turn in the *Symposium*. Indeed, his characterisation looks like a rebuttal of the portrayal of philosophers in his own comedies, unable to take the stage when initially called to do so. When he does eventually speak he supplies a beguiling myth of sexual attractiveness, with human beings initially conceived as having four legs and arms. The gods decide to split these early creatures in two, because, as Aristotle says, they believed these new beings had unfettered ambition, and they were scheming to overthrow their creators. Sexual attractiveness is a consequence of the desire of the divided halves to recover their original unity: 'love is born into every human being; it calls back the halves of our original nature together; it tries to make the one out of two, and heal the wound of human nature' (191d). This myth of original attraction was sufficiently compelling that we can still catch an echo of it in Freud's conception of Eros and Thanatos, where all matter has this impulse toward unification. Yet, the imagistic appeal of Aristophanes' idea is at least in part vitiated by some comic excessiveness, and the necessity of working out the anatomical logistics of cleaving these prototypes. Faces and necks have to be twisted round, navels stitched up, skin smoothed down, sexual organs placed on the front, and internal reproduction devised as an alternative to the previous model in which human eggs were externally fertilised after the example of cicadas. Zeus even declares that if humankind does not now display due deference to the immortals, they will be sliced once more 'to make their way on one leg, hopping' (190d).

The victorious Agathon courteously demurs from Aristophanes' view that Eros is a consequence of early disobedience, divine punishment and anatomical ingenuity. He returns to the idealism of Phaedrus' opening address, though now the god of love is conceived as the youngest rather than the oldest of divine beings. Love is personified as a supple youth, delicate, graceful, the inspirer of temperance, and a means of social cohesiveness. The playwright's rhetoric soars as he approaches the conclusion of his peroration, 'ornament of all gods and men, most beautiful leader and the best! Every man should follow Love, sing beautifully his hymns, and join with him in the song he sings that charm the mind of god or man' (197e). Unsurprisingly, Socrates is sceptical that love possesses any of the characteristics ascribed to it by the previous speakers. He begins by dismantling Agathon's claims on the nature of Eros. He states that love must be directed toward an object or property which the lover lacks, and it makes no sense, then, to speak of love being directed toward the beautiful *and* possessing the properties of the beautiful itself. Through the reported dialogue with Diotima, he rejects the stable states which Eros is customarily afforded precisely because love requires dynamic movement from one condition to another. Hence, love is described as a 'great spirit' (202e). It is situated between the mortal and immortal, and similarly positioned between wisdom and ignorance.

Along the way, other views are challenged. There is a combined repudiation of the arguments of Aristophanes and Eryximachus in the suggestion that the compulsion to conjoin only operates when the counterparty is deemed to be sufficiently good or desirable. Attraction is complemented by an equal and opposite principle of repulsion, such that 'people are even willing to cut off their own arms and legs if they think they are diseased' (205e). Love cannot be straightforwardly associated with honour in any improving sense. Diotima does not believe that Patroclus and other heroes were motivated by affection as Phaedrus proposed. No, they had their eyes firmly set on the prize of immortality, and without the prospect of timeless fame and honour, they would not have been prepared to make such a momentous sacrifice. On the other hand, love cannot be wholly associated with human and divine beings, because as soon as one adopts a materialistic and causal view of relations, one can see that the same principle is present throughout nature. 'Mortal nature seeks so far as possible to live forever, and be immortal. And this is possible only one way', she says, 'by reproduction, because it always leaves behind a new in place of the old' (207d).

Love in its highest forms, Diotima suggests, necessitates a conceptual change where the notion of the beautiful as the object of desire is substituted by that of the good. Love ultimately manifests itself in the seeking out of the pure knowledge of forms. This is to glimpse 'the Beautiful itself, absolute, pure, unmixed, not polluted by human flesh or colours or any other great nonsense of immorality' (211e). It is an expression of what Bloch regards as the defining characteristic of Platonic thought, 'the pure Jacob's ladder, of the pyramid of ideas rising with ever truer Being to ever higher perfection. After all, its apex is supposed to be the *idea of goodness*, as the sole and final definition projecting into, the mystically indefinite element of the highest Being'.[52] This, for Bloch, was no more than an exercise in wispy abstraction, a corollary to the rigid terms of the blueprint of such work as the *Republic* and the *Laws*, a denial of the possibility of any development beyond rational precepts of the former, and their codification in the statutes of the latter. Yet, the expression of this notion of love, goodness and higher knowledge is not necessarily the summation of the discussion in the *Symposium*, even as an aporetic device, and a soon as one adjusts one's perspective from the task of establishing a unity of thought and consistency toward a philosophical end, and one embraces instead the Nietzschean notion of a multiplicity of styles and purposes, then the dialogue's outcome can be understood as being somewhat different.

Socrates' views are not afforded absolute authority in the *Symposium*, even if they broadly conform to views expressed elsewhere in his dialogues. His narrative does not possess any more inherent logic or coherence than the preceding discussions; the status of his speech is rendered uncertain by its presentation as a reported conversation with the possibly fictitious Diotima. And if the closing section of the dialogue does not undercut Socrates' account of the 'pure Jacobs Ladder' of Eros ascending to abstract wisdom, then it does not offer a straightforward endorsement of his thesis either. The entrance of Alcibiades changes the tone of the discussion; and in his case, extreme intoxication facilitates candour. Alcibiades lambasts Socrates as the abandoned lover.

---

[52] Bloch, *Principle of Hope*, II, p. 846.

He recounts how Socrates has a passion for young men; how he rejected his own advances; how he instils in the young not a level-headed approach to rational analysis, but a desire to 'share in the madness, the Bacchic frenzy of philosophy' (281b). And yet Socrates still embodies all those values we should admire. He was involved in the Potidaea military campaign (in 432 BC); he can hold his drink; he had the fortitude to withstand the biting cold in the Potidaea expedition; and he was conspicuously brave (not in the warrior spirit of slaying foes, but in the companionship and care he provided for the wounded). And he is, for Alcibiades, an expression of inherent contrariness, the threadbare thinker, endlessly rattling on about 'pack asses, or blacksmiths, or cobblers, or tanners' (221e). But behind all this triteness are expositions of essential truth, he says, reaching for the analogy of a hollowed-out statue, 'if you go behind the surfaces, you realise no other arguments make any sense' (221e).

Yet in another shift, the rest of the company bursts out laughing when they recognise that Alcibiades' own contrary views are a consequence of him being still in love with his erstwhile mentor. More revellers turn up; some guests depart, and Aristodemus, as related by Apollodorus, recalls in the closing section an image of conviviality, not easily reconcilable with the opinions on the constitution of the ideal state as expressed in the *Republic*. He remembers the last figures who had not either departed or fallen asleep were Agathon, Aristophanes and Socrates. The philosopher and playwrights pass among themselves a large goblet of wine, while discussing tragedy and comedy (though not sufficiently distinctly for Apollodorus to recall their conversation). Perhaps no accident that it is Glaucon, Plato's brother and Socrates' principal interlocutor in the *Republic*, who initially hails Apollodorus and requests this account of the symposium, as though trying to conceive of the philosopher in a different and frankly more sociable context than when he attempted to establish the fundamental principles of the ideal society. For here, Eros is the sustaining idea, whereas in the *Republic* it has only a limited role as an adjunct to the sense of duty the guardians are supposed to display in their selfless service for the state.

As one of the more allusive of Plato's dialogues, the *Symposium* does not offer any decisive opinions, and even its method of elenchus is questionable to the extent to which the characteristic Socratic disproof can be regarded as being robust. We may be encouraged to accept broadly Socrates' arguments for the nature and phenomenal directedness of desire, but not at the expense of ongoing the qualifications of the dramatic framework, the second-hand account of its revelation, the inebriated state of the witnesses and speakers, and the fact that none of the views expressed are decisively overturned by any of the others. Philosophy and creative representation are severed in the *Republic*; but they are conjoined in congenial and celebratory libation in the *Symposium*. It is not the case, of course, that the *Symposium* offers an explicit model of the ideal state, but it *does* offer a compelling model in its own terms of the good society; and it encourages some thought, some consideration of what the ideal society might look like if it were established on the principles of Eros. Even if it does not correspond with Phaedrus' vision of 'a city or an army made up of lovers and boys', then it certainly suggests that Kallipolis must have the capacity for the expression of desire and its fulfilment. This would be to recommend a different interpretation of the foreshadowing of utopian thought and projection than that entertained by the Manuels, a parallel impetus, perhaps not so consciously referenced, not so readily traceable, but there nevertheless, in which the very qualities which are excluded or significantly restricted in the *Republic* and the *Laws* form the basis of an alternative social vision – the good society predicated on candid discussion, love and laughter; and to be realised, as we shall see, through an ostensibly literary milieu.

2

Oxymorus: Thomas More and Utopia

In his letter endorsing the second edition of Thomas More's *Concerning the Best State of a Commonwealth and the New Island of Utopia* (1516), the leading French Humanist scholar Guillaume Budé wrote to Thomas Lipset in Paris, probably at the behest of both More and Erasmus. Lipset was overseeing the publication of both the second edition of *Utopia* and Thomas Linacre's Latin translation from the Greek of the six books of Galen's *On Protecting One's Health*. Budé was thoroughly conversant with the tradition of *serio ludere* [serious play] to which More was evidently contributing, yet his letter of endorsement suggests he recognised that More's short book provided a notable expansion in the range and the sophistication of the extended learned joke over both its classical and modern predecessors. Budé's letter, which would become a standard paratextual item in the book's European editions in the early modern period, begins by describing *Utopia* as merely a pleasing adjunct, as a supplement to the major work of scholarship in the Galen, but by the letter's conclusion, the distinct impression is that *Utopia* has an equivalent if not a greater claim to significance than that of the prestigious medical treatise recently translated into Latin.[1] The letter weaves in and out of *Utopia*'s central themes, and offers a knowing emulation of its subtle ironical tone. Budé retraces the initial movement in More's introductory letter from autobiographical fact to a realm of apparent fiction. Budé recalls how he took the 'book with me to the country, and kept it in my hands as I bustled about, in constant activity, supervising the various workmen'.[2] The encounter supposedly produces a radical change in attitude: he becomes so enwrapped in the alternative egalitarian society of the Utopians that he 'almost forgot and even dismissed entirely the management of my household affairs' (p. 9). 'What nonsense', he thought, 'is all this bustle over getting and saving, this whole business of accumulating more and more' (p. 9). And the letter follows the development from *Utopia*'s first book to its second with a consideration of the nature of justice and codification of laws, especially as they relate to New Testament principles of 'mutual charity and community' (p. 13). He offers a jocular variant on More's etymological pun for utopia as 'nowhere' from the Greek 'ou' [no] and 'topos' [place] by suggesting that he has heard that the island is also described as 'Udepotia' (p.13), a derivation from the Greek 'Oedepote' [never].

---

[1] On the use of Budé's epistle in *Utopia*'s paratextual apparatus, see *Thomas More's* Utopia *in Early Modern Europe: Paratexts and Contexts*, ed. by Terence Cave (Manchester: Manchester University Press, 2008), p. 183, p. 229, p. 231, and pp. 277–79.

[2] Thomas More, *Utopia: Latin Text and English Translation*, ed. by George Logan, Robert M. Adams, and Clarence H. Miller, trans. by Robert M. Adams (Cambridge: Cambridge University Press, 1995), p. 9. Further in-text references are to this version of Budé's letter and to this edition of More's *Utopia*.

Budé thinks this island's principal advantages are 'equality of all good and evil things among the citizens [...] a fixed and unwavering dedication to peace and tranquillity; and utter contempt for gold and silver' (p. 13). He identifies a key benefit of such a reformation in human behaviour would be the doing away with statute and its ponderous interpretation (well aware that More's profession was as a lawyer): the 'immense weight of all those legal volumes, which occupy so many brilliant and solid minds for their whole lifetimes would suddenly turn to empty air, the paper food for worms or used to wrap parcels in shops' (p. 15). Yet, Budé also strikes a note of playful scepticism as to how such a state could be maintained given the undoubtedly aggressive temperaments of the surrounding peoples, 'what prevented those enemies', he wonders, 'from driving out justice and modesty under an onslaught of shameless effrontery' (p. 15)? And he indulges in some speculative psychology as to the text's principal motivations. He constructs his case on the basis that More had stylishly embellished this account of the ideal commonwealth, while portraying himself as only a 'humble artisan' (p. 17) so as to insulate himself from any prospective criticism. He speculates that the invented Portuguese explorer and enthusiastic documenter of Utopian manners, Raphael Hythloday 'might some day return, and be angry that More had left him only the husks for credit for his discovery' (p. 17). The following year, Budé wrote directly to More and attempted to distil the allusive and contrary impulses of the author and his short imaginative work into a single expressive term, a compact literary portrait. He is aware of the various homophonic possibilities of More's name in Latin. It can connote foolishness, morals, illness and death. Budé recommends that his correspondent should now go the whole hog, and change his name to 'Oxymorus'. And then he changes it for him anyway, with the valediction 'Vale mi Oxymore' [farewell my oxymoron].[3] The Latin 'oxymorus' conveys not only its familiar English sense of paradox and contradiction, but also preserves the dominant meaning in ancient Greek of pointed foolishness, and from there, to the guise of silliness, both as a means of obscuring and conveying a serious point.

More's visual depiction can be said to be singular in that there is only one extant contemporary likeness (even though it has existed in many different versions and in various preparatory drawings).[4] Hans Holbein the Younger's famous portrait of More, painted on oak panel, was completed in 1527 (see Fig. 2.1). The picture shows its subject in the middle of his public career; More had by then served as a diplomatic envoy and Privy Counsellor before being elected Speaker to the House of Commons in 1523 (he would succeed Cardinal Wolsey as Lord Chancellor in 1529). Holbein's elder brother, Ambrosius, had provided woodcut title-sheet illustrations for the early editions of *Utopia*, as well as for More and Erasmus's collection of Latin poems. The younger Holbein had travelled to England with a letter of introduction from Erasmus. It is generally assumed that Holbein stayed at More's Chelsea home during his first sojourn; and that his host provided the artist with his first commission.[5] Holbein's approach to his subject is realistic and minimally emblematic. The counsellor is situated in conventional

---

[3] Gvliemi Bvdaei, *Regiii Secretarii Epistoloae* (Basil, 1521), p.13 and p. 21, cited in Elizabeth McCutcheon, *My Dear Peter: The Ars Poetica and Hermeneutics for More's Utopia* (Angers: Moreana, 1983), pp. 13–14.

[4] The versions and the painting's provenance are considered by John Rowlands in his *Holbein: The Paintings of Hans Holbein the Younger* (Boston: Godine, 1985), pp. 132–33.

[5] See Oskar Bätschmann and Pascal Griener, *Hans Holbein*, (London: Reaktion, 1997), p. 158.

Figure 2.1 Hans Holbein the Younger, *Portrait of Sir Thomas More*, 1527, oil on oak, 74.2 cm x 59 cm, The Frick Collection, New York, Copyright The Frick Collection.

three-quarter view; he looks intently out of the painting to his left. He wears sumptuous robes of ruby and green velvet, trimmed with fur; and he has an engraved dark-stoned ring on his left forefinger. The painting's straightforward symbolism is in sharp contrast to the rich and multifarious allusion of the artist's most famous painting, *The Ambassadors* (1533), and indeed, is modest even when compared to Holbein's portrait of that other prominent low-born Tudor statesman, Thomas Cromwell (c. 1534). Holbein's version of More holds gently a folded slip of paper in his right hand, and a weighty gold chain is draped around his neck. The paper suggests affairs of state; and the eye-catching chain – realised in pin-sharp detail, constructed from double interlinked s-shaped pieces with a Tudor rose pendant – does not denote any particular public office, but rather confirms the sitter's steadfast commitment to public service.[6] The costume's refinement and expense is to be expected for someone of More's professional standing and rank. However, as Oskar Bätschmann and Pascal Griener have pointed out, there are signs of discussion between artist and sitter over the appropriate level of ostentation. The original flamboyant ruff cuffs of his official costume have been overpainted.[7]

More's portrait seems to have been a carefully calibrated exercise in establishing the sitter's social standing and commitment to public service, while also impressing on the spectator that he was not vain of his person or office. More wears a plain shirt underneath his splendid robes (and beneath that possibly a hair shirt). His lack of interest in worldly achievement is also suggested by Holbein's detailed rendering of the face and head. Underneath the elegant bonnet, the intensity and fixity of More's gaze conveys a sense of single-mindedness and pensiveness. More is also shown to be unshaven. He is apparently not concerned with personal appearance, even when being recorded for posterity, or perhaps he is sufficiently concerned to ensure that a certain disregard in this respect was evident in spite of the fineness of his official garments. The growth is scrupulously recorded with individual grey flecks discernible in his predominantly dark stubble. Here, then, was evidence of steadfast resistance to the temptations of hubris; that foundational flaw which More often condemned in his writings. In his attacks on Lutherans, for example, he followed St Augustine in insisting that pride is the mother of all heresies; in his reflective 'Treatise upon the Passion of Christ', a work composed in the Tower of London shortly before his execution for treason in 1535, he conceives of the Fall as a consequence of Adam and Eve being tainted by Satan's rebellious spirit, 'this false serpent bereft them by his deceitful train, poisoning them with his own pride'.[8] And the Utopians are praised right at the end of his short early work for their refusal to succumb to this debilitating vice: 'Pride is a serpent from hell', Raphael declares, 'that twines itself around the hearts of men, acting like a suckfish to draw and hold them back from choosing a better way of life' (p. 247). As an encapsulation of its subject, Holbein's portrait seems to supersede Budé's witty oxymoronic

---

[6] See Charles Ryskamp and others, *Paintings from the Frick Collection* (New York: Frick Collection, 1990), p. 37.
[7] See Bätschmann and Griener, *Hans Holbein*, p. 160.
[8] See *The Confutation of Tyndale's Answer*, ed. by Louis A. Schuster and others, 3 vols, *The Complete Works of Sir Thomas More* (Yale: Yale University Press, 1973), I, p. 662; and St. Thomas More, *The Tower Works: Devotional Writings*, ed. by Garry E. Haupt (New Haven: Yale University Press, 1980), p. 25.

interpretation of More with an image of sustained wary seriousness, now split between public office and devout conscience. And it was certainly a portrait which met with the sitter's approval. More wrote to Erasmus in December 1526, declaring that 'your painter, dearest Erasmus is a wonderful artist'.[9]

Holbein's depiction of More has been used to illustrate an extraordinary range of interpretations of the author and statesman. Modern perspectives have ranged from the attempt to uncover an underlying principle of unity out of apparent contradiction to those which are predicated on the deconstructionist principles that oppositional terms must constantly confound one another. This results in the inevitable conclusion that one cannot arrive at a stable and comprehensible view of this particular figure. R.W. Chambers' landmark biography from the mid-1930s updated the confident and singular interpretation of the Lord Chancellor stretching back to the earliest account, written by his son-in-law, William Roper. In this interpretation, More is the implacable defender of the true faith confronted by the destructive and spiritually corrosive heresies of Protestantism. As Roper recalls, More was 'a man of singular virtue and of a clear unspotted conscience'.[10] For Chambers, religious fidelity and unswerving conviction could be understood in analogical terms to stand for the necessity of conscience as a means of resisting state totalitarianism (and that dynamic of conscience confronting state power would also be central to his portrayal in Robert Bolt's play, *A Man for All Seasons*, 1960). However, More was already being treated as a steadfast defender of secular truth and decency by the Victorian era. A correspondent in the *Times* in 1866 remarks that More's life was 'the noblest and bravest in that corrupt court'.[11] More becomes the allusive self-conscious Renaissance performer in Stephen Greenblatt's 1980s New-Historicist thesis. His apparent contrariness is the central concern for some modern biographers. Peter Ackroyd's literary portrait is split between artistic sensitivity and Catholic zealotry; John Guy explored his subject's life through the oppositional drives of priestly celibacy and sexual gratification; and Richard Marius constructed an 'anti-biography' of his subject, in which More is a profusely suggestive figure, but also an essentially unknowable historical presence.[12]

What is striking, of course, is just how unfavourable the recent fictional representation of Thomas More has been. Hilary Mantel can lay claim to being the most significant historical novelist since Sir Walter Scott both in terms of the nineteenth-century view of Scott as the writer who rejuvenated a moribund genre, and in the sense advocated by Georgy Lukács in the twentieth century. Lukács credited Scott with charting a shift in widespread consciousness, utilising what he termed 'necessary anachronisms' in his fiction. This was an effective means of articulating contemporary concerns through the

---

[9] Quoted in Rowlands, *Holbein*, p. 70.
[10] William Roper, *The Life of Sir Thomas More*, in *Two Early Tudor Lives*, ed. by Richard S. Sylvester and Davis P. Harding (New Haven: Yale University Press, 1962), pp. 195–254 (p. 197).
[11] Anon., 'Exhibition of National Portraits at South Kensington', *The Times*, 19 April 1866, 6.
[12] R.W. Chambers, *Thomas More* (London: Cape: 1935); and Stephen Greenblatt, *Renaissance Self-Fashioning: From More to Shakespeare* (Chicago: University of Chicago Press, 1980), pp. 11–73; Peter Ackroyd, *The Life of Thomas More* (London: Vintage, 1999); John Guy, *Thomas More* (London: Edward Arnold, 2000) and Richard Marius, *Thomas More* (London: Collins, 1985). See also Michael Ackland's useful survey 'Modern Biographies of Sir Thomas More', in *A Companion to Thomas More*, ed. by A.D. Cousins and Damian Grace (Madison: Fairleigh Dickenson University Press, 2009), pp. 39–52.

distancing and estranging effects of historical representation.[13] The first part of Mantel's Tudor trilogy, *Wolf Hall* (2009) operates on the basis of a straightforward inversion of the standard view of More and his nemesis, Thomas Cromwell. Instead of More being portrayed as a principled man of conscience and defender of the faith, while Cromwell is a brutish political enforcer, Cromwell is now conceived as an indulgent family man, pragmatic reformer and conscientious steward of royal finances. More, by way of contrast, is tic-ridden, evasive and fanatical. The narrator records that when More was Lord Chancellor, he established a spy network in London, and undertook the judicial persecution of Protestants. More's self-flagellation is noted (a detail taken from Roper's early biography), and the narrator repeats the contentious claim that More confined and tortured suspected Lutheran heretics in his Chelsea home. Mantel's twenty-first-century construction of the Tudor Lord Chancellor possessed a certain immediacy and plausibility, such that the journalist Christopher Hitchens summarised More's portrayal, as a 'hybrid of Savonarola and Bartleby the Scrivener', a necessary historical antidote to 'the saccharine propaganda of *A Man for All Seasons*'.[14]

For *Wolf Hall*, Mantel evidently had Holbein's portrait of More in mind alongside that of Cromwell. These pictures now hang on opposite sides of a chimney breast in the Frick Collection in New York. However, Mantel selects another version of More's likeness for the key ekphrastic episode in her novel. Alongside the depiction of his single figure, Holbein also produced a group portrait of More's family. This painting was destroyed in a fire in the early eighteenth century, but the image survives as a contemporary compositional drawing with the figures identified in Latin by Holbein's associate and the former tutor to More's children, Nikolaus Kratzer (see Fig. 2.2).[15]

This preparatory drawing with its ascriptions was intended as a gift for Erasmus. The drawing shows the family gathered in what is usually assumed to be the central hall of More's house in Chelsea. More's seated figure is surrounded by his father, his daughters, adopted daughter, his son and his fiancée, his second wife, Dame Alice (with playful monkey at her side, a representative of the family's exotic menagerie) and the household fool, Henry Pattenson. The last of these has what looks like a deliberate Latin pun on the household name and constructive foolishness in the ascription: 'Thom: Mori Morio, An 40' [Thomas More's fool, aged 40]. The family probably appeared in the finished picture as calm and dutiful, rather than excessively pious. The household is evidently learned: five of the figures are either reading or holding books, with further volumes scattered at Margaret Roper's feet and placed on a window ledge. A musical instrument is either suspended in front of the hangings in the background, or intended as a motif in the fabric. Erasmus characterised Holbein's depiction of the family as being like 'Plato's Academy christianised'; and a Victorian

---

[13] Georg Lukács, *The Historical Novel*, trans. by Hannah and Stanley Mitchell (London: Merlin, 1989), p. 61 passim.
[14] Christopher Hitchens, *Arguably: Essays* (New York: Twelve, 2011), p. 150.
[15] See Susan Foister, *Holbein in England* (London: Tate, 2006), p. 34. The compositional drawing for Holbein's group portrait is in the Kunstmuseum, Basel, and there are further preparatory drawings in the Royal Collections, Windsor Castle. There is a 1787 etching after the Basel drawing by Christian de Mechel, with examples in the National Portrait Gallery, and the Royal Collections Trust.

Figure 2.2 Hans Holbein the Younger, *Preparatory Drawing for the Family Portrait of Thomas More*, 1527, pen and brush over chalk outline on Japanese paper, 38.9 cm x 52.4 cm, Kunstmuseum, Basel.

spectator interpreted More's household in similarly idealistic terms, of scholarship and communal love. 'That quiet, studious, cheerful house at Chelsea', he said, 'is the most blessed place we get a glimpse of all through Henry's troubled reign'.[16]

In *Wolf Hall*, Mantel imagines a visit to the Chelsea house by Cromwell, as one of Henry VIII's counsellors, and Stephen Gardiner, the king's master secretary in 1532, not long before More's resignation of the Lord Chancellorship over the 'Submission of the Clergy', the official instrument granting the monarchy the power of veto over ecclesiastical legislation. Mantel conjectures the family portrait was displayed in the front hallway to dramatic effect. The central conceit is that dinner with the Mores shows them in a very different light to the orderly, dignified and self-constrained family depicted in their group portrait. Mantel's Cromwell observes family tensions, unhealthy passions, and his host's failure to live up to his image as a sombre and indulgent head of a devout and scholarly household. Mantel's More demeans his resentful wife (with the monkey now cavorting on her lap). The meal becomes a synecdoche for the ascetic paterfamilias – a series of tepid dishes, smothered with the same 'gritty sauce like Thames mud'.[17] Dinner concludes abruptly and chaotically when the unhinged fool is ejected from the hall for his chuntering, only to reappear on the mezzanine as More's alter ego, from whence he pelts the family and their guests with bread while bellowing 'don't flinch masters I am pelting you with God'.[18]

An intriguing aspect of *Wolf Hall* is that while blackening More's reputation for the purpose of rehabilitating Cromwell's, the novel also utilises a number of literary devices and themes which are familiar from More's own writings, such as the use of irony in recuperative, dramatic and ambiguous modes; such as in a willingness to conflate fact and fiction, and in a commitment to the idea that fictional representation is capable of revealing salient truths not capable of demonstration through any straightforward documentary form of expression. Such themes and stylistic preoccupations periodically surface in More's prodigious output of history, biography, original poetry, translations of poems, religious tracts and pamphlets, but are realised in an especially sharp and succinct fashion in his early *Utopia*. Dedicated modern interpretations of the book's meaning and significance are broadly divided between those which regard the text as providing an attractive literary patina over some concrete political proposals; and those which regard the book as a predominantly fictional work in which political considerations are secondary. Hence, on the one side, George Logan argued More's *Utopia* has the stronger claim to being the foundational work of Western political science than Machiavelli's *The Prince* (written 1513, published 1532); and on the other side, Elizabeth McCutcheon stressed the narrative's complex and shifting qualities.[19] For McCutcheon, More's Latin prose was a vanishing point of sense, through its 'ambiguities and equivocations, his cryptic and otherwise understated allusions, his

---

[16] Erasmus quoted in translation in Bätschmann and Griener, *Hans Holbein*, p. 161; Anon., 'Exhibition of National Portraits at South Kensington', 6.
[17] Hilary Mantel, *Wolf Hall* (London: Fourth Estate, 2010), p. 230.
[18] Mantel, *Wolf Hall*, p. 234.
[19] See George M. Logan, *The Meaning of More's 'Utopia'* (Princeton: Princeton University Press, 1983), p. 105.

inverted sententiae and topoi, his tropes and figures – notably his hidden metaphoric transformations and turns'.[20] Yet, as this chapter will argue, one can conceive of the text's central definitional aspect is its amalgamation and inter-dependence of these factors, such that the literary requires the reality of the objective materials upon which it operates; and those materials are themselves illuminated by the allusive forms in which they are expressed. These qualities, in themselves, become essential aspects of literary idealism.

In the second half of the twentieth century, J.H. Hexter, Edward Surtz and George Logan convincingly reconstructed *Utopia*'s genesis. They identified its principal intellectual co-ordinates, and its intention as a specific type of Humanist literary production. By 1515, More had been appointed Undersheriff to the City of London. He was exceptionally busy with his legal career and young family. He had literary aspirations, but little time or the energy to write; and he had already been approached by the Crown to see if he would be interested in taking on an advisory position. In May 1515, he travelled to Bruges as part of a royal commission to negotiate a trade agreement with the appointees of Charles, Prince of Castile (who would become Holy Roman Emperor in 1519). The delegation's purpose was to resolve competitive difficulties between Flanders and England, and to endeavour to reduce or entirely remove trade tariffs between the states. Negotiations over the terms of access to European markets reached a point in which both teams of commissioners needed further instructions from their political masters. In the hiatus in negotiations, More visited Antwerp and met Peter Giles, a merchant, the city's chief secretary and a confidante of Erasmus. Giles would subsequently become one of the discussants in *Utopia*. It seems *Utopia*'s second book, in which the fictional Portuguese explorer Raphael Hythloday describes the social, political and economic circumstances of this island was substantially conceived and written during this interlude.

More probably decided to compose the first book once he returned to London in late summer 1516. Erasmus stayed with him in August of that year, so it is probable they collaborated on the text. It might have been that both More and Erasmus felt the first-hand report of the social structure and conventions of Utopia needed the addition of an extensive introduction and short conclusion so that the text met the rhetorical expectations of classical treatises, with readily identifiable components of exordium, peroration and conclusion.[21] As Paul Kristeller has pointed out, Humanist scholars were expected to produce works in the five associated disciplines of grammarian, rhetorician, poet, historian, and moral and political philosopher.[22] In the first phase of his literary career, More translated Lucian's satires as a grammarian; as a rhetorician, he composed intricate letters (in distinctive ironic style) in defence of Erasmus against charges from conservative theologians of irreligiosity and obscurantism; he wrote

---

[20] McCutcheon, *My Dear Peter*, pp. 21–22.
[21] Hexter's supposition; see his introduction to *Utopia*, ed. by Edward Surtz, S.J. and J.H. Hexter, *The Complete Works of St. Thomas More* (New Haven: Yale University Press, 1965), pp. xv–cxxiv (pp. xx–xxiii).
[22] P.O. Kristeller, 'Thomas More as a Renaissance Humanist', *Moreana; Thomas More and Renaissance Studies*, 65–66 (1980), 5–22.

Latin epigrams as a poet, and he undertook a biographical history of Richard III in Latin and English (starting as an anatomy of tyranny and ending as an exposé of necessary cruelty and deviancy required to gain and maintain power in a monarchical system). In this schema, *Utopia* could be classed as his contribution to moral and political philosophy. J.C. Davis perhaps overstates his case when he suggests that the account of the island Utopia in the second book should be viewed as no more than an adjunct to the significant discussion of society and justice in the first; but it is still plausible that the opening part, among its other evident functions, is intended to strengthen *Utopia*'s claim to being a work of trenchant political philosophy, rather than a mere flight of fancy.[23]

The first book, nevertheless, establishes the overall tone of the work, with its shifting frames of fact and fiction and apparent rebuttal of every argument advanced. The book provides an examination of the requirements and limitations of professional counsellors to European princes, whose power derives from a sense of dynastic entitlement and in the belief that the ruler's principal aim is self-aggrandisement and the expansion of territories. The first book prepares the reader for the extended account of Utopian society in Book Two, with brief descriptions of how other New-World nations manage their affairs in a more rational and efficient fashion than their Old-World counterparts. The title of Plato's *Republic* suggests in the original Greek that it is to be a work on the nature of the state and justice as much as an account of an ideal commonwealth. *Utopia*'s first book emulates this model by examining the nature of justice in Tudor England. In the book's interpolated dialogue, Hythloday recalls an exchange at the table of a fictionalised version of the late Cardinal Morton (More had served in the cardinal's household, admired him, and would include a further favourable portrait in his *History of King Richard III*). Hythloday commences one part of the discussion with a sardonic observation on unnatural developments in animal husbandry. 'Your sheep', Hythloday says, 'that commonly are so meek and eat so little; now, as I hear, they have become so greedy and fierce that they devour human beings themselves' (p. 63). This inverted trope whereby the gentlest of herbivores have become rapacious and carnivorous is an expression of interlinked anxieties over changes in English land usage and the rapid expansion of the wool trade. Hythloday's target, as Surtz points out, is the on-going practice of enclosure in which private owners systematically engross common land.[24] Hythloday highlights two manifestations of this unwelcome innovation: the establishment of the boundaries of properties through the planting of hedges and ditches, and the turning of arable land into pasture. Those who own land, the nobility, the gentry, private citizens, and even some orders of the church are motivated by the financial advantage of converting tracts of land to sheep farming. Wool can be sold for a substantial profit in English and continental European markets. The overall effect of the wool trade is to reduce the amount of land available for food production, and to encourage the elite to believe they have a right to live in ease from the profits generated by their holdings.

[23] J.C. Davis, *Utopia and the Ideal Society: A Study of English Utopian Writing, 1516-1700* (Cambridge: Cambridge University Press, 1981), p. 46.
[24] Edward Surtz, S.J., 'Commentary', in *Utopia, Complete Works of Thomas More*, ed. by Surtz and Hexter, pp. 257–570 (p. 325).

The consequence of the engrossment of large parts of England for personal profit is the high number of dispossessed commoners. These people have been either forcibly turned out of their villages and hamlets, or left with no other option but to abandon their communities, because without access to common pasture they have no means of sustaining themselves. The result of these developments is unquestionably a social menace. The steady stream of dispossessed individuals and families means the country is increasingly filled with those that have no stake or role in the wider community. Because they have no obligations, there are few restraints on their conduct. Hence, one sees an increase throughout the countryside of pauperism and vagrancy, and a steady accumulation of unmoored impoverished people in towns. Such excluded individuals may well cause social disorder, but Hythloday regards them as victims rather than the instigators of crime. The lawyer, however, openly admires the coherence and robustness of the English legal system through the rigorous prosecution of the laws with respect to theft. But he is also perplexed by current circumstances. Given that the punishment for this offence is so severe and so well-understood by the populace, he wonders why the capital sentence is not an effective deterrent, why 'so many thieves sprung up everywhere when so few of them escaped hanging' (p. 57).

The reason for this apparent anomaly is obvious to Hythloday, and he offers a sociological explanation for the seemingly endless hangings: people steal, not because they are inherently wicked and idle, but because they are desperate and hungry. The central defect of the English legal system is that it is skewed in the interests of the propertied. Rather than assuming a disinterested perspective on crime, English law assigns criminal responsibility to the individual, and pays *no* attention to prevailing social factors. The consequence is that common people are confronted with the invidious choice of stealing or starving, and are then executed because they unsurprisingly opt for the former. Hythloday argues executing thieves as a judicial measure fails on three grounds: first, it is not a deterrent, because the material pressures which give rise to the offences are such that the prospect of punishment cannot have any effect; second, executing criminals deprives the state of labour which could be used productively on public projects; and third, the punishment is disproportionate to the offence. English jurists, Hythloday declares, 'seem to imitate bad schoolmasters, who would rather whip their pupils than teach them. Severe and terrible punishments are enacted for theft, when it would be much better to enable every man to earn his own living, instead of being driven to the awful necessity of stealing and then dying for it' (p. 57).

From a modern perspective, Hythloday's demographic analysis is unconvincing. The major difficulties which had beset England for more than a century were not those of land use and capital markets due to enclosure, but the catastrophic decline in the population due to regular outbreaks of bubonic plague and other lethal infectious diseases. The result had been a chronic shortage of labour.[25] Some rural communities had been dispersed because of the engrossment of common land, but it is almost certain that the overall population of the English countryside had stabilised by the

---

[25] See Joyce Youings, *Sixteenth-Century England* (London: Allen Lane, 1984), pp. 130-53; and Christopher Dyer, *Making a Living in the Middle Ages: The People of Britain 850-1520* (New Haven: Yale University Press, 2002), pp. 271-97.

early sixteenth century, and the more common reason for abandonment of settlements was lack of economic viability rather than enclosure. Few English people starved in the late-medieval era, even during intermittent periods of famine; and shortage of labour maintained wage levels and depressed rents. More also characterises Hythloday in *Utopia*'s opening book as someone who tends to be swept along by his ideas, to work himself into such a state of righteous indignation that he fails to see how his remedies of political and social ills would be unworkable within the prevailing structures. It falls to More's more sombre and cautious literary persona to point out to the Portuguese traveller the shortcomings of his proposals. Nevertheless, Hythloday does provide cogent reasons as to why the legal system fails to address the problems with which it was confronted. The ethical basis of Hythloday's position probably derives from a combination of classical republican tradition (with its roots in Aristotle's inclusive political community) and empathetic New Testament virtues, with the personal requirement to act with charity, mercy and forgiveness. Whatever its historical and practical difficulties, Hythloday's analysis remains cogent in terms of its inferences from the judicial principles he assumes, and as a crux of distributive and retributive justice, whereby faults in the former lead to flawed reasoning in the latter. Hence, the unequal distribution of social goods gives rise to a retributive system which fails both on the grounds of proportionality and utility. One should not execute people for stealing when they have no choice in the matter; and theft is not an offence which merits a capital sentence.

Hythloday's remedy for social and economic ills in Utopia's first book is memorably direct and influential. He advocates the abandonment of private property and money as a means of determining worth as a mechanism for exchanging goods. Private ownership is incompatible with the principles of justice. 'Unless private property is entirely abolished', Hythloday says, 'there can be no fair or just distribution of goods, nor can the business of mortals be conducted happily. As long as private property remains, by far the largest and best part of the human race will be oppressed by a distressing and inescapable burden of poverty and anxieties' (p. 103). This position, of course, anticipates Utopian communism in Book Two. The examples of other communities which Hythloday provides in the first book similarly prepare the reader for the policies of the Utopians. The Polylerites, for example, have a rational system of criminal justice, where restitution for an offence is made directly to the victim of a crime rather than any stolen goods being commandeered by the state (as in England). Prisoners work on public construction projects, rather than being unproductively incarcerated. And these examples lead to the first book's other significant concern, the role of secular counsellors and the checks and balances on a ruler's authority.

Hythloday has some similarly radical suggestions for the way in which those who advise princes should behave. He argues that advocating purely practical measures for the maintenance of power to a ruler is unprincipled. It is plain wrong, he suggests, to recommend currency manipulation for the Crown's benefit (such as increasing the value when borrowing and devaluing when settling loans); or that counsellors should recommend the king's subjects be suppressed on the instrumental grounds that 'poverty and want blunt their spirits, makes them docile, and grinds out of the oppressed the lofty spirit of rebellion' (p. 91). He advocates instead that the king's sovereignty ultimately resides in his people. Employing another ovine allusion, he insists that it is the prince's 'duty to take more care of his people's welfare than his own, just as it is the duty of a shepherd who cares about his job to feed the sheep rather than himself' (pp. 91–93). Even if we set aside constitutional obligations to the populace, there are still sound reasons, he argues, why princes should concern themselves with the welfare of those they rule. Hythloday does not believe that a perpetual state of poverty will quell the rebelliousness of the dispossessed, rather it will make disorder more probable. 'Who is more eager to change things', he asks, 'than the man who is most discontented with his present position? Who is more reckless about creating disorder than the man who knows he has nothing to lose and thinks he may have something to gain?' (p. 93); and there are other matters of standing and obligation, which are not related either to constitutional requirements, or to the material advantage to the state and its finances. It is ultimately a matter of Christian virtue and reflected self-worth for the prince to demonstrate a concern for his subjects. More's literary persona has no doubt as to what reception Hythloday can expect if he were ever so foolhardy as to propose such policies to princes and their attendants. The powerful will remain 'stone deaf'. 'Academic philosophy', More bluntly concludes, 'is pleasant enough in the private conversation of close friends, but in councils of kings, where grave matters are debated with great authority, there is no room for it' (p. 95).

In his letter of endorsement for *Utopia*, the real-life Peter Giles highlighted the instructive comparison to be made between More's work and the most prominent classical projection of the ideal state. Giles suggested that the book should be 'studied by everyone as going far beyond Plato's Republic' (p. 25). And an anonymous encomiastic poem, also often reprinted alongside More's work, makes a similar point on the modern over-going of the ancient commonwealth – in the apparent rendering of the abstract into the concrete: '"No-Place" was once my name, I lay so far;/ But now with Plato's state I can compare,/ Perhaps outdo her (for what he only drew/ In empty words I have made live anew)' (p. 19). In practice, explicit derivations from Plato are scattered and incidental in *Utopia*, rather than being a matter of systematic revision or incorporation. Hythloday's travelling is initially compared to Plato's alleged Mediterranean journeying by the fictional Peter Giles. Hythloday describes noblemen as 'drones living idly off the labour of others' (p. 57); and the same metaphor is applied to oligarchs in Book Eight of the *Republic*.[26] When asserting that it is the counsellor's duty to speak truth to power, Hythloday cites the examples of both the *Republic* and the Utopians as alternative and viable social models; the property-less Utopians have a prototype in the property-less guardians; the Utopian emphasis on utility, such that all trades must contribute to collective wellbeing, has a corresponding expression in Plato's work; the small legal corpus in Utopia is consonant with the minimal legislative provision in Kallipolis, though not, of course with the extensive judicial provision of the ideal society in the *Laws*.

Nevertheless, there *are* noteworthy derivations from the *Laws* in *Utopia*, such as in the provision for potential Utopian spouses to view one another naked before making

---

[26] See *Republic*, trans. by G.M.A Grube rev. by C.D.C. Reeve, in *Plato: Complete Works*, ed. by John M. Cooper (Indianapolis: Hackett, 1997), pp. 971–1223 (p. 1164 passim).

a final commitment to the marriage, and the policy of distributing the population evenly between all the cities which comprise the polis. However, the most significant Platonic influence would seem to be on the role of philosophers in the governance of the ideal state. More's literary persona disparages Hythloday's political idealism by suggesting that he follows his 'friend Plato' in the chiastic formulation that 'commonwealths will be happy only when philosophers become kings and kings become philosophers' (p. 83). Yet, the conjectural basis of *Utopia* is the idea that intelligent, devout, well-educated men from ordinary backgrounds (More's grandfather was a successful London baker) are better suited to running modern states than the European nobility with their heritable claims and princely ambitions. The republican vision of Utopia seems, then, not only to be an imaginative projection of shared Humanist principles, but also a means of entertaining the idea that middle-ranking men could and perhaps should be entrusted with government, rather than merely being expected to advise their aristocratic masters.

Hythloday's account of the Utopians in Book Two is ostensibly a vision of a society in which a rational moral schema converges with the kinds of moral precepts one finds in orthodox Christian teaching. The island has approximately the same landmass as England, but is optimally shaped into a crescent with a large central harbour. It has planned urban development with fifty-four identical cities evenly distributed throughout the country. The Utopians are technologically ingenious. The original monarch Utopus, it is said, not only brought the population to their present and enduring 'high level of culture and humanity' (p. 111), but also enhanced their natural defences, by creating the island, cutting a channel between Utopia and the continent. The society is characterised by rationalist uniformity. The arrangements of land management are subject to similar symmetrical regulatory requirements. In the countryside, there are evenly-spaced large houses to accommodate farmworkers. These households, as Hythloday explains, are all run by 'a master and mistress, serious and mature persons' (p. 113); and it is the duty of all able-bodied citizens of the state to undertake agricultural labour on a two-year rota. Hythloday's early description of the cities and the countryside establishes the central principles by which the state operates. There is a material regularity with an equal distribution of labour, and due deference paid to the community's senior members. There is also an early introduction of the rational pragmatism of the Utopians in a variant on the farm rota. Most citizens undertake agricultural labour because they have to (even if most have a sense of civic duty). Those few individuals who actually enjoy tilling fields are permitted to carry on with it as long as they wish.

The overarching rational regulatory framework is complemented by a form of representative governance. Utopia is fundamentally republican in character; in keeping with the general high regard that such a broad-based system of political organisation was held by Humanist scholars in the early sixteenth century.[27] Each Utopian city

---

[27] On classical republican theory as the basis of Utopia's political institutions, see Quentin Skinner, 'Sir Thomas More's *Utopia* and the Language of Renaissance Humanism', in *The Language of Political Theory in Early Modern Europe*, ed. by Anthony Pagden (Cambridge: Cambridge University Press, 1987), pp. 123–58; and Logan, *The Meaning of More's Utopia*, pp. 190–95.

enjoys a high degree of political autonomy, so long as it abides by the same rules. Each group of thirty households elects a 'syphogrant' or 'phylarch' in modern usage (a realistic touch by More, suggesting that even in the ideal state political terminology will evolve). There is a further official, a tranibor, or head phylarch who presides over a group of ten syphogrants (the method of appointment is unspecified). The tranibors then elect by secret ballot the prince from four candidates to govern the city; and the prince usually holds this office for life. The tranibors and the prince meet on alternate days in the senate chamber, and two syphogrants are always present. The expectation is that governance will be routine, and the discussions cover the affairs of the city and the settlement of the few civil disputes. Important matters seem to be moved up and down the political levels. Policy decisions are referred downwards to the assembly of syphogrants, and from thence to all households in the city; state business can proceed in the opposite direction to be considered by the general council for the whole island. The governing council is constituted by the princes of each of the cities (though without any presiding presidential figure). Presumably, though it is never confirmed, this national body will be mainly concerned with formulating and implementing foreign policy.

The promotion of Utopian republicanism is intended to remedy the structural deficiencies of European monarchies in which, as the opening book suggests, there is little incentive for princes to govern in the interests of their subjects. Yet given the importance of proportionality as a basis for retributive justice in the opening book, one aspect of the Utopian criminal code as it applies to the practice of governance is particularly noteworthy. Hythloday declares that 'it is a capital offence to make plans on public business outside the senate or popular assembly' (p. 123). The severity of this punishment, it seems, is intended to deter the prince and his deputies from circumventing constitutional requirements to exercise power in their own interest rather than that of the public. Even so, there seems to be a glaring inconsistency between Hythloday's complaint about the severity of the punishment for those convicted of theft in the first book; and the endorsement of a capital sentence for conducting state business outside approved forums in the second. The reason for this draconian measure is never spelt out, but the assumption would seem to be that human beings are so constituted that they will always be tempted to act in their personal interest. The punishment for private consultation would seem to be a pragmatic measure, rather than the application of abstract principles for the assigning of a specific tariff to a specific action. The danger of holding such conversations *in camera* is that however innocuous this may be to begin with, such meetings will lead to the establishment of private arrangements. Such personal understandings with their reciprocal obligations will eventually undermine the state's institutions. The principle of proportionality needs to be applied to the probable consequence of an action rather than to the action per se. Furthermore, the circumstances of the Utopian statesman differ markedly from those of the half-starved English thief. The former can make a free and active choice as to how he behaves, whereas the latter cannot.

The political arrangements of the Utopians are, of course, of central importance to understanding what kind of constitutional arrangements will maximise the goods of the society as a whole. However, the second book's imaginative focus remains squarely on the society's customs and community organisation (in the sense that readers are encouraged to consider how they might fare should they find themselves inhabiting this society). The Utopians memorably live and work in extended households, which appear to be loosely modelled on More's own domestic arrangements. Younger members defer to their elders; there is a conventional demarcation of domestic labour with women taking responsibility for the cooking and cleaning. The society is earnest and active: everyone who is physically capable is expected to practise a useful trade, such as 'linen-making, masonry, metal-work, and carpentry' (p. 125). The exception to this rule is the small cohort of exceptionally-able scholars; they are permitted to study during the working day, and from whose ranks the rulers and administrators for the commonwealth are drawn. Leisure time is filled with productive, self-improving pursuits, such as learning a musical instrument, playing chess-like board games and attending early-morning lectures.

There are obviously differing degrees of authority and responsibility throughout Utopian society. However, the general commitment to the principles of egalitarianism is tellingly demonstrated by the citizens' appearance. As Hythloday reports, their dress is the 'same everywhere through the island'; and it has always been the same, 'except for the distinction between the sexes, and between married and unmarried persons' (p. 125). The uniform is not unattractive, apparently; it allows for free movement; and it functions equally well in warm and cold weather. The Utopian attitude to clothes, however, is also indicative of a wider commitment to equality aligned with utility and pragmatism. The demonstration of marital status is presumably of assistance for those unmarried members of the community who are in search of a spouse. The same principles of equality, utility and pragmatism also apply to work – if everyone does their fair share, then no-one has to labour for more than six hours a day, an arrangement which leaves everyone with plenty of time for rest and self-improvement.

While the social analysis of Utopia's first book might well have mistaken the key economic challenges of the early sixteenth century, the second book still demonstrates a keen awareness of the destabilising social effects of significant and rapid demographic change. The Utopian position is that just as the production of goods and services should remain constant across all the cities of the state, the population should also be stabilised. There is no consideration of the policies of selective breeding as advocated in the *Republic* (mechanised reproduction is restricted to a brief account of a chicken hatchery). Hythloday reports that the Utopians do recognise that birth and death rates are bound to fluctuate from one location to another; and Hythloday acknowledges that there may be periods when the population will decline sharply due to infectious diseases. The Utopians have a policy of forcibly relocating families from one urban centre to another to maintain an even distribution of citizens across the whole state; and they also have a colonial policy with established satellite communities in neighbouring counties. These outlying settlements act as a reservoir in the event of sudden population decline. Utopians are prepared to dismantle an entire colony rather than tolerate any significant fall in numbers in the mother country (More could not conceive of overpopulation as a social and economic difficulty, a persistent anxiety of utopian writers from the nineteenth century onwards). There are no observations in the book on the mechanism for achieving such substantial relocations, or on the psychological effects such enforced movements would have on the populace.

An effective novelistic aspect of *Utopia* is the way in which the reasons for Hythloday's initial outburst against private property are revealed in the second book. Hythloday openly admires the Utopians' common ownership and moneyless economy. The Utopian household is substantially a self-sufficient unit, producing many of the goods required for daily existence (including all of the clothing). The consequence of having a planned society with a fully-trained work force, a rotational system for agricultural production, and the expectation that most citizens will be employed for the public benefit is that the economy will produce a surplus of all necessary items. The Utopians do not have a domestic currency, because there is no need to establish relative values across a range of items. Each city has four market places. Citizens simply deposit surplus produce in these locations, and pick up those goods from the market their households require. More does not conceive of human beings as having a natural propensity 'to truck, barter and exchange' in the manner of Adam Smith; rather, he regards commercial transaction as a consequence of the unwarranted imposition of an arbitrary system of value which distorts the relationship of individuals belonging to the same community.[28] The contingent and artificial nature of material value is illustrated in Hythloday's well-known anecdote of the visiting delegation of Anemolian ambassadors to the federal capital, Amaurot. The foreign dignitaries parade through the city in golden cloth, and with 'heavy gold chains round their necks, gold jewels at their ears and on their fingers; and sparkling strings of pearls and gems in their caps' (p. 153). The ambassadors are disconcerted to find they are treated contemptuously by the capital's citizens, not realising that gold and precious stones occur naturally and abundantly on the island; and that the Utopians use golden chains to fetter their prisoners and slaves.

Just as Utopian clothing demonstrates the significance of practicality, equality and uniformity for this society, so their architecture demonstrates the preference of the public over the private. All Utopian houses are well proportioned, but designed to minimise privacy. 'Every house has a front door to the street and a back door to the garden', Hythloday reports, 'the double doors [...] open easily with a push of the hand and close again automatically – and so there is nothing private and exclusive' (p. 119). Still, the private is not an entirely unknown condition for the Utopians. The prohibition on rulers and officials holding clandestine discussions only extends to their consideration of civic affairs (so presumably they are free to talk about other matters). There is a residual sense of privacy in the relations of spouses; with some surprisingly liberal measures in place for securing initial and continuing nuptial contentment. And there is also a provision for divorce, should couples eventually find their spouse's company intolerable; although the requirements for such annulments are demanding. Nevertheless, the general expectation is that conduct remains open to public scrutiny. It seems Utopians are expected to internalise a sense of constant surveillance; as though they should be assessing the public benefit of any thought or action. It is as if Utopians believed they were being actually observed, as often they would be, by a senior family member.

[28] Adam Smith, *The Wealth of Nations, Books I–III* (London: Penguin, 1986), p. 117.

The corollary of the limitations on personal privacy is the restrictions on movement. Any individual Utopian must secure the permission and the appropriate documentation to be away from their home area prior to travelling. No specific reason is given for these strict edicts. It may be that the text merely reflects a common anxiety about the unregulated movement of large numbers of people across England and continental Europe. This would be interpreted as a sign of societal disorder and breakdown.[29] In any event, the restriction on free movement is consistent with a central policy which requires a stable output of labour; and the monitoring and maintenance of the population level in each Utopian city. In the cases of both unauthorised absence and engaging in sexual relations outside marriage, the penalties are harsh. If a citizen is found outside his home area without appropriate documentation, he is 'to be treated with contempt, brought back as a runaway, and severely punished. If he is bold enough to try it a second time, he is made a slave' (p. 145). Those who engage in pre-marital sex incur 'severe punishment on both the man and woman; and the guilty parties are forbidden to marry for their whole lives, unless the prince by his pardon mitigates the sentence' (p. 81). Adulterers fare even worse, and can expect to be condemned to the 'strictest form of slavery' (p. 191). If they are fortunately pardoned, and then so foolhardy as to repeat the offence, they will be executed.

These sentences seem out of keeping with the approach to justice in *Utopia*. No reasons are given for the draconian penalties, but their justification would presumably go something like this – the key difference between the state of Tudor England and the state of Utopia is that those at the bottom of English society have little option but to resort to stealing to survive, whereas the egalitarian provision of the Utopians, including a common education policy and lifelong welfare, means that everyone is properly fed and cared for. All Utopians understand the penalties for transgressing custom and law; and they have clear choices as to the ways they behave. Adulterers cannot argue their conduct should be excused on the grounds that they find themselves trapped in an unendurable relationship, because the social dispensation permits divorce. The principles of justice are predicated on abstract standards, but are also calibrated on the basis of necessary deterrence and final causes with respect to social effect. Unlicensed movement is problematic for a society which requires a regulated population. Given that the extended family is the fundamental unit of Utopian society, and the carnal instinct is so strong, the punishment needs to be sufficiently severe to deter citizens from acting in a fashion which would reduce orderly family life to a morass of jealousy, deception, passion and violent dispute.

As Logan points out, More's intellectual co-ordinates seem to have been an amalgamation of Epicurean and Stoical precepts combined with Christian notions of charity.[30] Hythloday reports that the principal concern of Utopian moral philosophy is 'human happiness, and whether it consists of one thing or many' (p. 159), and it

---

[29] See J.A. Sharpe, 'Economy and Society' in *The Sixteenth Century*, ed. by Patrick Collinson, Short Oxford History of the British Isles (Oxford: Oxford University Press, 2002), pp. 17–44 (pp. 36–39); and Robert Tittler, 'Society and Social Relations in British Provincial Towns', *A Companion to Tudor Britain*, ed. by Robert Tittler and Norman Jones (Oxford: Blackwell, 2004), pp. 363–80 (pp. 367–70).

[30] See Logan, *Meaning of More's Utopia*, especially pp. 154–66, also his edition of *Utopia*, p. 159n.

is thereby aligned with mainstream ethical reflection in the West from Aristotle onwards. Utopians have a hierarchical schema of pleasures with an acceptance of the need to gratify the body's desires and maintain good health. Hythloday describes the Utopians' attitude to health as 'the foundation of all the other pleasures, since by itself alone it can make life peaceful and desirable' (p. 173). Beyond these attributes, they advocate distinctive Ciceronian attributes expressed as 'the practice of the virtues and consciousness of the good life' (p. 175). Yet More clearly shared with Plato a belief in the necessity of a robust regulatory framework if such goods are to be realised; and that means ultimately the overall satisfaction of the community will take precedence over the happiness of any given individual. Citizens can certainly be happy, but only so long as their felicity conforms to the state's prescriptions for joyfulness. As Hythloday makes clear, some unfortunate Utopians will not achieve even a modicum of contentment. The great majority of the nation's slaves are former citizens, found guilty of heinous offences, presumably having been caught committing adultery, or having been picked up on more than one occasion outside their own district without the necessary paperwork.

More's encompassing commonwealth clearly rejects the most radical suggestion in Plato's *Republic*, that women in the guardian class should play an active role in the governance of the state. It is true that in Utopia women are not exclusively confined to the domestic sphere. They are expected to work for the commonwealth; they are granted the same educational opportunities as their male counterparts; they will eventually occupy senior positions in the home; some will serve as priests; and they can presumably initiate divorce proceedings alongside their discontented husbands. Nevertheless, there is still a conventional bias throughout Utopian society in favour of men. The head of the household is always a man, the work women undertake is suitable to feminine propensities; they are not excused the standard domestic obligations of raising children, cooking and cleaning; only a very few women of advanced years are appointed as priests; men are obliged to correct the errors of their wives; and the assumption is that all the rulers and senior state officials of the state are men. Dominic Baker-Smith suggests that the prohibition of family life in the guardian class in the *Republic* would have proved intolerable for many women, and as a consequence one should excuse this conventional understanding of the role of women as evidence of More's sensitivity to their natural propensities.[31] Yet that seems to be no more than special pleading for the socially conservative vision of the domestic unit in this society. Girls with an aptitude for scholarship and learning do have the opportunity in Utopia to pursue their academic interests, but in this respect, the commonwealth only succeeds in replicating the difficulties faced by the small coterie of highly-educated women in Tudor England (including More's own daughter, Margaret Roper). Such women had scant opportunity to use their learning and intellectual acumen outside of the household.[32]

---

[31] See Dominic Baker-Smith, *More's* Utopia (London: HarperCollins, 1991), p. 167.
[32] See Margaret Bowker's account of the constrained life More's daughter 'Roper [More], Margaret (1505–1544)', *Oxford Dictionary of National Biography*, Oxford University Press, 2004; online edn, May 2009 [http://www.oxforddnb.com/view/article/24071, accessed 11 April 2019].

As Hythloday often asserts, the Utopians are amiable and cultivated people. He brought a collection of classical works on one of his later trips to the island, and he suggests they avidly consumed the works of Plato, Aristotle, Homer, Sophocles, Euripides, Aristophanes, Plutarch, Lucian, Thucydides and Herodotus. However, as we have seen, the text also demonstrates the severity of their customs and laws. Two areas in which tensions between a benevolent and erudite outlook and harsh pragmatic conduct seem readily apparent, indeed seem to be advanced as an explicit means of testing the limitations of the idea of the perfect commonwealth, are in the Utopians' treatment of slaves, and in their policies toward potential and actual enemies. Hythloday makes no apology for the Utopians being a slave-owning society. Slavery is a common sentence for Utopians transgressing customs and laws. Native Utopian slaves are supplemented by foreign nationals captured in the course of battles with rival powers. This policy can once again be justified on the grounds of relative utility. It is evidently more productive to put those to work who would otherwise be imprisoned or hanged, as happens in Europe. Hythloday states that slaves who rebel will be summarily executed, but if they perform their allotted tasks without complaint, they will be treated well. Utopian slavery is not an inheritable condition; children are not bound with their parents; there is the possibility of manumission; and indeed, the circumstances of their bondage are often so favourable, Hythloday suggests, that there have been instances of 'free' but penurious foreigners asking to be enslaved to improve their lot.

One could further justify slavery in Utopia on the basis of historical precedent; that the examinations of ideal communities by Plato and Aristotle are predicated on the ready availability of slave labour. Both Old and New Testaments consider slavery as accepted social institutions, as well as supplying a series of theological metaphors; and while the accounts are undoubtedly complex in range and purpose, there is no explicit condemnation of enslavement in scripture (the abolitionist argument that slavery was incompatible with New Testament ethics did not emerge until the eighteenth century). David Brion Davies notes that one cannot even find specific objections to slavery in the seventeenth-century legal theories of Descartes, Malebranche, Spinoza, Pascal, Bayle or Fontanelle.[33] It is possible that slavery was a contemporary topic of discussion in the Netherlands at the time of More's visit to Antwerp, because of the large amount of sugar which was being imported into the city from the plantations of São Tomé.[34] Erasmus makes some condemnatory observations on the practice in his *Education of a Christian Prince* (1516). He insists that 'all slavery is pitiable and dishonourable', and suggests it is 'inappropriate for a Christian to acquire mastery over fellow-Christians, whom the laws did not intend to be slaves and whom Christ redeemed from all slavery'.[35] The presence of slavery in Utopia still looks anomalous. It is clear that much public work, and all of the most demeaning tasks would be undertaken by this subjugated workforce. And if it can be understood to satisfy a requirement for utility

---

[33] David Brion Davis, *The Problem of Slavery in Western Culture* (Oxford: Oxford University Press), p. 108. On biblical sanctions of slavery and the history of emancipation, see David Brion Davis, *Slavery and Human Progress* (Oxford: Oxford University Press, 1984), pp. 107–16, and pp. 129–53.

[34] Davis, *Slavery and Human Progress*, p. 63

[35] Erasmus, *The Education of a Christian Prince*, ed. by Lisa Jardine, trans. by Neil M. Cheshire and Michael J. Heath (Cambridge: Cambridge University Press, 1997), p. 24; p. 40.

in the sense of extracting useful public work from those criminals and enemies of the state which other societies execute, then it still does not make much sense in terms of the commonwealth's economic model. One cannot easily reconcile the practice of slavery with the insistence that if all citizens undertake their fair share of work there will be an equal distribution of social goods, and everyone will have adequate time for constructive leisure.

Part of the Hythloday's evidence for the general benign condition of Utopian slavery is the manumission of sentences. Even if one were to set aside the taxing question as to whether an objectionable measure can be rendered acceptable by good conditions and the prospect of liberation, this still leaves the difficulty that slaves are to be freed on an ad hoc basis. There is no clear indication at the outset as to how long a given sentence might be. In this respect, the criminal justice system of the Utopians seems to operate to the same capricious standards observed by European princes. Moreover, one class of slaves has almost no prospect of being manumitted, and their circumstances provide the clearest indication yet as to why slavery is necessary in the ideal state. The Utopians maintain bondsmen who butcher 'fish, meat and poultry' outside of the cities' boundaries. 'The Utopians feel', Hythloday says, 'that slaughtering of our fellow creatures gradually destroys the sense of compassion, the finest sentiment of which our human nature is capable' (p. 139). 'Besides', he adds, the Utopians 'don't allow anything dirty of filthy to be brought into the city lest the air become tainted by putrefaction and thus infectious' (p. 139). These slaves, then, must carry out those tasks which if they were allocated to Utopians would both expose them to dangerously unhygienic conditions and would desensitise them to such an extent they could no longer act as the suitably empathetic beings required for a dignified and well-mannered society. The passage suggests that the opposite also holds true, that the effect of admitting callous butchers as full members of the community would be to erode society's civilising principles.

The other area where the conduct of the Utopians appears dubious is in their foreign policy. They make extensive use of violent Zapoletes as mercenaries, while maintaining it would 'deserve very well of mankind if they could sweep from the face of the earth all the dregs of that vicious and disgusting race' (p. 221). They resort to espionage, targeted assassinations and bribes to encourage the officials of rival powers to turn on one another to subvert their governments. Utopians believe absolutely in their right to annexe adjacent territories and establish colonies when those lands are not being employed productively by their neighbours. Robert Adams thought More's account of the Utopians' foreign policy of deterrence aligned him with the mainstream Northern Humanist opinion of Erasmus, Colet and Vivet in detesting warfare. Adams believed that the principal aim of the aggressive and underhand policies outlined in More's book was to minimise the possibility of conflict on the basis that everyone understood any challenge to Utopia sovereignty would be met with an uncompromising response.[36] Hence, the Utopians do not tolerate any hostile actions toward their citizens. If any Utopian is killed

---

[36] Robert P. Adams, *The Better Part of Valor: More, Erasmus, Colet, and Vives, on Humanism, War, and Peace, 1496–1535* (Seattle: University of Washington Press, 1962), p. 153.

or seriously injured by a rival power, the state demands that the guilty party is surrendered to be enslaved or executed; and if these offenders are not given up, then the Utopians will declare war. However, it is difficult to reconcile such draconian policies with claims for pacifism. They invite the question – deliberately so one suspects – as to whether one can maintain a position of principled regulation with respect to one's own population and resort to unconstrained realpolitik when it comes to everyone else.

Eric Nelson has demonstrated how the trope of negation pervades *Utopia*, not merely as a matter of intriguing and engaging verbal playfulness, but as an overarching organising principle. He points out that Hythloday's name means that he is a disseminator of nonsense, and nearly everything he describes is intended to hollow out both meaning and being: '"Polylerites" are people of much (poly) nonsense (leros); Archorians are a people without a country (achorioi); Utopia is "no place" (outopos) [...] the title of the island's governor is Ademus, an official "without people" (ademos); the main river Anyder means "without water" (anudor), and it runs through the capital Amauro, the unknown city (amauros)'.[37] More's lexical pliancy informs the whole work. His name, Nelson suggests, is 'the most significant pun of all', connoting 'foolishness'. His literary persona ends up flatly dismissing Hythloday's opinions as nonsense.[38] Nelson interprets More's ingenious and persistent negation as a strategy for refuting one kind of concrete political-ethical settlement for the purposes of endorsing another. Greek nothingness is a means for More to refute a 'neo-Roman' version of republicanism; a vision of the good society 'synthesized out of the Codex of Justinian and the works of Cicero, Sallust, Livy and Tacitus', an intellectual tradition which 'provided for the framework for the Republicanism of City States'.[39] Nelson argues that Greek nothingness is an aspect of More's strategy to return to central aspects of Plato and Aristotle's projections of the good society, with an emphasis on the 'natural balance among elements' in humankind, a model of society which either abolished private property in the case of the former, or aimed for its 'temperate distribution' in the case of the latter.[40] This does not seem an improbable account of the book's political intentions, and Nelson's argument is certainly conducted with technical precision and deftness; but a consequence of such a rhetorical annulment is that there is no good reason why negation should end in the establishment of another concrete political theory. The persistent claim to nonsense and nowhere would seem to suggest that a more radical, indeed oxymoronic, rhetorical schema is being developed without the assurance of any republican backstop – both as a means of projecting the ideal society and of denying that any such society could be created. And if such a society were ever to be created, then it would not as a matter of its condition, be ideal. It is the formulation of a distinct type of aesthetic conceptual space, designated as Utopia, which enables such mutually incompatible notions to be proposed simultaneously.

In the twentieth century, grand utopian theorists tended to play down the shifting oppositional nature of More's text. Karl Mannheim, for example, conceived of *Utopia* as

---

[37] Eric Nelson, *The Greek Tradition in Republican Thought* (Cambridge: Cambridge University Press, 2004), p. 20; I have transliterated the Greek terms in Nelson's text.
[38] Nelson, *Greek Tradition*, p. 21.
[39] Nelson, *Greek Tradition*, p. 8.
[40] Nelson, *Greek Tradition*, p. 15.

a foundational work in a historical-literary tradition against which his own sense of the term's proper use could be tested. This literary tradition obstructed the proper sociological use of 'utopia' as a beneficial ideology, a schema of thought 'guided by wishful representation and a will to action'.[41] Ernst Bloch interpreted More's text as an anticipation of socialist utopianism, but it was also a work which avoided the static aspects of later projections of the ideal state. For all *Utopia*'s manifest faults (he describes it as 'dross' at one point), Bloch still believed the book was redeemed by its momentary revelations of 'the human tendency towards freedom – as a minimum of work and state, as a maximum of joy'.[42] One would expect on the basis of how their reading has been incorporated into *Utopia*'s standard reception that Frank and Fritzie Manuel would have provided an uncontentious interpretation of the book. They are now mainly remembered for suggesting that More was the earliest political theorist in the Western tradition to dignify physical labour in the ideal commonwealth.[43] Yet, to focus on this solitary aspect is to overlook one of *Utopia*'s more extraordinary readings from the last century. For what the Manuels were really drawn to was the contrast between Utopia's apparent urbanity and More's psychological state, especially after the existential threat of Lutheran heresy had become incontrovertible. Hence, the Manuels are interested in such details and habits as More's 'hair shirt, the self-flagellation with knotted ropes, the vigils, and fasts'. They recall More's subsequent persecution of heretics. They judged More's role in the burning of Protestants as recounted in Foxe's *Book of Martyrs* to be 'more true than false'; and his prolific writings excoriating William Tyndale were to be treated as a kind of visceral *Lex Taleonis*. More repudiated the foul heresy and the 'clumsy style' of Tyndale's translation of the Bible into English in suitably venomous fashion.[44]

What animates the figure of More in this interpretation was Thanatos as a fear of death; and Eros, as sexual passion sublimated into religious sensibility, and then articulated in such exquisite reflective devotional works as the *Dialogue of Comfort*. Any plausible account of More, the Manuels asserted, had to come to terms with these contrary impulses. 'Only a psychology that is undaunted by polarities and ambivalences and contrarieties and paradoxes', they declared, 'can presume to make sense of Thomas More without decapitating him psychically'.[45] And as mid-century Americans, they reached for their Freud to explain these contradictions. They quote Freud on the psychopathology of humour: 'by its repudiation of the possibility of suffering, [humour] takes its place in the great series of methods devised by the mind of man for evading the compulsion to suffer – a series which begins with neurosis and culminates in delusions, and includes intoxication, self-induced states of abstraction and ecstasy'.[46]

---

[41] Karl Mannheim, *Ideology and Utopia: An Introduction to the Sociology of Knowledge*, trans. by Louis Wirth and Edward A. Shils (New York: Harvest, [c. 1965]), p. 40.
[42] Ernst Bloch, *The Principle of Hope*, trans. by Neville Plaice, Stephen Plaice and Paul Night, 3 vols (Cambridge MA: MIT Press, 1986), II, p. 523.
[43] See Thomas More, *Utopia*, ed. by George M. Logan and Robert M. Adams, trans. by Robert M. Adams (Cambridge: Cambridge University Press, 1989), p. 43n.
[44] Frank E. Manuel and Fritzie P. Manuel, *Utopian Thought in the Western World* (Cambridge, MA: Belknap Press, 1979), p. 141, p. 139, p. 137.
[45] Manuel and Manuel, *Utopian Thought*, p. 139.
[46] Sigmund Freud *Collected Papers*, Vol. V (Miscellaneous Papers, 1888–1938), trans. by James Strachey (London: Hogarth Press, 1950), p. 217, quoted in Manuel and Manuel, *Utopian Thought*, p. 142.

The Manuels then added 'utopia-making as mental exercise' to this list of personal transformations and distractions.[47]

The most striking aspect of the Manuels' interpretation, however, is their insistence on the down-right avoidance of the book's central principles and wilful misreading in the subsequent utopian tradition. There are rejectionists, such as one can detect in the scientific and aristocratic visions of Bacon, Campanella and Cavendish. There are admirers who transform More and his best-known work into an endorsement of whatever cause they happen to believe in themselves. Hence they contemplate, 'William Morris turning him into a prophet of socialism, John Stuart Mill of utilitarianism, Karel Kautsky of communism, [...] Russell Ames of bourgeois democracy' (to which one could now add Rutger Bregman's citing of More's 'dream of free money' as a precursor to the policy of universal basic income).[48] Then there were eccentric literalists: such as in the attempt by the Mexican, Vasco de Quiroga to introduce a Utopian social programme into Indian villages in Santa Fe in the 1530s. Even forensic modern scholarship (such as Hexter's) misses its target. The expert 'has no sooner uttered a definitive judgement on the meaning than he feels the need to retract part of it'.[49] Literary interpretations fare no better, with all of these dismissed as being 'lop sided'. In this reading, More's concise early work is endlessly suggestive (with now a global reach, rather than merely a Western one). *Utopia* has become a postmodern artefact of absolute relativism, endorsing whatever one wishes to take from it. The Manuels' overall assessment of the influence of More's work in a study of the Utopian literature is that there is 'no *progeny* for *Utopia*, only epigone', only undistinguished offspring.[50] Psychic division may be at the centre of *Utopia* in this approach, but even that position is subject to its own moment of metanarrative qualification, as the Manuels conclude their own interpretation would not be received more favourably by the author than any other which had been bestowed on his best-known work.[51]

Nevertheless, we might still inquire further about such allusive features and the nature of such representation when it is associated with the ideal. As we have already seen, there are various derivations from Plato's considerations of the ideal state in *Utopia*. More follows the main reading of Plato's *Republic* in this period, insofar as he is interested in the dialogue's political and social principles. He makes no observations in either *Utopia* or the rest of his oeuvre on the *Republic*'s claims about the mendacious nature of art, that literary forms of expression and representation can only have an incidental relationship with the truth, and that poets and dramatists should be banished from the ideal city. More clearly had a lifelong interest in the revelatory capacity of art, and this extended to painting. He produced in collaboration with Erasmus, a number of ekphrastic epigrams in Latin. These were published in the Utopia-epigrammata edition in Basel in 1518, with the title-sheet illustrations by Ambrosius Holbein. Some poems produced in the same period of his literary career as *Utopia* treat the expressive possibilities of painting, and indeed, might

---

[47] Manuel and Manuel, *Utopian Thought*, p. 142.
[48] Manuel and Manuel, *Utopian Thought*, p. 145; see Rutger Bregman, *Utopia for Realists: And How We Can Get There*, trans. by Elizabeth Manton (London: Bloomsbury, 2017), p. 33.
[49] Manuel and Manuel, *Utopian Thought*, p. 146.
[50] Manuel and Manuel, *Utopian Thought*, p. 146.
[51] Manuel and Manuel, *Utopian Thought*, p. 145.

have been intended to accompany actual pictures. The visual principles as expressed in these poems are broadly mimetic and realist. He translates a Greek epigram, for example as 'this painting of you which Diodorus recently painted, Menodotus, is anyone's portrait rather than yours'. More then adds a poem of his own as a sequel, 'in that portrait of you [Menodotus], it is himself the painter has revealed, and so thoroughly that it resembles nobody as little as it resembles you'.[52] Elsewhere, the successful depiction of a sitter is apparently praised. 'Your likeness is so truly portrayed that it's not your portrait, but your mirror', More declares in one piece, although we may be expected to recall that a reflection is an inverted image.[53] In another poem, More describes a painting of a hare being chased by a hound. He mentions that viewers had complained that it was unclear which creature was which; and the artist had dispelled any perplexing ambiguity by simply writing 'this is the dog that the hare' underneath the respective animals.[54] The story, it seems, is intended as a whimsical illustration of the painter's ineptness (and those failings are those of not being able to reproduce accurately the appearance of things). However, it also seems to be indicative of an abiding sense in More's work that language is ultimately a more profound and revelatory means of communication and expression than that of visual representation.

Hythloday's description of what we might now term cultural activities in Utopia makes no mention of the visual arts; Utopians do not paint or sculpt for either religious or secular veneration; they study; they read and write; and they perform and listen to music. The role of the arts in this society is closer to the prescriptions of the *Laws* than the outright prohibition of the *Republic*. Socrates proposes for the city of Magnesia that creative activities should be conducted under a clear regulatory framework, and once the essential aspects of a given form have been uncovered then there should be no further embellishment or deviation from these norms merely to be novel and fashionable. The arts in Hythloday's Utopia would seem to have a secondary purpose to the political and social settlement; they are potentially improving and enjoyable, a means of attaining a state of temporary felicity, not to be prohibited or censored, but by the same token they are not activities central to the state's organisation, not a means in the perfect commonwealth to comment on the state. For the Manuels, *Utopia*'s principal literary qualities were its wit and humour, but one might well wish to add to these the book's extensive, inventive, and graduated irony as a means of turning, inflecting, illuminating the real without finally abandoning it to vertiginous literary deferral. And one can certainly approach More's use of this rhetorical technique in the same way that it subsequently appears in nineteenth-century Romantic discourse, as much as a recuperative measure, a means of intimating the underlying truth of a proposition in contradiction to all the available evidence, rather than as a means of suggesting the opposite of what has been ostensibly asserted.[55] *Utopia*'s irony could also be treated as

---

[52] *Latin Poems*, ed. and trans. by Clarence H. Miller and others, *The Complete Works of St. Thomas More* (New Haven: Yale University Press, 1984), p. 148.
[53] More, *Latin Poems*, p. 153.
[54] More, *Latin Poems*, p. 153.
[55] I have in mind Anne K. Mellor's exploration of 'artistic irony' in the works of Coleridge, Keats and Carlyle, see her *English Romantic Irony* (Cambridge, MA: Harvard University Press, 1980); see, in particular, pp. 15–17.

a way of exposing and reconciling the contradictions between the conflicting goods in a society, and the necessity of insisting on sharp divisions between its various categories. In this view, there has to be a clear distinction between who belongs to this society and who does not. The multiple optics provided by Morean irony become the means of simultaneously declaring and obscuring a position, enabling, for instance, one class to live in optimal conditions while another is debased.

Such literary deftness and subtlety would eventually be deployed against More himself. He was condemned by his Protestant foes as a fantasist and fabricator, rather than being righteously anchored in the literal interpretation of scripture as a sign of true faith. Foxe disputed the credibility of More's account of the recantation of the Protestant martyr, Thomas Bilney as '*per licentiam Poeticam*' [by poetic licence], and he sarcastically suggested all More's 'other tales' should be regarded as being equally untrustworthy.[56] Yet the literary ironic attributes of Utopia also have the effect of encouraging a reflection on the consequences of having a society which must rigidly adhere to its foundational principles. There are manifest divisions and difficulties which can be detected in connecting More's early literary career and subsequent actions as Lord Chancellor. However, irony in this recuperative mode allows us to read straightforwardly the rational calculus of the Utopians as the legitimation, indeed the necessity of taking extreme and ruthless action against those who threaten the settlement of the perfect state. There is, perhaps, some concomitant irony in the modern-day factual and fictional portrayal of More; a literary representation which has its own pictorial origins in the hanging of the Holbein portraits of More and Cromwell close to one another in the Frick Collection, almost as though they were intended as domestic pendants, and in the imaginative leap required in transfusing their attributes, as popularly understood, from one figure to the other.

Perhaps it is too outlandish to conclude that More's distinctive literary qualities have been expertly assimilated by his recent literary creator and denigrator. However, one might reflect upon Hilary Mantel's employment of a complex array of narrational conceits; the use of imaginative versions of actual figures for the purpose of examining allusive and multifaceted versions of truth; and the borrowing of a distinctive Morean cast of ironic expression and observation; especially in the dénouement to the episode in which Gardner and Cromwell visit the Lord Chancellor's home and witness the inverse of the ideal representation of the serious and devout extended Tudor household. They see the transformation of a portrait of love and kindness into its comic, chaotic, discontented and occasionally cruel obverse. After the account of the eventful supper with More and his family, Mantel imagines a meeting between Cromwell and Anne Boleyn at Westminster Palace; Gardner now having departed. 'Where have you been this evening?' the future queen asks the king's counsellor. Cromwell pauses, striving for a term as sufficiently freighted and symbolically resonant as Budé's early encapsulation of 'Oxymorus', searching for that 'necessary anachronism', a word which could carry with it a sense of millennial scepticism on attaining the ideal state – 'Utopia', he eventually replies.[57]

---

[56] *Foxe's Book of Martyrs: Select Narratives*, ed. by John N. King (Oxford: Oxford University Press, 2009), p. 12.
[57] Mantel, *Wolf Hall*, p. 236.

3

Hippophilia: Swift, Kant, and Eighteenth-Century Utopia

Of all the socially idealistic schemes produced in the eighteenth century one might argue that the most enduring and influential has been the doctrine of universal rights. Even if it lacked the theoretical innovation of the writings of Locke, Rousseau and Montesquieu, or indeed the pragmatic consideration of questions of implementation that one can find in the work of Jefferson and Lafayette, Thomas Paine's *The Rights of Man* (1791–92) remains a compellingly lucid manifesto for a rational social order. In defending the French Revolution from Burke's arguments that the overthrow of Bourbon monarchy and the abandonment of political tradition will inexorably result in chaos, Paine advocated a written constitution which enshrined universal rights, guaranteed equality of citizenship and promoted individual autonomy and majority rule. In *Agrarian Justice* (1797), Paine complemented this advocacy of rights and justice, with an outline for the common and comprehensive provision of the welfare state. Discussions of rights since the eighteenth century have been bedevilled by the tension between the claim to universalism on the one hand, and the restricted terms of their implementation on the other hand, either as a result of explicit policy or unconscious bias. The American constitution initially settled its bill of rights on the basis of the private ownership of property.

As Mary Wollstonecraft pointed out in her *Vindication of the Rights of Women* (1792), her riposte to Paine and others, constitutional radicalism did not usually extend to women, who were either implicitly or explicitly excluded from rights-based manifestos on the grounds of not being fully rational actors. Nevertheless, the doctrine of universal rights, for all its interpretative difficulties, for all the various instances when such rights have been adopted by narrow causes and eccentrically interpreted for regional and political gain, and for all the modern scepticism about the continuity between the general understanding of rights at the end of the eighteenth century and their comprehension and application in the second decade of the twenty-first century, such rights still provide a set of global standards by which humans, merely by reason of their humanity, are provided with an international standard to be able to live, think, act and consort freely.

It is generally accepted that the impetus for these modern international standards arose from the Nuremburg trials in 1945–46. As Mark Janis and others have pointed out, the tribunals' key judgement provided 'not only for the moral and political imperative that individuals be made legally responsible for violations of international law, but also evidence for the customary international legal rule that human rights ought to be protected at the level of international law'.[1] The judgement paved the way for the 1945 Charter of the United Nations; and thereafter to the key modern document of human rights, as a set of international legal standards in 1948 in the promulgation of the Universal Declaration of Human Rights, 'where the United Nations followed in the footsteps of Jefferson, Lafayette and Madison'.[2] The Declaration subsequently became the basis of super-national legal and judicial systems such as the European Commission and European Court of Human Rights. Article 1 of the Universal Declaration of Human Rights states 'all human beings are born free and equal in dignity and rights'.[3] Modern political scientists have recognised that the notion of dignity has become increasingly important in the discussion of rights, in their judicial application, and in the objections to the systematic persecution of a particular group that their dignity as well as their rights are being denied.

There is a temptation to regard 'dignity' as a vague and nebulous term, which merely provides an aspirational veneer to the more robust definitions of universal rights.[4] However, Jürgen Habermas argues that dignity in rights discourse should not be dismissed as an 'empty formula' or 'place holder'.[5] He suggests that there are significant examples of the codification of self-worth in the Judeo-Christian tradition. He gives the example of medieval theological discussion in which the underlying assumption is that 'everyone must face the last judgment'.[6] However, the key figure for the modern association of rights and dignity is Immanuel Kant. The notion of human dignity, Habermas argues, 'acquired its current canonical expression in Kant', and it is the Kantian conception of dignity and its link to rational capability which have found their 'way into texts of international law and recent national constitutions'.[7]

Habermas's argument on the Kantian aspect of modern universal right and dignity has a number of interlocking components. He gives the example of the determination of the Federal Constitutional Court on the Aviation Security Act. This legislation granted the German state the legal authority to intercept passenger planes. This was a peremptory measure to prevent hijacked aircraft being turned into missiles after the 9/11 attacks. The court judged the act unconstitutional, because 'with their lives being disposed of unilaterally by the state, the persons on board the aircraft . . . are denied the

---

[1] Mark W. Janis, Richard S. Kay and Anthony W. Bradley, *European Human Rights Law: Text and Materials*, 3rd edn (Oxford: Oxford University Press, 2008), p. 11.
[2] Janis, Kay and Bradley, *European Human Rights Law*, p. 11.
[3] United Nations, *Universal Declaration of Human Rights* [http://www.un.org/en/universal-declaration-human-rights/, accessed 31 August 2018].
[4] On the significance of dignity in modern human-rights theory, see indicatively, Kenneth Baynes, 'Toward a Political Conception of Human Rights', *Philosophy and Social Criticism*, 35 (2009), 371–90; Ernst Bloch, *Natural Law and Human Dignity*, trans. by Dennis J. Schmidt (Cambridge, MA: MIT Press, 1984), on Kant, pp. 66–75; Jack Donnelly, *Universal Human Rights in Theory and Practice*, 2nd edn (Ithaca, NY: Cornell University Press, 2003), pp. 111–20; and Christopher McCrudden, 'Human Dignity and Judicial Interpretation of Human Rights', *European Journal of International Law* 19 (2008), 655–724.
[5] Jürgen Habermas, 'The Concept of Human Dignity and the Realistic Utopia of Human Rights', *Metaphilosophy*, 41 (2010), 464–80 (466).
[6] Habermas, 'Concept of Human Dignity', 474.
[7] Habermas, 'Concept of Human Dignity', 465.

value which is due to a human being for his or her own sake'.[8] Habermas detects in this judgement an unmistakable echo of Kant's categorical imperative; that is, the maxim that the justification of any given action must lie in its capacity to be promoted to a universal tenet, and in the obligation on a sovereign body to treat human beings over whom they have jurisdiction as ends rather than means. In *The Metaphysics of Morals* (1797), Kant established the fundamental requirements of a just order for humans, whom he conceives universally as rational beings. Kant's definition of the theory of right is 'the sum total of those laws which can be incorporated into external legislation'; and the universal principle of right (from which all sovereign authority in a just civil society must ultimately derive) states that 'every action which by itself or by its maxim enables the freedom of each individuals' will to co-exist with the freedom of everyone else in accordance with the universal law is *right*.[9] Elsewhere, Kant provides an outline of the three a priori principles that any just political order should enshrine; these are: 'the freedom of every member of a society as a *human being*'; 'the equality of each with all others as a *subject*'; and 'the independence of each member of the commonwealth as a *citizen*'.[10]

It is these aspects of equality, rational capacity and reciprocal self-worth which equate with the modern conception of human dignity in international legislation and institutions. As Habermas acknowledges, these principles as a set of international standards are far from being unproblematic and uncontentious in their operations. There is the challenge of matching up the claims of human rights to the available enforceable structures of nation states and the universalising claims of the rights themselves; and there are difficulties in the ways in which international forums are co-opted for geo-political ends.[11] Yet it remains Habermas's contention that despite such obstacles, the institutionalising of human rights is to be welcomed as a means of maximising social goods and promoting international standards of justice (such as through the European Court of Human Rights and the International Criminal Court). And he casts this Enlightenment inheritance in explicitly utopian terms – the separation between the claim to rights free from considerations of time and space and the institutional structures which embody them. Hence, the distance between the aspiration and the actual practice of having a global body capable of both enshrining and giving legal force to human rights rooted in a sense of common dignity is described as a 'utopian gap'.[12] Habermas understands Kant's central contribution to the understanding of just and equitable political orders is that modern discourses of human rights 'constitute a realistic utopia insofar as they no longer paint a social utopia that guarantees collective happiness but anchor the ideal of a just society in the institutions of constitutional states themselves'.[13]

---

[8] Habermas, 'Concept of Human Dignity', 465.
[9] Immanuel Kant, *The Metaphysics of Morals*, in *Political Writings*, ed. by Hans Reiss, trans. by H.B. Nisbet, 2nd edn (Cambridge: Cambridge University Press, 1991), pp. 131–75 (p. 139).
[10] Immanuel Kant, 'On the Common Saying: "This May Be True in Theory, But It Does Not Apply in Practice"' (1793), in *Political Writings*, pp. 61–92 (p. 74).
[11] On contentiousness of human rights and the local interests in their promulgation, see Samuel Moyn, *The Last Utopia: Human Rights in History* (Cambridge MA: Belknap Press, 2012), especially pp. 120–75.
[12] Habermas, 'Concept of Human Dignity', 475.
[13] Habermas, 'Concept of Human Dignity', 476.

This Enlightenment project has its origins in Kant's famous dictum of emancipation, that the eighteenth century is the age in which traditional forms of authority are superseded by those which properly acknowledge human beings' rational will to self-determination.[14] That means for Habermas, in its twenty-first-century guise, the obligation to persevere in the explanation and defence of human rights – the ongoing endeavour in the modern world to realise 'the explosive political force of a concrete utopia'.[15]

At the centre of this analysis, then, is the claim that human rights with their Kantian core of reciprocity and dignity can maximise social goods by translating these aspects into an enforceable legal code. The Enlightenment project is realised in those international declarations which enshrine human rights and dignity; and this for Habermas is a claim for modern realistic utopianism with an eighteenth-century European provenance. However, the idea that the 1700s could be so readily associated with utopianism has had a chequered history. In the 1950s, A.L. Morton declared that 'utopian literature reached its lowest ebb in the eighteenth century'.[16] Intellectual historians and literary scholars such as Gregory Claeys, Alessa Johns, Nicole Pohl, Christine Rees and Jason Pearl have since demonstrated the variety and extensiveness of utopian projection in this period.[17] In what follows, I briefly consider some of these ideal communities. However, the main component of this chapter will be an examination of an author who is often considered to have a peripheral role at best in utopian projection, Jonathan Swift. Frank and Fritzie Manuel barely mention Swift in their landmark study, and when they do, he is portrayed as a convinced anti-utopian – an undoubtedly influential author who drove a coach and horses through everyone else's ideal theories without ever being saddled with one of his own.

However, the extensive body of recent textual scholarship on Swift has revealed a much greater debt to More's *Utopia* than has been previously acknowledged; and one can now consider his writings in general, and *Gulliver's Travels* (1726) in particular, as providing a significant reformulation of the principles and literary style of More's text. Furthermore, one can now situate *Gulliver's Travels* at the centre of the utopian imagination in the era, rather than being peripheral to it. This argument also entails examining the extent to which Swiftian satire tests the limits of idealistic projection. A seminal modern account of the paradigmatic elements of Swift's most famous work concludes with mid-twentieth-century genocide as an absolute denial of human rights and dignity. And it is out of that moment that the modern international order, with its Kantian rational basis and its explicit assertion of human dignity, comes into being,

---

[14] See Kant, 'An Answer to the Question: "What is Enlightenment?"' (1784), in *Political Writings*, pp. 54–60 (p. 54, p. 55).
[15] Habermas, 'Concept of Human Dignity', 466.
[16] A.L. Morton, *The English Utopia* (London: Lawrence & Wishart, 1969), p. 143.
[17] See *Utopias of the British Enlightenment*, ed. by Gregory Claeys (Cambridge: Cambridge University Press, 1994); *Modern British Utopias, 1700-1850*, ed. by Gregory Claeys, 8 vols (London: Pickering & Chatto, 1997); Alessa Johns, *Women's Utopias of the Eighteenth Century* (Urbana: University of Illinois Press, 2003); Nicole Pohl, *Women, Space and Utopia, 1600-1800* (Aldershot: Ashgate, 2006); Nicole Pohl, 'The Quest for Utopia in the Eighteenth Century', *Literature Compass*, 5 (2008), 685–706; Christine Rees, *Utopian Imagination and Eighteenth-Century Fiction* (Harlow: Longman, 1996); and Jason H. Pearl, *Utopian Geographies and the Early English Novel* (Charlottesville: University of Virginia Press, 2014).

Habermas's 'realistic utopia'. It may appear an idiosyncratic undertaking to consider the most influential Anglo-Irish satirist of the age alongside its leading European philosopher; although the latter was certainly aware of the former. Kant has scattered allusions to the 'sarcastic Swift' in his less formal writings; and he often turns to the author when in need of a maxim.[18] However, as I argue in what follows, both figures anticipate modern conceptions of the good society. In this account, Swift becomes an improbable companion to Kant, with the latter providing an influential version of the doctrine of universal rights rooted in human dignity, and the former producing a compelling meta-narrative on the limitations of universal reason as a means of achieving the ideal commonwealth.

What counts as utopian in this era, of course, still depends on what conceptual approach is taken to the texts and the parameters used in that definition. A common category is the fictionalised traveller tale with a maximally beneficial settlement. The genre has a significant origin in Daniel Defoe's *Robinson Crusoe* (1719), giving rise to authentic and spurious sequels, Robinsonades. These narratives contained, to a greater or lesser extent, politically idealistic attributes, though many are open to the objection that the protagonist's solitary circumstances mean there are insufficient social components to merit consideration as utopias. The conflation of traveller's tale with fantastic societies resulted in some remarkable works. Robert Patlock's *The Life and Adventures of Peter Watkins* (1751), for example, synthesised realistic description (the protagonist is described in impressive psychological detail) with fantastical utopianism. Watkins is assimilated into the winged race of Saas Doorpt Swangeanti, a republican society. The political upheavals late in the century resulted in many publications that shift the position of political pamphlets advocating an alternative and usually rights-based rational society towards a depiction of what that society might actually look like if put into practice. These blueprints were occasionally confounded by the author's particular circumstances and disposition. In *The Commonwealth of Reason* (1795), for example, William Hodgson produced a beguiling mixture of rational projection and frustrated outrage at his present imprisonment for sedition. Explicit philosophical investigations of the concept of the ideal state remained comparatively rare in Britain. The best-known is David Hume's 'The Idea of a Perfect Commonwealth' (1752). Hume dismisses the *Republic* and *Utopia*, as 'plainly imaginary', and focuses instead on James Harrington's *The Commonwealth of Oceana* (1656), which he suggests is 'the only valuable model of a commonwealth, that has yet been offered to the public'.[19] He proposes a number of fractional improvements to Harrington's agrarian system and rotational government. Elsewhere, Hume was sceptical as to the efficacy of such abstract schemas. In his *History of England*, written at roughly the same time as the essay, he stresses in his account of Harrington that the idea 'of a perfect and immortal commonwealth will always be found as chimerical as that of a perfect and immortal man'.[20]

---

[18] See Kant's indicative use of Swift in his *Anthropology from a Pragmatic Point of View*, trans. by Victor Lyle Dowdell, rev. edn (Carbondale: Southern Illinois University Press, 1978), p. 38, p. 39, and p. 120.

[19] David Hume, 'Idea of a Perfect Commonwealth', in *Essays: Moral Political and Literary*, ed. by Eugene F. Miller, revised edn (Indianapolis: Liberty Classics, 1987), pp. 512–29 (p. 514).

[20] David Hume, *History of England*, 6 vols (Indianapolis: Liberty Classics, 1983), VI, p. 153.

Nicole Pohl has suggested that the period also abounded in what she terms micro-utopias; projections of local communities, usually established as a sanctuary from a generally oppressive regime. As Pohl points out, these projections of small-scale ideal societies often appealed to female authors as a means of constructing attractive conceptual alternatives to male-dominated society. She charts the development of such projection from the satiric vision of Delarivière Manley in *New Atlantis* (1709), considered to be a 'utopian vision of a quasi-communistic, lesbian and separatist as well as aristocratic commonwealth'.[21] Also notable is Sarah Scott's popular and engaging novel, *Millennium Hall* (1762), which describes the founding and conduct of an all-women refuge in the south of England. The community's way of life is interspersed with a series of the personal histories of the hall's members. These describe the plight of intelligent and virtuous young middle-class women, who find themselves compromised and betrayed in their relations with an array of duplicitous and domineering fathers, suitors and spouses. And Mary Hamilton's *Munster Village* (1778) provides an account of feminist aristocratic generosity in which her protagonist uses an unexpected inheritance to establish a community school, and constructs a version of the good society on the basis of a common and robust educational system.

English poetry, especially in the first half of the century, could also offer a conceptual perspective on idealistic settlements. Alexander Pope's *An Essay on Man* (1733), for example, was intended as the first part of an uncompleted comprehensive treatise in verse on the nature of human beings and their place within the cosmos. Even in its partial form, the poem is an impressive if heterodox undertaking, an amalgamation of a variety of systems of natural philosophy and metaphysical speculation: Newtonian mechanics and optics and the Renaissance notion of the Great Chain of Being. However, the *Essay on Man* remains memorable for its deism and treatment of theodicy (the explanation as to why a benevolent God permits evil).[22] Pope's views on the function of apparent malevolence probably derived from authors such as Cicero, Seneca, Aurelius, Epictetus and Lucretius; and the poem's central position was also linked by Pope's contemporary continental European commentators to the speculative and possibly heretical views of Leibniz and Spinoza (even though Pope denied having first-hand knowledge of their works).[23] Yet the *Essay on Man*'s key intellectual success was to present its case on theodicy in compelling fashion; and Pope provided a particularly succinct and memorable formulation at the end of the poem's first epistle: 'All Nature is but Art, unknown to thee;/ All Chance, Direction, which thou canst not see;/ All Discord, Harmony, not understood;/ All partial Evil, universal Good:/ And, spite of Pride, in erring Reason's spite,/ One truth is clear, "Whatever is, is RIGHT"'.[24]

The poem argues that as human beings, we only have a limited grasp of the ways in which the universe operates as both a mechanical and moral entity. We cannot hope to

---

[21] Pohl, *Women, Space and Utopia*, p. 72.
[22] Tom Jones considers the poem's theistic attributes in the introduction to his edition of Alexander Pope, *An Essay on Man* (Princeton: Princeton University Press, 2016), pp. lvi–lxi.
[23] See Maynard Mack on the poem's classical influences in his introduction to *An Essay on Man*, Twickenham Edition of the Works of Alexander Pope (London: Methuen, 1950), pp. xi–lxxx. Miriam Leranbaum argued for the significant influence of Lucretius' *De Rerum Natura* on Pope's poem in her *Alexander Pope's 'Opus Magnum', 1729–1744* (Oxford: Clarendon Press, 1977), pp. 38–63.
[24] Pope, *Essay on Man*, ed. Jones, pp. 26–27, ll. 289–94.

attain the same omniscient perspective as our maker and enfold the whole majesty of creation within a single view. Even if we cannot uncover specific reasons for things turning out as they do, we can still be certain that every mystifying event has an ultimate cause; and we can be equally confident as a matter of syllogistic reasoning that God is the sum of perfection, that goodness is a perfection, and God as a consequence must be good. Hence, any fault we detect cannot be with the world as it is, but only with our dim and partial comprehension of it. Events that appear chaotic are mere local disturbances in a larger benign pattern; what strikes us as a discordant note is part of a universal harmony which we cannot detect; and any action we regard as being malign is the consequence of a local disturbance, a necessary flaw in the cosmic order. The passage builds toward its resounding climax, 'One truth is clear, "Whatever is, is RIGHT"', where the placement of the lapidary proposition in inverted commas after the caesura gives the impression of divine fiat. Overall, then, the poem suggests that we already inhabit an optimised state, but not one we can readily discern because of our limited perspective.

Of course, it was the central claim of Voltaire's *Candide* (1759) that such deistic thinking was facile and fallacious. Voltaire was aware of Pope's *Essay on Man* (he had admired the poem during his stay in England in the 1730s); but he left the poem untouched in his mordant tale, possibly because of his continued respect for its author.[25] His avoidance of the poem also looks like a tacit acknowledgement that for all the vivid presentational advantages such elevated verse possessed, it could not be regarded as being authoritative argument for theism. As his contemporaries understood, Voltaire's main target in *Candide* was the only work Leibniz published in his lifetime, *Theodicy: Essays on the Goodness of God the Freedom of Man and the Origin of Evil* (1710, Voltaire owned a copy). Pangloss's artless promotion of Leibnizian rational optimism has become a byword for a complacent vision of the world's benign organisation in the face of the overwhelming contrary evidence of warfare, natural disasters and widespread misery in Europe and the New World. Pangloss advocates the three key doctrines espoused in the *Theodicy* of pre-existing harmony of substances, the principle of sufficient reason (the minimum condition for things being as they are), and that the world as we encounter it must be optimally configured.

Theodicy was intended as a contribution to an ongoing philosophical debate with Pierre Bayle on the basis and coherence of his correspondent's system (Bayle died before he could read the essays). Leibniz's text, in fact, provides a lucid discussion of the fundamental nature of the substance of the universe; the means by which scriptural faith can be reconciled with a rational appreciation of God's works; and how free will is possible in a pre-ordained universe, especially as it applies to the evident presence and operation of the world. However, Leibniz made it clear he did not consider himself an utopist. He offered two versions of the ideal, even as he conceded that one must perforce be illusory. This world has to be perfect, for a beneficent deity would not have created any other (as a matter of conceptual as well as material perfection), yet this does not commit us to the position that we cannot even conceive of a state of being which is devoid of malice, just as we can, he suggests, still imagine sweetness without bitterness, a sustained chord without

---

[25] For Voltaire and Pope's personal and literary relationship, see Roger Pearson, *Voltaire Almighty: A Life in Pursuit of Freedom* (London: Bloomsbury, 2005), p. 63, p. 78, p. 79, and pp. 132–33.

a hint of dissonance, or a picture without the obscurity of a shadow. When Leibniz wishes to describe such a perfect state, he does so in conventional terms, conceding that 'one may imagine possible worlds without sin and without unhappiness, and one could make some like Utopian [...] romances'.[26] In other words, this ideal is a fantastical delusory state, a chimera as opposed to the ideal of his system of universal harmony, which must operate along the principles he outlines as a matter of rational necessity.

Leibniz may not have regarded himself as an utopist, but the Manuels certainly did. They sift a number of prominent European discourses for their utopian attributes. Rousseau, for instance, is the promoter of the 'commune moi' in which the idea of community is paradoxically focussed on subjective fulfilment; and the Marquis de Sade constructs a utopia of synchronic sexual gratification, 'the 120 days of Sodom is regulated like clockwork', such that 'split-second timing is required for carrying out the total sexual enterprise in its perfection'.[27] However, it is Leibniz who is regarded as *the* European utopian – though this judgement had little to do with either the *Theodicy*'s deistic programme, or Voltaire's subsequent assault upon it. Totality is the key. 'In Leibniz', they say, 'the philosopher, theologian, mathematician, diplomat, physicist, jurist, historian, and visionary are united. The man of universal knowledge was the man of universal utopia'; and his vision embraced plans 'for the founding of universities, the advancement of science, the conversion of non-Christians, the unity of churches'.[28] Leibniz also represents an important terminus – the final moment in which the Pansophic tradition which had drawn significantly on the works of More, Campanella and Bacon could be credibly envisioned. Hence Leibniz provides 'the Swan Song' of Christian utopia, the 'last great vision that derived its meaning from the love of God and the exploration of His world in all its dimensions, geological, historical, theological and scientific'.[29]

Swift, by way of contrast, only merits two asides in the Manuels' account of utopia. The immortal Struldbruggs in *Gulliver's Travels*' third part are regarded as 'one of the cruellest mockeries of man's utopian passion for longevity'; and the Yahoos in Part IV are deemed 'the most famous animals spawned by the utopian-dystopian imagination'.[30] The Manuels were right that Swift could not be straightforwardly inserted into an intellectual and literary lineage comprising More, Campanella and Bacon; and Swift himself certainly would not have considered those figures as constituting a unified tradition. Swift probably had not much more than a passing acquaintance with Campanella's writings (though he did own a copy of his aphorisms, part of Hugo de Groot's compilation, *Quaedam hactenus inedita* (1652)).[31] And he implicitly condemned Bacon. Whatever his undoubted merits as a constitutional author and erudite essayist, Bacon was still, for Swift, an archetypal modern and the perpetrator of fatuous scientific

---

[26] G.W. Leibniz, *Theodicy: Essays on the Goodness of God the Freedom of Man and the Origin of Evil*, ed. by Austen Farrer, trans. by E.M. Huggard (Chicago: Open Court, 1990), p. 129.
[27] Frank E. Manuel and Fritzie P. Manuel, *Utopian Thought in the Western World* (Cambridge, MA: Belknap Press, 1979), p. 542.
[28] Manuel and Manuel, *Utopian Thought*, p. 398.
[29] Manuel and Manuel, *Utopian Thought*, p. 410.
[30] Manuel and Manuel, *Utopian Thought*, p. 86; p. 774.
[31] See 'Campanella, Tommaso', in Dirk F. Passmann and Heinz J. Vienken, *The Library and Reading of Jonathan Swift: A Bio-Bibliographical Handbook*, 4 vols (Frankfurt am Main: Peter Lang, 2003), I, pp. 339–41.

optimism, the 'Troglodyte Philosopher' of his first significant work, *A Tale of a Tub* (1704).[32] However, Swift clearly saw himself as writing in a lineage with More, even if he had an imperfect grasp of what constituted that tradition. He probably first encountered More's work when in the service of Sir William Temple in the 1690s. Temple owned a first edition of *Utopia* and two editions of the *History of Richard the Third* (1543 and 1641).[33] And Swift subsequently acquired a copy of *Utopia* published in Holland in the early seventeenth century.[34] There is no evidence that he was aware of More's poetry, translations, devotional works or the attacks on Luther. Temple had praised More in his 'Essay on Popular Discontents' (posthumously edited and published by Swift in 1701); More is 'esteemed' in this work as one of 'the most extraordinary personages of their time, [who] fell all bloody sacrifices to the factions of their courts or their countries'.[35]

Swift followed Temple in venerating the Lord Chancellor. He owned a copy of Edward Herbert's *Life and Reigne of Henry VIII* (1649, to which he added a series of terse and pejorative handwritten marginalia that form an irate counter-narrative to what he considered to be Tudor propaganda). He variously refers to the king in his copy as 'a Dog, a true King', 'the profligate Dog of a King', and a 'Barbarous Dog'.[36] Herbert had provided a brief portrait of More, focussing on his alleged 'facetiousness', to which Swift retorts that More was the embodiment of principled resistance to despotism, insisting that he was 'the only Man of true Virtue that ever England produced'. And Swift responds to Herbert's account of More's execution by concluding 'here the detestable Tyrant [Henry VIII] murdered Virtue herself'.[37] His veneration is also apparent in *Gulliver's Travels*. In a rare passage without obvious satirical inflection, Gulliver spies More in a parade of spectral worthies in the work's third part. More is the only modern figure in this exalted group, sharing with his classical counterparts a reputation for unimpeachable virtue ultimately tied to political failure. These figures are collectively described by Gulliver as a '*Sextumvirate* to which all the Ages of the World cannot add a Seventh'.[38] Swift's respect for More and more broadly for humanist learning was also recognised by his contemporaries. In June 1737, William King sought to entice Swift to visit St Mary's Hall, Oxford with the prospect, should he accept, that the hall would then be able to 'boast a triumvirate that is not to be matched in any part of the known world, *Sir Thomas More, Erasmus*, and the *Drapier*' [a soubriquet attached to Swift after his authorship of the Drapier's Letters].[39]

---

[32] Jonathan Swift, *A Tale of a Tub and other Works*, ed. by Marcus Walsh, The Cambridge Edition of the Works of Jonathan Swift (Cambridge: Cambridge University Press, 2010), p. 118. See also p. lxxiii and p. 446 n. 8.
[33] See 'The Library of Sir William Temple: A Reconstruction', in Passmann and Vienken, *The Library and Reading of Jonathan Swift*, IV, pp. 185–215 (p. 213).
[34] See 'Thomas [More]', in Passmann and Vienken, *The Library and Reading of Jonathan Swift*, III, pp. 1833–42.
[35] *The Works of Sir William Temple Bart*, 4 vols (London: Clarke and others, 1757), III, pp. 32–66 (p. 36).
[36] 'Herbert, Edward', in Passmann and Vienken, *The Library and Reading of Jonathan Swift*, II, pp. 824–31 (p. 825, p. 825, p. 826)
[37] See 'Herbert, Edward', in Passmann and Vienken, *The Library and Reading of Jonathan Swift*, p. 826.
[38] Jonathan Swift, *Gulliver's Travels*, ed. by David Womersley, The Cambridge Edition of the Works of Jonathan Swift (Cambridge: Cambridge University Press, 2012), p. 292. All further in-text citations of *Gulliver's Travels* are to this edition.
[39] William King to Swift, 24 June 1737, *The Correspondence of Jonathan Swift*, ed. by Harold Williams, 5 vols (Oxford: Clarendon Press, 1963–1965, reissued 2012), V, pp. 53–54 (p. 54).

If More was to be esteemed for his personal example, his literary significance from Swift's perspective was exclusively dependent on *Utopia*. Swift seems to have drawn a sharp distinction between More's satirical work and the way in which the term 'utopia' was being used in contemporary parlance; and he produced some interesting commentary on the latter. In an early Pindaric ode to Sir William Temple, Swift amalgamates the notion of utopia as an unalloyed good place, with the idea of it being a distant island, and a colonial standpoint in which overseas territories are only there to be subjugated. His patron is cast as an intrepid moral pioneer, 'Tis you who must this land subdue'. He encourages Temple in the poem's apostrophe, 'the mighty Conquest's left for you,/ The Conquest and Discovery too:/ Search out the Utopian Ground/ Virtue's Terra Incognita'.[40] In 1727, the year after the publication of *Gulliver's Travels*, Swift writes despondently to Pope while suffering a debilitating bout of Ménière's disease (he asks to be excused for his 'wildness', being 'giddy and deaf'). He wishes that 'old friends' be reacquainted on the other side of the grave; and then observes that 'if I were to write an utopia for heaven, that would be one of my schemes'.[41] There seems here to be a deliberate conceptual misalignment between heavenly paradise and a secular perfected state. Yet, the intention is clear enough: if Swift were to design a future condition in the manner of an idealistic projector, then the re-acquaintance of long-standing friends would be a prerequisite.

The term 'utopia' also appears in his early faux treatise, *A Tritical Essay upon the Faculties of the Mind* (1711). Swift adopts in this satirical foray the persona of a modern progressive philosopher. As Valerie Rumbold notes, the treatise 'voices the self-assured babble that [Swift] identifies with modernity; a discourse buoyed up, in the absence of solid value, with entrepreneurial zeal'.[42] The title's key descriptor, 'Tritical', conflates 'trite' and 'critical', but to the credit of neither. As Rumbold goes on to observe, one can track in the treatise 'a significant overlap between the learned commonplace of humanist topics and the popular commonplace that consists of vernacular proverbs and sayings'.[43] A telling example of this shift between critical astuteness and triteness is in the use of 'utopia'. The narrator describes the 'Opinions of a Philosopher' as 'many Plagues of the Mind'; and he goes on to suggest that 'if Truth be not fled with *Astraea*, she is certain as hidden as the source of the *Nile*, and can be found only in *Utopia*'.[44] Astraea, Goddess of Justice, according to Ovid, flees the earth at the end of the Golden Age, and the world descends into mayhem. Thomas Browne had described the source of the Nile as 'being unknowne and drawne to a proverbiall obscurity'.[45] The allusion suggests both the proverbial sense of a fantastic unattainable state, with pejorative implications, but also the projection of a commonwealth in which certain types of political and social propositions can be constructively tested.

---

[40] 'Ode to the Honourable Sir William Temple' (1692), in *The Poems of Jonathan Swift*, ed. by Harold Williams, 2nd edn, 3 vols (Oxford: Clarendon Press, 1958), I, pp. 26–33 (p. 26).
[41] Swift to Alexander Pope, 24 June 1727, *Correspondence*, ed. by Williams, III, p. 242.
[42] Jonathan Swift, *Parodies, Hoaxes, Mock Treatises*, ed. by Valerie Rumbold, The Cambridge Edition of the Works of Jonathan Swift (Cambridge: Cambridge University Press, 2013), p. xliv.
[43] Swift, *Parodies, Hoaxes, Mock Treatises*, p. xliv.
[44] Swift, *Parodies, Hoaxes, Mock Treatises*, p. 26,
[45] Sir Thomas Browne, *Pseudoxia Epidemica*, ed. by Robin Robbins, 2 vols (Oxford: Clarendon Press, 1981), I, p. 497, quoted in Swift, *Parodies, Hoaxes, Mock Treatises*, p. 26, n. 37.

Yet it is in *Gulliver's Travels* that Swift both anatomises and extends the range of More's interrogative and darkly ludic idealism. Swift, of course, drew on an impressive range of classical and modern sources for the fashioning of what would come to be his most popular and enduring work, though many of these sources can be understood to resonate, overlap and intersect with More's projection and commentary on the perfect state. Swift, like More, was certainly intrigued by popular travel literature. It has been estimated that he either owned or read in the region of 370 travel narratives.[46] It seems probable he read such works principally in two periods: when he was a member of Temple's household (and the voyage motif in the Pindaric ode to his patron with the utopian allusion can be taken as indirect evidence of this), and while he was working on *Gulliver's Travels* in the early and mid-1720s.[47] There was a considerable diversity in this genre's quality and reliability, with the explorations of Richard Hakluyt and William Dampier at the more reputable end of the scale. Swift avidly consumed such writing in a not dissimilar fashion to some twentieth-century intellectuals' fondness for thrillers.[48] Realistic and improbable voyages offered imaginative stimulation and escapism; but Swift was distinctly ambivalent about such adventures, dismissing the entire genre in one splenetic outburst as an 'abundance of Trash'.[49] The commercial production of this literature often entailed parcelling up in one book a range of different voyages to different parts of the world, with no requirement for an explicit connection between one excursion and another.[50] These compilations clearly provided an effective and immediately recognisable model for *Gulliver's Travels*, with the book's global reach, and with its four distinct journeys to the miniscule land of Lilliput, the giants of Brobdingnag, the projectors of Laputa and other south-east Asian territories, and the notorious final sojourn in the land of horses. Swift could construct a narrative with thematic overlap in its four expeditions, safe in the knowledge that his readers would

---

[46] Figure derived on the basis of the entries in 'Index of Subjects: Travel Writing' in Passmann and Vienken, *The Library and Reading of Jonathan Swift*, IV, pp. 418–21.

[47] See Irwin Ehrenpreis, *Swift: The Man, His Works, and the Age*, 3 vols (London: Methuen, 1962–1983), III (1983), p. 329.

[48] I have in mind Bertrand Russell: 'Russell's consumption of thrillers was enormous, and a regular supply was fetched from the local library by his neighbour Crawshay-Williams. Traditionally, three of his four County Library tickets were available for fiction, and the fourth ear-marked for non-fiction. But Russell wanted four detective stories each time. "I was granted a special dispensation", Crawshay-Williams had written. "The County Council felt that Bertrand Russell was sufficiently cultured already"', Ronald W. Clark, *The Life of Bertrand Russell* (London: Jonathan Cape and Weidenfeld & Nicholson, 1975), p. 573.

[49] Swift to Charles Ford, 22 July 1722, *Correspondence*, II, pp. 430–32 (p. 431).

[50] See, indicatively, *A New Voyage to the East-Indies in the Years 1690 and 1691. Being a Full Description of the Isles of Maldives, Cicos, Andamants, and the Isle of Ascention; and All the Forts and Garrisons Now in Possession of the French. With an Account of the Customs, Manners, and Habits of the Indians by M. Duquesne. To Which is Added, a New Description of the Canary Islands, Cape Verd, Senegal, and Gambia, &c. Illustrated with Sculptures, Together with a New Map of the Indies, and Another of the Canaries* (London: Droig, 1696); and *An Account of Several Late Voyages & Discoveries To the South and North. Towards the Streights of Magellan, the South Seas, the Vast Tracts of Land Beyond Hollandia Nova, &c. Also Towards Nova Zembla, Greenland or Spitsberg, Groynland or Engrondland, &c. By Sir John Narborough, Captain Jasmen Tasman, Captain John Wood, and Frederick Marten of Hamburgh. To which are Annexed a Large Introduction and Supplement, Giving an Account of other Navigations to Those Regions of the Globe. The Whole Illustrated with Charts and Figures* (London: Sam Smith and Benjamin Walford, 1694).

not expect coherence and consistency or even consistent verisimilitude from a work in this genre, with sudden shifts between technical exactness and extraordinary fantasies.

Eighteenth-century French commentators first noted the extent of literary allusion in *Gulliver's Travels*. Voltaire portrays Swift as an effective dampener of Rabelaisian excess, 'Mr Swift is Rabelais in his right senses, and living good company', he proclaims, 'it is true he has not Rabelais's gaiety, but he has all the subtlety and judgement, the taste, the power to select, which are lacking in the Rector of Mendon'.[51] The Abbé Desfontaines contextualises the book in the preface to his French translation. He cites as significant precursors to Swift as 'Plato's *Republic*, Lucian's *True History*, and its supplement, the *Utopia* of Chancellor More, the *New Atlantis* of Chancellor Bacon, the *History of the Severambi*, the voyages of Sadeur and of Jacques Macé, and finally Cyrano de Bergerac's *Voyage in the Moon*'.[52] In this tradition, the most recent scholarly editor of *Gulliver's Travels*, David Womersley, identifies numerous allusions and derivations, reflecting Swift's extensive interest in classical political writing and history, embracing Aristotle, Plutarch and Xenophon as well as Plato. Swift also seems to have been conversant with the political theorising of the previous century in the writings of Hobbes, Locke, Milton, Bacon and Harrington. And then there was the significant but never acknowledged influence of Bernard Mandeville's *Fable of the Bees* (1714), both in *Gulliver's Travels* and elsewhere in Swift's bleak imaginings. Mandeville's central thesis was neatly encapsulated in the fable's subtitle, 'Private Vices, Publick Benefits'.[53] Almost all behaviour condemned by conventional moralists, Mandeville insisted, had wider social and economic advantages; and such 'benefits' ran in a continuous spectrum from the ever-changing tastes of the beau monde, which provided employment for legions of milliners, haberdashers, couturiers and hairdressers, to the criminality of thieves and other petty offenders, whose actions resulted in steady work for locksmiths and gaolers. In the course of his poem 'The Grumbling Hive; or, Knaves Turn'd Honest', which first advanced these ideas of exclusive economic interest, Mandeville describes the idea of living in a modern transactional society free of vice as '*a vain Eutopia seated in the Brain*'.[54] Mandeville's use of 'Eu' rather than the standard 'U' prefix dispensed with any ambiguity in the term, and reinforced the proverbial sense of utopia as a subjective and often pernicious fantasy. Swift could neither acknowledge, nor indeed sympathise with the economic opportunism of Mandeville's materialist and morally inert thesis, but his significant borrowings from the *Fable of the Bees*, including the repurposing of a shocking account of a sow consuming an infant, suggest

---

[51] Voltaire, *Mélange*, 'Lettre XXII', quoted in Swift, *The Critical Heritage*, ed. and trans. by Kathleen Williams (London: Routledge & Kegan Paul, 1970), p. 74. Swift's reception in France is summarised by Wilhelm Graeber, 'Swift's First Voyages to Europe: His Impact on Eighteenth-Century France', in *The Reception of Jonathan Swift in Europe*, ed. by Hermann J. Real (London: Thoemmes Continuum: 2005), pp. 5–16.

[52] Jonathan Swift, *Voyages de Capitaine Lemuel Gulliver*, trans. by Abbé Desfontaines (Paris, Amsterdam, 1787), p. xx–xxii [my translation], first published 1727.

[53] Bernard Mandeville, *The Fable of the Bees; or, Private Vices, Publick Benefits*, commentary by F.B. Kaye, 2 vols (Indianapolis: Liberty Fund, 1988), I, [p. 1].

[54] Mandeville, *Fable of the Bees*, I, p. 36.

he was both intrigued and imaginatively drawn to the book's iconoclasm, pungent anti-utopianism and rebarbative imagery.[55]

Womersley argues that Swift's observations in 'Some Few Thoughts Concerning the Repeal of the Test' (1733) were a coded response to the lack of any concrete results of his satire when it came to social modification. Rigorous arguments on church policy, Swift declares in this essay, 'will have little force under the present corruptions of mankind, because the authors treat this subject *tanquam in republica Platonis, et non in faece Romuli*' [as if in Plato's Republic, and not in impure Rome].[56] This comment, Womersley believes, is surely 'a bitter reflection on the effectiveness of *Gulliver's Travels*, Swift's own attempt (at least to some degree) to write in *republica Platonis*'.[57] One might qualify this observation by suggesting that in terms of direct influence and narrative dynamics, the book is more firmly rooted in More's idealism than Plato's Kallipolis. *Gulliver's Travels* begins with an introductory letter from the fictitious Richard Sympson, the book's supposed publisher. The device is reminiscent of More's opening letter to Peter Giles at the start of *Utopia*. It serves as a means of introducing the figure of the fabricated traveller, Lemuel Gulliver, as though he were a real person, and establishing the characteristic mingling of fact and fiction; it resembles More's presentation of Raphael Hythloday, his expert in nonsense. Sympson praises the travels and its author for their seeming candour, and in doing so, produces that indicative Swiftian alloy of the proverbial and the trite: 'there is an Air of Truth apparent through the whole', Swift/Symonds asserts, 'and indeed the Author was so distinguished for his Veracity, that it became a sort of Proverb among his Neighbours at Redriff [a port district in East London], when anyone affirmed a Thing to say it was true as if Mr. Gulliver had spoke it' (p. 16).

As in More, gambits of this kind are not merely intended as a perplexing play on the binary opposition of truth and invention, but also suggest the more engaging notion that the latter term does not necessarily cancel out the former (and vice versa). Swift evidently felt such playful Morean intricacies had not been sufficiently exploited or appreciated in this opening epistle; or perhaps he was following the textual progress of *Utopia* itself in the accumulation of paratextual missives for subsequent editions. In any event, Swift added a further autobiographical epistle 'A Letter from Capt. Gulliver to his Cousin Sympson' to the Dublin Faulkner edition of 1735. The letter is dated 2 April 1727; and that probably was roughly when it was written. This second epistle is a beguiling and narratively satisfactory variant on the preliminary letter in which Gulliver now attacks his own work and publisher; and it also serves as an outlet for the real author's frustrations – a barely concealed complaint to the real publisher about his excising of potentially incendiary passages for fear of prosecution, and for the numerous typographical errors which bedevilled the first and second editions.[58]

---

[55] Womersley makes the comparison between Mandeville's description of the sow in *Fable of the Bees*, I, p. 255 and Gulliver's description of the appearance of lice under a microscope in Part II of *Gulliver's Travels*, p. 159, n. 15.
[56] Quoted in Swift, *Gulliver's Travels*, p. 464.
[57] Swift, *Gulliver's Travels*, p. 464.
[58] See Womersley's account of the book's textual history in Swift, *Gulliver's Travels*, pp. 637–46.

Gulliver's Travels' second epistle also acknowledges the impotence of satirical writing. As Swift in the guise of Gulliver asserts 'I cannot learn that my Book hath produced one single Effect according to mine Intentions: I desired you would let me know by a Letter, when Party and Faction were extinguished; Judges learned and upright; Pleaders honest and modest, with some Tincture of Common Sense' (p. 10). And the additional letter provides some pleasing circularity and psychological continuity to the book, as Gulliver prefaces the work with the same slightly crazed zeal for the Houyhnhnms and vehement dislike for the Yahoos with which he concludes the fourth part. A reader who had not already finished the book might be bemused by an introductory discussion which required at least a cursory knowledge of the travels; but that would seem in some respects to be the main point, that the missive was a reassertion and elaboration of text which pivoted on conceptions of the ideal and the non-ideal; and that, in itself, was in keeping with Morean literary principles. The letter's date, 2 April 1727, as Womersley points, squarely places 'Gulliver between knavery and folly'.[59] The careful selection of the day should be read in the light of Swift's marginalia on his copy of Clarendon's *History of the Rebellion and the Civil Wars in England* (1702–4) that Charles I's issuing of writs for Parliament on 3 April 1640, that 'April 3rd [was] for knaves 1st for fools'.[60] Gulliver thus conflates foolery and knavery; but he also provides the possibility of revelation through folly in the manner of the conscious play on the Latin sense of More's name, as an amalgam of foolishness and insight in *Utopia* itself and its various paratextual endorsements.

The point about having sufficient alertness and the intellectual nimbleness to be able to appreciate fully the shifting sardonic allusiveness of the text would be made right in the middle of the letter. Gulliver/Swift complains that some critics 'are so bold as to think my Book of Travels a mere Fiction, out of my own Brain; and have gone so far as to drop Hints, that the *Houyhnhnms* and *Yahoos* have no more Existence than the inhabitants of *Utopia*' (p. 13). We can note that the phrasing here is reminiscent of Mandeville's attack in the *Grumbling Hive* on the subjective delusion of conceiving social affairs in idealistic terms, '*a vain Eutopia seated in the Brain*'. And we can also appreciate the elaborate play on truth and fiction – the 'truth' that the work is substantially a work of subjective invention (Swift's rather than Gulliver's), and that the rational loquacious horses and brute hominids have no more objective existence than the citizens of More's Nowhere. But there is still the suggestion, beyond a nod to facile idealism, that the book is engaged with the serious matter of identifying the good and just society; and the extent to which human beings are capable of achieving such a dignified goal.

There are allusions to *Utopia* throughout *Gulliver's Travels*. The central play on scale in Lilliput is anticipated by Hythloday's observation that humankind in general is 'colossal and bigger than any giant'.[61] Both the Lilliputians' distaste for personal

---

[59] Swift, *Gulliver's Travels*, p. 14, n. 49.
[60] On the marginalia, see 'Hyde, Edward, 1st Earl Clarendon' in Passmann and Vienken, *The Library and Reading of Jonathan Swift*, II, pp. 939–58 (p. 941).
[61] Thomas More, *Utopia: Latin Text and English Translation*, ed. by George M. Logan and others (Cambridge: Cambridge University Press, 1995), p. 157.

ornamentation and the Yahoos' fondness for precious stones have a prototype in the Utopians' distain for the jewels and precious metals which others covet. When describing the urban demographic organisation of Brobdingnag, Gulliver states that the nation has fifty-one cities, close to Utopia's fifty-four. As in Utopia, the elective republican components of their constitution operate on the basis of secret ballots. In the midst of an exchange with one of the professors in Laputa, in which Gulliver discusses 'the Kingdom of *Tribnia*, by the Natives called Langden' (p. 281) (obvious anagrams of Britain and England), he mentions the manipulation of credit for the government's advantage, which is similar to the economic policy attacked by Hythloday in *Utopia*'s first book. Hythloday complains, we may recall, that counsellors recommend currency manipulation to the prince, so that the value of money with respect to goods is inflated when revenues are collected and then devalued when debts are due to be settled. In other words, they put the interests of the ruler before those of his subjects. And the key name in the title of the third part of Gulliver's travels, 'Laputa' offers a dizzying set of puns and anagrams. 'La Puta' is Spanish for whore; but the term 'puta' also has a computational sense in early modern mathematical treatises written in Latin.[62] As Jenny Mezciems points out, there is also the possibly of a partial anagram of 'utopia' in 'la Puta', and the words 'whore' is contained within 'nowhere'.[63]

Swift also follows More's ironic mocking of the legal profession (though, of course, without the same personal investment). We may recall that it is a lawyer in *Utopia*'s opening book who praises the rigour with which thieves are prosecuted in Tudor England; and lawyers are then dispensed with in the perfect commonwealth, because the sources of civil discord have been removed, rendering litigation redundant. Gulliver momentarily assumes Hythloday's sense of social outrage when he describes to his Houyhnhnm master the inequality of Britain under Queen Anne, where 'the rich Man enjoyed the Fruit of the poor Man's Labour, and the latter were a Thousand to One in Proportion to the former' (p. 373). The Houyhnhnms' council sits for five or six days, the same period as the Utopians'. The Houyhnhnms' disdain for bestial Yahoos leads to the notorious question in their assembly as to 'whether the *Yahoos* should be exterminated from the Face of the Earth' (p. 408). The proposal has a noteworthy antecedent in the Utopians' attitude to the violent Zapoletes, whom they retain as mercenaries while holding it would 'deserve very well of mankind if they could sweep from the face of the earth all the dregs of that vicious and disgusting race'.[64] After Gulliver leaves the Houyhnhnms' land aboard a craft partially constructed from the stitched-together hides of Yahoos, he is eventually recovered from the Indian Ocean. The ship's captain, Pedro de Mendez, is Portuguese, the same nationality as Hythloday. De Mendez, a man of open mind, is described by Gulliver as 'a very courteous and generous Person'; he displays the same beneficent traits as More's explorer (p. 430). And the book's conclusion has an assault on what Gulliver conceives as the defining

---

[62] See Womersley's ingenious unpicking of the various possible meanings contained in the island's name in Swift, *Gulliver's Travels*, p. 217, n. 2.
[63] Jenny Mezciems, 'The Unity of Swift's "Voyage to Laputa": Structure as Meaning in Utopian Fiction', *MLR*, 72 (1977), 1–21 (6).
[64] More, *Utopia*, p. 211.

vice of human beings: 'when I behold a Lump of Deformity and Diseases both in Body and Mind (i.e. a person), smitten with *Pride*, it immediately breaks all the Measures of my Patience; neither shall I be able to comprehend how such an Animal and such a Vice could tally together' (pp. 443–44). Pride is explicitly attacked by Hythloday toward the end of *Utopia*, 'a serpent from hell that twines itself around the hearts of men'; and the sin was condemned as the principal human failing in More's subsequent devotional and polemical religious writing.[65]

One might object there is no cast-iron allusion to *Utopia* in any of these examples. There are other plausible prototypes. On the question as to whether the Yahoos should be exterminated, for example, there are sources alongside the ostensibly pacific Utopians' wish that the pathological Zapoletes could be extinguished, such as Jehovah's contemplation in Genesis of the eradication of his recent conscious creations; or Plutarch's account of the regular pogroms conducted by the Spartan secret police to ensure the Helot population remained subservient; or in Thucydides' familiar interpretation of the periodic Athenian plagues as evidence of divine anger and retribution for the city's collective sinful behaviour. However, even if some of these Morean allusions may be considered to be operating in a mode of instructive parallelism, rather than being explicit derivations, their sheer number still gives a sense of 'nowhere' being somewhat oxymoronically a constant presence in Swift's work. Utopia's interweaving of satire and social formal structure was not only to be revisited and imaginatively reinterpreted in *Gulliver's Travels*, but also thematically extended, such that the latent aspects of the earlier text were both exposed and roundly confronted by the later one. As we saw in chapter two, More provided examples in *Utopia*'s first book of various societies which organise their affairs in a more satisfactory fashion than their sixteenth-century European counterparts manage to do; and he did so as a means of preparing the reader for Hythloday's subsequent extended account of Utopia. In a similar fashion, *Gulliver's Travels* offers two significant episodes which reflect on social idealism before arriving at the sustained treatment of this topic in the fourth voyage. These are Gulliver's interview with the King of Brobdingnag in Part II, and the account of Laputa and the Academy of Lagado in Part III.

In the discussion between Gulliver and the King of Brobdingnag, Swift momentarily inverts the familiar polarity of utopian projection. Instead of the traveller arriving at a distant land which turns out to be a perfected version of their own county, Gulliver eulogises early eighteenth-century Britain as though it *were* a utopia; or at least offers an account in which the nation's constitutional arrangements seem to have been optimised. Gulliver addresses the patriotic English reader directly, expressing his wish that he possessed the forceful eloquence of the Greek orator, Demosthenes, and his Roman successor, Cicero, so that he might 'celebrate the Praise of my own dear native Country in a Style equal to its Merits and Felicity' (p. 179). He describes the temperate

---

[65] See Thomas More, *Utopia: Latin Text and English Translation*, ed. by George Logan, Robert M. Adams, and Clarence H. Miller, trans. by Robert M. Adams (Cambridge: Cambridge University Press, 1995), p. 247. For further representative discussions of pride, see *The Confutation of Tyndale's Answer*, ed. by Louis A. Schuster and others, 3 vols, *The Complete Works of Sir Thomas More* (New Haven: Yale University Press, 1973), I, p. 662; and St. Thomas More, *The Tower Works: Devotional Writings*, ed. by Garry E. Haupt (New Haven: Yale University Press, 1980), p. 25.

perfection of the British climate and the countryside's abundant fertility; he refers to the state as 'three mighty Kingdoms under one Sovereign' (p. 180, i.e. the arrangement for England, Scotland and Ireland prior to the Act of Union in 1707); the House of Lords is constituted by peers of the realm, who by inheritance, aptitude and learning seem to emulate the shrewdness and gravitas of the *Republic*'s governing elite; he expatiates on the 'extraordinary Care always taken of their Education in Arts and Arms, to qualify them for being Counsellors born' (p. 180). The bishops, as a branch of the Lords, are chosen for office on the basis of the 'Sanctity of their Lives, and the Depth of their Erudition' (p. 181). The House of Commons is populated by noble and earnest patriots, '*freely* picked and culled out by the People themselves' (p. 181); and the bicameral legislature constitutes 'the most august Assembly in *Europe*' (p. 181). Gulliver then examines the principles of the judiciary and English law, such that sagacious judges 'disputed Rights and Properties of Men, as well as for the Punishment of Vice and Protection of Innocence' (p. 182); and he includes accounts of those other aspects one might expect to see in a comprehensive survey of another nation: he comments on the size of the population, the scope of political and religious affiliations, 'Sports and Pastimes' (p. 182), and supplies a brief recent history of Great Britain and Ireland.

The king then asks a number of searching questions through which this idealistic vision of contemporary Britain is rapidly debunked. In the case of the peers, the king asks what exactly constitutes their education. He inquires as to whether stalwart obsequiousness rather than merit and qualification was not the easier route to a bishopric, such as in the example of 'slavish prostitute Chaplains to some Nobleman, whose Opinions they continued servilely to follow after they were admitted into that Assembly' (p. 183); he ask whether voters in parliamentary elections were not susceptible to financial inducement. He questions the judiciary's disinterestedness, and political interference in the operation of the law, 'whether Advocates and Orators had liberty to plead in Causes manifestly known to be unjust, vexatious, or oppressive' (p. 184, with the clear implication that lawyers behave in exactly these ways). He enquires about the state's economic foundations, while expressing scepticism on running a national economy on the basis of never-ending credit, a perplexity shared by the fiscally conservative Swift, as to 'how a Kingdom could run out of its Estate like a private Person' (p. 185). The king challenges the wisdom of spending vast sums on wars, and the liberal indulgence of dissenting and non-conformist groups when the unfettered expression of their views cannot be conducive to the public good.

The interview's conclusion is as savage as it is well known; and indeed, was the source for subsequent memorable visual adaptation (Gillray caricatured Napoleon as a miniscule Gulliver to George III's giant king in 1803).[66] The Brobdingnagian monarch places tiny Gulliver on the palm of his hand, and thanks him for projecting his native country as through a utopian prism: his presentation had been 'a most Admirable Panegyrick upon your Country' (p. 188). But this courtesy is merely a prelude to the wholesale demolition of this vision of the ideal state. He finishes with the brutal verdict that 'I cannot but conclude the Bulk of your Natives to be the most pernicious Race

---

[66] See Tim Clayton and Sheila O'Connell, *Bonaparte and the British: Prints and Propaganda in the Age of Napoleon* (London: British Museum, 2015), p. 119.

of little Odious Vermin that Nature ever suffered to Crawl upon the Surface of the Earth' (p. 189).

Womersley notes 'vermin' used in this context has a historical resonance. It had been employed in public discourse for describing dissenters in the 1670s, and the slur had also been applied to indigenous Irish Catholics.[67] In immediate literary terms, the king's description of British subjects anticipates the disgust with which the Houyhnhnms regard the Yahoos. There is almost always a shadow of satiric intent, of ironic detachment in Swift's utterances, even when the proposition seems to have no qualifying term or purpose. Some critics, for example, have even discerned a degree of irony in Swift's simplistically earnest pamphlet *A Project for the Advancement of Religion, and the Reformation of Manners* (1709), which advocates a system of surveillance to ensure the morality of publications and performance.[68] The King of Brobdingnag's closing observations on the wretchedness of the bulk of Gulliver's compatriots may appear incontrovertible. Yet, there is still a sense of disjuncture between the analysis and this closing judgement, of disproportionate response in the final coruscation of the majority of British subjects; that the opinion is out of kilter with the king's previous measured interrogation.

In *A Tale of a Tub*, Swift indicatively declared that 'when a Man's Fancy gets *astride* on his Reason [...] Common Sense is Kickt out of Doors'.[69] Hence effective personal and public governance is on the basis of sensible decision making in which reason and established consensus are respected. In the account of the flying island of Laputa in Part III, Gulliver uses a contemporary scientific term to describe its fantastic airborne movement, 'an Island in the Air, inhabited by Men who were able [...] to raise, or to sink, or to put it into a *progressive Motion*' (p. 223, my emphasis). Apart from being pleonastic, the phrase suggests that any such movement is not likely to be progressive in either literal or metaphorical senses. This section of the book satirises science as a means of ongoing social and intellectual improvement. The Laputian elite lack sufficient understanding and sense to organise their affairs satisfactorily. With one eye turned inward and the other heavenward, Laputian men inhabit a realm of abstraction and symbols, and have to be jolted from their airy speculations by a blow from one of their flappers. The section reads in part as though it were a repost to the central claim of Plato's *Republic* that those who excel at philosophical investigation are best suited by aptitude and temperament for the rigours of governance. Excessive astronomical and solipsistic reflection result in absurdities reminiscent of Restoration comedy – the chronically distracted men are habitually cuckolded by ground dwellers; the earthlings being indulged by the exasperated and presumably sexually-frustrated Laputian wives. And Laputian cuisine is singled out as a disconcerting and unappetising concoction on

---

[67] Swift, *Gulliver's Travels*, p. 189, n. 56.
[68] Michael Treadwell sifts the evidence for an ironical reading of this tract in his 'Swift's Relations with the London Book Trade to 1714', in *Author/Publisher Relations During the Eighteenth and Nineteenth Centuries*, ed. by Robin Myers and Michael Harris (Oxford: Oxford Polytechnic Press, 1983), pp. 1–36 (p. 15); see also Claude Rawson on this point in his *The Character of Swift's Satire: A Revised Focus* (Newark, NJ: University of Delaware Press, 1983), p. 46. Rawson agrees with Treadwell that the pamphlet should not be treated as being ironical.
[69] Swift, *A Tale of a Tub*, p. 110.

geometric principles, with a 'Shoulder of Mutton cut into an Æquilateral Triangle, a Piece of Beef into a Rhomboides; and a Pudding into a Cycloid' (p. 229); all served with bread shaped into 'Cones, Cylinders, Parallelograms, and several other Mathematical Figures' (p. 230).

The claims of a universal system of mathematics may result in culinary oddity, but the tendency toward abstraction also has more sinister implications. In a passage which is standardly interpreted as an analogy of the relationship of Great Britain to her Irish dependency, the flying island occasionally has to subdue a restive dominion. In these circumstances, 'the first and mildest Course', Gulliver reports, 'is by keeping the Island hovering over such a Town and the Lands about it; whereby he can deprive them of the Benefit of the Sun and the Rain, and consequently afflict the Inhabitants with Dearth and Diseases. And if their Crimes deserve it, they are at the same time pelted from above with great stones, against which they have no Defence, but by creeping into Cellars or Caves, while the Roofs of their Houses are beaten to Pieces' (pp. 246–47). This is a typical Swiftian litotes with aerial siege and bombardment described as the 'mildest' of the available strategies; and it serves as a prelude to the redundant measure of lowering the island to flatten the recalcitrant domain beneath it. Self-interest is dressed up as high principle. But the measure is never enacted, because 'it would render [government members] odious to the People, so it would be a great Damage to their own Estates that lie below' (p. 247).

The conceit of deluded principle and progressive circumstance is repeated in the subsequent account of the scientific pretentions of the Royal Academy. Swift imaginatively relocates the academy from London to Lagado (the capital of Balnibari). The city's description of houses 'strangely built', and with a population 'generally in rags' (p. 251) is reminiscent of Swift's general view of Dublin (as consistently described in his Irish pamphlets).[70] Despite Balnibari's dilapidated and mean circumstances, however, the academy is a hot-house of utopian projection. Gulliver reports on 'new Rules and Methods of Agriculture and Building, and new Instruments and Tools for all Trades and Manufacture, whereby, as they undertake, one man shall do the Work of Ten, a Palace may be built in a Week, of Materials so durable as to last for ever without repairing. All the Fruits of the Earth shall come to Maturity as Whatever Season we think fit to chuse' (p. 256). The schemes are then exposed as being either fraudulent, impractical or absurd. There are projects to erect a mill half-way up a hillside, extract sun-beams from cucumbers, reconstitute food from dung, and build houses from the roof downwards. The scepticism towards technological progress remains eye-catching from a modern standpoint, insofar as successive industrial and digital revolutions have delivered most of the technological and labour-saving benefits ironically envisioned by Swift; but those achievements do not necessarily overcome the second-order objection: that such schemes, even if they succeed, should not be treated as an unalloyed good. Indeed, a late example demonstrates that ingenious investigation when it is detached

---

[70] On these matters, see David Hayton and Adam Rounce's introduction to their edition of *Irish Political Writings after 1785: A Modest Proposal and Other Works*, ed. by D.W Hayton and Adam Rounce, The Cambridge Edition of the Works of Jonathan Swift (Cambridge: Cambridge University Press, 2018), pp. xxiii–cvii (especially, pp. lxviii–lxxiv).

from 'Common Sense' and 'Common Understanding' results in a Hogarthian spectre of animal cruelty. A physician proudly demonstrates to Gulliver his cure for colic by inflating a dog by means of bellows inserted into the animal's anus. The dog's intestines distend until the creature 'made so violent a Discharge, was very offensive to me and my Companions'; and Gulliver goes on to report that 'the Dog died on the Spot' (p. 264).

In James Joyce's totalising account of human experience, there is a strain of coprophilia such that excreta has its appropriate place and purpose in universal literary representation. Joyce expresses his attraction to feculence in an intimate letter to his future wife, Nora Barnacle. He recalls the erotic charge when she performs 'the most shameful and filthy act of the body'. He continues, 'you remember the day you pulled up your clothes and let me lie under looking up while you did it'.[71] This coprolite interest manifests itself in various allusions in the course of Joyce's *Ulysses* (1922), most memorably, according to Aida Yared, in the 'Lestrygonians' episode. Leopold Bloom, while walking from Sackville Street to Kildare Street in Dublin, 'transitions figuratively from mouth to anus', and he eventually 'emerges intact between gigantic gluteal hemispheres: the twin buildings of the National Library Museum'.[72] As his predecessor as ambivalent Irish writer, Swift could not so readily overcome the necessary abjection in constructing such an equivalence between human propensity and shit. Swift cannot really be described as being a coprophiliac; but he certainly matched Joyce in his compulsion to consider cloacae – as a simultaneous attraction and repulsion to filth and excrescence.

In *Gulliver's Travels*, in addition to the pungent image of the hapless dog expiring as it evacuates its bowels and the reconstruction of food from faecal residue, there is the account of Gulliver defecating in Lilliput. Gulliver records his disgust at the partridge-sized flies in Brobdingnag, as they alight on his 'Victuals', and leave 'their loathsome Excrement and Spawn behind' (p.153); and there is the Laputian professor advising statesmen to examine suspicious persons by taking 'a strict View of their Excrements, and from the Colour, the Odour, the Taste, the Consistence, the Crudeness, or Maturity of Digestion, form a Judgment of their Thoughts and Designs' (p. 280). However, as we might expect, the most sustained usage of excremental imagery occurs in the book's final and most contentious part, 'a Voyage to the Country of the Houyhnhnms'. In an early encounter with the bestial Yahoos, Gulliver, having provoked one of the creatures by striking him with the flat of his sword, takes shelter as the offended herd bespatter him from the canopy of trees in the manner of monkeys encountered by European travellers, discharging 'their Excrements on [his] Head' (p. 335). Later, Gulliver's attempt to inspect an infant male Yahoo has to be abandoned because when he held 'the odious Vermin in [his] Hands, it voided its filthy Excrements of a yellow liquid Substance, all over my Cloaths' (p. 399). And a metonymic adjective encapsulates all the violence and vileness of these creatures from Gulliver's perspective, when he describes the Yahoos to his Houyhnhnm master as being an 'execrable' race (p. 353).

---

[71] Joyce to Nora Barnacle Joyce, 2 December 1909, *Selected Letters of James Joyce*, ed. by Richard Ellmann (London: Faber and Faber, 1975), pp. 180–81 (p. 181).

[72] Aida Yared, 'Eating and Digesting "Lestrygonians": A Physiological Model of Reading', *James Joyce Quarterly*, 46 (2009), 469–79 (469).

At the centre of this section of Gulliver's narrative is his disgust at the recognition of kinship with the Yahoos. He expresses early on his 'Horror and Astonishment', when he observes in this vile creature 'a perfect human Figure' (p. 342). The biological closeness is subsequently affirmed when Gulliver is embraced by a young amorous female Yahoo while bathing, an encounter which removes the last vestige of doubt as to their common ancestry. He is no longer able to deny 'that I was a real *Yahoo*, in every Limb and Feature, since the Females had a natural Propensity to me as one of their own Species' (p. 401). And there is a subtle variant of satirical intent at this point as Gulliver almost concedes a reciprocal attractiveness. He acknowledges that 'her Countenance did not make an Appearance altogether so hideous as the rest of the Kind' (p. 401). Ian Higgins has taken issue with what became a standard interpretation of the Yahoos in the twentieth century as a commonplace pejorative perception of aboriginals in the European imagination, disseminated through travel literature from the seventeenth century onwards. Higgins argues instead that the Yahoos should be seen as an attempt to embody and project a sub-rational version of human nature in which Gulliver and by extension the reader is confronted with their intrinsic bestiality, 'a biological kinship with brutality', and that instinct becomes a handy repository for all that could be considered as foul, perverse and degrading from Swift's conservative and generally misanthropic perspective.[73]

Yet one might counter that the interpretation of the Yahoos as barbarians does not preclude their conception as an expression of common bestiality and vice versa. Swift's restless vision has a prismatic quality to it, such that the satirical sallies may be sustained on one topic on a single reference or an allusion only then to shift to another, as though the possibilities of any idea must be fully exploited, and part of that exploitation means that the referent is never stable with respect to the phenomena it describes, or with which it is imaginatively associated. All images, however vivid they may be, are subject to sequential refraction. Hence, Yahoos can stand for primitive savagery in one moment and the external projection of common bestial instinct in the next. The Yahoos can provide a broad allusion to Hobbesian anarchy devoid of the ordering presence of civil society, such that 'Battles have been fought between the *Yahoos* of several Neighbourhoods without any visible Cause: Those of one District watching all Opportunities to surprise the next before they are prepared' (p. 391). Yahoos provide the means for a wry if misogynistic exposure of what was usually regarded as socially-acquired behaviour as being, in fact, innate. Gulliver/Swift declares he 'could not reflect with some Amazement, and much Sorrow, that the Rudiments of *Lewdness, Coquetry, Censure and Scandal*, should have Place by Instinct in Womankind' (p. 397).

The odd male Yahoo is similarly afflicted by melancholy as a consequence of his spleen. Yahoos are on occasion, for Swift, a vision of the ragged, filthy and impoverished Irish. Gulliver's casual references to using Yahoo skins to re-sole his dilapidated shoes and to construct sails for his improvised craft at the end of his stay in the land of the Houyhnhnms can be interpreted as the point at which Gulliver loses touch with common humanity. However, the episode also anticipates the kind of social satiric instrumentalism which informs Swift's subsequent advocacy of extreme measures to

---

[73] Ian Higgins, *Jonathan Swift* (Tavistock: Northcote House, 2004), p. 70.

relieve the suffering of the immiserated Irish in his late and notorious pamphlets, *A Modest Proposal for Preventing the Children of Poor People from Being a Burthen to their Parents or Country; and for Making Them Beneficial to the Publick* (1729) and *A Proposal for Giving Badges to the Beggars in All the Parishes of Dublin* (1737). The former proposes that the flesh of impoverished Catholic infants should be marketed to and consumed by the Irish gentry as a means of alleviating poverty while stimulating the chronically sluggish Irish economy; and the latter advocates that beggars in Dublin be badged and shamed with foreigners expelled, on the basis that 'there is not a more undeserving, Vicious Race of human Kind than the Bulk of those who are reduced to Beggary'.[74]

Whatever significance one wishes to ascribe to each of the central aspects of the interpretation; as a version of the kinds of depictions of savage people in travel literature, as an expression of the negative perspective of indigenous Irish, or as a distillation of all that is intrinsically disgusting, execrable, about men and women in their fallen condition, it would still seem to be an ineluctable conclusion from this segment of the narrative that it is impossible, and indeed, futile to try to conceptualise human beings within a set of perfected circumstances. Nevertheless, that idea still provides Swift with various further satirical permutations. Gulliver reports that the etymology of the word 'Houyhnhnm' is '*the Perfection of Nature*' (p. 350), and Gulliver's equine master describes him on a full inspection of his physique as a 'perfect *Yahoo*' (p. 352). Gulliver's account of modern Britain and Europe to his unnamed Houyhnhnm benefactor merely confirms the earlier opinion of the King of Brobdingnag. Gulliver now recounts the horrors of contemporary life, including those consequences of the expanding global economy. 'We sent away the greatest Part of our necessary Things to other Countries, from whence in Return we brought the Materials of Diseases, Folly, and Vice, to spend among ourselves', he recalls, 'hence it follows of Necessity, that Vast Numbers of our People are compelled to seek their Livelihood by Begging, Robbing, Stealing, Cheating, Pimping, Forswearing, Flattering, Suborning, Forging, Gaming, Lying, Fawning, Hectoring, Voting, Scribling, Stargazing, Poysoning, Whoring, Canting, Libelling, Freethinking, and the like Occupations' (p. 375). Swift may draw on Mandeville throughout the course of *Gulliver's Travels*, but there are no public optimising advantages to this list of vices. The trap for this distinctly un-utopian vision of modernity snaps shut when Gulliver's equine master observes that the rational capacities of human beings have done nothing to ameliorate their Yahoo brutishness. Indeed, that 'small Pittance of Reason' (p. 389) which allows for close kinship, rather than absolute identity with these low creatures only makes matters worse – reason aggravates our '*natural* Corruptions', and encourages us 'to acquire new ones which Nature had not given us' (p. 389).

In the ostensible binary structure of this final section of *Gulliver's Travels*, the Houyhnhnms are presented as an ideal society of coolly detached and rational creatures, in opposition to the barbarously instinctual Yahoos. Reason does not operate in this equine community on the basis of a grand analytical schema, but rather leads to the Shaftesburian virtues of benevolence and friendship. As with Plato's *Republic*, this is a

---

[74] Swift, *A Proposal for Giving Badges to the Beggars in All the Parishes of Dublin*, in Swift, *Irish Political Writings*, pp. 305–19 (p. 312).

society which operates on the basis of rational judgement, rather than on a codified body of law. All citizens act in an egalitarian and selfless fashion. In a departure from the deceit required in the organisation of breeding arrangements in Kallipolis, Swift's hyper-rational horses submit to the selection of suitable partners for one another, so as to maximise the possibility of producing healthy, intelligent and considerate offspring. Education is exclusively rational; and the virtues instilled in colts and folds alike have a distinct Morean cast to them: '*Temperance, Industry, Exercise* and *Cleanliness*' (p. 405). And like More, there's no distinction to be drawn between the sexes when it comes to education. In common with Plato and Plutarch, Gulliver stresses the importance of physical exercise for a healthy society. The Houyhnhnms' language, Gulliver suggests, has no means of conceptualising falsehood; and the sole function of speech is naively referential (thereby ruling out the possibility of the shifting ironical and satirical expressiveness of *Gulliver's Travels*). The society is unlettered, and the one art form accorded any status is oral poetry. There is no money; and the only hierarchy the Houyhnhnms observe is a virtuous if self-perpetuating meritocracy. Their diet is a simple but nutritious combination of oats, hay and milk (which presumably results in inoffensive ordure). The horses seem to live in semi-rural circumstances, without technological labour-saving devices or medicine. When the time comes for one of their number to expire (and a combination of good breeding, sanitary conditions, and a healthy lifestyle means that disease is practically unknown in this felicitous state), they take themselves off to a secluded spot and reflect on a life well spent until the spirit eventually departs.

It was possible for eighteenth-century readers to view this portrait of equine utopia as being untroubled by irony. William Godwin, for example, regarded the Houyhnhnms' principles by which they conducted their quadrennial Representative Council of the Whole Nation as providing 'a more profound insight into the true principles of political justice than any preceding or contemporary author'.[75] Godwin was thinking of its similarity to the Amphitryonic council of ancient Greece (town-states in a political and cultural union), which 'possessed no authority but that which flowed from its personal character', and answering to the immediate needs of the populace.[76] He was not alone in this period in interpreting the land of the horses as a straightforward projection of the good and happy state; but it was the anti-utopianism of the bestial humanoids which attracted most attention. Jonathan Smedley allowed the last part to stand for the whole when he declared in 1728 that *Gulliver's Travels* was an 'unnatural *Romance*' made up 'of Folly and Extravagance'.[77] John Boyle, Swift's first biographer, complained that the fourth part expressed 'misanthropy that is intolerable', and that the whole edifice constituted a 'real insult upon mankind'.[78] Thomas Ogle dismissed the defence that extreme vices need to be painted in suitably lurid colours, observing that 'the morals of any individual are not likely to be amended by indiscriminate censure on the

---

[75] William Godwin, *Enquiry Concerning Political Justice; and its Influence on Modern Morals and Happiness*, ed. by Isaac Kramnick (Harmondsworth: Penguin, 1985), p. 552.
[76] Godwin, *Political Justice*, p. 552.
[77] Jonathan Smedley, *Gulliveriana: or, a Fourth Volume of Miscellanies* (London: Roberts, 1728), p. 329.
[78] John Boyle, Fifth Earl of Cork and Orrery, *Remarks on the Life and Writings of Dr Jonathan Swift*, ed. by João Fróes (Newark, DE : University of Delaware Press, 1998), p. 215, p. 217.

whole species'.[79] And Sir Walter Scott described the excessive bleakness of the vision as 'the deep and bitter misanthropy of a neglected age', and he explained this folly in social and biographical terms.[80] The misanthropy was a consequence of Swift living in Ireland, a detested land 'divided between petty tyrants and oppressed slaves'. Swift was 'a worshipper of that freedom and independence which he beheld daily being trampled upon' so that 'the unrestrained violence of his feelings drove him to loath the very species by whom such indignity was done and suffered'.[81] To these unfortunate circumstances, Scott added the debilitations of Ménière's disease, personal tragedy, professional disappointment and de facto banishment from England, the country in which 'he had found his hopes; and left his affections' – a list of such unremitting woe one must wonder that Swift was not even more misanthropic than he turned out to be.[82]

Godwin seemed to assume a provocative contrarian perspective on Swift's work by focussing on its idealistic aspects rather than considering its familiar dispiriting vision of humanity, although that interpretation still required a bamboozling conceptual elision. As Gulliver casually reported, the *only* matter the equine Representative Council of the Whole Nation ever debated, and indeed debated *every* time it convened was 'whether the *Yahoos* should be exterminated from the Face of the Earth' (p. 408). It is an indicatively shocking pronouncement, and not appreciably softened by the alternative measure proposed by Gulliver's equine master that they might consider gelding male Yahoos instead. The motion for extermination anticipates the suggestion of the modest proposal that the Irish gentry instigate a licensed and market-driven form of cannibalism for the purposes of economic stimulation, the relief of beggary and demographic control. An abiding concern of twentieth-century criticism was the scope of Swiftian misanthropy (the consensus has been that it was restricted rather than absolute), and whether or not the horse-land utopia was intended as a valid projection of the ideal state, or a bleak satire on it, consistent with all the other commonwealths which *Gulliver's Travels* proposed and then undercut. Terry Eagleton is surely right to suggest that Swift's myriad perspectives cannot be resolved into a unified whole, that 'the book cannot control the implications of its own satirical intentions', and that the same problem affects 'Swift's strategic cultural relativizing, in which one perspective objectifies another only to be dwindled and discredited by a third'.[83] But one might argue that such elements and textual strategies would only be problematic so long as one was persuaded that the book *should* exhibit the thematic cohesion of a realist novel, and that satire *should* function as a corrective toward a notional ethical mean, rather than constituting a dynamic method of examining the contrariness of human spirit, intention and desire.

[79] Thomas Ogle, 'George-Monck Berkeley's *Literary Relics*', *The Monthly Review*, 2nd series, 3 (1790), 242.
[80] Sir Walter Scott, 'Memoirs of Jonathan Swift D.D.', in *Works of Jonathan Swift*, ed. by Sir Walter Scott, 2nd edn, 19 vols (London: Bickers & Son, 1883), I, pp. 1–464 (p. 306).
[81] Scott, 'Memoirs of Jonathan Swift', p. 314.
[82] Scott, 'Memoirs of Jonathan Swift', p. 314.
[83] Terry Eagleton, *Heathcliff and the Great Hunger: Studies in Irish Culture* (London: Verso, 1996), p. 157.

One can, of course, also point to the multifarious ways in which this late suggestion that hominid vermin should be exterminated is both contained and hedged. We might note the genocidal policy is debated in the Houyhnhnm council, but not adopted (and there's no clear suggestion that this definitive solution will be agreed by any future assembly). Swift's contemporaries were well aware of the oddities, fancifulness and outrageousness masquerading as disinterested reportage in the genre of travel literature, that genre which Gulliver emulates while his author avidly consumed it and dismissed it as 'Trash'. Hence the suggestion is made in the context of a genre which carries with it a sense of the unreal and unreliable. The proposal is moreover made in the fantastical circumstances of horses being conceived as rational creatures. Horses may not be on the same level as the dim-witted talking asses of Lucian and Apuleius; but they are clearly still creatures of limited consciousness and minimal powers of reflection; even, as Swift evidently believed, such beasts deserve to be treated with all due care.[84] Gulliver becomes an increasingly unreliable witness as the narrative progresses; his obsequiousness and self-abasement in the company of the super-rational quadrupeds is at best unbecoming. And he is to be the final victim of the Swiftian satirical trap. Unable to overcome his equine predilections, he ends up at home in England, deranged, preferring the company of brute creatures in his stable, rather than practising the virtues of amity and benevolence with his own family. Yet there can be no complete security or certainty in this line of argument. For it is also the case that the book does connect ideas of utopia to the simplifying measure of eradication as a means of resolving political and ethnic difficulties.

I suggested earlier that if one were to look at the two most enduring and influential forms of utopian expression in the modern period, then one could look to the works of Kant and Swift, however anomalous this combination might appear to be. In the case of Swift, we can consider his significance as having three main components: first, there are the direct derivations and the development of the style and the ideas of More's *Utopia*; second, there is the extent to which his writing has had a significant influence on subsequent canonical utopian and anti-utopian writing; and third, there are the wider observations the text makes on ethnic distinctiveness, rational idealism and the prospect of genocide. As I have suggested, there are many allusions in *Gulliver's Travels* to More's *Utopia*, but beyond the direct references to the earlier work, there is the social, political and economic analysis of contemporary Britain to be set against the more successful arrangements of imaginary states. In *Utopia*, the construction of the ideal society must be at the cost of abandoning some principles; and that calls into question the supposed idealism of Nowhere. We can detect such conundrums in the Utopians attitude toward bondsmen and other non-citizens of the state. We may recall Utopians have a foreign policy where it is perfectly acceptable to subvert and destabilise the constitutional arrangement of a rival power; and the Utopians retain the services of another ethnic group as mercenaries even though they believe they would be doing humankind a great service 'if they could sweep from the face of the earth all the dregs of that vicious and disgusting race'. Clearly, Swift increases the number of satirical

---

[84] See Ehrenpreis, *Swift*, III, pp. 431–32.

perspectives on what could be considered the socially ideal; but it also seems at times as though there is a deliberate attempt to transform entirely the ironic mode of *Utopia's serio ludere* – to entertain the idea that *all* human beings are intrinsically 'vicious and disgusting'. Yet the ludic element in that imaginative configuration should not be entirely abandoned, even in the entertainment of such a bleak idea. The playful seriousness of More's work was now imbued with savage energy.

One can make the case for Swift having produced an extensive anatomy of utopian projection, stretching its expression to the point of collapse. If one were to survey the subsequent development of anglophone utopian and anti-utopian writing, then one might see the extent of Swift's influence. Godwin's *The Adventures of Caleb Williams* (1794) became a domestic version of Gulliver's international travelling; Thomas Carlyle's writings on modern Britain have Swift's savage vision of Ireland in view (as we will see in the next chapter); Samuel Butler's *Erewhon* (1872) is a de facto revision of Swiftian satirical utopianism for the Victorian era. The bisection of humanity into Eloi and Matlocks in H.G. Wells' *The Time Machine* (1895) looks like a radical reformulation of the split into the rational and bestial in Houyhnhnms and Yahoos. George Orwell declared that 'the dreary world of the Houyhnhnms was about as good a Utopia as Swift could construct'; and he was less than impressed by Swift's reactionary conundrum, 'a Tory anarchist, despising authority, while disbelieving liberty'.[85] Nevertheless, Orwell still declared Swift 'one of the writers I admire with least reserve, and *Gulliver's Travels* in particular is a book which seems impossible for me to grow tired of'.[86] And indeed, *Nineteen Eighty-Four* (1949) possesses the remorseless logic of Swift's satire. Aldous Huxley is evidently Swiftian in his account on technological progress and in his views on the primitive in *Brave New World* (1932); and in Margaret Atwood's MaddAddam trilogy (2004–13), a key utopian/dystopian romance of the early twenty-first century, the central sardonic premise is that if one wishes to create the perfect society then the essential requirement of this position is that the bestial human race needs to be eradicated; which is merely to pass finally the quadrennially debated motion of the Houyhnhnm assembly.

Yet one might suggest that the most significant aspect of the work is its imaginative presentation of a set of ideas that became central for the consideration of the West in the twentieth century. Kant's advocacy of universal reason can be understood to manifest itself in the doctrine of human rights and the eventual enshrining of those principles in the first article of the declaration adopted by the United Nations in 1946, with its parallel claim for human dignity. This is the interconnectedness of right and dignity which Habermas regards as being a fundamental condition for the creation of a 'realistic utopia'. Swift, however, offers an alternative set of perspectives on idealism, sovereign reason, the fundamental attributes of human beings, and the probable outcome of rational utopianism. In the closing section of *Gulliver's Travels*, and in those late Irish pamphlets, *A Modest Proposal*, and *A Proposal for Giving Badges to the Beggars*

---

[85] 'Politics vs Literature', in *The Collected Essays, Journalism and Letters of George Orwell: Volume 4, In Front of Your Nose*, ed. by Sonia Orwell and Ian Angus (Harmondsworth: Penguin, 1971), pp. 241–60 (p. 256, p. 253).

[86] Orwell, 'Politics vs Literature', p. 257.

in All the Parishes of Dublin, Swift certainly does not endorse, but is still prepared to toy with the idea of extermination. Writing on Swift in 1946, Orwell could only bring himself to note that the Yahoos 'occupy the same place in [the Houyhnhnms'] community in Nazi Germany – anger and hatred'.[87] Claude Rawson has provided the most sustained consideration of Swift's blackest satire as an anticipation of the horrors of the Holocaust. The central thread of this discussion combines the insight on the apparent simplicity and decisiveness for resolving social difficulties, and that strand in late Swiftian thought which connects Gulliver's use of Yahoo hides for his shoe soles, the manufacture of his improvised craft to the instrumentalism of the butchery of poor children for foodstuffs and the necessity of eradicating beggars from Dublin streets. This aspect of Swift's oeuvre revealed an appreciation of the instincts and calculations which can result in genocide. In the case of the Nazis, the upshot was the Final Solution, exemplified in Himmler's declaration on the 'necessity of making the Jews Disappear from the face of the earth ["dieses Volk von der Erde verschwinden zu Lassen"]', but also the macabre spectacle in which body parts are fashioned to make tables and chairs, even a copy of *Mein Kampf* allegedly bound in human skin.[88]

Rawson concludes that Swift was essentially a compassionate man, who objected vehemently to the waste and carnage of military conflict. As such, he would have abhorred the Nazis' vicious cruelty. Swift contemplated genocide without really believing such actions could ever be taken in practice, just as the Houyhnhnms debated the extermination of the Yahoos, but never approved this murderous proposal. And one might add further caveats – Swift lacked a word with the modern legal force of 'genocide'; the term was not coined until 1946. The Houyhnhnms are devoid of technology (without even wheels and carriages); and the Final Solution was the murder of Jews and others on an industrial scale. Yet the multiple perspectives of Swift's satire certainly cannot be resolved into a unified vision; and the tactic of shock and outrage does not dispel the visceral attraction to the idea of eradicating those people and groups whom one thoroughly detests, the vermin supposedly devoid of intrinsic dignity, as a cruel but necessary step for the foundation of a pure society. It was the 1940s that the ideas of mass extermination and universal rights were to have their immediate successive moments. Instrumental reason coupled to loathing which resulted in extermination was followed by the response in international law that *all* human beings are intrinsically rational and sentient beings whose rights demand the upholding and safeguarding of their inherent dignity – in other words, Habermas's 'realistic utopia'.

The formal and informal consideration of genocide from the 1940s onwards often contains a reference both to universal dignity and the assaults upon it. Hence, Vann Nath, a rare survivor of the S-21 prison in Phnom Penh during the Khmer Rouge mass killings in the mid-1970s, summed up his debasement to a UN Tribunal as having 'lost

---

[87] Orwell, 'Politics vs Literature', p. 225.
[88] Cited in Claude Rawson, *God, Gulliver, and Genocide: Barbarism and the European Imagination, 1492-1945* (Oxford: Oxford University Press, 2001), p. 287. See also p. 372, n. 82 in the same for the multiple sources of this quotation.

his dignity'.[89] Noam Schimmel argued that survivors of the 1994 Rwandan genocide have a 'right' to resettlement outside their native country, because 'there is no greater moral obligation, no clearer expression of human solidarity and compassion than to enable these genocide survivors to live in freedom and safety without fear and with their dignity honored and restored'.[90] Nils Muižnieks, the Council of Europe Commissioner for Human Rights, complained of the lack of support for the victims' relatives and survivors of the 1995 Srebrenica genocide. The political culture of Serbia and the Republika Srpska, he argued, 'breeds contempt for the victims' human rights and dignity'.[91] And the International Criminal Court's indictment of the alleged perpetrators of the Darfur Genocide (often referred to as the first genocide of the twenty-first century) included 'charges of murder; attacks against the civilian population; destruction of property; rape; pillaging; and outrage upon personal dignity'.[92]

It was the animating irony of Samuel Johnson's account of the final period of Swift's life to suggest that an author who assumed a pervasive misanthropic attitude should have been stripped of all semblance of personal 'dignity' in his final years. Johnson reports with grim satisfaction that the dean in his unsound state was reduced to being exhibited as a curiosity by his servants for the entertainment of the paying public, as '*Swift* expires a Driv'ler and a Show'.[93] Swift's modern biographers have discredited this undignified concluding tableaux.[94] As we might expect, Swift's own use of 'dignity' includes the common eighteenth-century sense of an ecclesiastical preferment, but in the main, he remains close to the principal senses of its Latin root 'dignitas'; that is, as an allusion to rank of elevation, or to the inherent noble qualities of the exceptional individual. However, he often inflects both usages with characteristic wit and irony. Swift writes, for example, early in his career that 'dignity, high station, or great Riches are in some sort necessary to old Men, in order to keep the younger at a Distance; who are otherwise too apt to insult them on the Score of their Age'.[95] He comments caustically on the Whig journalist, Richard Steele, in *The Publick Spirit of the Whigs* (1714) that 'to *France* [Steele] hath given Leave to invade the *Empire* next Spring with two hundred thousand Men; and does at last he deals to *France* the *Imperial* Dignity, and so farewel *Liberty*'.[96] And in a letter to Archbishop King he provides an apposite

---

[89] Associated Press, 'Khmer Rouge Survivor Tells of Horrific Conditions at Torture Centre', *Guardian*, 29 July 2009, [https://www.theguardian.com/world/2009/jun/29/cambodia, accessed 5 September 2018].

[90] Noam Schimmel, 'A Safe Place to Call Home: Securing the Right of Rwandan Genocide Survivors to Resettlement outside Rwanda', *The Journal of Humanitarian Assistance*, 4 April 2010 [https://sites.tufts.edu/jha/archives/688, accessed 5 September 2018].

[91] Nils Muižnieks 'Addressing the Needs of the Victims of the Srebrenica Genocide must be the Priority', Commissioner for Human Rights, Council of Europe, 7 July 2015, [https://www.coe.int/en/web/commissioner/-/addressing-the-needs-of-the-victims-of-the-srebrenica-genocide-must-be-the-priority, accessed 5 September 2018].

[92] 'Darfur, Sudan, Situation in Darfur, Sudan, ICC-02/05', International Criminal Court [https://www.icc-cpi.int/darfur, accessed 5 September 2018].

[93] *The Vanity of Human Wishes*, in *The Poems of Samuel Johnson*, ed. by David Nichol Smith and Edward L. McAdam, 2nd edn (Oxford: Clarendon Press, 1974), pp. 110–33 (p. 130, l. 318).

[94] See Ehrenpreis, *Swift*, III, p. 920.

[95] *Thoughts on Various Subjects*, in the *Prose Works of Jonathan Swift*, ed. by Herbert Davis, 14 vols (Oxford: Basil Blackwell, 1939–1968), IV (1957), pp. 241–56 (p. 246).

[96] *The Publick Spirit of the Whigs*, in the *Prose Works of Jonathan Swift*, VIII (1953), pp. 27–68 (p. 61).

maxim, that he is 'in some Doubt, whether a Fall from a Horse be suitable to the Dignity of an Archbishop. It is one of the chief Advantages in a great Station, that one is exempt from common Accidents of that Kind'.[97]

The modern sense of dignity as a universal human attribute does not appear in Johnson's *Dictionary*, but it does occur notably in Swift's 'Hints Towards an Essay on Conversation' (1762), which contemplates the significance of reason and romance. The essay concludes with the observation that the latter is 'no ill Ingredient to preserve and exalt the Dignity of human Nature, without which it is apt to degenerate into every Thing that is sordid, vicious, and low'.[98] And one of Swift's earliest biographers surmised that the central impetus of his writings was to serve a similar common interest, 'to stimulate mankind to sustain their dignity as rational and moral beings'.[99] Just as modern biographical opinion has dispensed with the sordid spectacle of the ageing Swift *non compos mentis* being exhibited by his servants, so it has focussed instead on another more reliable closing vignette; that the dean's final words were: 'I am a fool'.[100] This valedictory utterance can be interpreted in more than one way: as a random expression of his deranged mind, or a last moment of lucidity in his diminished mental condition. However, the phrase also has the ring of a closing irony, as a return to More in the deliberate folly of attempting to fashion the ideal state which perforce cannot exist, and in the conviction that the 'truth' can be revealed by an expert in nonsense – an enterprise in which Swift had persevered through his life, with all its savage implications.

---

[97] Swift to Archbishop King, 3 January 1713, *Correspondence*, I, pp. 327–29 (p. 329).
[98] 'Hints Towards an Essay on Conversation', in *Prose Works of Jonathan Swift*, IV (1957), pp. 85–95 (p. 95).
[99] Jonathan Hawkesworth, 'An Account of the Life of the Reverend Jonathan Swift, D.D.', in *The Works of Dr Jonathan Swift*, 12 vols (London: Bowyer and others, 1768), I, pp. 1–76 (p. 75).
[100] Quoted in Ehrenpreis, *Swift*, III, p. 918.

4

The Machine Age: Carlyle to Morris

When Thomas Carlyle was a student at the University of Edinburgh in the early 1800s, his Swiftian acerbity led him to be nicknamed 'Jonathan' and 'The Doctor' by his peers.[1] Carlyle refers to Swift intermittently in his writings. He argues in an early essay that Swift employed 'a simple irony' when compared to Shakespeare, but then suggested that Swift 'had genuine humour too, and of no unloving sort, though cased like Ben Jonson's, in a most bitter and caustic rind'.[2] He deployed Swift's put down of Dryden in the *Battle of the Books* (1704), 'a helmet of rusty iron, dark, grim, gigantic; and within it at the furthest corner, is a head no bigger than a walnut' to demonstrate the disparity of baroque edifice and meagre revelation in Kantian philosophy.[3] In his essay on Robert Burns, he borrows a Swiftian epitaph for the maligned and disdained poet, 'Burns now sleeps', he declares, '"where bitter indignation can no longer lacerate his heart"'.[4] Even when there is no explicit reference, Swift's influence can still be detected. The early *Sartor Resartus* (1831) in which a fictional editor struggles with a philosophy of clothes as a means of both exemplifying and parodying German idealism is indebted to the digressive and allegorical structure of Swift's *Tale of the Tub* (1704). Carlyle used anthropomorphic horses at least twice in his writings, seemingly taking his cue from the final part of *Gulliver's Travels* (1726). In *Past and Present* (1843), Carlyle insists that his own Victorian industrial present has inverted social standards when it come horses and men: 'the four-footed worker has already *got* all that the two-legged worker is clamouring for!'[5] He goes on to complain of 'such a Platitude of a World, in which all working horses could be well fed, and innumerable working men should die starved' (p. 22). And in 'The Present Time', the first of the incendiary *Latter-Day Pamphlets* (1850), he has refined speaking horses complain about burdensome labour to suggest that emancipation and liberal philanthropism will not alleviate the immiserated circumstances of the populations of the west of Ireland and the Caribbean.

---

[1] See Fred Kaplan, *Thomas Carlyle: A Biography* (Cambridge: Cambridge University Press, 1983), p. 34. See also David R. Sorenson, 'Swift, Jonathan', in the *Carlyle Encyclopedia*, ed. by Mark Cumming (Madison: Fairleigh Dickinson University Press, 2004), pp. 456–57.
[2] Thomas Carlyle, 'John Paul Friedrich Richter', in *Critical and Miscellaneous Essays*, 5 vols (London: Chapman and Hall, 1899), I, pp. 1–25 (p. 17).
[3] *The Life of Schiller, Comprehending an Examination of his Works*, in *The Works of Thomas Carlyle*, 30 vols (London: Chapman and Hall, 1896–1899), XXV (1897), p. 113.
[4] Thomas Carlyle, 'Robert Burns', *Critical and Miscellaneous Essays*, I, pp. 258–318 (p. 305).
[5] Thomas Carlyle, *Past and Present*, in *Works*, X (1897), p. 22. All further in-text references are to this edition.

However, it is in the opening chapter of *Past and Present*, entitled 'Midas', that Swiftian allusion is at its most arresting. Carlyle describes a report in the newspapers of an Irish family, 'a Mother and a Father are arraigned and found guilty of poisoning three of their children to defraud "a burial-society" of some £3 8s due on the death of each child' (p. 4). Not unusually in these circumstances, Carlyle refracts contemporary experience through a literary or cultural allusion. In this instance, he recalls Dante's description of Count Ugolino in the *Inferno* (written 1320), condemned to Hell's lowest circle for treachery. Fixed in the Cocytus's ice for eternity, Ugolino feeds on the skull of his oppressor, Cardinal Ruggieri. Ugolino tells the poet that he and his children were incarcerated without food and water on the cardinal's orders. The young children pled with their father to eat them once they perished; and Ugolino recalls ambiguously 'I called them after they were dead. Then fasting did more than grief had done'.[6] The allusion to the *Inferno* suggests a troubling amalgam of grief and utility which is supposed to apply to wider Victorian society as much as to the culpable parents. Carlyle speculates on the dismal calculus which led the Stockport family to taking this grim course of action, 'and now Tom being killed, and all spent and eaten. Is it poor little starveling Jack that must go, or poor little starveling Will' (p. 4). The metaphor of Tom being 'eaten', rather than being murdered, and the profits from the scam being used to purchase foodstuffs is of a piece with traditional associations of poor Irish and cannibalism. Carlyle acknowledges that casual racial slurs will be aimed at the guilty couple '"Brutal Savages, degraded Irish", mutters the idle reader of the newspaper' (p. 4). However, there is to be no general exculpation. This crime besmirches us all, an inevitable consequence of industrialisation and instrumental economic relations. 'We are deep sunk here in our dark cellar', Carlyle declares, 'and help is far' (p. 4). If Count Ugolino establishes the context for this episode, then its more obvious antecedent is Swift's *A Modest Proposal* (1729), with the suggestion that the well-to-do Irish should take to eating poor children as an effective means of alleviating vagrancy and poverty and boosting domestic output. Yet, as Carlyle's reflections imply, the spectre of a wider society consuming its impoverished children has moved from the realm of savage if improbable satire in Swift's pamphlet to something uncomfortably close to documentary fact in contemporary England.

It is generally accepted that the nineteenth century represents a highpoint for utopian expression in Britain and America, certainly in terms of the number of imaginative works produced.[7] The reasons for this expansion are complex and multifarious, but the central dynamic would seem to have been the perception of deep-seated social difficulties alongside the widespread countervailing conviction that the very forces which produced such challenging circumstances also held out the possibility of radical change and improvement. Industrialisation had produced appalling inequality; the underlying economic structure resulted in exceptional differentials in commodity prices, unpredictable cycles of economic performance, and the conviction that the current order condemned the majority of the populace to a short life of poor

---

[6] Dante Alighieri, *The Divine Comedy: Inferno*, trans. by Charles S. Singleton (Princeton: Princeton University Press, 1980), p. 353 (xxxiii.75).

[7] See indicatively Krishan Kumar, *Utopianism* (Milton Keynes: Open University Press, 1991), p. 60.

health and grim endeavour. The utopian socialist, Charles Fourier, claimed his inclusive and extensive reimagining of the ways in which modern society should operate had its origin in an observation on the price differential of an apple in Paris and his home province. He noted fourteen sous bought a single apple at a restaurant in Paris when the same amount would buy a hundred of superior quality in Franche-Comté. Apples, he suggested, had three significant moments in humankind's development. The first two were symbols of destructiveness, in the eating of the fruit of the tree of knowledge in Eden, and in the Judgment of Paris, the root cause of the Trojan War. The third was a symbol of enlightenment, the spur for Newton's discovering the gravitational laws. Fourier's apple was to be the fourth in this series. Following Newton's epiphany, the apple inspired Fourier to apply scientific principles to uncover the fundamental movements by which society operated, and then by extension to consider how social structure could be optimised to maximise the benefits for all its citizens. Fourier made clear in *Theory of the Four Movements* (1808) his intention to 'deliver the human race from civilised barbarism and savagery, ensure it more happiness than it ever dared dream of and open up the realm of nature's mysteries from which it thought it was for ever excluded'.[8]

Although their theories had different emphases, the utopian socialists, Henri de Saint-Simon, Fourier and August Comte, along with Robert Owen as the leading British advocate of social reform all held with the view that contemporary society possessed both the means and will for significant reorganisation. The proselytising zeal of these theorists and their acolytes was exemplified by Saint-Simon when he declared in his *Reorganisation of European Society* (1814): 'a time will undoubtedly come when all the nations of Europe feel that questions of general interest should predominate over those of merely national. The poverty with which society is now oppressed will diminish; the troubles with which peace is now menaced will disappear; wars will cease', he wrote, 'the golden age of the human race is not behind but before us.'[9] As we saw in the opening chapter, Marx had an ambivalent relationship with 'utopian socialists' (Marx coined the term). He lauded their attempt to place the understanding of modern society on a scientific footing, while condemning their complacency in holding that society could be perfected through the reconciliation of class antagonisms, rather than by overthrowing the existing order, with the proletariat playing a crucial role in their own emancipation.[10] Revolution in Marxian doctrine still required international organisation, albeit under the forces of historical determinism. John Stuart Mill, the century's leading British philosopher of liberalism, similarly sympathised with the reformatory intentions of the Saint-Simonists (the followers and champions of Saint-Simon's theories, especially active throughout Europe after his death in 1835). For Mill,

---

[8] Charles Fourier, *The Theory of Four Movements*, ed. by Gareth Stedman Jones and Ian Patterson, and trans. by Ian Patterson (Cambridge: Cambridge University Press, 1996), p. 23.
[9] See *The Utopian Vision of Charles Fourier: Selected Texts on Work, Love, and Passionate Attraction*, trans. and ed. by Jonathan Beecher and Richard Bienvenu (Columbia, Miss: University of Missouri Press, 1971), p. 1. The analogy is also discussed by Frank E. Manuel and Fritzie P. Manuel, *Utopian Thought in the Western World* (Cambridge, MA: Belknap Press, 1978), p. 641.
[10] *Manifesto of the Communist Party*, in Karl Marx, *Later Political Writings*, ed. and trans. by Terrell Carver, pp. 1–30 (pp. 27–29).

however, the construction of the ideal society required reorganisation on a constitutional level which took account of the propensities of human beings as individuals. In *Considerations of Representative Government* (1861), Mill indicatively argued that the 'ideally best polity' was a comprehensively enfranchised liberal democracy. 'It is evident', he declares, 'that the only government which can fully satisfy all the exigencies of the social state is one which the whole people participate', but since this would only be practicable for small conurbations, it follows for the nation state, 'that the ideal type of a perfect government must be representative'.[11]

Like Swift, Carlyle would initially seem to have slim claim to be considered a utopist; and indeed even more so given that his corpus can be set against the predominant progressive spirit of the age (in an epoch in which it was not a risible notion that a single defining historical characteristic could be identified); an age in which social reformation and idealism were unavoidable facets of intellectual life in Britain, Europe and America. Carlyle wrote little on either Plato or Aristotle. There is nothing in his oeuvre on More, Campanella or Andrea. Bacon is praised as a moralist and appears notably as Kepler's correspondent in his *History of Friedrich II of Prussia, Called Frederick the Great* (1858). Leibniz is dealt with curtly in the same work, dismissed as he attempts to drum some metaphysics into the future Enlightenment monarch. Carlyle hazards at the boy's incredulity at this philosophical tutorial: 'Sublime *Théodicée* (Leibnitzian "justification of the ways of God") was not an article this individual had the least read of, nor at any time the least value for. "Justify? What doomed dog questions then? Are you for Bedlam then?"'[12] Carlyle produced at great labour a three-volume work on Cromwell's life and letters, but said next to nothing on Harrington's commonwealth ideology in the course of it. The word 'utopia' appears only once in his voluminous correspondence – in a letter to Ralph Waldo Emerson in 1835. In the midst of speculation as to whether he might undertake a lecturing tour in the United States, Carlyle thinks that when he 'sets foot in American land it will be no utopia' (with the implication that the new nation was treated as exactly that by many of his compatriots); and he fancies 'America [is] mainly a new Commercial England with a fuller pantry', and with 'the same unquenchable, almost frightfully unresting spirit of endeavour, directed (woe is me) to the making of money, or money's work'.[13] On those occasions when an explicit utopian image does occur, it is usually as an aspersion on a fantasy of replete idleness, such as in the questionable account of the effect of Sir Walter Scott's antiquarian collection, *Minstrelsy of the Scottish Border* (1802–3) on the literary culture of the new century, the misguided attempt to establish 'a bright Eldorado, – or else some fat beatific land of Cockaigne, and Paradise of Donothings'.[14]

---

[11] John Stuart Mill, *On Liberty* and *Considerations of Representative Government*, ed. by R.B. McCallum (Oxford: Blackwell, 1945), p. 151.
[12] Thomas Carlyle, *History of Friedrich II of Prussia, Called Frederick the Great*, in *Works*, XII (1897), p. 31.
[13] Thomas Carlyle to Ralph Waldo Emerson, 3 February 1835, *The Carlyle Letters Online* [http://carlyleletters.dukeupress.edu/clo/content/vol8/#lt-18350203-TC-RWE-01?term=%20utopia%20, accessed 6 November 2018].
[14] Thomas Carlyle, 'Sir Walter Scott', in *Critical and Miscellaneous Essays*, IV, pp. 22–88 (p. 50).

However, like his sometime friend and antagonist, J.S. Mill, Carlyle was initially intrigued by the Saint-Simonists. In July 1830, he received a parcel of books from Gustave d'Eichthal, a leading light in the Saint-Simonian society in Paris. Eichthal did not know to whom he was writing. Carlyle's first major essay on contemporary social themes, 'Signs of the Times' had been published anonymously in *The Edinburgh Review* in 1829. Eichthal directed the package of Saint-Simon's publications to the essay's author care of the journal. The parcel was then forwarded to Carlyle in Dumfriesshire. Eichthal evidently believed that the author of 'Signs of the Times' would at worst be a fellow traveller and could even perhaps be recruited to their cause of social-religious transformation. Carlyle's response was qualified endorsement. In the books, he finds 'nothing to dissent from, the spirit at least meets my entire sympathy'; and he recognises the society's prospectus has been established 'in logical sequence and coherence, with precision and noble zeal'; but he also obliquely acknowledges the underlying tensions in this project to reconcile the energies of divine revelation with trenchant analysis. He wonders 'how in your minds, Scientific insight has transformed itself into Religion; or in what sense, not of exaggerated metaphor, men of cultivated talent, strong power of thought, and far above all superstition and deception, use these extraordinary words: Dieu est revenu à la France en saint-simon, et la France annoncera au monde le Dieu nouveau [God has returned to France in saint-simon, and France will announce the new God to the world]'.[15] Even though Carlyle makes it explicit that his own views proceed from a different set of principles, he did eventually agree to translate Saint-Simon's *Nouveau Christianisme* (1825), describing the work to his brother, John, as 'a heterodox Pamphlet', and to provide a short introduction to it; but no publisher was interested in the tract; and thereafter Carlyle maintained his distance from the Saint-Simonists.[16]

Yet, if one were to adjust the framework of this question and consider the position of Carlyle's approach to social idealism and the extent to which those ideas are consistently subjected to conceptual pressure, then it is apparent there *is* a significant utopian strand to his work. In the era's most prominent and idiosyncratic social criticism, Carlyle effectively defined the central categories through which modern times should be comprehended; and the key tropes, recurring in various combinations throughout his writings were temporal specificity, history, industry, heroism, work and organisation. For William Morris, who at the end of the century would produce the most influential of utopian romances out of an amalgamation of Chaucerian dream vision, utopian-socialist communitarianism, anarchist and Marxist theory for overthrowing the bourgeoisie and pre-Raphaelite aestheticism, Carlyle remained a champion, both in terms of the analysis of contemporary social difficulty, in the unstinting opposition to mechanisation, and in the utilisation of a holistic medieval community for the purposes

---

[15] Carlyle to Gustave d'Eichthal, 9 August 1830, *Carlyle Letters Online*, [http://carlyleletters.dukeupress.edu/clo/content/vol5/#lt-18300809-TC-GE-01?term=%20saint-simon%20, accessed 6 November 2018].

[16] Carlyle to John Carlyle, 19 December 1830, *Carlyle Letters Online*, [http://carlyleletters.dukeupress.edu/clo/content/vol5/#lt-18301219-TC-JAC-01?term=%20saint-simon%20, accessed 6 November 2018].

of offering a viable alternative to the current industrial age. It was this contraposing of historical communities which, as his contemporaries recognised, gave rise to his most significant work of social commentary, *Past and Present*.

There was initially a sense of the incidental to Carlyle's social writings, or that at least such commentary should be seen as a supplementary aspect of literary analysis and reflection. His early essays established him as the major conduit of German letters for an anglophone audience. He wrote articles from the late 1820s onwards on Richte, Goethe (repeatedly), Werner, Heine, Novelis, German playwrights; and he produced an overview of the contemporary field in 'The State of German Literature' (1827, for which Goethe provided ample assistance by sending packets of relevant recent volumes). The essays were mainly published in the journals *The Edinburgh Review* and *The Foreign Review*. They were ostensibly book reviews of recent German publications, biographies and editions of authors' works. 'The State of German Literature' is an account of two works by Frantz Horn, his three-volume history of German poetry from the age of Luther and a book on modern 'polite literature', considered in this account as a sequel to the history. Carlyle's technique in these pieces was to use the works under review as a springboard for a wide-ranging consideration of literary and cultural matters. In the 'State of German Literature', Horn is dealt with summarily as an earnest author, but suffering from an affected style and with no capacity to discuss poetry, rather than merely poets.[17] Carlyle's central intention in this article is to disprove the central claim of an earlier French study of German literature by Père Bouhours that German literature lacked spirit. The English reader is to be disabused of the notion that German literature has no appropriate standard of taste, that it is nothing more than a composite 'of faring contrasts, vulgar horrors, and all sorts of showy exaggeration'.[18] Recent German writing has not been a constant parade of 'wizards and ruined towers, with mailed knights, secret tribunals, monks, spectres, and banditti'.[19] To think this makes no more sense than believing that the English literary canon could be justifiably represented by the Gothic extravagances of Horace Walpole, Monk Knight, Anne Radcliffe and Mary Shelley. One only needs to contemplate the poise, eloquence and sophistication of Wieland's verse to see how erroneous this view must be; and Kloptock similarly exhibits in his poetry an assured and nuanced aesthetic judgement, with 'his clear enthusiasm, his azure purity, and heavenly if still somewhat cold and lunar light'.[20]

Carlyle was not by any means an uncritical promotor of German letters. In an essay on three modern playwrights, he ends with a broth metaphor: these plays do not provide nourishment for the soul of humankind, being merely 'the froth and scum of German literature'. But German creative genius in its purest form was moving, transcendent, luminescent and was a richer font than anything to be found in its anglophone counterpart.[21] Sir Walter Scott was at his best in the initial part of his career before his

---

[17] See Thomas Carlyle, 'The State of German Literature', in *Critical and Miscellaneous Essays*, I, pp. 26–86 (p. 26).
[18] Carlyle, 'The State of German Literature', p, 37.
[19] Carlyle, 'The State of German Literature', p. 37.
[20] Carlyle, 'The State of German Literature', p. 47.
[21] Thomas Carlyle, 'Modern German Playwrights', in *Critical and Miscellaneous Essays*, I, pp. 355–95 (p. 395).

artistry was subjugated to economic necessity; and his earliest works had the indelible stamp of their fine German antecedents.[22] Writing in the 1820s, Carlyle concedes that Wordsworth 'is no ordinary man', and that his assorted rural portraits in verse have laudable qualities; but they still 'sink into whining drivellers beside *Rösselmann the Priest, Ulric the Smith, Hans of the Wall,* and other sturdy confederates of Rütli' – all characters from Schiller's drama of the Swiss Revolution, *Wilhelm Tell* (1804).[23] German literature also does not deserve its reputation for fractured parochialism with as many works translated into German as there are into English. And German Romantic literature has been buttressed by an expanding body of aesthetic theory, with Lessing's comparative explorations of temporal and spatial relations in epic poetry and sculpture in *Laocoön* (1766), with Winkelmann's *History of Art in Antiquity* (1764), and Schiller's *On the Aesthetic Education of Man* (1795), from which Carlyle translates extended passages in the 'State of German Literature'. The creator, in this view, 'strives by uniting the possible with the necessary, to produce the ideal. This lets him imprint and express in fiction and truth; imprint it in the sport of his imagination and the earnestness of his actions; imprint it in all sensible and spiritual forms, and cast it silently into everlasting time'.[24]

After the early Swiftian experimental satire on German idealism, *Sartor Resartus*, Carlyle's creative energies were directed toward critical, historical and social forms of literary endeavour. In all these undertakings, the 'truth' of whatever was under consideration was to be revealed through the imminence of its imaginative treatment; and that was especially apparent in his views on historiography. In 'On History' (1830), Carlyle provided a conspectus of what he believed a historian should be doing; and that meant disputing the orthodox view of the discipline, that of 'philosophy teaching by experience', as well as resisting the notion that history was the melding of a series of external observations into a coherent progressive narrative; and that stood as a direct refutation of the Whig historiography of Stubbs and Macaulay.[25] Events are simultaneous not successive, not linked together by a causative chain as might be uncovered by a natural scientist. History, at bottom, is incomprehensible; and it is the historian's responsibility to exemplify this diffuse phenomenon rather than attempting to fashion it into a readily graspable whole. History, he says, is 'an ever living, ever-working Chaos of Being, wherein shape after shape bodies itself forth from innumerable elements. And this Chaos as boundless as the habitation and duration of man, unfathomable as the soul and destiny of man, is what the historian will depict'.[26] This meant adopting an ambivalent relationship to the past (another persistent feature of Carlyle's writings); that the historical specificity of a given period had to be gauged and set explicitly alongside the circumstances and concerns of the modern era.

One certainly had to acknowledge there were significant psychical differences in human beings living in different periods; yet there was still the requirement to trace the

---

[22] See Carlyle, 'Sir Walter Scott', pp. 51–59.
[23] Thomas Carlyle, *Life of Schiller*, p. 175.
[24] Carlyle, 'The State of German Literature', p. 58.
[25] Carlyle, 'On History', in *Critical and Miscellaneous Essays*, II, pp. 83–95 (p. 85).
[26] Carlyle, 'On History', p. 88.

threads of continuity between one epoch and another. 'Our clock strikes when there is a change from hour to hour; but no hammer in the Horlogue of Time peals through the universe when there is a change from Era to Era', he declares in familiar vatic style.[27] And he is just as convinced that it is the 'Artist in History', who can reveal the essential characteristics of the age investigated. One should revere those historical artists 'who inform and ennoble the humblest department with an Idea of the Whole, and habitually know that only the Whole is the Partial to be truly discerned'.[28] These principles were vividly put into practice in his *The French Revolution: A History* (1837), which charted the revolution's lurching progress from the death of Louis XV to Napoleon's crushing of the insurrection of the 13 Vendémiaire. Carlyle refuted the view that the ideals of the revolution were worth fighting for. The epoch's terminus was an act of individual decisiveness, not the consequence of predictable causes. When history was not being considered as being chaotic, it was being treated as cyclical. Carlyle dissolved the distance between past and present in the *French Revolution* by employing throughout the present historic tense, pitching his readers into the immediacy of the turbulent events he sought to describe, sometimes assuming the personae of witnesses in the crowd to upheavals and massacres; but at the same time, Carlyle continually reminded his reader through the extensive use of hints and allusions that there were instructive parallels to be drawn between the convulsions of France in the 1790s, and the detrimental effects of rapid economic and industrial development at the beginning of the Victorian era.

It is unclear whether the final declaration of the *French Revolution* is meant to be the author or Napoleon speaking. When the 'Whiff of Grapeshot' subdues the last vestige of opposition to the general's forces, the speaker declares 'behold you have it; and the thing we specifically call French Revolution is blown into space by it – become a thing that was!'.[29] However, what is key here is that history, so far as it was susceptible to ideas of will and spirit, was to be embodied in great men. These ideas on the hero, the historically transformative individual were present from Carlyle's early essays; they can be seen to inform his judgements of Heine and Goethe, with the latter described as 'a clear and universal *Man*'.[30] And, the notion of the heroic is similarly employed to the demerit of Voltaire, whom for all his notable attributes cannot rise above the pettiness and rancour of his age. 'Greatness', Carlyle says of Voltaire's case, 'implies several conditions, the existence of which might be difficult to demonstrate'.[31] And for Carlyle's compatriot, Robert Burns, there is partial greatness alloyed to unfulfilled heroic potential, such that one needs to place the poetry in the context of the life, which was in the entirety of his art and being, 'but a fragment', as 'the plan of a mighty edifice had been sketched; some columns, porticos, firm masses of building, stand completed, the rest more or less clearly indicated'.[32] This strand of historical reverence, however, had its clearest statement in his lecture series *On Heroes and Hero-worship and the Heroic in*

---

[27] Carlyle, 'On History', p. 88.
[28] Carlyle, 'On History', p. 90.
[29] Thomas Carlyle, *The French Revolution: a History*, in *Works*, IV (1896), p. 320.
[30] Thomas Carlyle, 'Goethe', in *Critical and Miscellaneous Essays*, I, pp. 198–257 (p. 208).
[31] Thomas Carlyle, 'Voltaire', in *Critical and Miscellaneous Essays*, I, pp. 396–468 (p. 407).
[32] Carlyle, 'Burns', p. 291.

History (1841), in which Carlyle endeavoured to provide, if not a systematic treatment of his topic, then at least a broad categorisation of his guiding dictum that 'universal history, the history of what man has accompanied in this world is at bottom this history of the Great Men, who have worked here'; and that manifested itself in presentations on the heroic in divinity, prophet, poet, priest (including the Calvinist John Knox), man of letters, and kingship (including Cromwell in the Protectorate, as well as Napoleon).[33]

In the context of his early writings on the excesses of German idealism, the critical examination of European literature, the manifestation of the chaotic flux of universal history, and the distillation of the historical actions through the will of great men, his initial social critique, 'Signs of the Times' (1829) still has the sense of an unexpected departure. It was a concentrated expression of the background social elements, which intermittently surfaced in his literary and historical writing. And its startling impact was due to the combination of concise phrasing, rhetorical confidence and the articulation of a widely-held sense of unease over the current circumstances in Britain. We live in an era of crisis, he suggests, borne of the rapid changes in social organisation and standards, where the diagnosis and solutions range from the apocalyptic to the instrumental, 'as the Millenarians have come forth on the right hand and the Millites on the left. The fifth monarchy men prophesy from the Bible, and the Utilitarians from Bentham'.[34] These seemed to offer contrasting views as a matter of social prophesy, for whereas the former trumpeted 1860 as the year when the earth would be enveloped in a maelstrom; the latter offered the brittle, superfluous utopia of '"the greatest-happiness principle"', 'to make a heaven of earth, in a still shorter time'.[35] Yet Carlyle's startling idea was the suggestion that these two apparent opposing forces should be considered as *one*, as a confluence of systematic apocalyptic intention and revelation, 'a rage of prophesy'.[36] The essay's second significant idea was the notion that the epoch's principal 'sign' was pervasive mechanisation.

The mechanical was not just the literal shift in the increasing use of technology for the production of goods, services and for transportation, though it was certainly that in the references to Lancashire weavers, stream packets and steam-driven threshers; it was, rather, the defining characteristic of the present, the application of a 'single epithet', which would not identify 'an Heroical, Devotional, Philosophical, or Moral Age, but above all others, the Mechanical Age'.[37] The paradoxical mechanical spirit had suffused all aspects of contemporary life. One might expect this in the rise of science; or rather, from his perspective the rise of one species of science at the expense of another – the moral sciences decay as the physical ones predominate, 'the science of the age, in short, is physical, chemical, physiological; in all shapes mechanical'; mathematics is no longer concerned with the such pure endeavours as the revelation of Platonic forms, but rather with applied practical applications.[38] This trend could similarly be detected in British philosophy, where Thomas Reid's common-sense philosophy had extended Hume's

---

[33] Thomas Carlyle, *On Heroes and Hero-Worship, and the Hero in History*, in *Works*, V (1897), p. 1.
[34] Thomas Carlyle, 'Signs of the Times', in *Critical and Miscellaneous Essays*, II, pp. 56–95, (p. 58).
[35] Carlyle, 'Signs of the Times', p. 58.
[36] Carlyle, 'Signs of the Times', p. 58.
[37] Carlyle, 'Signs of the Times', p. 59.
[38] Carlyle, 'Signs of the Times', p. 63.

inductive psychology into the 'bottomless abysses of Atheism and Fatalism'; and the end-point of such a mechanical analogical endeavour can be glimpsed in the proposal by the French empiricist who claims 'as the liver secretes bile, so does the brain secrete thought'.[39] The same deadening causative spirit pervades politics and civil government ('the Machine of Society'), the church in both established and non-conformist incarnations operates on a materialist basis; there are hard profit-making motives behind the claims of Bible societies to a higher calling, and the Anglican community has perfected sacerdotal ritual as a series of automatic operations. Not even art and literature in Britain effectively challenge the pre-eminence of this mechanical spirit. In a nod to Swift's suspicions of secular institutions, Carlyle suggests that 'in defect of Raphaels and Angelos, and Mozarts, we have Royal Academies of Painting, Sculpture, Music; whereby the languishing spirit of Art may be strengthened as by the more generous diet of a public kitchen'.[40]

'Signs of the Times' finishes with an attack on what Carlyle terms 'a *faint* dilettantism', by which he means the attraction to a superficial mode of being; there are general imprecations to finding a faith that is not a form of worship of the machine and the supposed progress in both material and figurative senses it was intended to bring about.[41] Yet the self-conscious nature of this polemic does not articulate a clear alternative to the pre-eminent aspect of the modern age it identifies. One can understand now just how such an open-ended diagnosis would be attractive to the Saint-Simonists, where the essay's call for a renewal of faith could be seen to be answered in the emergence of a new religion of utopian socialism, and the advocacy of a moral and social science which was emphatically *not* the physical sciences. When Carlyle undertook his book-length analysis of modernity in *Past and Present*, there was a clearer sense of what that social alternative might look like, even though the book's idealism remained qualified and problematic. *Past and Present* was written as a distraction from an intended heroic biography of Oliver Cromwell, on which Carlyle could not make progress in the 1840s, eventually consigning the manuscript and its accompanying notes to embers in his living-room hearth.

The coincidental, off-the-cuff, semi-improvisational *Past and Present* can be regarded as Carlyle's most successful work, as though the free play of his mind, when not really working on the book he was supposed to be working on, allowed him to synthesise themes, forms and interests developed over the previous fifteen years: the stylistic plurality and philosophical idealism of *Sartor Resartus*, the anti-industrial polemic of 'Signs of the Times', the historical fabulation of the *French Revolution*; and the significant dynamic of the hero and his worshipper. Carlyle worked on the book initially in clandestine fashion, maintaining the fiction that he was still writing on Cromwell, until his wife, Jane Welsh Carlyle, discovered among his papers hieroglyphics and various oblique allusions to an Abbot Samson. Who, she demanded, was this medieval abbot, and what had he to do with the seventeenth-century commonwealth.[42]

---

[39] Carlyle, 'Signs of the Times', p. 65, p. 65.
[40] Carlyle, 'Signs of the Times', p. 62.
[41] Carlyle, 'Signs of the Times', p. 81.
[42] See Kaplan, *Thomas Carlyle*, pp. 296–97.

As Carlyle reveals in the book's early stages, Samson was the leader of a thirteenth-century monastic community at St Edmund's Abbey; the remains of which stood close to a modern workhouse at St Ives in Cambridgeshire (Carlyle had inspected both while undertaking field research for the stalled Cromwell project). He had also been intrigued by a recently published slim Latin chronicle of this community by one of its friars, Jocelyn of Brakelond, which, as he says, has survived 'Henry the Eighth, Putney [i.e. Thomas] Cromwell, the Dissolution of the monasteries, and all accidents of malice and neglect for six centuries or so' (p. 42).

However, this usage is a typical Carlylean synecdoche in which the wider and more significant deciphering of this short work will take place through the unfolding of its modern social implications. In *Past and Present*, Carlyle establishes Jocelyn's chronicle as having an affecting revelatory quality. He compares it to 'a magical speculum', a small concave mirror in which the intricacies and the momentary exchanges on both every-day and more significant events can be glimpsed, an instrument 'much gone to rust, indeed yet in fragments still clear; wherein the marvellous image of his existence does still shadow itself' (p. 43). The cultural, social, and psychological separation between then and now is configured in terms of recent bounds in palaeontology and the developing fossil record, a topical subject. We should approach this work, Carlyle suggests with a hint of whimsy, as though it were 'a deep-buried Mastodon, some fossil Megatherion, Ichthyosaurus, were to begin to *speak* from amid its rock-swathings, never so indistinctly' (p. 43).

The other significant comparison Carlyle makes in this portion of the narrative is between Jocelyn and James Boswell (referred to as 'Bozzy'), Samuel Johnson's biographer. Carlyle had reviewed Croker's landmark edition of the *Life of Johnson* in 1832. He considered the biography as an instance of the dynamic of the hero and hero-worship, with the hero for these purposes as a man of letters. For Carlyle, Johnson was an exemplary eighteenth-century figure, resisting the swelling tide of mechanisation, one of few who possessed genuine insight, who 'saw into the Things themselves, and could walk as men having an eternal loadstar, and with their feet on sure paths'.[43] Boswell, on the other hand, was all surface, 'vain, heedless, a babbler; had much of the sycophant, alternating with the braggadocio, curiously spiced too with an all-pervading dash of the coxcomb'.[44] Yet 'Bozzy' was the essential acolyte, transforming Johnsonian spiritual resistance into a tangible literary form; despite his failings, Boswell was 'a practical witness, or real *martyr*, to this high everlasting truth'.[45] Even though Jocelyn does not suffer from Boswell's personal flaws; the friar's text is problematic because of its temporal distance. Jocelyn's 'light is most feeble', he says, 'intermittent, and requires the intensest kindest inspection; otherwise it will disclose mere vacant haze' (p. 44); and it is, of course, Carlyle's ambition to subject this slim memoir to such a focussed and incisive reading that it will bring clarity, immediacy and modern social relevance to this work.

---

[43] Thomas Carlyle, 'Boswell's Life of Johnson', in *Critical and Miscellaneous Essays*, III, pp. 62–135 (p. 89).
[44] Carlyle, 'Boswell's Life of Johnson', p. 69.
[45] Carlyle, 'Boswell's Life of Johnson', p. 74.

As with the palaeontological reference, the book's medievalism was to pick up on a historicising trend in Victorian culture which had been prominent in literary sources from the turn of the century onwards. The epoch had been used as a setting for Coleridge in his Gothic fragments, *Christabel* (1797); as a frequent backdrop to Keats's poetry; and as the setting for a number of Sir Walter Scott's works, ballad collections, narrative verse, and novels (in terms of sales, Scott was the most popular literary author in the United Kingdom throughout the nineteenth century); and Augustus Pugin had published his manifesto for medieval Gothic revivalism in architecture, *Contrasts*, in 1836.[46] It seems Carlyle intended in *Past and Present* to dispel much of the vacant haze which he detected in the contemporary literary usage of medievalism, and bestow upon it a new and dynamic mode of social criticism. However, as Isobel Armstrong has pointed out, whatever distinctiveness Carlyle was attempting to introduce into his account of the Middle Ages, then the central structuring dynamic of the text remains between a medieval period conceived as a holistic ideal and the soot-black commercial Victorian present.[47]

Alert to objections of this kind, Carlyle, explicitly rejects in quick order the notion of the monastery as an arcadia, or a precursor to some modern perfected model of republicanism; yet the denial does not have quite the same conviction as the claim for historical fidelity in the *French Revolution*. 'This England of the Year 1200', he declares, 'was no chimerical vacuity; or dreamland, peopled with mere vaporous Fantasms' (p. 44). And conventional utopian imagery, in a kind of reverse psychological manoeuvre, is associated with the awful present rather than the alluring past. Hence in an attack on modern economic principles whereby wages and prices are determined by supply and demand, Carlyle declares that financial institutions and labour markets cannot supply anything of spiritual value, even if 'the demand been in thunder and earthquake, with gold Eldorados and Mohametan paradises for the reward' (p. 186); and later Carlyle's archetypal Tory politician, 'Sir Jabesh Windbag, Mr Facing-both-ways, Viscount Mealymouth' bends and flexes as he strives to stay on the right side of public opinion and parliamentary majorities. He is characterised as 'Columbus minded to sail to the indistinct country of NOWHERE' (p.223).

Beyond a residual sense of transcendental idealism, it would be difficult to draw out much of a comparison between Carlyle's vatic mode of social prophesy and, say, Leibniz's rationally constructed universe with its syllogistic derivation of the optimal arrangement of the world as we encounter it. However, both the *Theodicy* and *Past and Present* are confronted with the same problem of invoking a category of the ideal, and then having to impose limitations upon it. Carlyle includes a brief conjectural and cyclical history of the inevitable consequences of principles coming into contact with concrete forms, that all ideals are subject to mutability and decay; and that all monastic orders will eventually become 'diseased corpulent bodies fallen idiotic, which merely eat and sleep; *ready* for "dissolution", by Henry the Eight or some other' (p. 58). Abbot

---

[46] On Scott's prodigious sales, see William St Clair, *The Reading Nation in the Romantic Period* (Cambridge: Cambridge University Press, 2004), p. 209, p. 221, and pp. 245–46.

[47] See Isobel Armstrong, *Victorian Poetry: Poetry, Poetics and Politics* (London: Routledge, 1996), p. 237.

Samson's community may be some way off from this dilapidation, but Carlyle still suggests that the reader prepare him or herself 'to see the Ideal not sleeping in the aether like a bird-of-paradise, but roosting as the common wood-fowl do in an imperfect, uncomfortable, more or less contemptible manner' (p. 58).

Carlyle relates and interprets the rise of Samson, his almost accidental appointment on his overwhelmed predecessor's death; his struggles to improve the abbey's parlous finances, to impose a meaningful structure on his community's disjointed lives, to manage and collect the various tithes from the not especially productive farms, and to negotiate within the intricate lattice of political and economic interests of feudal knights, Pope's legatees, viscounts, bishops and kings. Monks are refractory, knights and farmers are out to cheat him; the neighbouring dean has set up a rival mill on his glebe land to undercut the cost of production of flour for the local townspeople; and he has to stand up to the monarch, Richard, Coeur de Lion, in a marriage dispute. Samson is certainly not successful in all his endeavours; and the chronic stresses of office take their toll on his health and appearance. Yet he is the embodiment of the Carlylean heroic, through the application of vision, charisma, courage, guile, political expediency and good governance within a beneficial social system – an aristocratic feudalism with an even dusting of undisputed Christian faith, which, however imperfect, at least allowed for personal relations, not narrowly defined by the modern standards of cash transaction as 'the sole nexus of man with man' (p. 186).

Of course, as much as Carlyle protests against the notion of idealism in this narrow window onto the community at St Edmund's in the thirteenth century; it is intended to be just that; and Jocelyn's narrative is refracted and animated by Carlyle's vital and selective treatment of it. This portrait of an 'ideal' community is as much a matter of vibrant essential interpretation as historical fact, a certain literary contingency and selectivity is necessary to overcome the inertia of conventional interpretation, a causative empirical version of historical analysis, which leaves past time 'as one infinite incredible grey void, without sun, stars, heath fires, and candlelight' (p.107). For Carlyle, the foundations of the successful community are faith beyond material relations, a society which is not characterised by what he terms the 'valet-world', a combination of a shallow and cynical disregard for proper forms of authority and deference to sham figures (such as politicians); and a form of heroic leadership which Carlyle identifies in the inherent characteristics of the abbot of devoutness and steadfastness, 'a skilful man; full of cunning, insights, lively interests; always discerning the road to his object, be it circuit be it short-cut, and victoriously traveling forward thereon' (p. 159). The answer to Jane Carlyle's early exasperated inquiry as to the identity and significance of Samson when her husband was supposed to be working on a study of the protector, emerges in the later part of the text in the oblique comparisons of the abbot and Cromwell. The former is essentially a precursor to the latter. The heroic ideal and capacity for social reformation could be more straightforwardly extracted from Jocelyn's distant slim memoir, than from the more recent complex and contorted history of the English civil war and the seventeenth-century commonwealth.

There is an anticipation of Engel's notions of estrangement and alienation in Carlyle's opening description of the inhabitants of the modern workhouse of St Ives, as a community which on initial viewing appears to be composed of robust men of thoughtful disposition; but which on closer inspection suffer a kind of modern enchantment, a 'torpor', 'in the eyes and brows of these men', he says, 'hung the gloomiest expression, not of anger, but of grief and shame, and manifold inarticulate distress and weariness' (p. 2). The contemporary reader is supposed to see this as a current social ill, a waste of life and labour, with these ostensibly charitable institutions having been established throughout the nation. Of course, the reader is also meant to notice that the episode's more significant aspect lies in its symbolic resonances, as these dispirited figures encapsulate a shame and lethargy, emblematic of the age; a dismal spectacle to which no receptive and sensible being could be entirely immune. Medieval vitality is then counterpoised with modern spiritual inertness. As one might expect of a text which is intended, at least on one level, to be a significant exercise in contemporary social commentary, Carlyle included considerations of the major political concerns and movements of the 1830s and 1840s; such as Chartism, the demand for labour rights (generally against), the Great Reform Act for suffrage and urban representation (ambivalent), and the Corn Laws, protective tariff legislation to maintain the price of domestic grain above a certain threshold (adamantly against on the grounds that it disproportionality penalises the poorest member of society by inflating the price of standard foodstuffs).

Yet, as an exercise in social and political analysis, *Past and Present* either rejects or dismantles the terms in which such an examination might be reasonably conducted. The notion of 'Fact' (capitalised throughout the book), for example, is subjected to the kind of persistent sceptical interrogation subsequently championed by twentieth-century deconstructionists with the intention of denying a secure and stable meaning for any given term. 'Fact', it seems, was to be demolished as the documentary basis of other social explanatory discourses, such as those branches of political economy and philosophy which were predominantly reliant on an empirical-statistical methodology. 'Fact', so far as can be rendered meaningful in this discourse, is a matter of intuitive conviction beyond the reach of sets of data and such matters as legal entitlement; 'in the ever-whirling chaos of Formulas', he declares, 'we have quietly lost sight of Fact' (p. 176). We must '*feel* it by and by' (p. 176). And the 'Fact' is that land, which is fundamentally neither a commodity, nor a political power-base, but as we should have learnt from the period of Abbot Samson, 'the Land is *Mother* of us all; nourishes, shelters, gladdens, lovingly enriches us all' (p. 174). This attack on the cogency of any notion of objective facticity has its corollary in the wholesale rejection of the kinds of social and personal goods advocated by radical reformers; and especially those of a utopian bent. The idea that justice can be found in legal mechanism or a constitutional settlement can readily be discarded; the notion of the 'just' is not to be encapsulated in any transparent form of expression, 'for the unembodied Justice is of Heaven; a Spirt and Divinity of Heaven,–*in*visible to all but the noble and pure soul' (p. 14). And the pursuit of happiness is presented as a matter of conceptual confusion between material satisfaction and the proper aims of the virtuous life. Modern society and its would-be reformers have erroneously substituted a 'Greatest-Happiness Principle' for a 'Greatest-Nobleness Principle' (p. 154).

Near the beginning of *Past and Present*, Carlyle proclaims 'that he who dwells in the temporary Semblances, and does not penetrate into the eternal Substance, will *not* answer the Sphinx-riddle of Today, or of any Day' (p. 13). The allusion, of course is to the plague which had afflicted Thebes at the beginning of Sophocles *Oedipus Tyrannos*, and which is lifted when the newly arrived Oedipus was able to solve the Sphinx's conundrum. The implicit promise of *Past and Present* is that it will offer diagnosis and remedy for spiritual wastage of industrial modernity; and much of the force of this discourse is a consequence of the extraordinary energetic variety of style; where form itself is intended to be substantive; where expression is intended as a significant means of bringing the reader to a proper understanding of the matters under consideration. Modern critics have expressed both bewilderment and disdain at the array of registers employed in Carlyle's works, or indeed have, on occasion, merely skated over matters of rhetorical profuseness.[48] Carlyle cited his extensive reading of modern German literature as a formal influence, although the rapid movement and ostensibly obscure mode of energetic discussion was also a feature of journalism in the first half of the nineteenth century; and such stylistic heterodoxy did not seem so strange to his contemporary readership.

Carlyle's dominant mode of address is a combination of Old Testament prophet and Church of Scotland minister; his idiom is deliberately arcane with liberal use of 'thee' and 'thou'; it is noisily declarative with propositional structures and frequent exclamation marks, as though preaching to the kirk congregation. He can then quickly moderate these lapidary declarations to a softer, more intimate mode, as though now solemnly leading the discussion in chapel, cued by addresses to his readers as 'brethren'. There are contemplative passages, indicated by a 'Yes' at the beginning of a paragraph, as though the reader has introduced some plausible caveat to what has just been proposed. The tone is by turns, scolding, scoffing, ironic and sardonic. There is also the residual Presbyterian suspicion of the graven image. Carlyle rarely provides large-scale constructed and integrated pictures of a scene or episode. His writing, however, is always, highly associative and improvisational such that once a set of ideas have been placed together, he will usually return to them, trying them out in different combinations; and the links between successive passages are rarely a matter of straightforward inference or causation. The great digressive arcs of his discussion invariably return to one of the key anchoring terms of the social analysis; and most of these have the purpose of encapsulating the woes of the modern age, such as 'Laissez-Faire', 'Mammonism' and 'Dilettantism'.

It would seem that the overall purpose of this highly distinctive form of address was not only to mount a sweeping critique of the industrial epoch with its poor driven to the desperate measure of poisoning their children for meagre financial gain, and with its workhouses full of men of torpid hopelessness. Two points on which Marx would subsequently concur with Carlyle's conservative social vision was on the generally destructive and debilitating condition of industrial capitalism; and that as a system

---

[48] See G. Robert Stange, 'Refractions of *Past and Present*' (1976), in *The Critical Response to Thomas Carlyle's Major Works*, ed. by D.J. Trela and Rodger L. Tarr (Westport, CT: Greenwood, 1997), pp. 169–80 for a consideration of Carlyle's stylistic profusion; and Chris R. Vanden Bossche, *Carlyle and the Search for Authority* (Columbus: Ohio State University Press, 1991) for a study which is predominantly interested in the content rather than the style of Carlyle's works.

it would require a more substantial challenge than hoping for amelioration from within. Carlyle, of course, aimed at spiritual rejuvenation rather than a revolutionary overthrowing of the present social-economic order. And the style of the discussion seems intended to provoke and reveal a sense of spiritual richness and vitality that is both masked and deadened by the modern world; that if the dualism of the idealism and matter could be brought into a fruitful tension in the course of the discussion, then the multifaceted discourse, which was always prodding, prompting, instructing and goading the reader toward some noumenal notion of the perfected individual and social being, would be apprehended somewhere beyond the expressive limitations of language itself. Many Victorians found this type of hyperventilated social commentary attractive, though not without reservation. Elizabeth Barrett Browning recognised the centrality of style in Carlylean prognostication, 'pre-eminently true' she says, in his case that 'speech is the man'; and she lauded his genius, his originality of mind; and for 'having knocked out his window from the blind wall of his century'.[49] Carlyle's election by students of the University of Edinburgh to the position of Rector late in his career in 1865 was evidence of his continued influence with a youthful socially-engaged audience (his inaugural address greeted with tumultuous applause, 'everyone was on his feet, arms waving, caps flying, students surging forward to touch him as he had apparently touched their hearts').[50] But that praise must stand against his abandonment of the ethical decency of the kind encapsulated by Abbot Samson in the vitriolic attacks on progressive liberal causes in the 1850s.

Evidently, Carlyle's intention in *Past and Present* to unpick 'the Sphinx-riddle of Today' resulted neither in a clear-cut diagnosis, nor in a manifesto of practical measures for social transformation. The book's gnomic prose looks as though it offers an embellishment on rather than a solution to the Sphinx-riddle of modernity it adumbrates. It is not unreasonable to suggest that the success of the Carlyle's socio-aesthetic discussion of modern times significantly lay for all its riddling difficulty in its capacity to produce a resonant and compelling response to the sense of disquiet and confusion Victorian's felt about their own historical moment, about industrial modernity, about time and space, about the need for a sense of faith, which cannot find convincing expression either though the institutions and liturgical conventions of mainstream Christianity or in pamphlets on social policy. Barrett Browning sums up Carlyle's whole enterprise as 'the philosophy of disillusionment', and marvels half-mockingly at his 'continual contemplation of a soul beating its tiny wings amidst the place vapours of infinity'.[51] Yet, the political and social ideal still sits squarely at the centre of *Past and Present*; to be glimpsed fitfully and dimly in the speculum of Brother Jocelyn's memoir of his abbot and monastic medieval community. Its distance from the present, and the once removed nature of the account ensure that the attentive reader will not mistake the book as a call for a return to the society of the Middle Ages; but by the same token, the reader should be assured that the precondition for the fashioning the good society in the modern age is the recovery of

---

[49] [Elizabeth Barrett Browning], 'Thomas Carlyle', in *A New Spirit of the Age*, ed. by R.H. Horne, 2 vols (London: Smith, Elder: 1844), II, pp. 253–80 (p. 258, p. 256).
[50] Kaplan, *Thomas Carlyle*, p. 469.
[51] [Barrett Browning], 'Thomas Carlyle', p. 268.

such principles as faith, community beyond mammon, and a suitable recognition and deference to the genuinely heroic.

If the lyrical intensity of *Past and Present*'s vision allowed for an affective revelatory element to its account of modern social ills – allowed for a sense of truth beyond such statements that could be factually corroborated, then there was also not much of an indication as to what kind of reformation should take place in practice, or indeed, how any such reformation might come about. One contemporary, William Henry Smith, dryly observed that the student of Carlylean social nostrums 'opens his tablets to put down the precious sum of wisdom he has learned [from the book], pauses – finds his pencil motionless, and leaves his table still a blank', a 'nowhere' now devoid of any critical utopian content.[52] And some proposals are, frankly, so insipid and improbable that it seems doubtful even their author took them seriously. Carlyle has a chapter toward the book's end, entitled 'Captains of Industry' (he coined the phrase), in which he suggests modern industrial magnates should seek to follow the example of Abbot Samson – as though they could collectively fashion themselves into an elite custodial class, capable of disinterested guardianship in the manner of Plato's *Republic*.

The experience of the twentieth century provided good reasons to be sceptical of societies that put heroism and hero-worship at their centre, and that encourage determined charismatic rulers to operate outside of standard constitutional arrangements. The rise of political populism in the twenty-first century has done little to temper such suspicions. Nevertheless, there is also a means of turning this discussion on its head in keeping with the characteristic dualisms of the text itself. Just as the book moves between spirit and matter, past and present, idealism and current English woes, so then the dynamic of self to the social is reversed. Rather than being a highly distinctive and imaginative anatomy of modern society, that society becomes the means for an elaboration of self; the means by which the author can be displayed in an inflated spectral form, a Broken spectre, as he suggests in a letter to Ralph Waldo Emerson, 'there is a decided likeness of myself recognisable in it [Emmerson's review of *Past and Present*], but so enlarged, so transfigured – the most delicious, the most dangerous thing'.[53]

It remains a moot point as to whether Carlyle actually ever envisaged the overthrowing of the industrial age. Henry Smith was surely correct to suggest that the consumer of vatic social criticism has a right to expect some concrete suggestions as to what the improved social order might actually look like. There is a Nietzschean complexion to Carlyle's thought insofar as one can apply the German contemporary's principles of social transformation, that the extent of the personal and collective change of attitude and consciousness will be so profound that one cannot readily glimpse them from the narrow and debilitating circumstances of the present age.[54]

---

[52] [William Henry Smith], 'Past and Present by Carlyle', *Blackwood's Edinburgh Magazine*, 54 (1843), 121–38 (122).

[53] Carlyle to Ralph Waldo Emerson, 31 October 1843, *Carlyle Letters Online*, [http://carlyleletters.dukeupress.edu/clo/content/vol17/#lt-18431031-TC-RWE-01?term=%20most%20dangerous%20thing%20, accessed 8 November 2018]. Emerson reviewed *Past and Present* in *The Dial*, 4 (1843), 96–102.

[54] I have in mind Nietzsche's notion of overcoming, see his *Thus Spoke Zarathustra*, trans. by R. J. Hollingdale (London: Penguin, 1969), especially 'Of the Three Metamorphosis', pp. 54–56.

Moreover, Carlyle has a residual sense of progressiveness; history may be cyclical and chaotic, but that does mean that one should be actively seeking to return to a simpler age; it is not industrialisation per se, which is the principal problem with the nation's current condition; it is the stubborn 'Fact' that industry and unregulated commerce have become the master metaphors for the way in which British society operates. What is required in the Carlylean reformation is the reassertion of spirit, not the wholesale rejection of modernity through the dismantlement of machinery. There is the remaining question of how the aesthetic as a category functions in Carlyle's social thought. Carlyle did not advocate literature as a civilising force in the face of impeding social chaos in the manner of Matthew Arnold; and he did not regard the aesthetic as a sphere which operated by a different set of rules and standards from those which governed the rest of society, as suggested by Walter Pater, and then polemically embraced by Oscar Wilde at the century's end.

The aesthetic is predominantly understood, or at least generally assumed to be a literary endeavour in Carlyle's works. Literature as a means to the ideal is on one level a matter of stylistic suffusion through his works; but it also collectively seems to be the example of modern German literature so far as one is able to consider that as a totality; and that seems to require an image which spectrally defies its own boundaries, such as his own self-image as a Brocken spectre, 'the most delicious and dangerous thing', a literature of spirt and value, but instructively and revelatory at one remove from the English present. At the end of his 1831 essay surveying the history of German poetry, he tends toward vatic abstraction, a billowing evocation, 'what form so omnipotent an element will assume; how long it will welter to and froe with wild anarchy, what constitution and organisation it will fashion for itself; for what depends on it, the depths of time, is a subject of prophetic conjecture'.[55] Yet, the essay's close offers a rather more surprising concrete utopian proposal, and indeed one with a markedly modern resonance when Carlyle identifies 'a tendency' within the best of such literary expression, 'to a universal European Commonweal that the wisest in all nations will communicate and coöperate'.[56]

In his account of William Morris's political transformation, E.P. Thompson took a dim view of Carlyle's social vision, 'a negative critic', he states bluntly, 'not only reactionary, but actively malign'.[57] Carlyle's beneficial influence on Morris could be understood as a consequence of one of his very few 'gleams of profoundest revolutionary insight' piercing the clouds of 'pretentious mysticism, white-hot moral indignation, pious mumbo-jumbo'.[58] This shaft of revolutionary light was the operation of cash-nexus, the reduction of all human value to those of instrumental economic exchange. This central idea would periodically resurface in Morris's writings, such as in the relatively late Socialist lectures, where he would declare that modern capitalist society a misnomer, not a society at all, more akin to a permanent state of war. Fiona MacCarthy

---

[55] Thomas Carlyle, 'Historic Survey of German Poetry', in *Critical and Miscellaneous Essays*, II, pp. 333–70 (p. 370).
[56] Carlyle, 'Historic Survey of German Poetry', p. 370.
[57] E.P. Thompson, *William Morris: Romantic to Revolutionary*, rev. edn (London: Merlin Press, 1976), p. 29.
[58] Thompson, *William Morris*, p. 29.

produces a more comprehensive account of Morris than Thompson. She focuses on Morris's first encounter with Carlyle's writings while a student at Oxford. She points out John Ruskin had a much more profound and enduring influence on Morris than Carlyle. The former was the source of hope and light. Ruskin's criticism was 'ecstatic', with his plan to establish a Guild of St George with the transposing of the 'laws and methods of life already proven in the great cities of Venice and Florence at the high point of their cultural achievements'.[59] MacCarthy uses that most indicative terms of Carlylean praise to describe the effect of Ruskin's life and writings as 'heroic', containing a whole series of [...] emblematic episodes'.[60] By way of contrast, the '"ferocity" of Carlyle's gloom stood as a warning to him'.[61] The promotion of a furious destructiveness, which left the young Morris suggesting Carlyle needed to have someone constantly beside him (in the manner of a Laputian flapper), to periodically remind the Victorian seer of the proper function of social criticism.[62]

Morris's references to Carlyle in his correspondence, however, produce a rather more nuanced and indulgent picture of his influence. A sense of pessimism is certainly apparent in a relatively late letter to Georgiana Burne-Jones in which Morris discusses reading Carlyle's autobiographical work, *Reminiscences* (1881). Morris reveals that he has being taken aback 'by the ferocity of [Carlyle's] gloom'; and he goes on to 'confess that I had no idea of it until I read this book'.[63] However, in other letters, Morris tends to be more receptive. He acknowledges Carlyle's role in translating Goethe and in the popularising of Richter in Britain; and Morris indirectly communicated with Carlyle in the 1870s, eventually persuading him to join the S.P.A.B. (Society for the Preservation of Ancient Buildings).[64] When Morris produced for the *Pall Mall Gazette* in 1886 a list of the 100 books which he considered as having most influenced him, he included Thomas Carlyle's works in a group with Ruskin's works, Grimm's Teutonic mythology and More's *Utopia*.[65] When he wrote to George Howard in 1882 about J.A. Froude's recently published biography of Carlyle, he took a different view to that expressed to Georgiana Burne-Jones. He reports that he found the biography 'deeply interesting', and that 'I fare to feel as if [Carlyle] were on the right side in spite of all faults'.[66] He had written to his daughter in February 1881, shortly after the sage's death. 'So Carlyle is off to learn the great secret at last', he says, 'though his work is over it is a kind of a miss to him'.[67] That reference to the 'great secret' to be resolved in death seems to be an allusion to Carlyle's pronouncement in *Past and Present* that 'he who

---

[59] Fiona MacCarthy, *William Morris: A Life for our Time* (London: Faber and Faber, 1994), p. 71.
[60] MacCarthy, *William Morris*, p. 71.
[61] MacCarthy, *William Morris*, p. 71.
[62] MacCarthy, *William Morris*, p. 71.
[63] Morris to Georgina Burne-Jones, 6 July 1881, *Collected Letters of William Morris*, ed. by Norman Kelvin, 4 vols (Princeton: Princeton University Press, 1984–96), II, part 1 (1987), pp. 52–53 (p. 52).
[64] See Carlyle to William Frend de Morgan, 3 April 1877, *Collected Letters of William Morris*, I, p. 361. De Morgan interceded on Morris's behalf.
[65] See Morris to Editor of the *Pall Mall Gazette*, 2 February 1886, in *Collected Letters of William Morris*, II, part 1 (1987), pp. 514–17 (p. 517).
[66] Morris to Georgiana Burne-Jones, 23 August 1882, *Collected Letters of William Morris*, II, part 1, pp. 120–21 (p. 121).
[67] Morris to Jane Morris, 10 February [1881], *Collected Letters of William Morris*, II, part 1, pp. 14–15 (p. 14).

dwells in the temporary Semblances, and does not penetrate into the eternal substance, will *not* answer the Sphinx-riddle of Today, or of any Day'. As if to emphasise the metonymic centrality of *Past and Present* to Morris and his works, a copy of this book still sits prominently in a display of his effects from his time as student in Oxford. No longer dwelling in a temporary state, Carlyle is presumably considered to be at a sufficient vantage point to be able to solve his own Sphinx-riddle, a task his contemporaries believed he was incapable of doing during his lifetime; and while it clearly possesses many other influences and objectives, one way of approaching William Morris's late socialist romance, *News from Nowhere* (1890) is as an attempt to solve Carlyle's enigmatic secret of industrial modernity by reconfiguring *Past and Present*'s medieval idealism.

Morris was of his age in his abiding interest in the medieval period. There is childhood apocrypha attesting to his early assumption of his lifetime interest in this epoch. The middle child of a wealthy London broker, Morris allegedly read his way through the collected works of Sir Walter Scott by the time he was seven; and he rode around Epping Forest on a pony in his bespoke miniature suit of armour.[68] His characteristic medieval outlook developed through his reading of Chaucer and Malory's *Morte d'Arthur*, his experience of Oxford as a student, a city, he suggested, which still looked like a medieval conurbation in the 1830s; the formation with likeminded friends of the 'brotherhood', with the conscious association in its title with both monastic order and craft guild. Medieval topics, shapes, motifs and patterns recur in his artworks, such as in the design for murals at the Oxford Union in the late 1850s, in the production of stained-glass windows for private homes and churches from the 1860s onwards, replete with angelic imagery and Arthurian themes, in his tapestry weaving, and in the establishment of the Kelmscott Press in 1891, with the intention of producing vellum-bound volumes, with the look and feel of sumptuous incunabula.

Morris's writing was similarly suffused with medieval sources and expressive modes. 'The Story of an Unknown Church' (1856) is an indicative dream vision, related by a thirteenth-century master mason who is carving a relief of the Last Judgement on a new church associated with an abbey. His early collection of lyric and narrative verses, *The Defence of Guinevere and other Poems* (1858) was significantly indebted to Malory (and then refracted through a subjective Keatsian sensibility). He frequently celebrated and promoted medieval standards in his critical writings. In a lecture on architecture in 1889, he declared without qualification that the Gothic was 'the most completely organic form the world has ever seen'.[69] And in an address on pottery from the same period he identified the principal aspect of aesthetic creation in the Middle Ages in northern Europe: 'nor was it any longer as in the Greece of Pericles, wherein no thought might be expressed that could not be expressed in perfect form. Art was free. Whatever a man thought of, that he might bring to light by the labour of his hands, to

---

[68] See MacCarthy, *William Morris*, pp. 5–6, and Fiona MacCarthy, 'Morris, William (1834–1896), designer, author, and visionary socialist' *Oxford Dictionary of National Biography*, [http://www.oxforddnb.com/view/10.1093/ref:odnb/9780198614128.001.0001/odnb-9780198614128-e-19322, accessed 27 April 2019].

[69] William Morris, 'Gothic Architecture', in *News from Nowhere and Other Writings*, ed. by Clive Wilmer (London: Penguin, 1993), pp. 330–48 (p. 332).

be praised and wondered by his fellows.'[70] And in its oxymoronically constructed progressive medievalism, his late socialist romance *News from Nowhere* offered both a digest and reimagining of Morris's central themes and preoccupations with this epoch.

Clive Wilmer suggests that *News from Nowhere* can be fruitfully approached as Morris's attempt to reconcile Ruskin's aesthetics with Marx's theories of social emancipation including dialectical materialism, as the engine of significant historical progress.[71] This is to see the text as a working through of the two dominant strands in Morris's life with his Pauline conversion to active socialism on joining the Democratic Socialists in 1883, then being amalgamated with his longstanding belief in the centrality of art to all worthwhile human endeavours. The well-known influence on Morris at the time of writing were, as the title suggests, More's *Utopia* (which he misinterpreted as a medieval romance, seemingly unaware of its ludic irony) and Edward Bellamy's *Looking Backward 2000-1887* (1888), the most popular of American literary socialist utopias, which Morris reviewed in his paper, *The Commonweal* in 1889; but he had also read and enjoyed Samuel Butler's *Erewhon* (1872) in the 1880s as well.[72] Butler's romance was the most successful reformulation of Swiftian utopian satiric principles in the Victorian era.

Erewhon follows Swift by having the protagonist travel to a far-away land only to encounter a version of his homeland when he gets there; and then Butler examines that almost familiar society though an outrageous conceit. Butler's strikingly imaginative manoeuvre was to invert middle-class Victorian attitudes to medicine and law, such that criminals (mainly the white-collared variety) undergo a curative treatment for illegal action; while the ill (mainly the urban poor) are prosecuted in the courts for their ailments. Butler's title, of course, is almost an anagram of 'nowhere' backwards; and that sense of 'almost' seems also to stand metonymically for the text as a whole – 'almost' a fully worked through satire on an inverted utopian Victoriana. Butler's contemporaries recognised the anomalous nature of this undertaking, such that when Butler was being idealistic he was compelled to introduce a satirical note; and when he was being satirical he was unable to abandon his idealism.[73] The book is at its Swiftian best in its account of Erewhonian trials, a scathing critique of the English criminal justice system (and High Court judges' conduct); and in its examination of Victorian middle-class mores through the inverted standards of health and crime. It would seem, however, the work's two germane aspects from Morris's perspective were those which were not fully integrated into the main narrative: the association of utopianism with beauty, and the extended explanation as to why the Erewhonians abolished machinery.

---

[70] 'Art and the Beauty of the Earth. A Lecture Delivered at Burslem Town Hall on October 13, 1881', in *Collected Works of William Morris*, ed. by May Morris (London: Longmans Green, 1910–1915), XXII, *Hopes and Fears for Art, Lectures on Art and Industry* (1912), pp. 155–74 (p. 158).
[71] See Morris, *News from Nowhere and Other Writings*, ed. Wilmer, p. xxxiii.
[72] See MacCarthy, *William Morris*, p. 584.
[73] See Hans-Peter Breuer and Roger Parsell, *Samuel Butler: An Annotated Bibliography of Writings about Him* (New York: Garland, 1990), pp. xv–xvii.

Butler's first-person narrator remarks upon the physical attractiveness of the Erewhonians on his initial encounter with them, 'abashed in the presence of such a splendid type – a compound of all that is best in Egyptian, Greek and Italian' (p. 79); while this is little more than a standard arcadian topos given an exotic southern European and oriental caste, his description of landscape is more imaginative. Butler trained as a painter and his narrator describes his initial sighting of an Erewhonian hamlet in the lyrical and spacious terms of the landscapes of the medieval artist Giovanni Bellini (Butler's favourite painter).[74] The narrator suggests his access to Erewhonian society was eventually eased because he was comely. Beauty exemplifies harmonious social relations. The Erewhonian dislike of machines and clock time is apparent early in the tale when the narrator is imprisoned for possessing a fob watch. Erewhonian hostility to mechanisation is explained toward the conclusion in the 'Book of the Machines' (which started out as a journal article when Butler was working as a sheep farmer in New Zealand). The book, an ancient tract archived in the Colleges of Unreason, establishes the reasons why all mechanisms should be banned. The account of potential machine development was predicated on Darwin's evolutionary theory in *The Origin of Species* (1849, 1872). The 'Book of Machines' gives the example of molluscs when considering the evolutionary advantages of consciousness. Molluscs have insignificant awareness when compared with human beings, but under appropriate conditions (where incremental increases in consciousness confer an evolutionary benefit) and given sufficient time, there is no reason why molluscs' successors would not eventually match Homo sapiens in their capacity for self-awareness. And if that is true of the evolution of organic forms, then one cannot rule out the same developments taking place in inorganic entities. Think of a watch: 'examine its beautiful structure; observe the intelligent play of the minute members which compose it; yet this little creature is a development of the cumbrous clocks that preceded it; it is no deterioration from them'.[75]

The prima facie objection to this line of argument is that it confuses identity with analogy. The book counters such an objection in two ways: first, it insists that to argue machines cannot reproduce themselves like living organisms is to take too narrow a view of reproduction. Organic reproduction assumes many different forms; and the model of one set of machines producing another is not so outrageous as soon as one contemplates the variety produced by meiosis; and moreover, technological development possesses its own impetus. Human ingenuity and labour has become subservient to the development and maintenance of such devices. It is not just that machines have the features of living things; 'the vapour engine must be fed with food and consume it by fire even as man consumes it; it supports combustion by air as man supports it; it has a pulse and circulation as man has' (p. 208); it is also that humankind had entered into a bonded relationship with such mechanisation. Human beings have become increasingly like machines; and machines increasingly like human beings. The choice presented by

---

[74] Butler's artistic preferences are discussed extensively by Elinor S. Shaffer in her *Erewhons of the Eye: Samuel Butler as Painter, Photographer and Art Critic* (London: Reaktion, 1988).
[75] Samuel Butler, *Erewhon; or, Over the Range*, ed. by Peter Mudford (London: Penguin, 1985), p. 202. Further in-text references are to this edition.

the 'Book of the Machines' is stark: humankind either has to undergo a period of considerable hardship and deprivation through the abolition of all devices, or risk eventually being enslaved or hunted to extinction by advanced automata (that staple dystopian scenario of twentieth-century science fiction). As the narrator reports, the Erewhonians eventually took the former option, but the consequence was an all-consuming civil war which only resulted in the machine-less state after decades of destruction.

There is little evidence of satire or humour in Bellamy's influential, *Looking Backward 2000–1887*; though it shares with Butler's text a sentimental romance between the protagonist and a conventional representation of attractive and responsible young Victorian womanhood. And Bellamy's narrative has the more striking conclusion with the defamiliarising device of his time-travelling protagonist, Julian West, returning to nineteenth-century Boston from the city's perfected future at the turn of the millennium. Having grown accustomed to the light, spacious and efficient metropolis on the cusp of the twenty-first century, West sees the Victorian city now in apocalyptic terms, dirty, cramped, unsanitary, inegalitarian and miserable, with the newspapers full of reports of warfare and civil unrest. Julian is fortunate enough to waken from this nightmare of late nineteenth-century America to realise that he truly has been transported to the perfected urban future, and counts his blessings as a consequence. The device for this transiting was to take the standard nineteenth-century American progressive motif of heading westward, and transform it into an image of social rather than geographic movement. Julian undergoes the Poe-like fate at the romance's beginning, entombed in a catatonic state, only to be fortuitously disinterred and revivified at end of the twentieth century.

Bellamy, a trained lawyer and practising journalist, had encountered socialist theories in a visit to Germany in the 1870s; and he was able to select and combine these experiences to provide an American utopian vision of compelling imaginative force. In keeping with the approach of the Saint-Simonists, there is the belief that social conflict can be resolved without recourse to violent revolution; and as with the Saint-Simonists and the later Robert Owen, there is conviction in the benefits of rational efficiency. Bellamy's urban utopia is a monopoly technologised society with an industrial army of obligatory if limited service. Money has been replaced by a system of credit (which looks like a version of the anarchist Pierre-Joseph Proudhon's elaborate system of chits and credit notes to replace cash). The population eats in large refectories. Washing and cleaning are centralised services free at the point of delivery; and while families still live in conventional domestic units, everyone has modest but comfortable accommodation in properly designed suburbs.

As Arthur Lipow observes, the nationalist movement inspired by Bellamy's romance, at its peak in the 1880s and 1890s 'consisted of a loose federation of 165 clubs with five or six thousand members'.[76] The radical appeal of Bellamy's social vision was that it seemed to offer an achievable alternative to the intractable inequality and economic insecurity of nineteenth-century capitalism with its long periods of depressed conditions; and to

---

[76] Arthur Lipow, *Authoritarian Socialism in America: Edward Bellamy & the Nationalist Movement* (Berkeley: University of California Press, 1982), pp. 119–20.

achieve this reformation in such a way that it did not require violent insurrection (in a nation where civil war was a recent memory), and in which the evident benefits of capitalism, such as ready access to department stores with a wide range of attractive goods, did not as a matter of equality and solidarity need to be foregone.[77] While Morris could see the ingenuity and humour in Butler's satirical vision of a utopian society which emphasised the importance of beauty and supplied an extensive explanation as to why the Erewhonians felt it necessary to dispense with machinery, he was not so well disposed to *Looking Backward*. In his review of the romance in the *Commonweal*, Morris concedes that 'Mr Bellamy has faced the difficulties of economical reconstruction with courage'; but he also cautions that the book should not be taken as the 'Socialist bible for reconstruction'.[78] His principal objections to the work are that it is complacent in its belief that economic and social change can come about merely by relying on the ultimate rationalising efficiencies of market forces; that the model of work proposed in this future state seems to be no less alienating and unpleasant than the current one; that the vision of technologised urban future seems to have banished any significant notion of artistic practice. 'Art', Morris suggests, 'is not a mere adjunct of life which free and happy men can do without, but the necessary expression and indispensable instrument of human happiness'.[79] If one were to define the main problem of modernity as living in the machine age, then Bellamy, by this reckoning, produces a curious solution by double-downing on mechanisation in this future state, where there is no conception in *Looking Backward* 'of anything else than the *machinery* of society'.[80]

It is, of course, understandable to see *News from Nowhere* as Morris's explicit retort to Bellamy as to what the socialist future should look like; and irrespective of how events will eventually turn out, it is still a good idea to recognise what are and what are not appropriate aims for the process of social reformation. Morris, however, was also clear in his book review about the subjective nature of all idealistic projection: 'the only safe way of reading a Utopia', he claims, 'is to consider it as the expression of the temperament of its author'.[81] *News from Nowhere* certainly provides an effective digest of Morris's social and artistic views by the early 1890s, as well as more direct autobiographical referents. His two main figures, Richard Guest, the traveller from grim Victorian London, and old Hammond, his host and principal explicator of the harmonious socialist future, are both versions of himself. The book opens with Guest, whom like Morris is a member of the Socialist League, returning from a League meeting in central London to Hammersmith, where Morris had his London residence. The meeting, held on a weekday winter evening, is poorly attended and indicative of the divided state of revolutionary politics 'for the rest, there were six persons present, and consequently six section of the party were represented, four of which had strong

---

[77] On the reception of *Looking Backward*, and the dissemination of its ideas, see Silvia E. Bowman, *The Year 2000: A Critical Biography of Edward Bellamy* (New York: Bookman Associates, 1958), pp. 119–38.
[78] William Morris '"Looking Backward": A Review of *Looking Backward* by Edward Bellamy', in *News from Nowhere and Other Writings*, ed. Wilmer, pp. 351–58 (p. 358, p. 358).
[79] Morris, 'Looking Backward', p. 358.
[80] Morris, 'Looking Backward', p. 356.
[81] Morris, 'Looking Backward', p. 354.

but divergent anarchist opinions'. After the meeting, Guest travels home by underground train, described as 'that vapour bath of hurried and discontented humanity'.[82] The watery theme is continued by association at the beginning of the second chapter, entitled 'A Morning Bath'. Guest awakens early and is taken for a swim in the Thames by a boatman. He immediately notices the water is unusually clear and sparkling; fish have return to the polluted river; and the stern iron suspension bridge across the river at Hammersmith (recently opened in 1887) has been replaced by an elegant stone structure, even finer than the Ponte Vecchio. Guest recognises the extent of the changes when the boatman refuses payment; he good humouredly explains that 'you see this ferrying about the water is my *business*, which I would do for anybody' (p. 12).

Morris was not content with the style of *Looking Backward*. He reports that Bellamy described the use of the romance genre as mere 'sugar coating to the pill'; whereas Morris's use of a medieval dream vision in *News from Nowhere* to imagine a socialist future is in earnest, such that form and style cannot be readily divorced from narrative content.[83] As the vision unfolds, it becomes apparent that Guest has been transported to London at some point in the twenty-second century (the book is hazy as to exactly when); and the dreamer gradually acquires a clear view of this society, through both direct observation and in discussion with various interlocutors, notably the elderly and sagacious Hammond. The perfected future society is a secular imaginative version of the Middle Ages, certainly in its dress and overall appearance. Hammond suggests the intention has been to capture the vital organic completeness of the era, for its people in which 'heaven and the life of the next world was such a reality, that it became to them part of life upon earth; which accordingly they loved and adorned, in spite of the ascetic doctrines of their formal creed, which bad them contemn it' (p. 158). This is a society in which anarchic principles have been applied in a rather idiosyncratic aestheticised fashion, in the belief that human beings are intrinsically creative and collaborative creatures; and the happy and just world will be that which has dispensed with all the conventional political, economic, legal and coercive state apparatuses. There is to be no police, no army, no system of civil and criminal justice, and no schools. All people are equal, where communities collectively arrive at decisions which effect their lives. Children learn through their natural propensities for inquiry; though this is a society that puts as much store by traditional crafts as thatching as academic aptitude and achievement.

Morris was sceptical about Bellamy's projection of 'Boston beautified' and his occasional passing allusions to villages beyond its city limits. He reimagines a future London beautified as though it were series of medieval hamlets, with a residual sense of nineteenth-century socialist-utopian self-sufficient secular communities, such as the Owenite Good Harmony and Fourier's Phalanges. Beautifying London meant reconsidering the metropolis as a garden city; and disposing with the great majority of Victorian buildings, though some fine structures were kept, irrespective of their original dubious function. The modern Gothic Houses of Parliament are retained as

---

[82] Morris, *News from Nowhere*, ed. Wilmer (1993), p. 43. All further in-text references are to this edition.
[83] Morris, 'Looking Backward', pp. 353–54.

the communal storehouse for manure; and Westminster Cathedral, now cleared of all its superstitious Anglican clutter, has been preserved for the intricate fineness of its interior. Like Bellamy's Erewhonians, modern Londoners have been beautified, rendered more attractive, healthier and longer-lived than their Victorian counterparts. Anarchic and communitarian principles are not seen to be at odds with this utopia's forceful individualism, where radical freedom equates to a broad scope for self-expression, demonstrated through the radiant medieval costumes which some of its citizens elect to wear (and the only implied restraint on such expression is an intuitive judgement on the infringement of someone else's scope for expression or action). Even though the principal goods of this society are freedom, equality and happiness, this does not mean that violent offences are unheard of. The social imperative is to bring the offender to a proper comprehension and sense of atonement for the destructive consequences of their actions; and not to exact some arbitrary form of retribution for the sake of either demonstrating social disapproval, or for providing a salient deterrent to others from following the same destructive path. When Guest asks about habitual killers, Hammond loftily dismisses the idea, 'in a society where there is no punishment to evade, no law to triumph over, remorse will certainly follow transgression' (p.114); and if a killer turns out to be ill or mad, then he will be restrained until deemed cured.

The two central elements in this society, however, are the attitude to work and personal relations, and the respective distribution of libidinal energies between them. All work has been aestheticised; and the value of any object is purely dependent on the subjective artistic pleasure invested in it. Hence the example of the pipe which Guest acquires *gratis* from a tobacco shop, an object of iconic exquisiteness, 'carved out of some hard wood very elaborately, and mounted in gold sprinkle with little gems [...] something like the best kind of Japanese work, but better' (p. 73). Guest wonders at first how he could possibly afford it, before Hammond warns him against 'another exhibition of extinct commercial morality' (p. 74). This is a small and intricate demonstration of the necessary amalgamation of art and utility. The craftsman takes pleasure in the creation of a piece which has a practical function in the smoking of tobacco; and the pleasure of its subsequent use is enhanced by the fineness of the pipe's design and execution. One area in which Morris departed from Ruskin's aesthetic views was the extent to which medieval craftsmen found their work fulfilling.[84] It is not just the claim in *News from Nowhere* that intricate craftmanship is inherently pleasurable; but also that even hard manual labour can be conceived as being satisfying in the right circumstances. On encountering workmen repairing a road, Guest comments that they were 'strong young men, looking much like an Oxford boating party would have looked in the days I remembered, and not troubled with their work' (p. 82); and the appealing combination of physical exertion and sensual delight is confirmed when Guest notices that 'beside them lay a good big basket that had hints about it of cold pie and wine; a

---

[84] On Ruskin's views on the hardships of labour and the complexities in aligning pleasure with work, see, for example, his *Pre-Raphaelitism* (1851), in *'A New and Noble School': Ruskin and the Pre-Raphaelites*, ed. by Steven Wildman (London: Pallas Athene, 2012), pp. 63–105 (pp. 67–73), and his *Fors Clavigera: Letters to the Workmen and Labourers of Great Britain*, ed. by Dinah Birch (Edinburgh: Edinburgh University Press, 2000), pp. 131–43 and pp. 314–22. See also P.D. Anthony, *John Ruskin's Labour: A Study of Social Theory* (Cambridge: Cambridge University Press, 1983), pp. 148–72.

half-dozen of young women stood by watching the work or the workers, both of which were worth watching' (p. 82).

Morris is aligned with Fourier to the extent that both believed in the significance that work could be pleasurable; and they both argued against the imposition of standard expectations on sexual relations, although Fourier's unpublished writings on sexual mores were much more radical than Morris in this respect. For Fourier, one had to accept the polymorphous nature of human sexuality, and social structures had to flow along the contours of such desires, rather than imposing a heterosexual monogamous norm, which had the consequence of rendering society dissatisfied and hypocritical in the pursuit of extra-marital affairs, effectively institutionalising deception as the basis for intimate relationships.[85] In Morris's more restrained version of Victorian sexual revolution, the key matter was to detach personal relations from considerations of contract and property; but without entirely disposing of the notion of marriage as the basis of an enduring and fulfilling partnership. The experience of Hammond's son, Dick, is a case in point – once married to Clara she left him for another man; and they are now planning to be married again. Social institutions cannot eliminate unhappiness, but they can be configured in such a way that they do not add to the sum of distress and anxiety when relationships run into difficulties; and by being sufficiently pliant to offer couples the possibility of coming to a satisfactory arrangement in their personal affairs. As Morris suggests, utopia cannot escape subjective impulses; and the examples of both Clara and Ellen (an attractive guide and confidante of Guest) reflect Morris's own difficulties in his marriage to Jane Burden in the former, and romantic wish-fulfilment in the latter.

Morris's views on relations remain in twenty-first-century parlance robustly heteronormative. Women in *News from Nowhere* are young and attractive, free-spirited, and enjoy tending to the needs of men. Victorian demands for rights for women and universal suffrage are spurned as incidental manifestations of an oppressive bourgeois ideology. The late appearance of the commanding figure of a women sculptor reads exactly as to what it is: a belated addition to the book in response to the complaints from Morris's female supporters about the general passivity of the women depicted in the romance's serialised version in the *Commonweal*. The female sculptor serves as an indication of autonomous womanhood; and in her modest use of machinery to cut stone; she also provides a late qualification to the utopian abjuring of all technology. Now machines are permissible when no pleasure can be realistically produced in the execution of a particular activity. As much as Morris's vision of women can be seen to be staid, there is a defence for it in that he pursued a life-long celebration of the domestic in wallpaper pattern design, furniture construction and his championing of the traditional feminine arts of weaving and embroidery. There is self-evidently a qualitative difference between insisting that the proper place for women is a domestic

---

[85] See Frank E. Manuel, *The Prophets of Paris* (Cambridge, MA: Harvard University Press, 1962), pp. 218–19; and Jonathan Beecher, 'Women's Rights and Women's Liberation in Charles Fourier's Early Writings', in *Utopian Moments: Reading Utopian Texts*, ed. by Miguel A. Ramiro Avilés and J.C. Davis (London: Bloomsbury Academic, 2012), pp. 92–98 (especially pp. 97–98).

environment, and the proper place for *all* future people should be the home, because Morris envisages the home or home-like spaces are where almost all creative satisfying labour will be undertaken.

Mathew Beaumont correctly observes that Morris's overhauling of Bellamy was a matter of substituting one promissory note of the ideal future for another.[86] Yet Morris, following Marx, believed that profound social transformation was not possible without violent confrontation. He had lost faith in the 1870s in the possibility of conventional political parties being able to effect significant change within a democratic system, having come to the view that all governments will continue to support the pre-existing commercial interests at a point of social jeopardy.[87] The prospect of revolution had become more distant between the serial publication of *News from Nowhere* in the *Commonweal* and the book version, moving from the early twentieth century in the former to 1952 in the latter. When it does happen, it will be the consequence of the breakdown of capitalism which leads to a catastrophic collapse in employment and wages. Recent upheavals are refashioned as part of a twentieth-century conjectural history. The spark for the future revolution is imagined as a massacre in Trafalgar Square. A riot had in fact broken out in the Square in February 1886 after a mass protest of the unemployed. Morris charts in his imaginative history, the various revolutionary and counter-revolutionary surges through the 1950s until the forces of freedom prevail. The civil war will be extraordinarily destructive; and the final utopian settlement will take decades to be realised.

If its historical determinism roots *News from Nowhere* in a certain version of the future, which opens up the text to unfavourable comparisons as to what actually transpired in the twentieth century, then the end of the romance seems, initially at least, to expose Morris to a further objection – that social analysis has given way to wish-fulfilment. The narrative's closing segment is an account of a boat trip upstream on the Thames, in which Guest and his friends visit a number of towns and places along the riverside: Runnymede, Bisham, Caversham and Port Meadow in Oxford, before arriving at the final destination of an old house by the Thames, modelled on Morris's summer residence, Kelmscott Manor in Gloucestershire. The river has a mytho-poetic quality to it with the journey as an attempt to encapsulate an essential rural Englishness. Morris in his poetic sequence *The Earthly Paradise* (1868–70) had described Pygmalion the sculptor creating the statue with which he falls in love as it comes to life; so here in the romance of *News from Nowhere*, the artist creates the whole of future society, which can elicit the same charged emotional response; an idealised vision of society to be animated and adored. As Morris suggests in his review of *Looking Backward*, the subjective plays a significant role in the construction of all ideal societies; and then one must presumably trust that others will find one's own vision just as compelling. But the autobiographical is also directly realised in this romance in Guest's utopian questing, in the sage-like Old Hammond and in Dick Hammond's troubled

---

[86] Matthew Beaumont, *Utopia, Ltd.: Ideologies of Social Dreaming in England 1870–1900* (London: Haymarket, 2009), p. 179.
[87] See Nicholas Salmon, 'The Political Activist', in *William Morris* (London: Philip Wilson, 1996), ed. by Linda Parry, pp. 58–65.

marriage to Clara. Morris also seems to make a final spectral doubling appearance as the dream fades. He comes across a shadowy figure who looks not unlike his ageing Victorian self. 'I came upon a figure strangely contrasting with the joyous beautiful people', Guest records, 'it was a man who looked old, but I knew from habit, now half-forgotten, was really not much more than fifty. His face was rugged and grimed rather than dirty; his eyes dull and bleared; his body bent; his calves thin and spindly' (p. 227).

The subtitle of *News from Nowhere*, an 'Era of Repose', has struck commentators as being notably incongruous with the career of the indefatigably energetic Morris. But it may well have been on the mind of his secretary, Sydney Cockerell, when he viewed his employer's remains, shortly after he died in October 1896. Cockerell recorded in his diary that Morris in death underwent a remarkable transformation, 'the face was singularly beautiful', he observed, 'but the repose of it made it the more unlike what I had known' – in effect, Morris beautified.[88] If there is the spectre of a final dissolution at the end of *News from Nowhere*, then this cannot be said to be at the expense of the sensuous; and it would be Morris's singular triumph to recognise that in the age of the machine, a compelling vision of the alternative society requires the animating forces of the subjective; and more importantly, the artist's implicit trust in a communal passion, which cannot be readily translated into a set of analytical propositions or explicit social dicta. The text's ending in which Guest sombrely awakes back in his own bed 'in dingy Hammersmith' (p. 228) is a final retort to Bellamy's apparent hopefulness in having his protagonist awake from his nineteenth-century Boston nightmare to find that he is once again safely ensconced in his blissful future state; and thereby implying there was a degree of inevitability in the process of social amelioration which Bellamy had envisaged. Morris's closing line that it is his hope that 'if others can see it as I have seen it, then it may be called a vision rather than a dream' (p. 228) proved prescient. His social-artistic vision did have a widespread influence on politicians, artists, urban planners and designers throughout the twentieth century. Widely read in Russia before the revolution; it also made its mark on prominent left-leaning twentieth-century academics, such as R.H. Tawney and E.P. Thompson. Reformist politicians, such as Keir Hardy (the first socialist MP) and Clement Attlee (the first Labour Prime Minister) acknowledged a debt.[89] The principles the book espoused influenced the Garden City Movement, English artists as diverse as Eric Gill and Osbert Lancaster, the design theory of Christopher Fry in the 1920s, Ethel Mairet's couture in the 1930s and Terence Conran's furniture in the 1950s.[90]

News from Nowhere can certainly be interpreted as a late distillation of Morris's aesthetic and socialist thinking, as a rejection of the technologised urban version of the future offered by Bellamy, and indeed, as a decisive response to Plato's view of the ideal polis in the *Republic*; for this is a thoroughly aestheticised society, in which all human beings have creative and imaginative freedom. Art has moved from the role of necessary

---

[88] Sydney Cockerell, Ms Diary, 3 October 1896, British Library, Add Ms 52633, f. 61ʳ.
[89] Fiona MacCarthy discusses Morris's social and political influence in her *William Morris*, pp. xvi-xviii.
[90] See Fiona MacCarthy, *Anarchy and Beauty: William Morris and his Legacy, 1860-1960* (London: National Portrait Gallery, 2014); and Roger Fry, *Vision and Design* (London: Chatto and Windus, 1920).

mimetic deception to the central aspect of everybody's life, even if the definition of art is practical and intricate rather than grand and dramatic. Yet ultimately, the text seems to offer a plausible set of responses to Carlyle's questions on the machine age in *Past and Present*; those questions which Carlyle was able to pose forcibly, but unable for his contemporaries to provide entirely convincing answers. *News from Nowhere*'s response to the 'Sphinx-riddle of Today' was to suggest that the holistic organic vision of the Middle Ages needed to be detached from its historical specificity, while retaining its idealistic aspect and *Past and Present*'s comparative structure. Instead of looking backward to the ideal state, one now needed to look forward to its achievement; and if one were thoroughly disenchanted with industrial modernity, then one had to find a plausible means of explaining how society might progress beyond it – that necessitated writing something akin to the history of the future in which one envisaged both the stages and consequences of social transformation. Morris certainly would not dispute the Carlylean doctrine of faith, but that sense of faith had to be invested in the aesthetic vision of the era of repose. For his admirers, Morris could certainly be seen to embody Carlylean qualities of heroism in the positive sense of personal example, unceasing endeavour and clear-sighted social vision. And if Morris substituted Carlyle's Broken Spectre for his own less ominous spectral presence in *News from Nowhere*, then there was still the Carlylean vatic strain to his works – the Abbot Samson for his epoch.

Yet, there was also an anomalous aspect to *News from Nowhere*. As Gregory Claeys points out that for all its subsequent influence, the organic communitarianism of Morris's romance was out of keeping with mainstream utopian writing in the last decade of the nineteenth century.[91] It was not so much that the machine age could be considered to have decisively passed; but rather it could no longer be considered as the master metaphor for the era in the way constituted by Carlyle and then inherited by Morris. If the machine was still *the* epochal symbol, then its principal referents seemed to have shifted. Morris could admire Butler's satire on the Darwinian evolution of machines, but that did not require him to address the status and implications of the theories in his own imagining of a future perfect state. For utopian writers toward the century's end, technology was increasingly considered not just in the context of capitalism as the prevailing economic social system, but also in the context of Darwin's theories and their social applications in the writings of Spencer and Huxley, along with Galton's racial ideas. Such theories constituted a wider sense of scientific transformation rather than being strictly concerned with its mechanical application. Such concerns would repeatedly surface in the work of H.G. Wells, the most influential utopian and anti-utopian English writer as the new century commenced.

---

[91] See *Late Victorian Utopias: A Prospectus*, ed. by Gregory Claeys, 6 vols (London: Pickering & Chatto, 2009), I, p. ix.

5

English Triptych: Wells, Huxley, Orwell

There is an autobiographical allusion in H.G. Wells' novel, *Tono-Bungay* (1909). George Ponderevo's mother finds herself in the same situation as Wells' parent. She has had to return to domestic service, now accompanied by her son, in the Sussex country house where she worked before her marriage. Bookish George finds solace from his socially embarrassed circumstances in the library of Bladesover House. He mentions reading, *inter alia*, Paine's *Rights of Man* and *Common Sense*, both judged 'excellent books'.[1] He describes his encounter with *Gulliver's Travels* 'strong meat for a boy perhaps, but not too strong I hold'. He says that as a consequence he 'hated Swift for the Houyhnhnms and never quite liked a horse afterwards'.[2] He reads *Candide* and *Rasselas*, and Gibbon's *The History of the Decline and Fall of the Roman Empire*. Morris's idealistic writings, important elsewhere in Wells' oeuvre, are restricted to a single reference, all forming part of his auto-didactic learning, 'scraps', he says, of social theory, which led him as a youth to a dangerously naïve outlook.[3] Carlyle is included in the mix; and George's entrepreneurial Uncle Edward improbably claims the sage had advanced a test for economic solvency before expostulating along with many perplexed Victorians, 'Lord, what a book that *French Revolution* of his is!'[4] More intriguing still is George's early interest in the ideal state. He remembers that he had precociously attempted a translation of Plato's *Republic* in the Bladesover library, but made little headway, 'being much too young for that', preferring instead the Gothic cruelty and extravagance of Beckford's oriental romance, *Vathek*.[5] William Bentham, the socially elevated and well-educated protagonist of Wells' *The Research Magnificent* (1915), has a sustained admiration for the *Republic*, revealing that he had been in thrall to Plato since he was a student at Cambridge, and his political dialogue is the initial offering in the novel's central romantic relationship, 'it was a matter of course that my first public gift to Amanda', Bentham writes in his memoir, 'should be his REPUBLIC. I love Amanda transfigured in that dream'.[6]

In 'Modern Fiction' (1925), Virginia Woolf was scathing about the older generation of Edwardian novelists, including Arnold Bennett, John Galsworthy and H.G. Wells.

---

[1] H.G. Wells, *Tono-Bungay*, ed. by Patrick Parrinder (London: Penguin, 2005), p. 26.
[2] Wells, *Tono-Bungay*, p. 26.
[3] Wells, *Tono-Bungay*, p. 164.
[4] Wells, *Tono-Bungay*, p. 136.
[5] Wells, *Tono-Bungay*, p. 27.
[6] H.G. Wells, *The Research Magnificent* (London: Macmillan, 1915), p. 313.

These writers, she believed, never overcame the cultural and social norms which they ostensibly opposed. They 'have excited so many hopes and disappointed them so persistently that our gratitude largely takes the form of thanking them for having shown us what they might have done but have not done'.[7] Formal and lexical conventionality bespoke a mind-set which could not adequately express the experience of modernity on a subjective, social or artistic level. Woolf principally had in mind the limitations of Wells' social fiction; and the sense that for all his attempts at casting off traditional morality and examining the sensual and erotic in mainstream narrative fiction, these endeavours only led him to affirm with trivial variants standard relationships between the sexes. A decade later she added an acid PS to a letter to her sister that she had turned down an invitation to be the president of the P.E.N. [Poets, Essayists, Novelists] Club in succession to Wells. She declared in the postscript the proposed succession constituted 'just about the greatest insult that could be offered to a writer, or a human being'.[8] However, as her diary reveals, Wells was also a source of ongoing fascination. Woolf is better disposed in her account of dinner with the seventy-year-old Wells in January 1937. She listens to his 'old man's talk, mellower than I remember, eyes a little bleared'. He is, despite his celebrity, 'conscious of his lack of distinction; prone to snap at any pretence; introduced my father the professional cricketer'. She then has Wells concede much of his prolific output had been 'trash', has him say 'that he has done a vast mass of work & think it won't all die'; and surmises that 'he is a humane man in some corner; also brutal; also entirely without poetry'.[9]

There is some irony in Woolf's discussion of Wells in 'Modern Fiction', with the suggestion that it was precisely modernity in its intrinsic and aesthetic aspects which Wells was never able to fully grasp. For Wells was *the* modern storyteller of the late nineteenth century. In his early scientific romances, he married the imaginative possibilities of scientific ideas to a romance form which suggested social allegory, but never with such exactness that it entirely dissipated its more potent symbolic resonances. Wells is sometimes portrayed as a scientist manqué, a writer who under different circumstances would have pursued an academic career in zoology or biology, following the example of T.H. Huxley, Darwin's leading supporter, who taught Wells at the Normal School of Science in South Kensington in the 1880s. Yet, Wells was drawn to the imaginative possibilities of scientific thinking and innovation as a kind of literary aesthetic rather than to the systematic and laborious procedures required to test hypotheses under laboratory conditions. Like his protagonist, George Ponderevo, having worked hard to gain a scholarship at a science college, Wells left the Normal School without a degree. And science as an imaginative resource was to be set against what it could usually be understood to determine, both in the nature of matter and the laws governing time and space.

---

[7] 'Modern Fiction', in *The Complete Essays of Virginia Woolf*, 6 vols, ed. by Andrew McNeillie and Stuart N. Clarke (London: Hogarth, 1994–1996), IV (1994), pp. 157–66 (p. 158).
[8] Woolf to Virginia Bell, 17 July [1935], *Letters of Virginia Woolf*, ed. by Nigel Nicholson, 6 vols (London: Hogarth, 1975–1980), *The Sickle Side of the Moon: 1932–1935*, V (1979), pp. 415–17 (p. 417).
[9] Virginia Woolf, *A Moment's Liberty: The Shorter Diary*, ed. by Anne Olivier Bell (London: Hogarth, 1990), p. 405.

Hence in Wells' *The Invisible Man* (1896), the unstable and impoverished scientist, Griffin, explains the fantastic conceit that a potion could render him invisible. The justification is a series of brilliant analogies of the complexities and liminal nature of visibility. The variable opacity and translucence of a glass box depends on the reflection and refraction of light and the angle of view. Powdered glass is immediately visible in air, but vanishes in water, because the refractive index of glass is close to that of the liquid. There are many examples of fauna with transparent corpora, such as jelly fish and sea larvae; and even much of the human body can be seen through. 'The whole fabric of man', Griffin points out, 'except the red of the blood and the black pigment of hair, are all made up of transparent colourless tissue'.[10] The apparently incredible is thus rendered conceptually plausible, only requiring a minor biological adjustment to switch off the relatively few light-absorbing properties of the human body – a scenario made more credible by Wells making Griffin an albino. And one can glimpse in this romance a semblance of social criticism in the young scientist's impoverished circumstances where invisibility suggests estrangement and alienation; a widespread indifference to the subject, as though much of the population of nineteenth-century England from a political and institutional perspective remained unseen.

That sense of analogy is at its sharpest in *The War of the Worlds* (1897), with both its warning on the way in which advanced technology can be utilised for offensive and oppressive purposes; and the straightforward fashion in which the conquering and destructive Martians can be deciphered as European colonialists. One can detect a Swiftian animus in the narrator's implicit endorsement of the Martian mission to eradicate humans, with only a late abandonment of that misanthropic position, when the alien force is destroyed by microbial infection. The romance's striking and unexpected conclusion pitches physics, applied mechanics and advanced technology against epidemiology and biology (Wells' favoured scientific discipline), but at the expense of inverting the usual direction of fatal infection in colonial encounters, such as in the epidemics of measles, smallpox and cocoliztli which afflicted Aztecs after the arrival of European colonists in the sixteenth century. The stark Manichaeism of *The Time Machine* (1895) provides a more suggestive, if less exact, comparison with contemporary class relations in the vision of a distantly future society divided between the arcadian Eloi, with their 'Dresden-China type of prettiness', and the machine-like arachnid Morlocks in their sightless underworld.[11] The class element is indicated by the time traveller who attempts some 'Carlyle-like scorn of this wretched aristocracy in decay'; but still found the Eloi 'had kept too much of the human form not to claim my sympathy and to make me perforce a sharer in their degradation and fear'.[12] The social division seems to run in this instance through a vision of the Victorian industrial proletariat, who have undergone a strange biological revolution, merging with the machines they tend. The Morlocks have subjugated their erstwhile bourgeois masters, rendering them not only anxious and tractable, but ultimately as a food source, as 'mere fatted cattle'.[13]

---

[10] H.G. Wells, *The Invisible Man*, ed. by Andy Sawyer (London: Penguin, 2005), p. 91.
[11] H.G. Wells, *The Time Machine*, ed. by Patrick Parrinder (London: Penguin, 2005), p. 24.
[12] Wells, *Time Machine*, p. 62.
[13] Wells, *Time Machine*, p. 62.

Biological revolution is at the heart of Wells' most visceral and compelling scientific romance from this period, *The Island of Dr Moreau* (1896). He revises Shelley's Victor Frankenstein in the guise of the surgeon Moreau. Like Frankenstein, Moreau undertakes a Promethean project, but rather than attempting to create life, he transforms species, fashioning original beings from various mammals. Moreau creates his tribe of 'beast people' on a Pacific island through vivisecting an ape, puma, leopard, sloth and others, 'craven and wrought into new shapes'.[14] Moreau concedes that it was an aesthetic impulse, which compelled him to turn his surgical and scientific training to the production of hominid creatures, as he remarks 'there is something in the human form that appeals to the artistic turn of mind more powerfully than any animal can'.[15] But there are also alternative experiments which result in a chimera with an overtone of original sin, the production of 'a limbless thing with a horrible face that writhed along the ground in a serpentine fashion', an uncontrollably violent beast, which eventually must be shot.[16] Other beast men with their imposed and constructed consciousness are initially more pliant. They are subject to commandments, 'The Law', a means of imposing a minimal standard of human conduct on the 'beast folk'. This is 'a strange litany', which the tribe routinely chants until the tale's later stages, when the creatures rebel and revert to their previous incarnations, but not in a way which observes a standard taxonomy – Moreau's creativity has meant one species possesses traits which rightly belong to another, and 'that a generalised animalism appeared through the specific disposition'.[17] The first-person narrator, Edward Prendick, documents their violent rebellion and progressive loss of human characteristics, 'the dwindling shreds of the humanity [...] a momentary recrudescence of speech perhaps, an unexpected dexterity of the forefeet, a pitiful attempt to walk erect'.[18]

The story's conclusion is reminiscent of *Gulliver's Travels*, but with no trace of a satire on hippophilia. The traumatised Prendick, having returned to London, thinks he detects everywhere the bestial substratum of his fellow citizens, 'prowling women [who] would mew after me', 'weary pale workers go coughing by me, with tired eyes and eager paces like wounded deer dripping blood'; and when visiting a chapel, he believes 'the preacher gibbers as the ape man had done'.[19] The *Island of Dr Moreau* evidently touches a late Victorian nerve on the cruelties of vivisection. As Alan Bates points out 'by the century's end, anti-vivisection had become a humanitarian *cause célèbre*, a mainstream issue with great public support and many societies dedicated to it'.[20] One can also detect a scepticism over the Victorian enthusiasm for missionary work in which the possibility of transformative and salvific Christian encounter with so-called primitive peoples is called into question; and beyond that, the novella's final chapter offers a Conradian perspective on the brittle carapace of civilisation with a destructive

---

[14] H.G. Wells, *The Island of Dr Moreau*, ed. by Patrick Parrinder (London: Penguin, 2012), p. 71.
[15] Wells, *Island of Dr Moreau*, p. 71.
[16] Wells, *Island of Dr Moreau*, p. 76.
[17] Wells, *Island of Dr Moreau*, p. 59, p. 125.
[18] Wells, *Island of Dr Moreau*, p. 125.
[19] Wells, *Island of Dr Moreau*, p. 133.
[20] A.W.H. Bates, *Anti-Vivisection and the Profession of Medicine: A Social History* (Basingstoke: Palgrave Macmillan, 2017), p. 14.

animalism lurking behind modern social exchanges; Prendick records his 'horror' at these London encounters. One might agree with Woolf that such works are an examination of brutishness and cornered humanity. If poetry is neither discussed, nor exemplified in this romance, then the notion of the creative is put under pressure as the animating force for Moreau's attempt to fashion a beauteous form from bestial materials.

Yevgeny Zamyatin, author of *We*, an influence on the plot and dénouement of Orwell's *Nineteen Eighty-Four*, produced an essay on Wells in 1924 while overseeing translations of the author's works into Russian. Zamyatin lauded Wells as a modern mythmaker, creating 'a species of fairy tale reflecting the endless prospect of technological change and the rigorously logical demands of scientific culture', as Patrick Parrinder puts it.[21] His stories were the literary equivalent of the recent re-conception of terrain through aerial photography. 'There is nothing more urban, nothing more of the day, more contemporary than the airplane', Zamyatin declares, and he knows 'of no English writer more contemporary than Wells'.[22] However, as a self-conscious avant-garde author, Zamyatin shared Woolf's scepticism when it came to Wells' social fiction. He found these novels derivative and old-fashioned when compared to the fantastic revelatory modernity of his romances. This, however, is to be rather dyspeptic. Wells certainly utilised standard nineteenth-century literary forms, such as the Dickensian bildungsroman as a means of exploring social norms through the protagonist's developing sense of self. And Dickensian realism was then compounded with the naturalism of Hardy and Gissing (a friend of Wells in the 1890s). What is striking in novels such as *Tono-Bungay* and the *Research Magnificent* is the working through of conflicting perspectives, even when these are never quite resolved. In these books, there is the possibility of individual transformation while holding at the same time with the contrary view that most lives are fixed by the circumstances into which they are born. In the *History of Mr Polly* (1910), this tension is played out in a whimsical fashion as Polly finds himself continually defying convention in spite of himself (attempting suicide, burning down his shop and abandoning his wife). Indeed, Wells' petit-bourgeois hero seems to anticipate Joyce's protagonists insofar as he attempts to make sense of the modern world and his place within it through punning and extravagant word play, even though his expressiveness is severely and poignantly restricted by his patchy education. And there are remarkable generic and geographical dislocations, such as George Ponderevo's African expedition in *Tono-Bungay*, which anticipates a similarly dramatic and unexpected narrative shift at the end of Evelyn Waugh's *A Handful of Dust* (1934). Wells' modernity, however, was especially evident in the utopian strain of his writings, and explicitly declared in the title of his *A Modern Utopia* (1905).

Elements of Wells' utopianism can be glimpsed in the nineteenth-century romances. At the end of the *Island of Dr Moreau*, Prendick withdraws into a comforting cocoon

---

[21] Patrick Parrinder, 'Imagining the Future: Zamyatin and Wells', *Science Fiction Studies*, 1 (1973) [https://www.depauw.edu/sfs/backissues/1/parrinder1art.htm, accessed 19 December 2018].

[22] Yevgeny Zamyatin, *A Soviet Heretic: Essays*, trans. and ed. by Mirra Ginsburg (Chicago: University of Chicago Press, 1970), p. 285.

of non-biological scientific research (chemistry by day, astronomy by night). And the *War of the Worlds* suggests Martian invasion has had unexpected benefits, 'the gifts to human science it has brought are enormous, and it has done much to promote the conception of the commonweal of mankind', and that notion is subsequently linked to romantic love – as the closing sentence reveals that the extraordinary personal conclusion to this global adventure has been 'to hold my wife's hand again, and to think that I have counted her, and she had counted me among the dead'.[23] Though, Wells, of course, was one of the earliest writers to imagine the uses of technology to produce a totalitarian vision of a future society (even though he never uses the terms 'dystopia', 'dystopian' or 'anti-utopia'), and his first full-length exploration of the future state took this darker turn. In *When the Sleeper Awakes* (1898), Wells inverted the dynamic of Bellamy's *Looking Backward* (1888), so that his suicidal Victorian everyman awakens in an advanced society where the monopolising impetus of nineteenth-century capitalism has not led to the industrial army and a rational egalitarian provision, but to modern urban bondage under the heel of the global Machiavellian dictator, Ostrog. As Wells describes it in the retrospective preface from the early 1920s, the novel 'resolves itself into as vigorous an imagination as the writer's quality permitted of this world of base servitude in hypertrophied cities'.[24] Wells' preface indicates a certain ambivalence. Writing from the perspective of the post-war era, 1898 'now appeared a remote and comparatively happy year'; and while the story 'is a nightmare of capitalism triumphant', it is also a flawed prospectus, given that it assumes 'an intelligence, a power of combination, and a *wickedness* in the class of rich financiers and industrial organisers, such as this class does not possess, and probably cannot possess'.[25] When Wells subsequently recognised the imaginative and strategic limitations of businessmen and entrepreneurs, the future capitalist overlord Ostrog, he suggests, 'gave way to the reality which I drew on Uncle Ponderevo in *Tono-Bungay*', a comic portrait, although not without tragic overtones, of a haphazard contemporary businessman who makes and loses a fortune in the manufacture and marketing of a Coca-Cola-like tonic, invested with bogus therapeutic properties.[26]

For Krishan Kumar, Wells was *the* utopist of the twentieth century (a marker of canonical division between the nineteenth-century utopian 'twilight' with which the Manuals concluded their study, and its rebirth in the 1900s). Wells' thinking and writing was subject to a pendulum swing, an optimistic perspective on a technologised future followed by a grim warning of the oppressive capabilities of scientific advancement. Hence, Kumar observes, *The Time Machine* was broadly anti-utopian and his first work of sociological speculation, *Anticipations* (1900) was 'resolutely utopian in character'.[27] His novel, *First Men in the Moon* (1901) attacks the notion of a future technologised civilisation, followed by the optimism of *A Modern Utopia* (1905). The social despondency of *The New Machiavelli* (1911) and *Marriage* (1912) 'were

---

[23] H.G. Wells, *War of the Worlds*, ed. by Patrick Parrinder (London: Penguin, 2012), p. 189.
[24] H.G. Wells, *The Sleeper Awakes* and *Men like Gods* (London: Odhams Press, [c. 1921]), [p. 7]. Wells omitted the initial 'When' from the former's title for the 1910 edition.
[25] Wells, *Sleeper Awakes* and *Men like Gods*, [p. 7].
[26] Wells, *Sleeper Awakes* and *Men like Gods*, [p. 8].
[27] Krishan Kumar, *Utopia and Anti-Utopia in Modern Times* (Oxford: Blackwell, 1987), p. 178.

succeeded by a strong reaffirmation of the utopian faith in The *World Set Free* (1914)', and so on.[28] If one were to accept the argument for the centrality of Wells' writing for the development of twentieth-century conceptions of literary and social idealism; then one might still have reservations about an argument that suggests Wells wrote in the same fashion as Samuel Johnson, attempting through the tick-tock of contrary positions to produce a semblance of thematic equilibrium. It seems, however, such a satisfactory resolution lay beyond the scope of these various projections; and the opposing case was often disruptively present in the same work. In the relatively late *The Shape of Things to Come* (1933), the perfected technological civilisation under the Air Dictatorship eventually comes about, but only after another global conflagration, and an era of a rural destitution, disease and brigandage, as an explicit retort to William Morris's machine-less anarchic arcadia. There were also complications of tone. In *Anticipations*, Wells' first attempt at futurology, he predicts the aggregation of urban centres and suburbs with high-speed transport to create vast metropolises; he foresees the waning of the nation state as a means of geo-political organisation; he thinks women will become more prominent in the work place; and there will be liberalisation of marriage and the legislation governing divorce; but at the same time, there is an unapologetic enthusiasm for the eugenic elimination of the urban poor; and Wells wrote with relish on further mechanisation of armaments and warfare in a manner which would appear crass and jingoistic by the middle of the following decade.

Nevertheless, Wells still remains the central utopian figure in the first half of the twentieth century; and along with George Orwell and Aldous Huxley established the major ideas which would shape the depictions of ideal society in anglophone literature until at least the 1960s. This is not to claim that there is an exclusive right to significant ideas within a literary field, and one could also include the works of other British authors such as E.M. Forster, Hilaire Belloc, Charlotte Haldane and Katharine Burdekin; and American writers, such as Malcolm Bradbury, B.F Skinner and Isaac Asimov; but the proposition remains that many of the key discussions and defining ideas of literary utopianism take place between these writers. Huxley and Orwell both wrote disdainfully of Wells, and while these younger authors self-evidently produced canonical works in this genre, almost all of their own influential utopian and anti-utopian fiction was produced in response to a Wellsian vision of such themes and ideas. Both Huxley and Orwell followed Wells in enabling the flow of ideas on perfected social forms from those writings which dealt explicitly with such matters as social fiction and journalism. As such, their utopianism cannot be narrowly defined in those books where it can be seen to be immediately apparent. These writers are conceived as an English triptych for the purposes of this discussion; that is, as a set of three inter-connected panels on a common theme, with Wells as the central image, and Orwell and Huxley to either side. Described as 'English' precisely because the conception of national identity and social class remained significant aspects, even as they all wrote in opposition to the British state and imperial mission. For these authors, utopia and its discontents was a matter of shaping the possibilities of that project in response to the political and social upheavals of the first

---

[28] Kumar, *Utopia and Anti-Utopia in Modern Times*, p. 178.

half of the twentieth century; but also one which required the active rejection of much that had gone before on the grounds of irrelevance and misguided thinking – a process which Wells explicitly commenced in *A Modern Utopia*.

Written in 1905, the same year as Wells completed his social comedy, *Kipps*, *A Modern Utopia* attempts to synthesise discursive and analytical components with the familiar attributes of narrative fiction; 'the entertainment before you', he informs the reader near the beginning, 'is neither the set drama of the work of fiction you are accustomed to read, nor the set lecturing of an essay you are accustomed to evade, but a hybrid of the two'.[29] 'Set drama' is noteworthy, because Wells had briefly been a theatre critic, and playwriting and theatrical production are significant for *Kipps'* plot. However, theatre is rapidly succeeded with a developing medium better adapted to the imaginative display and analysis of the new century. Wells invites the reader to consider the narrator and his travelling companion as though they were watching a cinematograph; that is, the illuminated rapid display of successive photographs which results in the illusion of movement, a precursor to cinema, the seminal art form of the twentieth century. When Wells envisages his central figures 'going to and fro in front of circle of a rather defective lantern, which sometimes jams and sometimes goes out of focus, but which does occasionally succeed in displaying on the screen a momentary moving picture of Utopian conditions' (p. 8), he might have expected his contemporaries to detect an allusion to Plato's cave in the *Republic* through the flickering outlines of figures before an artificial source of light. However, the more telling suggestion is to newness in the means of relation, as a statement of artistic and social intent; that the amalgam of modern fiction and modern fact was intended to result in the modern ideal state.

After some deliberation, Wells settled on having a fictionalised version of himself as narrator, referred to throughout as 'the Voice' (a referent first used for the protagonist in the *Invisible Man*). The domestic and international aspects of his *A Modern Utopia* are apparent in its *mise-en-scène*: two English gentlemen on a walking holiday in Switzerland (the germ was a tour Wells undertook to that country in 1903 with Graham Wallas, the educationalist and Fabian socialist, portrayed as a disgruntled botanist in this book). Wells updated the standard device of having a traveller visit a distant land only to find that it was a significantly altered version of their native country. In this instance, the Voice and his companion arrive on a planet near the star Sirius, eight light years away. The planet is earth perfected. The inter-stellar transit, however, is achieved purely 'by an act of imagination', authorial fiat, rather than space travel. The world just tilts as the Voice and his companion walk through the Lucendro Pass in the Leopantine Alps. There are few initial signs of momentous transformation. Clouds and landscape remain the same, though they quickly begin to notice the occasional new building, that the dress and speech of the locals have changed; and that when they look up at the night sky, the constellations are unfamiliar.

Early on, Wells constructs a canon of utopian writing into which he can add his own projection. He writes that 'the cardinal assumption of all Utopian speculations old and

---

[29] H.G. Wells, *A Modern Utopia*, ed. by Gregory Claeys (London: Penguin, 2005), pp. 7–8. All subsequent in-text references are to this edition.

new; the Republic and the Laws of Plato, and More's Utopia, Howell's implicit Alturia, and Bellamy's future Boston, Comte's great Western Republic, Hetzka's Freeland, Cabet's Icaria and Campanella's City of God are built [...] on the hypothesis of complete emancipation of community of men from tradition, from habits, from legal bonds' (p. 13). Yet, he is equally clear that he intends to emancipate his own work from the utopian tradition in which he has just situated his own work. The canon is too uniform with 'handsome, but characterless buildings, symmetrical and perfect cultivations, and a multitude of people, happy, healthy, beautifully dressed' (p. 14). These models function as restricted communities, which means utopianism can only ever apply to the relatively low numbers who belong to a particular polis. Mobility is an essential facet of modern labour; and as such, one must immediately reject the defining restriction of *Utopia*. More, Cabet and Morris were wrong to reject money as a means of setting the value of goods and exchanging them. Harrington is mistaken to believe rotating governors will result in strong and stable government. Morris is a *bête noir*, offering a vision of free co-operative humanity out of keeping with any known form of social interaction; and Morris is badly mistaken in believing beauty is inimical to industrial design. In utopia, the Voice says, 'a man who designs a tram road will be a cultivated man, an artist craftsman' (p. 79). Two texts which the Voice admires are Plato's *Republic* and Bacon's *New Atlantis* (1627): the former on the grounds of its rational approach to social organisation, and the latter because of the portrayal of the House of Salomon which places science at the centre of the ideal community. *A Modern Utopia* is not technologically futuristic, not a work which seeks to replace trains with some not-yet-invented form of rapid transport; rather, the rail network is to be optimised in terms of the possibilities of contemporary engineering. However, it is an abstracted conception of motion which Wells believes separates the modern utopia from *all* its predecessors – that the global utopian state should be regarded as a kinetic rather than a static entity.

Wells saw the kinetic as shaping 'not as a permanent state, but a hopeful stage leading to a long ascent of stages' (p. 11). However, the kinetic is given a compellingly imaginative treatment in this work in the development of a single world state as the only means of producing a just society. Wells anticipates globalisation when he suggests that no territory at the beginning of the twentieth century can be regarded as being isolated, though he is less convincing when he insists that the inevitable consequence of such inter-connectedness is to have a world state, a single government for the whole planet. The kinetic is also the basis for a suggestive model of economic relations even though its actual operation remains vague. Money is still required in the modern utopia to facilitate transactions. The Voice provides what at first appears to be an arcane account of the uses of gold as a means of exchange. However, the passage's topic is not 'gold' per se, but the gold specie standard; that is, the means by which currencies from the late nineteenth century, such as sterling and the dollar, were pegged to gold's international market value.[30] Wells highlights the instability of a system prone to rapid

---

[30] See Ted Wilson, *Battles for the Standard: Bimetallism and the Spread of the Gold Standard in the Nineteenth Century* (Aldershot: Ashgate, 2000), pp. 1-18; and Steven Bryan, *The Gold Standard at the Turn of the Twentieth Century: Rising Powers, Global Money, and the Age of Empire* (New York: Columbia University Press, 2010), pp. 17-31.

fluctuations in the availability of bullion. He proposes instead, in keeping with the principles of a parallel universal society where physics underpins theories of sociology and politics, that the standard economic measure in this utopia should be a unit of energy. This would serve as the basis of all transactions between the centralised state authorities as the owner of all the major utilities and power supplies, and local private providers of goods and services. Wells does not foresee the circumstances in which energy prices might be prone to sudden fluctuation as a consequence of mismatches in supply and demand; and he does not explain how determining a unit of energy as the economic predicate would achieve more stability in the financial system than one based on the availability of a precious metal. However, he does recognise that the transference between state-owned utilities and private contractors would necessitate an enormous centralised administration. A distinctive feature of this perfected global society, then, is its extensive bureaucracy, and especially as it is applied to the oversight and management of the population.

The Voice acknowledges that the general trend in the real world alongside any thought of an ideal one was toward larger states and a rapidly rising population. The two major challenges of the universal utopian state are the means to enable the general mobility of the citizens, and indeed to encourage them to relocate to those regions where there is a demand for labour and services; and the facilitation of such movement alongside the effective tracking of the population. Labour will move from areas of low productivity to those where there are shortages, because of need and opportunity. Thomas More, having lived through an age where demographic decline was a source of social instability, ensured in Utopia that there was a stable central population by replenishing cities from colonial outliers should there be a demographic collapse. As an avowed Malthusian, Wells believed the major threat to the modern world was overpopulation, where numbers would outstrip agricultural capacity to feed them. He believed the global population of 1.6 billion at the beginning of the twentieth century was nearing capacity. Shortfall in production will result not only in the misery of extensive malnourishment, but there will also be widespread social and political upheaval in the absence of security over food.[31] The Voice observes the utopian diet is mainly vegetarian on grounds of health and sustainability. However, the main means of avoiding a Malthusian calamity is by controlling population size, which necessitates accurate census data, and a reliable means for tracking every citizen. Even though Wells' utopia is unlike More's in scale and socio-economic vision; it does share the earlier work's concerns over food supplies. Both consider the means for optimising distribution of the population throughout their territories, and requiring surveillance of all their citizens. For More, this monitoring takes the form of mutual

---

[31] On Malthus's influence in the nineteenth century and neo-Malthusian theories, see William Peterson, *Malthus* (London: Heinemann, 1979), pp. 218–39, and G.R. Searle, 'Socialism and Malthusianism in Late Victorian and Edwardian Britain', in *Malthus: Past and Present*, ed. by Jacques Dupâquier, Antoinette Fauve-Chamoux and Eugene Grebenik (London: Academic Press, 1983), pp. 341–56. The global population in the late nineteenth century and early twentieth century is discussed by Massimo Livi-Bacci in his *A Concise History of World Population*, trans. by Carl Ipsen, 2nd edn (Oxford: Blackwell, 1997), pp. 112–58.

oversight, and a vernacular architecture to minimise private space. For Wells, it takes the form of a vast bureaucracy of clerks, personal identity documents, ledgers and index cards.

Some of the Modern Utopia's measures for population control, especially those which apply to women, are progressive. Women in the global state enjoy equal access to education and employment; they are paid the same rate as their male counterparts; they are encouraged to marry later (and cannot do so before the age of twenty-one); there is state-provided contraception, and childcare through universal benefits; the care and education of all children are ultimately the state's responsibility. The extensive use of surveillance as a means of maintaining a stable population level has its corollary in the racial theories which underpin this perfected universal society. The Voice dismisses Plato's horse-breeding tactics for enhancing the athleticism and intelligence of the guardian class as uncivilised and unworkable. There is also an explicit rejection of the idea that one race can be considered inherently superior to another. The Voice forcefully distinguishes between cultural markers and inherited characteristics, and dismisses any straightforward correlation between ethnicity and intellect.

However, there is still a prominent eugenicist strain to this work. Wells contemplates the bemused reception the alien Voice and botanist are likely to receive on this parallel planet: 'who in the name of Galton and Bertillon', one fancies a Utopian exclaiming, 'are *you*'? Francis Galton, inventor of Eugenics and the statistical notion of recession to the mean and Alphonse Bertillon, inventor of the mug shot and the personal metric identification system, anthropometry, are names which have passed into popular parlance in the Modern Utopia. Bertillon is significant because of the need for accurate identification and record-keeping in Utopia, and Galton, for the promotion of selective breeding as a means of enhancing the genetic stock. Joseph Conrad, along with other friends and acquaintances, warned Wells of the inconsistencies and difficulties in utilising Galton's theories, though he would continue to discuss and apply them in a more-or-less supportive fashion well into the 1930s. In this instance, he argues that social pressures will encourage most citizens to adopt a responsible attitude in the selection of sexual partners and numbers of children; but the genetically-flawed lower orders are still prohibited from reproducing, with the prospect of enforced sterilisation should they continue to burden the world state with defective offspring.

Aware of the controversy such ideas would provoke, Wells puts some terse objections into his reader's mouth: '"harsh", you say, and "poor humanity"' (p. 127). The Voice answers such criticism by appealing to rational organisation, and by making a comparative argument on relative benefit. One should not let sentiment cloud one's judgement on the necessity of maximising goods for the overwhelming majority of the population (he is utilitarian in this respect). The only alternative to demographic controls and sanctions on lower-order reproduction is 'your terrestrial slums and asylums' (p. 127). In his qualified socialist manifesto *New Worlds for Old* (1908), Wells would provide a detailed account of just such contemporary urban deprivation in a catalogue of destitute households in Edinburgh, taken from a report of the Charity Organisation Society. In a *Modern Utopia* Wells struggled with hierarchical social structure. He was reluctant to acknowledge the authoritarianism required for such a system to be maintained. Plato's tripartite division is reworked in this scheme as a four-tiered social schema in which the Poietic ('creative' in ancient Greek) is the apex, followed in descending order by the Kinetic, the Dull and the Base.

The Poietic are an imaginative class, with minds ranging 'beyond the known and accepted'; it includes artists and scientists, 'when the invention or discovery is primarily beauty then we have the artistic type of Poietic mind; when it is not so, we have the true scientific man' (p. 179). The Kinetic is proposed as a kind of mean, exemplifying the modern state's vigour. Its members are, he says, 'often very clever and capable people, but they do not, and they do not desire to do new things' (the exasperating botanist travelling companion is placed in this category). The Kinetic can be further divided into two, with able administrators on the one side, and energetic performers on the other, those 'great actors, and popular politicians, and preachers' (p. 181). Beneath the Kinetic are the Dull (possibly a minority in this properly-educated world). These are 'stupid people, the incompetent people, the formal imitative people', and this class counts 'neither for the work nor the direction of the state' (p. 181); and at the bottom is the Base, which vaguely suggests the pathological with the inclusion of the 'egotistical', the 'cruel', and those lacking 'moral sense' (p. 181). Yet having proposed this clear demarcation, Wells then muddies the waters, as these classes do not apply straightforwardly to any given individual. *Modern Utopia* perversely implies 'everywhere and in everything, margins and elasticities, a certain universal compensatory looseness of play' (p. 182) – a pliancy which would subsequently be abandoned in the strict social categorisation, 'the pitiless benevolent grip of the Air *Dictatorship*' in the *Shape of Things to Come*.

Wells began *New Worlds for Old* with a series of epigraphs, including this striking expostulation from the Duke of Rutland: 'undiluted atheism', his Grace thunders, 'I know of no language sufficiently potent to express fully my absolute detestation of what I believe to be the most poisonous doctrine ever put forward, namely Socialism'.[32] In response to such denunciations, Wells declares that he regards himself to be a socialist, 'but by no means a fantastical and uncritical adherent'.[33] His own hybrid doctrine required a robust and active role of the state on health and social welfare (especially when it came to the guardianship of children); the nationalisation of large public services (such as railways); the sweeping away of the savings and investments of the middle class (a bamboozling deception by financial institutions); but he does not suggest private property should be entirely abolished. In the Modern Utopia, the state has a more extensive role than in this essay on contemporary ills; but the Utopians still hold onto their houses. However, Wells was keen to dispense with all contemporary political orthodoxy in *Modern Utopia*'s aggregated social vision. Hence individualism and socialism are *both* declared 'in the absolute, absurdities; the one would make men the slaves of the violent rich, the other slaves of the State official' (p. 64). The undemocratic system of governance Wells proposed instead attracted

---

[32] H.G. Wells, *New Worlds for Old* (London: Constable, 1908), p. [i].
[33] Wells, *New Worlds for Old*, p. 1.

much contemporary comment in its promotion of a self-appointed global elite, the Samurai, who were to emulate the disinterested example of Plato's guardians.[34]

In addition to the Platonic allusions and Japanese swordsmen, the Samurai are compared to Knights Templar and Cromwell's Ironsides. They also have similar features to Schiller's elite classicists, Carlyle's Captains of Industry and the public-service ethos of senior British civil servants. Unlike their Platonic predecessors, the Samurai can marry, own a modest amount of property, and hold down jobs alongside their governmental responsibilities. They have the appurtenances of a masonic order; they abide by a rigorous code of personal conduct, 'The Rule' (prone to some accidental irony given that it is not unlike Moreau's 'The Law'). The *Republic* was an argument for the pre-eminence of philosophers in the ideal state; and it should not surprise us that creativity in both aesthetic and scientific fields as Wells' own attributes and aspirations are the hallmarks of the Poietic class from which the Samurai are drawn. The parallelism, whereby each earthly human has his or her corresponding self in Utopia, enables Wells to employ the Gothic figure of the doppelgänger, but in keeping with this perfected state, the double has been shorn of its sinister nineteenth-century connotations. The Voice enjoys convivial discussions with his utopian counterpart in the latter's London home. His 'better self' is, of course, 'a little taller [...] younger looking and sounder looking' (p, 167). As one might expect, the double of Wells' literary persona turns out to be a Samurai (presently conducting a report into penal reform); and it is his doppelgänger who explains the system of voluntary governance.

If the double no longer has a sinister connotation, then it seems, as John Huntington has suggested, it still possesses an unsettling amorous connotation in 'love's shadow'.[35] *A Modern Utopia* finishes with another imaginative shift between parallel states. In the concluding chapter, entitled 'The bubble bursts', the Voice's companion spies in a London park the double of his former lover walking alongside the double of his romantic rival. The botanist's unhealed heart and reluctance to conceive of the world as appearing one way and configured in another dispels this utopian mirage. Wells returns his central characters to earth with an abrupt perspectival change, from the fine buildings of perfected London to the pandemonium of the early twentieth-century metropolis as a 'sullen roar' fills their ears (p. 237). In a borrowing from Julian West's hallucinatory nightmare in *Looking Backward*, they see newspaper headlines proclaiming the state of the modern world: 'Massacre in Odessa/ Discovery of Human Remains at Chestrey/ Shocking lynching outrage in New York state/ German intrigues get a set-back/ The Birthday Honours – Full List' (p. 239). The Voice prophesies 'there will be many utopias' (p. 245), while still insisting the inevitable progression of all of these will be toward the World State.

---

[34] See Sydney Olivier, 'Review of *A Modern Utopia*', *Fabian News*, 15 (1905), 38–39, reprinted in *H.G. Wells: The Critical Heritage*, ed. by Patrick Parrinder (London: Routledge & Kegan Paul, 1972), pp. 110–12; R. Mayor, 'Review of *A Modern Utopia*', *Independent Review*, 7 (1905), 235–40, in *Wells: Critical Heritage*, pp.112–17; John Batchelor, *H.G. Wells* (Cambridge: Cambridge University Press, 1985), pp. 63–64; and Justin E.A. Busch, *The Utopian Vision of H.G. Wells* (Jefferson: McFarland, 2009), p. 216.

[35] John Huntington, 'H.G. Wells: Problems of an Amorous Utopian', in *H.G. Wells under Revision*, ed. by Patrick Parrinder and Christopher Rolfe (Selinsgrove: Susquehanna University Press, 1990), pp. 168–80 (p. 171).

Yet, for Wells, there was also a persistent manifestation of the utopian in the real world. London certainly appears to George Ponderevo in *Tono-Bungay* as a wasteland in which the population 'went to and fro on pavements that had always a thin veneer of greasy, slippery mud, under grey skies that showed no gleam of hope of them, but dinginess until they died'; but within a few pages he is describing the city as having 'hugely handsome buildings and vistas and distances, a London of gardens and labyrinthine tall museums, of old trees and remote palaces and artificial waters'.[36] The same dynamic is apparent in *New Worlds for Old*, but in the opposite direction. Wells walks with a companion along the Thames Embankment. He summarises the evening prospect as being 'beautiful', a vista of modern urban perfection, 'the rich black archings of Waterloo Bridge, the rippled lights upon the silent-flowing river, the lattice of girders and shifting trains of Charing Cross Bridge'.[37] That sense of wonder and pleasure, however, rapidly dissipates as soon as they realise every bench along the waterfront is occupied by the homeless. One unfortunate occupant encapsulates the city's bleakness, a 'ghastly long white neck and white face that lopped backward, choked in some nightmare, awakened, clutched with bony hand bony throat, and sat up and stared angrily as we passed'.[38]

As Ruth Levitas notes, a significant interpretative consideration in a *Modern Utopia* is the extent to which the objectives of sociology as an emergent field are treated idealistically. There is the endeavour to expound social ideas with rigour and fused with a compelling imaginative form. Wells, she points out, was lobbying unsuccessfully to gain a professorship in sociology at the LSE at the time of writing.[39] The glaring inconsistencies in a *Modern Utopia*, however, still tend to undermine the book's sociological credentials. The perfected equivalence is compromised by the alternate global history in which 'Jesus Christ had been born into a liberal and progressive Roman Empire that spread from the Arctic Ocean to the Bight of Benin' (p. 175); and the notion that racial distinctions have broken down cannot be easily reconciled with the idea that there is an exact equivalence of individuals. Despite the claim that the Voice understands that it is delusional to believe in 'English superiority', the reformulation of the class system for the global state; and the fact that the representative of the Samurai is a sombre and public-spirited English gentleman in his own image suggest otherwise. The closing reference to impermanence of the bubble film would seem to be a reflexive acknowledgement of such conceptual difficulties. Wells was certainly alert to the contrary case in his fiction. Indeed, one way of interpreting William Benham's fate in the *Research Magnificent* is as a doomed attempt to lead the virtuous elective life of the Samurai; the novel ends with his death in a futile intervention in a racial industrial dispute in South Africa.

As Wells predicted in a *Modern Utopia*, there would be many different utopias in the twentieth century; and he was determined to explore a good number of the alternatives

---

[36] Wells *Tono-Bungay*, p. 93, p. 106.
[37] Wells, *New Worlds for Old*, p. 16.
[38] Wells, *New Worlds for Old*, pp. 17–18.
[39] See Ruth Levitas, *Utopia as Method: The Imaginary Reconstruction of Society* (Basingstoke: Palgrave Macmillan, 2013), pp. 83–84. On Wells' sociology and style, see also Nathan Waddell in his *Modernist Nowheres: Politics and Utopia in Early Modernist Writing, 1900-1920* (Basingstoke: Palgrave Macmillan, 2012), pp. 17–20.

himself. He is at his most fanciful in *Men like Gods* (1923). His unprepossessing hero, Mr Barnstable, is the beleaguered assistant editor of the reformist journal, the *Liberal*. Just as the Voice has his utopian epiphany in the cleansing Swiss air of a walking holiday, so Barnstable has his transformative encounter with the ideal when he inadvertently drives into a multi-dimensional portal just outside Slough while taking a holiday from dispiriting journalism and a wearisome home life in the summer of 1921 – a turbulent year, the rebellion against British rule in Ireland ended in the establishment of Ulster and the Free State, the number of unemployed in Britain surpassed one million with lockouts in the coal mining industry, and Lenin began the New Economic Policy in Russia during extreme famine.[40] The utopia of *Men like Gods* is an arcadia in which microbes, pestilent insects, arachnids and reptiles have been eradicated. This utopia is imagined within conventional notions of the beautiful in harmony and symmetry of form alongside the benefits which applied science can bestow on both the appearance and function of the world, such that the Utopians' marvellous technological achievements are either hidden, or blended sympathetically into the surrounding countryside. The novel's central purpose is not so much to present a realistic or realisable vision of an alternate world, but to use the distancing perspective of the ideal to challenge conventional thinking on politics, economic organisation and social and sexual mores. However, *Men like Gods* is mainly memorable for two reasons: that it is an imaginative even whimsical evocation of an improved society abstracted from the requirement of concrete social proposals; and that it provides a rare meditation on personal tragedy in the perfect society.

The Utopian, Lychnis, who cares for the injured Barnstable in the novel's closing stages is still afflicted by the loss of her family in a boating accident long after the event. Barnstable thinks she would make an admirable nurse in twentieth-century England, where her enduring sadness would be put to productive use in tending for others (her name means 'red flower' in Latin, and has a common root with the Greek 'luknos', 'lamp', a nursing symbol). However, Lychnis's inability to overcome her grief is judged from the Utopian's perspective as a personal failing. Pity is an atavistic trait. Yet the account of Lychnis's conduct is both awkward and intriguing precisely because she cannot be properly understood in the framework which is provided to make sense of her experience. The narrative suggests protracted suffering has no place in a society where the rational, the harmonious and beautiful prevail. At the same time, there is a tacit acknowledgement that the propensities she exhibits and her mournful response to catastrophe cannot be dismissed as merely being wayward and eccentric, without accepting that to do so would mean denying that suffering can have any place in this ideal world. She turns out to be both contemptible and sympathetic.

For Ernst Bloch, *Men like Gods* encapsulated the significant defects in Wells' utopian fiction. It was, he said, the perplexing demonstration of 'the frolicking life like that of naked piano teachers in Arcadia'.[41] Wells, in Bloch's view, was too trusting of blind authority, investing too much faith in the benefits of technology; and too keen to

---

[40] See Martin Gilbert, *A History of the Twentieth Century: Volume 1, 1900–1933* (London: Harper Collins, 1997), pp. 602–24.
[41] Ernst Bloch, *The Principle of Hope*, trans. by Neville Plaice, Stephen Plaice and Paul Knight, 3 vols (Cambridge, MA: MIT Press, 1995), II, p. 617.

establish a fixed set of future or parallel prospects, rather than trying to trace out or exemplify the implications of a transformatory consciousness. Wells was certainly candid in his utopian projection, just as he was in the articulation of anti-utopias (with the *Shape of Things to Come* becoming the sequential expression of both poles). Anticipation meant for him being explicit about what that alternative state would actually look like. Wells has been oxymoronically characterised as a 'utopian pessimist'.[42] And indeed it is possible to conceive of his utopianism and anti-utopianism as being subject to a kind of entropic flux in which the utopian became a mean to impose a form of order in a universe which has a tendency toward chaos. That pessimism became more pronounced as he aged. However, Wells did take a more pragmatic step at the beginning of the Second World War. In *The Rights of Man* (1940) he sets out ten rights for all citizens of the modern world, including freedom of movement, the right to education, freedom from torture and mutilation, and freedom of expression. He concluded by stating that 'the provisions and principles embodied in this Declaration shall be more fully defined in a code of fundamental human rights, which shall be made easily accessible to everyone'.[43] Wells was a contributor to the Sankey Declaration of the Rights of Man; and, as such, can be regarded as an architect of the 1948 UN Declaration of Human Rights (adopted two years after his death); the document, as we saw in chapter three, which Jürgen Habermas declared to be the key international expression of a 'realistic utopia' in the post-war period.

One might approach *Island* (1962), Aldous Huxley's last novel, as a decisive casting off of Wellsian influence (a process commenced in his fiction from the late 1930s in works such as *Eyeless in Gaza* (1935), *Ends and Means* (1937), and *Grey Eminence* (1941)). However, Plato is still there through negative inflection right at the end. The native Palanese, Lakshmi, is in the final stages of terminal cancer. She is asked by her daughter-in-law about what is on her mind. She replies '"Socrates"', '"Gibber, Gibber, Gibber – even when he's actually swallowed the stuff. Don't let me talk"', she says, '"Help me get out of my own light"'.[44] The reference is to Plato's *Phaedo*, the dialogue in which Socrates, having been sentenced to death for impiety and corrupting youth, drinks the hemlock. In fact, having discussed immortality, purification of the soul and the realm of eternal ideas, Socrates says almost nothing once he has drained the cup. However, Lakshmi's terminal outburst suggests irritation with Socratic dialogue as a prolix disquisition which fails to provide a satisfactory resolution to the ethical and metaphysical conundrums it raises. Plato's influence can also be detected indirectly in Huxley's debut novel, *Crome Yellow* (1921). Its protagonist is a young diffident poet, Denis Stone, a version of Huxley himself. The country house, Crome, is based on the gatherings of Huxley's patroness Lady Ottoline Morrell at Garsington Manor, near Oxford. This community falls short of the expected standards of a virtuous and harmonious society, but Denis still sees it as eminently desirable, and suffers in the

---

[42] Lyman Tower Sargent: *Utopianism: A Very Short Introduction* (Oxford: Oxford University Press, 2010), p. 26.

[43] H.G. Wells, *The Rights of Man; or, What Are We Fighting for?* (London: Penguin, 2016), p. 82.

[44] Aldous Huxley, *Island* (London: Vintage, 2005), p. 255. All subsequent in-text citations are to this edition.

conclusion the same fate of the poets in the *Republic*, of being exiled, forced in his case to catch the train back to London, a circumstance he likens to death.

Crome Yellow also contains Huxley's earliest discussion of a technological society liberated from natural reproduction and the obligations of kinship. A house guest, Scogan, possibly modelled on the geneticist J.B.S. Haldane and Bertrand Russell, advocates an extreme form of scientism for the benefit of humankind. The most remarkable achievement, he declares, will be the development of 'the means of disassociating love from propagation'. He looks forward to a time in which 'an impersonal generation will take the place of Nature's hideous system. In vast state incubators, rows upon rows of gravid bottles, will supply the world with the population it requires. The family will disappear; [...]; and Eros, beautifully and irresponsibly free, will flit like a gay butterfly from flower to flower through a sunlit world'.[45] The vision, of course, would form the basis of *Brave New World* (1932). Huxley, brother of the biologist Julian Huxley and nephew of Darwin's supporter and Wells' lecturer, T.H. Huxley, was conversant with the scientific discoveries and discussion of the 1920s and early 1930s, but he objected to the socially progressive claims which were made for science. The Eton- and Oxford-educated Aldous was patricianly dismissive of Wells, writing in 1927 that he struck him 'as a rather horrid, vulgar man', though the authors corresponded and were on dining terms in the 1920s and 1930s, even after the publication of *Brave New World*.[46] Huxley's principal objection to Wells was as the standard bearer of a populist utopian future; and he revealed to an acquaintance in May 1931 that he was 'writing a novel about the future – on the horror of the Wellsian Utopia and a revolt against it'.[47]

This assessment turned out to be somewhat awry. The 'horror' of the future society is tempered by *Brave New World*'s notionally attractive aspects, as well as its sardonic and ludic tone. The 'revolt' is modest and ineffectual. Huxley's brilliance was to mesh Wellsian technological faith with what he judged to be the superficial and materialist nature of 1920s America. He had first visited the United States in 1926, and was beguiled by the energetic brashness of California, with its unapologetic commercialism, wealth, neon signage, speak easies, jazz, automobiles, celebrities and Hollywood moviemaking. He describes to one correspondent his encounter with the 'soulless' if 'exquisitely pretty flappers' on Venice Beach, 'dressed in bathing costumes so tight that every contour of the Mount of Venus and Vale of Bliss was plainly visible'.[48] In his travel narrative *Jesting Pilate* (1926), he bathetically repurposed the title of James 'BV' Thomson's poem of Victorian London, *The City of Dreadful Night*, (1880) to conceive of modern-day Los Angeles as 'the City of Dreadful Joy'; a modern utopia, 'its light-hearted people', he observes, 'are unaware of war or pestilence or famine or revolution, have never in their safe and still half-empty Eldorado known anything but

---

[45] Aldous Huxley, *Crome Yellow* (London: Vintage, 2004), p. 23.
[46] Huxley to Robert Nichols, 18 January 1927, *Letters of Aldous Huxley*, ed. by Grover Smith (London: Chatto & Windus, 1969), pp. 281–82 (p. 281); see Nicholas Murray, *Aldous Huxley: An English Intellectual* (London: Abacus, 2009), p. 196.
[47] Huxley to Kethevan Roberts, 18 May 1931, Huxley, *Letters*, p. 348.
[48] Huxley to Mary Hutchison undated, quoted in Murray, *Huxley*, p. 182.

prosperous peace, contentment, universal acceptance'.[49] Yet America was not just an expression of zany sunlit gaudiness. In his essays in the 1920s Huxley developed a Spengler-like conviction on the decline of Western civilisation; and he believed the emergent United States as the pre-eminent global power was hastening that demise. If one were to contemplate a futuristic unitary society then the chances were that in appearance and cultural standards, it was going to look and feel like the West Coast. 'The future of America is the future of the world', he proclaimed in the opening to an essay in *Harper's Magazine* in August 1928, and then proceeded to lambast what he perceived as its dim-witted populism, a culture in which people 'given food, drink, the company of their fellows, sexual enjoyment, and plenty of noisy distractions [...] are happy'.[50]

Wells, as we have seen, admired aspects of Plato's *Republic* and Bacon's *New Atlantis* as a model of social integration in the former and a vision of community with institutional science at its core in the latter. *Brave New World* extends and imaginatively reconfigures these elements to striking purpose. The Platonic substratum, however, is more tightly conceived than anywhere to be found in Wells; and the novel's central and innovative conceit of biotechnological innovation and social conditioning renders Plato's Kallipolis plausible in imaginative terms. The motto above the Central London Hatchery and Conditioning Centre in the opening paragraph, 'Community, Identity, Stability' is a concise explication of the Republic's central principles in the pursuit of the central objective of a stable polis, where all members of society are expected to contribute to the 'good' of the community, and where identity refers to the capacity to express the collective identification with the state and given class, rather than as a marker of unique individuality.[51] Families are abolished; the hierarchical nature of society is rendered immutable on an individual and collective basis. All citizens perform allotted roles, according to their predestined attributes. The elite cadre of alpha pluses is ultimately directed by a philosopher ruler in the guise of the World Controller, Mustapha Mond. The Controller reworks Plato's analogy of the cave, having experienced his own moment of speculative enlightenment only to realise that his social obligations required him to return to the occluded world of public service and governance. And Plato's exiling of poets is reworked in Mond's detailed explanation to John the Savage as to why Shakespeare as an exemplary artist must be banished from the ideal state.

If *Brave New World* can be read as Huxley's satiric attempt to outdo Wells in Platonic emulation, then the Platonic components were still refracted through Wells' use of such devices; and particularly as they appeared in a *Modern Utopia*. The Brave New World of A.F. 632, like the Modern Utopia, is a global state. Huxley followed Wells in extending the hierarchically arranged social classes. Wells has four and Huxley five (along with gradations). And both have a special class for those who refuse to conform. The impending banishment of the dissenting intellectuals Bernard Marx and Helmoltz

---

[49] Aldous Huxley, *Jesting Pilate: The Diary of a Journey* (London: Chatto & Windus, 1948), p. 267, p. 268.
[50] Aldous Huxley, 'The Outlook for American Culture: Some Reflections in a Machine Age', *Harper's Magazine*, 155 (August, 1927), 265–72 (p. 265, p. 267).
[51] Aldous Huxley, *Brave New World* (London: Flamingo, 1994), p. 1. All subsequent in-text references are to this edition.

Watson to Iceland in the novel's closing stages is a revised version of the lowest stratum in Wells' scheme, 'The Base', in which those individuals who lack 'moral sense' are assigned, and those placed in this class are also banished to remote islands. The diffuse application of Eugenics in *A Modern Utopia* is applied more rigorously in *Brave New World*. And we may recall that the popular expostulations refer to the eugenic and to identifying the social aspects in the interjection of 'who in the name of Galton and Bertillon are you' are picked up in the various similar colloquial allusions in Huxley's novel to the industrialist and car manufacturer, Henry Ford, the foundational figure and guiding light for this perfectly engineered society.

Huxley had read the industrialist's autobiography, *My Life and Work* (1922), on a liner crossing the Pacific to San Francisco in 1926. Ford offered in this work a kind of rough-and-ready Nietzschean overcoming by declaring 'history is bunk'; a proclamation, which Huxley then used as an opening gambit in a 1931 essay 'On the Charms of History and the Future of the Past'. The pronouncement becomes one of the World Controller's utopian dicta. However, it was Ford's detailed descriptions of production techniques which was to have the more significant influence. Assembly-lines dramatically reduced costs. Cars became standardised mass-market items (by 1909, the Ford company was only producing the Model T). Huxley recognised the usefulness of having a workforce adapted to mundane repetitive tasks; but then transferred the idea of assembly-line production to the population itself, whereby sufficient numbers of each type could be produced by biotechnological means to meet social economic targets. And there is also the idealistic model of the life-cycle of manufactured goods. Just as one might expect a given device to operate for a given number of years, so human beings are similarly commodified, carefully maintained in a youthful state until their sixtieth year, and then they promptly expire on the principle that 'ending is better than mending' (p. 44). The conflation of categories is one of the novel's hallmarks. Hence the ingenious play with the ideas of production and consumption. Delta infants undergo Pavlovian conditioning by electric shock to develop a strong aversion to nature, while at same time they have a love of country sports instilled in them, 'so that they consume manufactured articles as well as sports' (p. 19).

Much of *Brave New World*'s sardonic élan is a consequence of the imaginative fulfilment of Huxley's prediction that America's future would be the world's future, and with Huxley's lurid Los Angeles transposed to London. Promiscuity is a social obligation, expressed in the mantra that everyone belongs to everyone else; relationships are ephemeral; and there are Dionysian rituals, 'Orgy Porgies' in which the self dissolves into a libidinous whole. The most witty observations are on the English establishment operating in a similarly uninhibited fashion. After Bernard and Lenina become celebrities, Bernard's advances to the headmistress of Eton are warmly received, and the 'pneumatic' flapper-like Lenina is pursued by an array of dignitaries, spending 'one week-end with the Ford Chief-Justice, and another with the Arch-Community Songster of Canterbury. The President of Industrial and External Secretions was perpetually on the phone, and she had been to Deauville with the Deputy Governor of the Bank of Europe' (p. 149). The background noise of American radio jingles and commercials becomes the sleep-conditioning mechanism of hypnopaedia (its discovery is one of the many co-incidental jokes), said to have been discovered when a sleeping boy memorised a radio broadcast by a 'curious old writer', George Bernard Shaw, discussing 'his own genius' (p. 21)). And what Huxley regarded as infantile hedonism of jazz and Hollywood talkies is transformed into wailing sexophones and the all-consuming sensuousness of the feelies, with the zipper as emblem for modernity and easy sex.

So, the central premise of *Brave New World* is that people should be shaped to meet the needs of the state rather than the state existing to satisfy the intrinsic needs and wants of its populace. Stability is the ultimate social goal, though all individuals should at least be contented with their lot – given that they are generically adapted and conditioned to their respective ranks and roles; and if there should be any momentary distress which cannot be diffused through mindless saturation in popular culture, then one still has ready recourse to the opioid-like Soma to relieve any remaining low spirits. Yet Huxley is careful to suggest that not all autonomous thought and unexpected action has been entirely eliminated in this engineered society, otherwise there would be no need to have a police force (deployed to quell the Delta riot instigated by the Savage's throwing away of their narcotic). There is a stark metaphysical divide between human capacities and the organisational requirements in the Fordian utopia. Bernard Marx anticipates the Savage's Shakespearian perspective when he hovers in a helicopter with Lenina above the English Channel, and broods over the gloomy vista, 'the rushing emptiness of the night, by the black foam-flecked water heaving beneath them, by the pale face of the moon, so haggard and distracted among the hastening clouds' (p. 81). He regards the sublime sea as co-extensive with his present bleak mood, and the stormy panorama leads to a discussion of solitariness and the nature of freedom. Bernard rejects the illusions of false happiness and yearns for a radical sense of liberation beyond the confines of his conditioning; Lenina breezily insists that he is making no sense; and anyway 'I am free', she says, 'free to have the most wonderful time' (p. 83). She is correct, of course, in terms of the dovetailing of conditioned expectation and hedonistic opportunity within the global state. On the other hand, Bernard expresses a standard Romantic trope on the necessity of solitude for the realisation of the imaginative self through the contemplation of nature.

When it comes to literature and aesthetic standards, Huxley advances a position somewhere between Matthew Arnold's proposition that Shakespeare is a means of disseminating sweetness and light, a binding set of civilising values for the fractured polity, and Harold Bloom's view of Shakespeare as a repository of human insight and expression at the centre of the English canon. In the set-piece exchange between the Savage and the World Controller, Mond, the Controller acknowledges the end of suffering and the optimised nature of the stable society equates to the end of history, and the end of history requires the prohibition on those ideas which cannot be reconciled to the existing order. The Controller points out in their discussion of *Othello*, a play from which the Savage liberally quotes and has seen grotesquely bowdlerised in a feely, that 'you can't make tragedies without social instability. The world's stable now. People are happy; they get what they want, and they never want what they can't get. They're well off; they're safe; they're never ill; they're not afraid of death.' (pp. 200–1) One can certainly have a society, he concedes, in which there is a possibility of a rich and complex aesthetic experience; and one can have a society constructed on the robust foundations of continuing stability, prosperity and contentment; but one cannot have both; hence, no Shakespeare. The discussion subsequently turns to the matter of rights. The Controller presents an image of the alternative non-utopian society, suggesting that John's bold declaration of his inalienable right to unhappiness should be placed alongside 'the right to have syphilis and cancer; the right to have too little to eat; the right to be lousy; the right to live in constant apprehension of what may happen tomorrow; the right to catch typhoid; the right to be tortured by unspeakable pains of every kind.' The exchange has a sharp but inconclusive conclusion, as the Savage insists he would claim them all; and the Controller mordantly retorts, 'you're welcome' (p. 219).

It is an intriguing proposition that the good of stability and happiness of the society can be attained by the biotechnological means of manufacturing people on the model of the twentieth-century industrial production line so that they are entirely fitted to their allotted social and economic roles; but these standard utopian benefits can only be achieved at the price of the great majority of these people being unable to think, act, respond and feel in the ways one might regard as being intrinsically human; and those that are blessed with the full complement of attributes, including higher consciousness, the alpha plusses, are obligated in the manner of Plato's guardians to maintain the status quo of the integrated hierarchical society. *Brave New World*'s continuing suggestiveness lies partially in the fact that none of the oppositions it proposes, such as the Controller's discussion with the Savage, are entirely resolved; and every position which is advanced is then subject to destabilising qualification or detraction.

The apparent opposition of science and literature in the above exchange is moderated by the scene's opening in which the Controller is censoring a biological article, because its findings are not consonant with the state's social principles. Fordian utopianism may be brutally deterministic, but conventional modes of reproduction, family life, and the process of ageing are shown in an equally dismal light through the experiences of Linda and John in the Rousseauvian reservation in New Mexico. Bernard's rebellion and his general unusualness may be explained by a possible procedural error in his conception, and his social opposition lacks conviction (happy to enjoy the fruits of celebrity after recovering the Savage). Mond, the overlord of this department of the global state, is portrayed as urbane and moderate, a figure apparently modelled on Sir Alfred Mond, first chairman of ICI (Huxley had met Mond in 1930, describing the ICI plant at Billingham as a triumph of large-scale industrial organisation). The Savage's defence of the revelatory powers of Shakespearian drama and the triumph of individual freedom are comically and then tragically undercut by his inappropriate spouting of lines from the plays, his strange emulation of the characters, and his excessiveness (with some self-flagellation worthy of Sir Thomas More). Huxley himself charted the book's shifting tone; having revealed at the outset that *Brave New World* was a work on 'the horror of the Wellsian Utopia and the revolt against it'; he described the book to his father on its completion 'as a comic, or at least satirical novel'.[52]

---

[52] Huxley to Leonard Huxley, 24 August 1931, Huxley, *Letters*, pp. 351–52 (p. 351).

David Bradshaw reminds us that for all its utopian futurism and Wellsian critique, *Brave New World* is rooted in the early 1930s, a novel written against the backdrop of the 1929 Wall Street Crash, the ensuing depression, rising unemployment, the formation of a national government in Britain, and the rapid depreciation of sterling leading to the abandonment of the Gold Standard in September 1931.[53] Huxley gives a sense of the intellectual and political currents of the era in his use of given names and surnames in the book, such as Ford (sometimes referred to as Freud), Marx, Trotsky, Benito (as in Mussolini), Lenina (for Lenin), Bakunin and Engels. If Huxley could be judged to be uncannily prescient in his account of the technical achievements of genetic manipulation and the crassness and ubiquity of consumerism in the age of high capitalism, then it is notably understated, indeed anachronistically disengaged, when it comes to the defining conditions of its own period, economic chaos, the rise of national socialism in Germany, and Stalin's consolidation of power in the USSR. Wells' major utopian and anti-utopian foray from the same period, *The Shape of Things to Come*, treated such matters directly. And one might add that the Jazz Age with its flappers had all but disappeared by the depression-hit 1930s. As William Morris observed in his review of *Looking Backward*, utopian authors invariably construct ideal states in their own image; and one might speculate the extent to which the utopian and anti-utopian vision of *Brave New World* offers a diffuse portrait of Huxley as cosmopolitan English intellectual who was both repelled and attracted to the glitzy sensual allure of Southern California, the 'dreadful joy' of Los Angeles; and who would in due course be drawn to its pellucid light, to live in that city, write for the Hollywood studios, and eventually produce his alternative utopian vision there. While satirising the awfulness of the Wellsian utopia, the regimentation of the future global state could still appear attractive when set against the fraught state of world affairs in 1932.

Huxley periodically returned to *Brave New World* in subsequent works. He had revisited the text in the light of the Second World War, writing a new introduction to the novel in 1946 in which he began to consider, contra the spirt of the age, as to how one might conceive of a positive utopia as an antidote to the earlier Wellsian future. His ideas were impressionistic at this stage, notions of a kind of transfigured Mills in 'Higher Utilitarianism' married to anarchist and communitarian principles, 'politics Kropotkinesque and co-operative'.[54] As David Dunaway points out an early indication that Huxley would attempt to write a positive utopia was in a letter to Humphry Osmond in 1953; though he then put the project aside as he experimented with Mescaline, and recorded its perceptual effects in *Doors of Perception* (1954) and *Heaven and Hell* (1956).[55] He began working in earnest on *Island*, as a kind of palimpsestic sequel to *Brave New World* in the late 1950s. The book was written against the background of Huxley's diagnoses of mouth cancer and a fire at the Huxleys' home in the Hollywood Hills which destroyed nearly all their possessions, although Huxley and

---

[53] See David Bradshaw's introduction to *The Hidden Huxley: Contempt and Compassion for the Masses*, ed. by David Bradshaw (London: Faber and Faber, 1994), pp. vii–xxvi (especially, pp. xii–xx).

[54] *Writers at Work: The Paris Review Interviews*, ed. by George Plimpton, 2nd series (New York: Viking, 1963), p. 199, quoted in David King Dunaway, *Huxley in Hollywood* (London: Bloomsbury, 1989), p. 395.

[55] See Dunaway, *Huxley in Hollywood*, pp. 395–96.

his wife managed to save *Island*'s manuscript from the flames. And, as Huxley acknowledged, the book's difficult gestation was due to two other factors: that it was 'always a great deal easier to write about the negative than about positive things, easier to criticise negative things than to set up positives'; and the problem of striking an effective balance between fable and exposition in the novel of ideas.[56]

Will Farnaby, *Island*'s protagonist, seems to have been borrowed from the fiction of Huxley's compatriot and contemporary, Graham Greene. The novel begins with Farnaby being awoken by a Mynah bird calling 'Attention' (a recurrent motif). Farnaby is the alcoholic Englishman abroad; and the reader has the sense from the beginning that the protagonist will be confronted with a moral dilemma which he won't be able to resolve. Farnaby is washed up, figuratively and literally. He is a journalist with a faltering career. He is guilt-ridden over an affair in England with Babs, the separation from his wife, Molly, and her subsequent death in a car crash. Farnaby is also washed up, Crusoe-like, on Pala, a 'hypothetical' equatorial island, said to be located between Ceylon (Sri Lanka) and Sumatra.[57] Farnaby's boat sank when he was heading to the island as an agent of a tycoon who wants the island's pacific collaborative regime to be replaced with one more amenable to his business and commercial interests. Farnaby learns about holistic Palanese society along with the reader. He gradually recovers his health; he overcomes his extreme morbidity and misanthropic fixation (a compulsion to regard human beings as maggots); and he achieves a degree of psychological resilience and insight into his circumstances.

Farnaby encounters a small group of characters in the course of the novel. On the one side, there are those who uphold the traditions and principles of Palanese society; and on the other, those who wish to modernise the state for the purpose of securing power, and their own commercial advantage. Huxley is clear that Pala is a just society, established to maximise the goods of freedom and happiness for its citizens. Its success has been to resolve the Malthusian dilemma, to remain a community of a size proportionate to its available resources. In a variant of the amalgamation of the antithetical economic systems of Soviet command economy and unimpeded American capitalism in *Brave New World*, Pala is an effective blend of selective Western science and technology and Eastern spirituality. Modern Pala has its origins in the meeting of a nineteenth-century Scottish doctor, escaping from his strict Calvinistic background, and the current Raja's great grandfather. Tantric Buddhism is combined with the mind-expanding opportunities afforded by a mescaline-like psychedelic substance, and a progressive agricultural policy, centred on the Pala advanced plant-breeding centre, modelled on Rothamstead, the main UK agricultural research centre in Hertfordshire (then as now). The Palanese have adopted a permissive approach to sexual relations (contraception is freely available, sex education starts early and is factual and comprehensive). They have a flexible notion of the constitution and the family's obligations as the fundamental unit of social organisation. The responsibility for raising children is spread across the kinship network. A Palanese explains to Farnaby that the

---

[56] Interview with Huxley 18 March 1957, UCLA library special collections, quoted in Dunaway, *Huxley in Hollywood*, p. 396.
[57] Huxley to Ian Parsons, 8 January 1961, quoted in Murray, *Huxley*, p. 437.

nuclear family affords a certain freedom, but it is limited. Your children, she says, 'are foisted on you by hereditary predestination. You can't get rid of them, can't take a holiday from them, can't go to anyone else for a change of moral or psychological air. It's freedom, if you like – but freedom in a telephone booth' (p. 91).

The basis of Palanese society is enlightened collectivism. There is widespread appreciation of the need to avoid the artificial wants of modern consumer society; and there is an educational policy which means that the great majority of the island's population appreciates the value of those goods they possess in abundance – peace, stability, freedom and happiness. The Palanese accept the necessary sacrifices the protection of such goods entail in terms of forgoing wealth and material possessions. *Island* reworks the Romantic aesthetic which underpins both Bernard Marx's desire to gaze meditatively at the sublime seascape of the storm-tossed English Channel, and Huxley's account of his experimentation with Mescaline in *Doors of Perception*. In his essay on the effects of the naturally occurring hallucinatory alkaloid, he suggests that the drug's most significant property is its capacity to shift the usual parameters of sensory experience, and to encounter the world in a revelatory state (Huxley refers to the example of William Blake as a visionary artist, though the detailed examination of the physiological and psychological record of narcotic effect are reminiscent of Thomas de Quincey's confessional narratives). In *Island*, moksha-medicine is the successor to Soma, but this substance is a means for the wide dissemination of Romantic aesthetic insight. Palanese research into the drug 'has clearly shown that quite ordinary people are perfectly capable of having visionary or even fully liberating experiences' (p. 172).

Will has an epiphany when he takes moksha-medicine near the novel's conclusion. There is a distinctive abstraction of form, where 'the inner illumination was swallowed up in another kind of light. The fountains of forms. The coloured orbs in their conscious arrays and purposefully changing lattices gave place to a static composition of uprights and diagonals, of planes and curved cylinders' (p. 269). Huxley leaves his reader in no doubt as to the transformative power of this experience, as Will is said to be 'like a blind man newly healed and confronted for the first time by the mystery of light and colour, he stared with uncomprehending astonishment' (p. 269). For here, there is supposed to be the attempt to distil all meaningful experience; and to take attentiveness as a byword for the fusion of inner and outward perception. The elaboration of this inner state is the incidental experience of Pala itself – just being in the streets, of being sufficiently alert to the everyday in all its sensuous plenitude. Will immerses himself in 'the spaces between the tall buildings [which] echoed with a confusion of English and Palanese, of talk and laughter, of street cries and whistled tunes, of dogs barking, parrots screaming. Perched on one of the pink gazebos a pair of the Mynah birds calling indefatigably for attention and compassion. From an open-air kitchen at the centre of the square rose the appetising smell of food on the fire. Onions, turmeric, fish frying, cakes baking' (p. 241).

Island's utopian perspective is to evaluate the failings of the modern world (as though one were resident in this idealised alternative community), and to view the world beyond Pala as though it were the diametric opposite of the stable organised state; a kind of global dystopia, a mixture of the malice, perversity and accident, which renders many lives insufferable. In a passage reminiscent of Mond's address to the Savage, Will indicatively recounts the inferno-like horrors he has encountered in the course of his journalistic career: the treatment of the black population in Apartheid South Africa, 'the man in the San Quentin gas chamber, mangled bodies in an Algerian farmhouse, and everywhere mobs, everywhere policemen and paratroopers, everywhere those dark-skinned children, stick-legged, pot-bellied, with flies on their raw eyelids, everywhere the nauseating smell of hunger and disease, the awful stench of death' (p. 232). And Huxley also suggests the influence of Marx, Darwin and Freud as grand theorists of capital, evolution and the unconscious has been broadly malign. Marx is condemned for devising a system which leads to totalitarianism in the name of emancipation; Darwin is the prophet of dismal biological determinism; and Freud had reduced the splendour of the human psyche to the brute stimulation of mouth and anus.

If the account of the pervasive awfulness of the modern world seems to correspond with alarming acuity with the list of horrors provided by Mustapha Mond in response to the Savage's insistence on the right to unhappiness, then it also seems that Huxley intended in *Island* to provide a valedictory alternative to the hierarchical Neoplatonic society with its engineered populace; and that switch is signalled by the Palanese attitude to art. It transpires that playwrights are not banished from this ideal society for being liars, or for writing about a human state dominated by fate and suffering. On Pala, canonical works of the Western tradition have been refashioned to the circumstances and expectations of their own compassionate and tolerant society. So, in the Palanese version of Sophocles' *Oedipus*, Jocasta does not commit suicide, and the Theban king does not blind himself when he finally recognises his incest and parricide. Oedipus and Jocasta comprehend their offences; but there are no symbolic implications to their tragedy, because they did not know, nor indeed could have known of the circumstances which led to their taboo relationship; and so they cannot be held culpable. It remains a moot point as to how much dramatic power such an adaptation would retain (and indeed how this differs significantly from the bowdlerised feelie version of *Othello* in *Brave New World*), but it does stand as a rapprochement of art and the ideal society; and as a further sceptical observation on the universal application of Freudian theory as psycho-sexual process, when the myth which gives its name to his most famous complex has been comprehensively revised.

Yet, Huxley could not entirely embrace *Island*'s optimistic social vision. In the conclusion, Pala is overrun by the military forces of the neighbouring island of Rendang in a *coup d'état*; and a leading light of this pacific community is assassinated. Farnaby could have alerted the Palanese to their impending danger; but spiritual rejuvenation, attention to one's psychological needs, and a sensitivity to the world around him did not apparently extend to acting decisively in defence of the principles he had recently embraced. Farnaby may be like one of Greene's tormented English protagonists overseas; but he does not provide their characteristic act of closing self-sacrifice (and the reasons for his inaction are not disclosed). The novel finishes with the drawing together of opposites. The opening call of the Mynah birds for 'Attention', an invitation for spiritual observance, is transformed in the final sentence into the characteristic bark of a military order.

Island's contemporary reviews were mixed. Writing in *The Spectator*, P.N. Furbank detested the Palanese, describing them as 'priggish and arch, sententious, censorious and smug. They are some of the most disagreeable Utopians I have met'; and Frank Kermode commented bathetically in the *Partisan Review* that 'reviewers ought to watch their superlatives, but *Island*, it is reasonable to say, must be one of the worst novels ever written'.[58] Other reviewers were more sympathetic, Wayne Booth thought it a welcome provocation to reflection on current social norms, and a vast improvement on B.F. Skinner's 'simple-minded' behaviourism in *Walden Two* (1948).[59] As Nicholas Murray notes, Huxley was well aware of the book's limitations; he had wondered when writing *Island* whether he was constitutionally suited to narrative fiction, and posited a transcendental intellect which could satisfactorily reconcile art and science.[60] Huxley had produced a model of subjectivity and social relations quite unlike anything to be found in Wells' utopianism; and the short-term anticipatory vision of *Island* would prove more prophetic than that of *Brave New World* both in its description of social and sexual liberation and the consolidation of right-wing juntas in Latin America, southern Europe and Indonesia. In terms of broad outlook, however, the demise of a modern paradise would seem itself to be only a minor variant on the Wellsian outlook. As Huxley established himself at the end of his career as a pessimistic utopian to his predecessor's utopian pessimism.

Both Woolf and Huxley's criticisms of Wells look mild when compared to Orwell's wartime essay 'Wells, Hitler and the World State' (1941). Orwell was infuriated by what he saw as Wells' complacency in underestimating the threat of Nazi Germany and its forces, and of being blindly inconsistent in endorsing fundamental human rights 'of anti-totalitarian tendency' in the Sankey Declaration while still promoting his long-held views on the necessity of a World State, along with 'federal world control of air power'.[61] Wells would then dismiss anyone who could not see the obvious rightness of his proposals. Orwell thought Wells deluded to believe in the inevitable march toward global utopianism, because the idea lacked the visceral attractiveness to persuade anyone to fight for it. Wells' world was one of false oppositions, 'on the one side science, order, progress, internationalism, aeroplanes, steel, concrete, hygiene: on the other side war, nationalism, religion, monarchy, peasants, Greek professors, poets, horses'.[62] Such dichotomies have no purchase. Orwell asks what has kept Britain going over the last year: 'in part, no doubt, some vague idea about a better future', he answers, 'but chiefly the atavistic attitude of patriotism, the ingrained feeling of the English-speaking people, they are superior to foreigners'.[63] It is facile to equate science with progress. 'The aeroplane', he says, 'which has been looked forward to as a civilizing influence, but in practice, has hardly been used except for dropping bombs, is a symbol of the

---

[58] P.N. Furbank, 'Review in the *Spectator*, 30 March 1962', in *Aldous Huxley: The Critical Heritage*, ed. by Donald Watt (London: Routledge & Kegan Paul, 1975), pp. 449–50 (p. 450); and Frank Kermode, 'Review in *Partisan Review*, Summer 1962', in *Huxley: Critical Heritage*, pp. 453–54 (p. 454).

[59] Wayne C. Booth, 'Review in *Yale Review*, 51 (1962)', in *Huxley: Critical Heritage*, pp. 451–52 (p. 452).

[60] See Murray, *Huxley*, pp. 444–45.

[61] George Orwell, 'Wells, Hitler and the World State', in *Essays* (London: Penguin, 2000), pp. 188–93 (p. 188).

[62] Orwell, 'Wells', p. 191.

[63] Orwell, 'Wells', p. 190.

fact'. Orwell concedes his polemic is Oedipal, a 'sort of parricide', that he should acknowledge Wells' influence in confronting the Edwardian conventions of his own youth, 'the world of pedants, clergymen, and golfers'; and that up to the outbreak of the First World War, Wells must be judged 'a true prophet'.[64] Thereafter his oracular powers waned, no grasp of Fascism, and 'too sane to understand the modern world'.[65] Since 1920, Wells had busied himself 'slaying paper dragons'. His 'greatest achievement' was never his utopianism, but his social novels, which 'stopped short of the other war, and never really began again'.[66]

Wells understandably eventually responded to this line of attack in terse and pungent fashion.[67] Yet Orwell's parricide remained incomplete, and the central conceit of Orwell's best-known work *Nineteen Eighty-Four* (1949) is strikingly Wellsian in the consideration of a romance within a rigid social structure and in the intersection of social and utopian fiction. The only moment of radiant colour in a world of systematic dullness is when bold, gamine Julia from the fiction department of the Ministry of Truth, surreptitiously slips a piece of folded paper into Winston Smith's hand as she passes him in the corridor. In Oceania's artless world, the words possess lyrical intensity, a haiku, as the narrator closely aligned with Winston's perspective reveals the three words written in 'large unformed handwriting: *I love you*'.[68] The middle-aged English everyman with aches and pains, thinning hair, with his poor teeth, with his ongoing attempt to reconstruct a personal history from shards of personal memory, scratching away at his diary just out of the sight of the telescreen, is, of course, bewildered by this most improbable approach; and the exchange instigates their doomed romance, the start of the central narrative strand in which the expression of sexual desire and elective emotional attachment to one another have become for the residual middle class, the members of the Outer Party, a political crime.

Orwell was clearly narratively and stylistically influenced by Wells. George Bowling, the first-person protagonist of his cusp-of-the-war novel, *Coming Up for Air* (1939), is a figure from the same provincial shop-keeping background as those featured in *Kipps* and the *History of Mr Polly*. The novel similarly charts George's ascent into the middle class. Orwell is critical of the constraints and perversions of capitalism in the 1920s and 1930s in a manner reminiscent of Wells' economic and social analysis from the Edwardian era; and the literary indebtedness is reflexively indicated. Bowling states that given the similarity in Polly's and his background, 'Wells was the author who made the biggest impression on me'.[69] Gordon Comstock, would-be poet in *Keep the Aspidistra Flying* (1936), may not be a Wellsian figure, but the novel has a Wellsian dynamic to it, with some of *Tono-Bungay*'s naturalism at the beginning and *Kipps*'

---

[64] Orwell, 'Wells', p. 191.
[65] Orwell, 'Wells', p. 192.
[66] Orwell, 'Wells', p. 196.
[67] After a repeating the substance of these charges in a talk on the BBC Indian service, Wells wrote to Orwell: 'I don't say that at all. Read my earlier works, you shit'; see Norman and Jeanne Mackenzie, *The Time Traveller: The Life of H.G. Wells* (London: Weidenfeld and Nicholson, 1973), pp. 430–31.
[68] George Orwell, *Nineteen Eighty-Four* (London: Penguin, 1989), p.113. All subsequent in-text references are to this edition.
[69] George Orwell, *Coming Up for Air* (London: Penguin, 2000), p. 124.

social comedy toward its end. Gordon is the artist in the age of depressive rather than high capitalism, and his contradictory behaviour is a consequence of the warping effect of the cash nexus. He is the scion of a moribund middle class (uncles and aunts either all dead or gone mad without offspring). The notion of the ideal for Orwell, however, tended to tilt toward the retrospective arcadian rather than the utopian; or on occasion, as a fusion of georgic principles with the perfect commonwealth.

A balanced and egalitarian rural community can be glimpsed in Orwell's Soviet parable, *Animal Farm* (1945). After Man's overthrow, and before Napoleon's ascent to absolute power, there was a state in which each animal 'worked according to his capacity', and 'the quarrelling and biting and jealousy which had been normal features of life in the old days had almost disappeared'.[70] The animals adopt a flag for their fledgling state, with a green background 'to represent the green fields of England'.[71] The arcadian is significant in both Orwell's fiction and journalism in the 1930s. There is the piscine eclogue at the centre of *Coming Up for Air*, with George sharing the author's adopted given name and his passion for fishing. Angling becomes a symbol for a kind of essential rural Englishness in the novel, under threat from 1930s commerce and urbanisation, and which may be completely eradicated in the coming war. Middle-aged George returns to his childhood home to find that an ancient pool he wanted to fish has been turned into a waste-pit for a salubrious housing estate. *Homage to Catalonia* (1938), Orwell's account of the Spanish Civil War, concludes with an image of Southern England as arcadia. Having returned from war-torn Spain, he observes that England has 'probably the sleekest landscape in the world', and this England is once more a childhood idyll, 'railway-cuttings, smothered in wild flowers, the deep meadows where the great shining horses browse and meditate, the slow moving streams bordered by the willows, the green bosoms of the elms, the larkspurs in the cottage gardens; and then the huge peaceful wilderness of outer London'.[72] However, the picturesque Home Counties also stand for fatal complacency, the manifestation of 'the deep, deep sleep of England' from which Orwell fears 'we shall never wake till we are jerked out of it by the roar of bombs'.[73]

Orwell developed his views on the positive animating force of essential Englishness in his 'The Lion and the Unicorn: Socialism and the English Genius' (1940, which one might read as a companion piece to his essay on Wells). He drew together in this article an array of strands of opinion and argument, which would not usually be regarded as being compatible with one another: political principles of international socialism with English patriotism, an instinctual account of the nation coupled with adamantine economic and social analysis; an insistence of the inherent civility and peacefulness with some necessary belligerence; and a nationalist nostalgia linked to a blueprint for an egalitarian settlement to be implemented should Britain prevail in the current conflict. England, in this view (and Orwell does not draw any clear distinction between Englishness and Britishness), is constituted by an incidental appeal to fragmentary impressionism, validated by the expectation of the tacit assent of his domestic

---

[70] George Orwell, *Animal Farm; A Fairy Story* (London: Penguin, 2013), p. 20, p. 21.
[71] Orwell, *Animal Farm*, p. 21.
[72] Orwell, *Homage to Catalonia* (London: Penguin, 2000), p. 196.
[73] Orwell, *Homage to Catalonia*, p. 196.

readership. Essential Englishness, he says, is 'somehow bound up with solid breakfasts and gloomy Sundays, smoky towns and winding roads, green fields, and pillar boxes'.[74] Britain is an extended family, with reciprocal ties of affection and obligation; but with the caveat that if the nation is to be viewed as a family, then it should also be acknowledged that the wrong members are in charge (the traditional elite). There is self-conscious naivety, recuperated by ironic knowingness to the trust Orwell places in the 'common people', depicted as bearers of a rich and raucous counter-culture, manifested in the 'comic coloured postcards that you see in the window of cheap stationers' shops'.[75] Such images encapsulate for him their defining features, 'their old fashioned snobberies, their mixture of bawdiness and hypocrisy, their extreme gentleness, their deeply moral attitude to all life'.[76]

The ambivalent expression of traditional English working-class culture reappears in *Nineteen Eighty-Four* in Winston's expressions of disgust and exasperation at the Proles while at the same time recognising that any hope for social transformation of the state of Oceania lies with this strata. The Proles, he believes, still have the capability of challenging the iron grip of the party, because they remain beyond its instruments of direct control; and because they still have conventional kinship networks; they possess beauty and valour, epitomised by the worker-woman seen by Winston and Julia from Charrington's shop shortly before their arrest. Winston reiterates an observation on the Stakhanovite horse, Boxer, in *Animal Farm* that the proletariat possessed the strength to overthrow the existing order. Yet that view is rebutted by O'Brien during Winston's interrogation that no successful revolution has ever arisen from the lowest social class. Oceania's static totalitarian settlement is anticipated by George Bowling in *Coming Up for Air* when he suggests the outcome of the impending war will be 'a kind of hate-world, slogan-world [...]. The secret cells where the electric light burns night and day, and the detectives watching you while you sleep. And the processions and posters with enormous faces, and the crowds of million people all cheering for the Leader into thinking that they really worship him'.[77] In *Homage to Catalonia* Orwell observed in 1930s Britain that 'the gangster gramophone of continental politics is still a rarity, and the notion of "liquidating" or "eliminating" your enemy does not yet seem natural', with the implication of not-yet in England.[78] He subsequently explained he wrote *Nineteen Eighty-Four* as a warning that just because England had resisted Fascism in the 1930s and 1940s, it would be complacent to believe there was any divine prohibition on the emergence of home-grown totalitarianism.[79]

One can detect significant similarities in the visions of *Animal Farm* and *Nineteen Eighty-Four*, both in the identifications of Napoleon and Big Brother with Stalin and Snowball and Emmanuel Goldstein with Trotsky. Indeed, one can discern an extension

---

[74] 'The Lion and the Unicorn: Socialism and the English Genius', in George Orwell, *Essays* (London: Penguin, 2000), pp. 138–87 (p. 139). Further in-text references are to this edition.
[75] Orwell, 'Lion and Unicorn', p. 162.
[76] Orwell, 'Lion and Unicorn', p. 142.
[77] Orwell, *Coming Up for Air*, p. 157.
[78] Orwell, *Homage to Catalonia*, p. 159.
[79] See 'Last of Orwell's Statements on *1984*', in George Orwell, *Seeing Things as They Are: Selected Journalism and Other Writings*, ed. by Peter Davison (London: Harvill Secker, 2014), p. 449.

of the symbolism of the farm's flag representing the green fields of England with Winston's bucolic dream of the 'Golden country', and the way in which the reviving intimacy of Winston and Julia is associated with the summer countryside outside London. Yet, of course, the direction of travel is entirely different: the parable's dénouement is the return of the same capitalist order which had been overthrown in the animals' revolution, so the novel ends with the impossibility of distinguishing pigs from men and men from pigs. In *Nineteen Eighty-Four*, there is the preservation of central features of Stalin's rule of the USSR, as Orwell understood them, with the explicit utopian framing of the Soviet Union in the 1930s, centralised economic planning, cult of personality, infallibility of party, governance by fear, show trials, purges, erasure of disgraced officials from photographs, and the routine detention of ordinary citizens, who were then either liquidated or sent to forced labour camps. Totalitarianism was then conflated with Blitz-damaged London in 1948, with rationing and the dreariness of much post-war experience, captured by the shortage of razor blades, and the uniform branding for dismal monopolised goods, Victory cigarettes, Victory tea and Victory gin. There is the imagined continuation of the V2-rocket strikes on London between September 1944 and March 1945 into perpetual conflict. Having written about warfare since the late 1930s, Orwell found it difficult to break the habit. His vision of permanent remote conflict between super-states had its contemporary resonances in those lower-level conflagrations which immediately succeeded the Second World War, with the first war in Vietnam from 1945, First Indochina War, and the Greek Civil War from 1946 (the first proxy conflict of the Cold War).

Keep the Aspidistra Flying remains Orwell's most effusive literary creation. Gordon Comstock, the protagonist, is writing his long Johnsonian poem, 'London Pleasures'. He works in a second-hand bookshop in the Charing Cross Road, surrounded by the dusty tomes of eminent Victorians, Carlyle, Pater, Ruskin and Stevenson. He attacks socialism by suggesting that it is like Huxley's *Brave New World*, 'only not so amusing: four hours a day in a model factory, tightening up bolt number 6003. Rations served out in greaseproof paper at communal kitchen. Community hikes from Marx Hostel to Lenin Hostel and back.'[80] Gordon quotes Baudelaire; and wanders through a symbolic forest in Berkshire. At one point a limousine full of gilded youth sweeps past him in central London, as though they were the *jeunesse dorée* from Waugh's *Vile Bodies* (1930). Community hikes, of course, are a facet of Julia's party life in *Nineteen Eighty-Four*. Yet the overall direction of Orwell's dystopia is in the opposite direction to his 1930s literary satire. The philologist, Syme, subtracts rather than adds words to the state-approved dictionary; and the poet, Ampleforth, with his keen sense of prosody, spends his working life removing literary ambiguity, symbolism and nuance – producing ideologically pure versions of canonical poems for state anthologies. As Steven Connor suggests, the novel's logic seems to cancel out its own narrative, rendering the whole enterprise as an 'unbook', un-writing itself as it goes along in much the same way that Winston Smith is systematically rendered by O'Brien as an '*unperson*'.[81]

---

[80] George Orwell, *Keep the Aspidistra Flying* (London: Penguin, 2000), p. 97.
[81] Steven Connor, *The English Novel in History 1950–1995* (London: Routledge, 1996), p. 212.

That sense of entropic writing, of entrapment, can be expressed another way. Orwell's Eton contemporary, Steven Runciman, noted that he felt more 'pity for the human condition than for the individual human'.[82] As Runciman was almost certainly aware, this was pretty much an inversion of Jonathan Swift's opinion of himself. Swift declared to Alexander Pope in 1727 that 'I hate and detest that animal called man, although I heartily love John, Peter, Thomas and so forth'.[83] Yet the space between those perspectives on reflection can seem slight. Orwell, as we saw in chapter three, admired Swift; and there is a distinctly Swiftian cast to *Nineteen Eighty-Four* in the systematic and detailed progression of a set of proposals, expressed in journalistic prose, which do not allow for any conceptual escape from what is being suggested. Just as there is a meticulous logic to Swift's *A Modest Proposal* – so there is a remorseless animated completeness to the system of social control devised by Ingsoc, of surveillance, indoctrination, arbitrary disappearances, torture and control of the present through the overwriting of the past, so that nearly all 'facts' and even those bits of misinformation which were once taken to be 'facts' are reduced to the seamless orthodoxy underpinning the party's current position. Yet the novel's central animating force, despite these literary and political illusions, still seems to be Wells; and it is possible to read the text as an extended rejoinder to Wells' early vision and its refraction of Plato – a modern dystopia to match his modern utopia.

The stability of Wells' global state is reimagined as the stability of three power blocs perpetually at war where it is the ongoing conflicts which counter-intuitively produce the sense of security between each combatant. The extensive bureaucracy of the Modern Utopia becomes the ministries of *Nineteen Eighty-Four* with the bureaucratisation of every aspect of one's life. The state has been able to achieve Thomas More's goal of the eradication of privacy; as Winston reads in Goldstein's *The Theory and Practice of Oligarchical Collectivism* (partially penned by O'Brien), 'with the development of television, and the technical advance which made it possible to receive and transmit simultaneously on the same instrument, private life came to an end' (p. 214). The influence of Plato can be detected in the pyramidic structure of three classes of Inner Party, Outer Party and the Proles, and with virtually no exchange of personnel between them. As O'Brien subsequently makes clear during Winston's re-education, meaningful art will be banished, insofar as there 'will be no distinction between beauty and ugliness' (p. 280); and the state of Oceania shares the Platonic hostility to the family, echoed by Wells. Like Plato's Kallipolis and the Modern Utopia, there is no codified body of law. The family will be abolished (except as an extension of the thought police), and the Platonic state's asceticism in the *Republic* will be extended into all sexual activity with Wellsian bureaucratic nicety and some sweeping scientific optimism. O'Brien proclaims 'the sex instinct will be eradicated. Procreation will be an

---

[82] Quoted in Minoo Dinshaw, *Outlandish Knight: The Byzantine Life of Steven Runciman* (London: Allen Lane, 2016), p. 33.
[83] Swift to Alexander Pope, 29 September 1725, in *The Correspondence of Jonathan Swift*, ed. by David Woolley, 4 vols (Frankfurt am Main: Peter Lang, 1997–2007), II (1997), pp. 606–9 (pp. 606–7); Woolley notes that the epigram is contained in 'the most celebrated passage in Swift's correspondence accessible to the reading public since 1741', p. 609, n. 7.

animal formality like the renewal of a ration card. We shall abolish the orgasm. Our neurologists are at work on it now' (p. 280).

Where there is convergence between a *Modern Utopia* and *Nineteen Eighty-Four* is in the response to the nineteenth-century vision of pastoral idealism. Big Brother denigrates Morris as much as Wells. The brotherhood, the supposed opposition which Winston and Julia attempt to join, has an echo of Morris's Pre-Raphaelite brotherhood. The world of Ingsoc, O'Brien proclaims, 'is the exact opposite of the stupid hedonistic Utopias the old reformers imagined' (p. 279). Yet at that point there is a departure from all utopian principles, as O'Brien confesses the party's only aim is the consolidation and maintenance of power; and this is to be achieved through hatred – 'a world of fear and treachery and torment' (p. 279). The striking aspect of this particular vision is not just the employment of the expression and devices of twentieth-century utopianism as popularised by Wells, but that Orwell produced an original account in which the dystopian is presented not merely as the negative of the ideal beneficent settlement. The utopian opposite is constructed originally in full and candid consciousness, a social blueprint in which all its implications have been unapologetically worked through. There is no pretence to the anti-utopian being merely the accidental consequence of good intentions gone awry, or as a necessary evil on the way to future stability, equality and happiness. Winston's recurrent use of a phrase which he associates with O'Brien 'we shall meet in the place where there is no darkness' may seem to afford a final allusion to the description of Pandemonium in Milton's *Paradise Lost*, 'no light but only darkness visible/ Served only to discover sights of woe'; yet that is not so much a manoeuvre to place the narrative within an explicit Christian schema as to provide a further symbolic resonance to twentieth-century totalitarianism.[84]

However much we may be tempted to see *Nineteen Eighty-Four* as an inversion of Wellsian utopian principles, it still remains possible to conceive of the novel as imaginatively reconfiguring many of the same elements: the relationship of the self to the social whole, the exploration of love in the future state (like much of Wells' fiction, *Nineteen Eighty-Four* is a story of a failed romance), the nature of authority and one's response to it, and the prophetic capabilities of narrative fiction. Huxley claimed in a letter to Orwell that *Brave New World* would prove a more accurate prophesy than *Nineteen Eighty-Four* (and he believed its explication of systematic torment had its origins in the works of Sade).[85] That claim to pre-eminence has become increasingly open to question in the developing capacities of some twenty-first-century states, especially those with authoritarian tendencies, to employ digital apparatuses and media to monitor the movements and interactions of their populations.[86] Yet one could, if one were so inclined, also see Orwell's own ending in Wellsian terms. When terminally ill in University College Hospital London in 1949, there was a plan to move Orwell to a sanatorium in Switzerland. His friend, the journalist Malcolm Muggeridge,

---

[84] Milton, *Paradise Lost*, ed. by Alastair Fowler, rev. 2nd edn (Harlow: Pearson Education, 2007), p. 64 (ll. 62–63).
[85] Huxley to Orwell, *Letters*, pp. 604–5.
[86] See, for example, 'Big Data, Big Brother: China Invents the Digital Totalitarian State: The Worrying Implications of its Social-Credit System', *The Economist*, 17 December 2016 [https://www.economist.com/briefing/2016/12/17/china-invents-the-digital-totalitarian-state, accessed 11 April 2019].

recalled that Orwell kept a fishing rod in his room in anticipation of this journey and the final forlorn hope of recovery, the hope for a return to the perfect personal state of Bowling's piscine eclogue, a symbol of light and tranquillity in opposition to chaos and darkness, that elemental struggle in which all utopianism must eventually find its place. It was a circumstance in keeping with the conclusion of Wells' *Tono-Bungay*, with a lyricism never appreciated by Woolf, when weary George Ponderevo endeavours to reconcile himself to his allusive ideal, to encapsulate the flux of the world all around him. 'We are all things that make and pass', he reflects, 'striving upon a hidden mission, out to the open sea'.[87]

---

[87] Wells, *Tono-Bungay*, p. 389.

6

Post-Utopia: America in the 1970s

Don Siegel's best-known film, *Dirty Harry* (1971), begins with the camera focussed on a star badge emblazoned on the memorial plaque in the San Francisco Hall of Justice. It then pans down the list of the city's fallen police officers. The camera cuts to a fish-eye view of a muzzle interspersed with the rifleman's point of view as he looks through the cross-hairs of a telescopic sight. The cumulative effect is disorientating: the rifleman is apparently looking directly downwards from the top of a skyscraper at a sundeck pool situated atop the roof of another tall building (the sense of menace heightened by Lalo Schifrin's atonal score). The sharply-angled camera tracks a young woman in a yellow crimped swimsuit as she crawls across the pool. The scene reaches its climax with a muffled shot, a tell-tale trace of blood, and with the swimmer rotating slowly. The next wide-angle take introduces the protagonist, the police detective Harry Callaghan (Clint Eastwood), as he enters through the roof hatch to inspect the crime scene; there is the first instance of the movie's grim humour: the viewer can just make out a sign in the background, it warns swimmers that they enter the pool at their own risk.

The most memorable image from the opening sequence, however, is when Callaghan climbs to the top of the other skyscraper. He uses his pen to retrieve a spent rifle case from the roof-top gravel. The camera then swings expansively around the detective to reveal a sublime view of San Francisco, with the rich azure of the bay and Golden Gate Bridge. On a cloudless spring day, the solitary figure appears to be set against a backdrop of the New Jerusalem, a city of refulgent whiteness. Harry stands there – 1970s icon – tall, lean, hint of ruggedness, longish hair and attired as though he were a traditional school teacher. The film's early success seems to have been dependent on a kind of heterotopic displacement – that the audience recognised they were being presented with the mythological expectations of the western; but those familiar pioneering virtues of toughness, resilience, independence, an innate sense of the difference between right and wrong, a readiness to act decisively in the interests of justice, were now set against the bewildering kaleidoscope of contemporary American life.

Dirty Harry might have been a novel conflation of western and thriller; but as a thriller it was short on suspense with the perpetrator revealed in the opening scene. The shooter is a demented blackmailer calling himself 'Scorpio' (Andy Robinson), who demands $100,000 from City Hall, otherwise he will kidnap and murder randomly selected San Francisco citizens (which he duly does). Callaghan pursues his quarry, eventually trapping him and, indeed, beating him to extract a confession on the Kezar Stadium's floodlit playing field (near Golden Gate Park). Callaghan subsequently discovers that the murderer has been freed, because he had not followed appropriate procedures for arresting suspects; and because the evidence he gathered was inadmissible without the necessary warrants. The film's conclusion sees Scorpio hijack a school bus. Contravening his orders, Callaghan intercepts the vehicle. When the bus is finally halted, he chases Scorpio to a lake, where in spite of the location's general downbeat appearance, there is still a suggestion of an arcadia in the setting of bulrushes and lapping waters – even of piscine eclogue – with a teenage boy fishing on the bank. Scorpio takes the boy hostage, and Callaghan, trusting his aim, shoots his revolver, winging the sociopathic killer. The youth runs off. Harry recites a speech he has honed for moments of independent justice of this kind. He denigrates his felled opponent in the style of a Homeric warrior before administering the *coup de grâce*. In a final moment of disgust at the modern world, Harry throws his star-shaped police badge into the lake, as though it were Excalibur.

On *Dirty Harry*'s release, critics of a liberal persuasion lambasted the movie as an exercise in distasteful right-wing propaganda. While acknowledging the iconographic aspects of Eastwood's portrayal ('saint cop', 'Camelot cop'), Pauline Kael condemned the movie for its latent fascism, concluding that the whole enterprise had been 'deeply immoral'.[1] The film's surface narrative could be readily translated into symbolic form in which the solitary man is convinced of his own rectitude, with an infallible ability to discern good from evil. Self-serving politicians capitulate at the first sign of threat, and then extoll the rights of the accused while ignoring those of the victims.[2] If Siegel's film could be condemned as being reactionary, then it was equally offensive in its moral reductionism. It dispensed with any sense of social complexity to reveal a stark Manicheanism of the you're-either-for-us-or-against-us variety. It was not difficult to see which cultural group the film had in its sights. Siegel told the youthful, long-haired and pacific Robinson that he had cast him as the psychopath, rather than the pot-bellied, balding, middle-aged degenerate specified in the film's script, because he took to his 'choirboy' looks; though he might equally have observed that he was struck by Robinson's ability to combine a cherubic appearance with wide-eyed cackling mania.[3] But everyone understood that Scorpio, with his unkempt hair, dishevelled apparel, multiple beaded bracelets and leather belt with peace-badge buckle, was supposed to be a hippy, a representative of 1960s American counterculture.

No accident either that the film is set in San Francisco and the Bay Area. From the middle of the 1960s, the conurbation was a hub for opposition to mainstream America. The University of California Berkeley became a byword for student protest, academic dissent and revolutionary fervour. The Black Panthers, the most militant group in

---

[1] Pauline Kael, 'Saint Cop', *The New Yorker*, 15 January, 78–82, reprinted in *Deeper into the Movies: The Essential Kael Collection, from '69–'72* (London: Marion Boyars, 1996), pp. 385–88 (p. 388). See also Dennis Bingham's discussion of the film along the same lines, in his *Acting Male: Masculinities in the Films of James Stewart, Jack Nicholson and Clint Eastwood* (New Brunswick, NJ: Rutgers University Press, 1994), pp. 180–95.

[2] See Joe Street's account of the law-enforcement and political backdrop to *Dirty Harry* in his 'Dirty Harry's San Francisco', *The Sixties: A Journal of History, Politics, and Culture*, 5 (2012), 1–21 (pp. 9–12).

[3] Andy Robinson discusses the original characterisation and his casting by Siegel in the documentary *Dirty Harry: The Original* (Warner Brothers, 2008).

pursuance of the cause of African-American liberation, was founded by Bobby Seale and Huey Newton in Oakland in 1966. By the mid-1960s, the run-down quarter of Haight-Ashbury on the eastern side of Golden Gate Park in San Francisco was attracting a youthful vivid community, espousing an ersatz philosophy of peace, love, tolerance and happiness. Haight historian, Charles Perry, has described the district's social economic organisation by the mid-1960s as being a collective of the nation's 'first urban agricultural communes'.[4] This was to extend a nineteenth-century tradition of rural religious communities with idealistic principles into twentieth-century cosmopolitanism. However, the community could also be seen as a collective expression of Morris's anarchist principles. For there was the more-or-less spontaneous attempt to ruralise the modern city. These latter-day communards were committed to, if not entirely dispensing with cash, then getting by with as little of it as possible. They could disregard conventional morality, constructing new-style social units from collective amity and personal desire, rather than being subjected to the obligations of blood relations, and the expectations of the nuclear family. Individual distinctiveness and an intrinsic sunniness of temperament could be exhibited through one's clothes. Morris's characterful bin man declared his radiant sense of being by dressing as a medieval baron, and his sartorial expressiveness found its modern equivalent in the ad-hoc costumes of Haight's inhabitants, often assembled from the district's second-hand clothes shops.[5]

This new world was to be an 'epoch of rest', inasmuch as it was not to be subjected to the requirements of capitalist labour. Work was, in theory, to be of the aestheticised communitarian kind. It was to be embodied in the art of performance and participation, most clearly expressed through music with the emergence of such performers as The Grateful Dead, Jefferson Airplane, Quicksilver Messenger Service, Janis Joplin, and Big Brother and the Holding Company. But music as an art form was also to be complemented by street theatre, mime troupes, dance performances and poetry recitals. If Morris seemed to provide the template for a creative, leisured and radically free society, then the hippies and their fellow travellers also looked to Herbert Marcuse's writings for a conceptual justification for a liberated and libidinous modern society. In *Eros and Civilization* (1956), Marcuse proposed that the classical psychoanalytical assumption that civilisation was dependent on subjugation of instincts was not consistent with much of what Freud had actually said about the fundamental psychological condition of the human subject. Marcuse advocated a reconfiguration of advanced society, such that civilisation should not be conceived as necessarily repressive, but as an extension of libidinous instinct.

Giving free rein to Eros would not inevitably result in disaster. Far from it: 'under non-repressive conditions', Marcuse suggested, 'sexuality tends to "grow into" Eros – that is to say, toward self-sublimation in lasting and expanding relations'.[6] And 'Eros',

---

[4] Charles Perry, *The Haight-Ashbury: A History* (New York: Wenner Books, 2005), p. 260.
[5] Perry, *Haight-Ashbury*, p. 6. See also Jim Marshall's contemporary photographs of the area in his *The Haight: Love, Rock, and Revolution* (San Rafael, CA: Insight Editions, 2014), pp. 50–51, 64, 69, 97, 98, 100, and 102.
[6] Herbert Marcuse, *Eros and Civilisation: A Philosophical Inquiry into Freud* (London: Ark, 1987), p. 222.

when freed from the constraints of modern instrumentalism, 'strives for eternalizing itself in a permanent *order*'.⁷ We should no longer be confronted with the choice of either living under oppressive civilisation or reverting to 'prehistoric savagery'.⁸ Society could be utopian, not in any dead-end fantastical sense, but in the concrete opportunity of establishing peaceable, happy and orderly communities, entirely consonant with our fundamental psycho-sexual drives.⁹ Jerry Garcia, a lead member of The Grateful Dead, summed up this spirit of Eros and intrinsic order, when he declared in 1967 that 'we inherited the evil and wars, but chose to ignore to death, rather than try to kill off everyone who does not see Utopia as we do. The movement of Joy is spreading and we are glad to be a part of it'.¹⁰

An aspect of the Haight community, unforeseen by either Morris or Marcuse, was the extensive use of drugs as a means of personal transformation. Marijuana seems to have been ubiquitous; smoked to maintain a certain hazy mellowness. The other significant substance was the synthetic hallucinogen, LSD (legal until 1967).¹¹ Extensive use of LSD in the Bay Area by the mid-1960s was a consequence of two interlinked factors: its high-profile advocacy by the former pharmacological scientist Timothy Leary and the rumbustious novelist, Ken Kesey, and the drug's widespread availability, which by the later part of the decade was being manufactured locally and distributed at low cost. In his acerbic history of the era (written not long after the decade came to a close), William O'Neill characterised Leary as a figure of distorted religious zeal. Extending Huxley's drug proselytising in *Doors of Perception* (1954), Leary had insisted that the 'heightened awareness stimulated by "consciousness-expanding" drugs brought undreamed-of sensual pleasures [...]. Even better, drugs promoted peace, wisdom, and unity with the universe'.¹²

In *The Electric Kool-Aid Acid Test* (1968), the journalist Tom Wolfe attempted to recreate what he termed 'the mental atmosphere and subjective reality' of Kesey and his followers.¹³ Kesey had enjoyed considerable success with his debut novel on a patient rebellion in an Oregon mental hospital, *One Flew over the Cuckoo's Nest* (1962). He had originally taken LSD as part of drug trial for the US military when he was a postgraduate creative-writing student. By 1964, he had established an alternative commune in La Honda, west of San Jose, with a group of like-minded revellers, known as the Merry Pranksters.¹⁴ Wolfe retrospectively charted their acid-suffused excursions in their psychedelically-painted school bus, named 'Further'. Kesey and the Pranksters

---

⁷ Marcuse, *Eros and Civilisation*, p. 222.
⁸ Marcuse, *Eros and Civilisation*, p. 154.
⁹ Marcuse, *Eros and Civilisation*, p. 154.
¹⁰ Jerry Garcia, in the first edition of the Grateful Dead's newsletter, *The Olompali Sunday Times*, March 1967, quoted in Peter Richardson, *No Simple Highway: A Cultural History of the Grateful Dead* (New York: St Martin's Press, 2015), p. 91.
¹¹ On the criminalisation of LSD in the USA and Canada, see Erika Dyck's *Psychedelic Psychiatry: LSD from Clinic to Campus* (Baltimore: Johns Hopkins University Press, 2008), pp. 128–132, and pp. 136–37.
¹² William L. O'Neill, *Coming Apart: An Informal History of America in the 1960's* (Chicago: Ivan R. Dee, 2005), p. 239. See also Dyck, *Psychedelic Psychiatry*, pp. 101–18.
¹³ Tom Wolfe, *The Electric Kool-Aid Acid Test* (London: Black Swan, 1995), p. 367.
¹⁴ See Alex Gibney and Alison Ellwood's documentary film, drawing on the Pranksters' contemporary footage, *Magic Trip: Ken Kesey's Search for a Kool Place* (A&E Indie Films, 2011).

travelled to New York, ostensibly for the launch of his second novel, *Sometimes a Great Notion* (1964), and to attend the 1964 World Fair, but really as a kind of collective mind-expanding homage to Jack Kerouac's *On the Road* (1957). Among many escapades, there is an account of the group's attendance in Day-Glo costumes at a Californian Unitarian Church conference near Monterey. In a typical prankster affront, Kesey outraged his audience by trampling on the American flag during an address on emotional dependency, only then to produce a moment of patriotic affirmation when he held aloft the Stars and Stripes and led the communal singing of 'America the Beautiful'. The episode was indicative of Kesey's modus operandi as insightful and provocative jester. Sage-like foolishness was to be combined with the carnivalesque, as a state of celebration, liberation and misrule. Yet, for all Kesey's oppositional energy and ethos, as Wolfe makes clear, there was always a strong sense of American uniqueness and patriotism to his saturnalia.

The beginning of the end for Haight counterculture has been traced to its greatest success. In January 1967, 'the Human Be-In', an all-day festival was held in Golden Gate Park, opened by Beat poet Alan Ginsburg. He chanted 'We are One'; and over twenty thousand hippies turned up, peacefully eating, drinking, dropping acid, listening to San Francisco bands; and at the end of it all, they collectively cleared up the litter before heading home. However, as Geoff Guinn notes, 'if the neighbourhood was Eden for hippies, then the San Francisco media inadvertently became the serpent'.[15] The event was covered extensively by the local press; and these accounts with television and photo-journalist pieces were then distributed nationally.[16] The result was that the Haight became celebrated as an alternative idyll. Whereas prior to its national coverage the district attracted only a handful of penniless youngsters every day, in the months after the Be-In numbers rose rapidly to over 300 a day. The conservative city authorities were unsympathetic to the new arrivals. The increased population contained psychotic and criminal elements; and a hard-drug culture rapidly took hold in the district. It was, as Guinn notes, a dispiriting and rapid downward spiral from the highpoint of the 'hippie utopia' of the festival.[17] Yet, the central difficulty for Guinn was not so much the press reporting the emergence of this loosely-associated Californian community, committed to the principles of peace, love, freedom and happiness, but rather Charles Manson's orchestration of bizarre murders in and around Los Angeles in the decade's closing year.

Manson was a petty criminal from the Mid-West. By a circuitous route, he ended up living with a young librarian in Berkeley in 1967; and while entertaining thoughts of a career as a musician, he took to preaching in the Haight. According to Guinn, he was a charismatic orator whose street philosophy was a potpourri of 'Beatles song lyrics, biblical passages, Scientology, and the Dale Carnegie technique of presenting everything dramatically'.[18] Manson gradually acquired a group of young female acolytes. At the end of 1967 he and his 'family' relocated to the Los Angeles area in order to fulfil his

---

[15] Jeff Guin, *Manson: The Life and Times of Charles Manson* (London: Simon & Shuster, 2014), p. 91.
[16] See Marshall's photographs of the event in *The Haight: Love, Rock, and Revolution*, pp. 120–27.
[17] Guin, *Manson*, p. 92.
[18] Guin, *Manson*, p. 95.

ambition of becoming more famous than the Beatles. By 1969, the family was living in a ranch in the Santa Susannah Mountains, north of the San Fernando Valley. Manson devised a doctrine of 'Helter Skelter' after a song on the Beatles' *White Album* (1968), which he interpreted as a prophecy of race war. Manson believed social chaos needed to be brought about as a prelude to the New Age (in which his musical genius would be acknowledged). He instructed family members to commit a series of ritualised murders for which he intended the Black Panthers should be blamed. On 9 August 1969, Manson family members murdered the actress Sharon Tate and five others at her Bel-Air residence. The following night, family members randomly selected and killed a middle-aged supermarket executive and his wife at their home in the Los Feliz district of Los Angeles. They carved the word 'War' on the dead man's abdomen, and scrawled various provocative slogans in blood around the house, including a misspelt 'Healter Skelter' on the fridge door.

Manson was arrested and charged in December 1969, and went on trial for multiple homicides in June 1970. The proceedings and Manson's disruptive behaviour in court receiving global coverage. The Republican president, Richard Nixon, made political capital out of the events, fulminating that the accused was made 'to look like a glamorous figure to the young people he brought into his operations [...] the judge seemed to be a villain'.[19] The beliefs and actions of Manson and his associates could be co-opted to a narrative in which the kind of anarchic society to which hippies aspired did not result in Eros, but in Thanatos; not in the dizzy carnivalesque of the Merry Pranksters 'doing their thing', but in the drug-addled macabre of the Manson family. O'Neill had no doubt that Manson's conduct exemplified 1960s counterculture. The wilful abandonment of reason and convention had its inevitable upshot. Manson, he concluded, was the symbol 'of the repressed hostility, authoritarianism, perversity, and mindless paranoia that underlay much of the hippie ethic'.[20]

Siegel's *Dirty Harry* is said to be based on the Zodiac series of unsolved murders in California from 1968 onwards.[21] However, the film's casting and principal photography took place against the backdrop of Manson's arrest and trial.[22] And Andy Robinson, who played Scorpio, also bore a striking resemblance to the infamous defendant. Yet the film does not allow for any straightforward opposition of its central figures. *Dirty Harry* maintained a conceptual distance between the viewer and its titular character, such that events are never viewed straightforwardly from the detective's perspective. The film also suggests an uncomfortable equivalence between its principal figures: Callaghan tortures his suspect in the football stadium; and his rage at injustice shades into sadistic delight in the extraction of a confession. The film closes with a mirroring of the initial sequence, but with Callaghan now cast as the killer. There is a medium shot of Scorpio's body floating in the lake, reminiscent of the young woman in the pool,

---

[19] Richard Nixon's speech is quoted in Vincent Bugliosi, *Helter Skelter: The Shocking Story of the Manson Murders* (London: Arrow, 1992), p. 439.
[20] O'Neill, *Coming Apart*, p. 264.
[21] See Robert Tanitch, *Eastwood* (London: Cassell, 2005), p. 77.
[22] Manson and other family members were formally sentenced on 19 April 1971, see Guin, *Manson*, p. 385. Principal photography on *Dirty Harry* started the same month, see Patrick McGilligan, *Clint: The Life and Legend* (London: HarperCollins, 1999), p. 207.

and the final close-up of Harry's sheriff-like badge is a reminder of the ornament at the top of the memorial to San Francisco police officers, with which the film begins.[23]

Just as *Dirty Harry*'s dénouement seems to anticipate the demise of American counterculture, the movie does not fully endorse the conservative conspectus which its protagonist inconsistently embodies. One might, moreover, regard the film as providing a sceptical commentary on two rival versions of post-war American idealism. On the one side, there is the image of American decency of the Eisenhower era of the 1950s; and on the other side, revolutionary counterculture of the 1960s. If the film seemed to exemplify the irreconcilable tensions of America in a period of social upheaval, race riots and the Vietnam War, then it also seemed to capture a growing mood of despondency across the political spectrum with the recognition that by the 1970s America was in a post-utopian moment. The opportunity to create the good society from both perspectives had been squandered.[24] Post-war American economic expansion was clearly at an end. Oil prices quadrupled in 1973 and food prices rose by 40 per cent in two years. The economy defied standard analysis by having no growth, rising unemployment, *and* being inflationary simultaneously (termed 'slumpflation'). Median household income fell for the first time since the Second World War.[25] The progressive spirit of the 1960s ebbed away. Leading members of the Black Panthers met violent deaths. The issues which animated political opposition lost their potency, particularly the war in Vietnam. President Nixon introduced the Vietnamisation policy in 1969, reducing direct American involvement in the conflict. The draft was replaced with a lottery system, and federal judges refused to prosecute draft resisters. In the same period, the conservative political elite were in turmoil. The Watergate investigations resulted in the imprisonment of prominent Republican figures, as well as the eventual impeachment and resignation of Nixon as president in 1974. Personal narratives tend to underscore that sense of terminus of what might be termed the long 1960s.[26] An editor of San Francisco radical journals recalls he took a job mid-decade at 'Yellow Cab to rethink what I was doing with my life.'[27] A prominent figure in the highly

---

[23] For Siegel's technical and conceptual prowess, see Andrew Sarris's 'Don Siegel: The Pro among the Pod People', *Film Comment*, September to October 1991, 34–38.

[24] For an alternative Marxian perspective on American utopian periodisation, see M. Keith Booker, *The Post-Utopian Imagination: American Culture in the Long 1950s* (Westport, CT: Greenwood Press, 2002), especially pp. 5–10.

[25] The changing circumstances of the USA economy from 1945 to 1980 are considered by Gary M. Watson and Hugh Rockoff in their *History of the American Economy*, 10th edn (Mason, OH: South Western Thomson, 2005), pp. 565–88. See also Stephen K. McNees' self-explanatory 'A Brief Overview of Post Wold-War II Expansions', in *History of the U.S. Economy since World War II*, ed. by Harold G. Vatter and John F. Walker (Armonk: NY: Sharpe, 1996), pp. 48–51. Walter W. Heller offers a succinct account of the factors which led to the 1970s downturn in his 'Activist Government: Key to Growth', in Vatter and Walker, pp. 283–88. For contemporary perspectives on 'slumpflation' or 'stagflation' (the preferred term in the UK), see 'Inflation: Seeking Antidotes to a Global Plague', *Time*, 8 April 1974, 18–25, and 'Getting Ready for an Economic Doomsday', *The Economist*, 31 August 1974, 37–38.

[26] For an overview of the social and political challenges of the period, see James T. Patterson's chapter, 'Unsettling Times: from Nixon to Reagan', in his *America in the Twentieth Century: A History*, 5th edn (Belmont, CA: Thomson Wadsworth, 2000), pp. 445–87.

[27] Peter Booth Wiley, interviewed in San Francisco, 12 August 2015, and email, Wiley to the author, 19 August 2015. See also Wiley's 'Where Did All the Flower's Go?: The View from the Street in Bernal Heights', in *Ten Years that Shook the City: San Francisco, 1968–1978*, ed. by Chris Carlsson (San Francisco: City Lights Books, 2011), pp. 95–107.

politicised and theatrical Yippies (Youth International Movement), who spent the late 1960s protesting, writing for alternative newspaper, the *Berkeley Barb*, and visiting Hanoi and Havana, moved with her young family to the Catskills in 1974, she said, 'for a quieter life'.[28]

These apparently unpromising circumstances for utopian composition also paradoxically made the mid-1970s one of significance for utopian literary projection, precisely because it was the first time in the Western tradition that the notion of the good society seemed to have been in reach for so many of the state's citizens. Yet, the waning of counterculture and the discrediting of conventional politics meant that writers interested in this genre had to self-reflexively consider what an ideal society might look like, just at the point at which the possibility of establishing such a social and economic settlement seemed to have vanished. Three American novels in particular, written in short order in the mid-1970s (and considered consecutively in what follows), extended the capacity for expressiveness and reflection in the genre of utopian fiction, and encapsulated the weariness and irreconcilable difficulties of their era. These works are Eric Callenbach's landmark account of ecological utopianism, *Ecotopia* (1975), Ursula K. Le Guin's examination of the psychological and social implications of standard utopian topoi from the perspective of the late twentieth century, *The Dispossessed* (1974), and Marge Piercy's mixture of melodrama, criminal biography, feminist polemic, asylum novel and utopian romance, *Woman on the Edge of Time* (1976).

Callenbach's *Ecotopia* is set in 1999; and, as such, occupies the same future era as Bellamy's projection of Victorian Boston at the start of the second millennium. *Ecotopia* has a first-person narrator, William Weston (with a surname reminiscent of Bellamy's Julian West). Weston is a north-eastern journalist, filing copy to his Manhattan paper from San Francisco, part of an independent state on the western seaboard of North America, which seceded from the rest of the United States at the end of the 1970s, and now has little contact with its former nation. The novel has two alternate strands. Weston produces reports to be published in his newspaper, and these are interspersed with personal reflections recorded in his journal. Weston has a complicated private life, a divorced and resentful wife (the mother of his daughter), a materialistic mistress in New York; and he embarks on a tempestuous relationship with one of the Ecotopians, the tree-loving Marissa. Weston's progress is similar to that of Will Farnaby, Huxley's protagonist in *Island* (1962), from being a cynical self-centred journalist to adopting a more candid and relaxed outlook; and Weston ultimately chooses to make his life in *Ecotopia*, rather than returning to the industrial and corporate United States. As Callenbach conceded, the novel suffered technical shortcomings with many of the characters drawn sketchily and the plot assembled haphazardly.[29] However, the novel proved markedly popular on its publication; and that success was a consequence of

---

[28] Judith Gumbo, interviewed in Berkeley, 13 August 2015.
[29] Callenbach acknowledges the novel's technical shortcomings in an afterword written in 2004. He also notes that his Ecotopian prequel *Ecotopia Emerging* (1981), intended to address these narrative deficiencies, made little impact; see Ernest Callenbach, *Ecotopia* (Berkeley, CA: Heyday, 2014), p. 169.

Callenbach adopting and developing a range of contemporary environmental ideas, and expressing them in an appealing utopian format.

The ecological movement of the 1970s, to which *Ecotopia* gave imaginative impetus, can be understood to have significant origins in the work of the American Paul Goodman in his *Growing up Absurd* (1960) and *Communitas* (1960), with roots in the anarchist thought of Proudhon and Kropotkin. Goodman both opposed the way in which large corporations dominated and structured American life and offered detailed proposals for the development of decentralised communities and forms of industrial production, which operated on a personal and local level. In the late 1960s ecological ideas were formulated and disseminated in America through the establishment of journals such as *Whole Earth Catalog* and *Mother Earth News*. Friends of the Earth was founded as an anti-nuclear campaigning organisation in San Francisco in 1969, the first Earth Day advocating environmental reform was held in 1970 (as a response to a massive oil spillage off the coast of Santa Barbara), and E.F. Schumacher's influential *Small is Beautiful*, which counsels the use of sustainable alternative technologies on both moral and practical environmental grounds, was published in 1973. Callenbach's novel was clearly intended as a contribution to contemporary environmental discussion and the personal and psychological advantages of an ecological lifestyle. However, *Ecotopia* was also a work that sought to refashion the Romantic nature writings of Henry David Thoreau and John Muir from the nineteenth and early twentieth centuries. By doing so, the novel was part of that strand of American culture which regarded wilderness as a common birthright. Marissa is a member of a committee which cares for thousands of acres of mixed woodland, and she affirms to Weston a Thoreauvian doctrine of sylvan belonging. 'The forest is my home', she declares, 'among the trees you're safe, you can be free' (p. 50).[30] And Weston's observation on 'a gentle ordinary-looking young man, not visibly drugged leaning against a large oak and muttering "Brother Tree"' is reminiscent of Muir's anthropomorphic and mythopoeic contemplation of giant sequoia in Yosemite.[31]

There is an anarchic disdain for urban conurbations in Callenbach's novel, on the grounds that such places produce estranged and alienated inhabitants, and dense populations inevitably cause environmental damage. In *Ecotopia*, cities have been thoroughly ruralised, and the urban populations have dispersed throughout the new state of their own volition. 'New minicities grew up in favourable locations', Weston reports, 'Napa, on its winding, Seine-like river, at last pollution-free; Carquinez-Martinez stretching out along rolling hills down to the Strait. [...] Old city residential areas were abandoned and razed, and the land turned to parks and reforested' (p. 62). The state has not been entirely dismantled in this new nation; however, executive powers have been strictly curtailed. Hospitals and schools function on a community level; factory farms have been abolished, 'and commune and extended family farms are encouraged' (p. 62). Families are bound together by mutual affection and candid

---

[30] See, indicatively, Henry David Thoreau on industry and solitude in *Walden* (Oxford: Oxford University Press, 1997), ed. by Stephen Fender, pp. 102–17, and pp. 123–26.

[31] Callenbach, *Ecotopia*, p. 58. Further in-text citations are to this edition of the novel. See John Muir, *The Yosemite* (1912), selected in *Journeys in the Wilderness: A John Muir Reader* (Edinburgh: Birlinn, 2009), pp. 427–503 (pp. 467–78).

feeling, rather than by social obligation and blood ties. Life is not governed by clock time, but shaped by the length of the day and the season. Watches have not been banned as in machine-adverse Erewhon, but Weston notes that few Ecotopians bother to wear them. There has been a progressive discarding of the redundant materialism of late twentieth-century society. Weston suggests it was the middle aged at the point of the great change who found it hardest to adapt to the new order when the acquisition of goods was no longer deemed an appropriate aspiration, although there is no blanket ban on the ownership of private property in this society.

If the forests serve in *Ecotopia* as a symbol for the progressive greening of the state, then they still retain a practical purpose. Trees are treasured, but also sustainably logged for paper, lumber and as a substitute for aluminium and synthetics. Technology is embraced insofar as it enhances people's lives without causing environmental damage. Wood is processed by Ecotopian scientists to produce biodegradable plastics. Any device deemed harmful to the planet is banned; so, there are no microwave ovens or cars running on gasoline. Freeways have been converted into railway tracks (with rapid magnetic-levitation trains). Oil and gas power plants have been shut down, because of emissions, and atomic-fission reactors phased out because of their radioactive by-products. Solar, wave and thermal power have been developed. Weston admires the hot springs in northern California as a kind of ecologically satisfying alternative to the Victorian blast furnace. 'It is a hellish scene', he observes, 'billows of steam issue from pipes and wells, with loud hissing noises; the earth seems to be about to explode' (p. 103). Yet, despite its sublime appearance, the system meets the key requirements of geo-thermal efficiency and integrated secondary usage: 'cost is low, it adds virtually no pollutants to the atmosphere, and only a small amount of warm water to the run-off in nearby streams – one of which has become the site of swimming resorts that are even open in winter' (p. 103). When Weston discards successive drafts of his newspaper report, Marissa upbraids him for wasting paper. Ecotopian households separate all their trash to be processed and reused.

Underpinning Callenbach's environmental vision is a model of stable-state economics. As Richard Frye has noted, Callenbach's views in this respect were almost identical to those of the ecological economist, Herman Daly, who produced his key work on this topic in 1977.[32] Both Callenbach and Daly dismiss the central tenet of orthodox capitalism that a healthy economy must be one which is growing. The notion that an expanding GDP is an indication of financial well-being is predicated on two key errors from their perspective: it assumes an inexhaustible supply of natural resources; and the central mechanisms of commercial enterprise are inherently self-regulating. Both Callenbach and Daly argue for a profound change in the relationship of society to environment, from exploitative dominion to dynamic equilibrium – a reconciling of the aspirations and requirements of human beings with their ecological responsibilities.[33] Daly suggests that faced with finite resources the supposed principal

---

[32] See Richard Frye, 'The Economics of Utopia', *Alternative Futures: The Journal of Utopian Studies*, 3 (1980), 71–81 (p. 71).

[33] On economic equilibria, see Herman E. Daly, *Steady-state Economics*, 2nd edn (London: Earthscan, 1992), p. 69, and pp. 122–23.

good of never-ending economic growth is as unachievable as it is undesirable (a position he denigrates as 'growthmania'). The fundamental tenet of the good society is the even maintenance of supply and demand, whereby output matches input, and consumption equals production.[34]

From an economic ecological perspective, global aims should be to decrease production and achieve a more equal distribution of social and economic goods. 'If people count equally and the marginal utility of income diminishes for each person', Daly states, 'then the presumption is that an equal distribution of wealth and income would maximise the interpersonal sum of utility and service'.[35] The fall in economic production in Ecotopia at the time of secession was precipitous, 30 per cent of GDP. Weston describes the chaos which ensued with capital flight and collapsing markets and conglomerates. However, he also suggests the systemic shock provided the opportunity to restructure the economy on a sound ecological basis, and to render society more equal and just. The experience of developed nations in the early part of the twenty-first century suggests there are in practice scant benefits to such a sharp contraction. There is little discernible change to overall wealth distribution; and the young and the poor are effected disproportionately.[36] Although Callenbach's position is certainly consistent with his earlier *Living Poor with Style* (1972), a manual for sustainability, drawing on the necessary parsimony of his own Depression-era childhood. Callenbach does not at any point discuss Ecotopia's fundamental economic system; but one can surmise that he intends it to be a restricted version of American capitalism, complemented by some modern European social provision. Ecotopians still use money for the exchange of goods and services, though their bank notes have been beautified. They are 'very Romantic in style, [with] lush, Rousseau-like scenes, almost tropical, with strange beasts and wondrous plants' (p. 81), a currency rendered sufficiently exotic to obscure its residual instrumentalism.[37]

Ecotopia's descriptions of vigorous lovemaking are of a piece with its sense of psychological and libidinal freedom as a necessary condition for the fulfilled society. In practice, couples are 'generally monogamous', Weston reports, 'except for four holidays each year, at the solstices and equinoxes, when sexual promiscuity is widespread' (p. 66). Sexual relations are conceived predominantly as being heterosexual; and as Naomi Jacobs has pointed out, there is minimal engagement with 1970s feminism (of which Callenbach must have been aware as a founder of *Film Quarterly* and an editor at the University of California Press in Berkeley).[38] Female characters are still largely defined by how they look; and they behave stereotypically (such as bursting into tears when challenged). The Ecotopian president is a woman, but her appearance suggests that a combination of attractiveness and authority would be an inappropriate

---

[34] Daly, *Steady-state Economics*, p. 183.
[35] Daly, *Steady-state Economics*, p. 81.
[36] I have in mind Greece after the sovereign debt crisis in 2009. See *The Politics of Extreme Austerity: Greece in the Eurozone Crisis*, ed. by Georgios Karyotis and Roman Gerodimos (Basingstoke: Palgrave Macmillan, 2015), especially Athanasia Chalari, 'Reorganising Everyday Greek Social Reality: Subjective Experiences of the Greek Crisis', pp. 160–78.
[37] An allusion to the post-impressionist painter, Henri Rousseau, rather than to Jean-Jacques.
[38] See Naomi Jacobs, 'Failures of the Imagination in Ecotopia', *Extrapolation*, 38 (1997), 318–26 (p. 321).

conflation of gender types; as Weston observes the president is 'rather plain and a trifle stout' (p. 147).

Race relations are dealt with cursorily. The secession of the Pacific North West is followed with the new state's own internal moment of separation along racial lines, as African-American Ecotopians choose to found their own autonomous communities. The departure was consistent with urban black separationist policy as advocated by Malcolm X, but remains hard to reconcile with Ecotopia's general co-operative spirit; and merely confirms race as a defining social and cultural division in the new social order. Equally anomalous is the attitude to violence. Weston describes ritualised war games as a central component of Ecotopian life. He is initially taken aback by these conflagrations, describing them as 'Ecotopia's Dark Side' (p. 71); though he is eventually persuaded to participate in them (and wounded as a result). Marissa makes the case for the visceral necessity and candour in such savagery, when she claims of American military technology that 'we had to develop it because we can no longer bear just to bayonet a man' (pp. 58–59). The games suggest a repudiation of a Marcusian view of a co-operative human psychology with a return to Freud. Violence is a defining constitutive drive, even if it is ultimately weaker than the libido.[39] For Callenbach, aggression is clearly an intrinsic aspect of human beings, and hence requires a means of release through ritualised combat even in this pacific ecological community.

It remains a moot point as to whether such observations on instinctual savagery are best accepted as a universal claim for the propensities of human beings; or more restrictively as an acknowledgement of the enduring aspects of American foundational mythology – of the occasional necessity to resort to arms and force in the pioneering endeavour of the great push westward through the nineteenth century. The inability to realise fully the anarchic elements of the projections of the ideal state, along with its conventional sexual politics and acceptance of violence as an immutable trait led Heinz Tschachler to criticise *Ecotopia* as a work of eco-totalitarianism, the product of 'despotic reason' applied to green concerns.[40] Tschachler is clearly not concerned with the role of *Ecotopia* as an early and influential proponent of discrete environmental policies which would come to be regarded as being conventional by the early part of the twenty-first century. Theses measures include sustainable manufacturing, energy efficiency, recycling, restrictions on cars (and the move to electric vehicles), promotion of public transport, pedestrian precincts and urban bicycle schemes; though the wider economic principles of a steady-state system are still not widely accepted.

Indeed, when Callenbach reflected on the influence of Ecotopia in the second decade of the twenty-first century he would highlight the adoption of pragmatic measures rather than its overarching idealised vision.[41] There is, however, another way of viewing the limitations of the social reformulation in *Ecotopia*. In this interpretation, the book provided a version of the environmental state which had the potential both to

---

[39] See Erich Fromm, *The Anatomy of Human Destructiveness* (London: Pimlico, 1997), p. 356.
[40] See Heinz Tschachler, 'Despotic Reason in Arcadia? Ernest Callenbach's Ecological Utopias', *Science Fiction Studies*, 11 (1984), 304–17.
[41] *Ecotopia or Bust – Ernest Callenbach* (2009), [https://www.youtube.com/watch?v=pczXBYJuab0&t=1454s, accessed 28 January 2019]

reconcile and transcend the conflict between conservative and radical conspectuses of the ideal state in 1970s America, to offer a new departure, in which renewable technologies could be seen to be beneficial to the environment and for which a commercial case could also be made. As the ecological historian Hal Rothman points out, it was not that the green movement and the causes of environmentalism were uncontentious in the America of the mid and late 1970s. However, the idea that the environment needed protecting was an area of public policy which enjoyed significant bipartisan support. Richard and Pat Nixon marked the first Earth Day in 1970 by planting a tree in the grounds of the White House. That semblance of political consensus lasted until the accident at the Three Mile Island nuclear power plant in 1979, and President Ronald Reagan's appointment of free-marketeer James Watt as his first Secretary of the Interior in 1981.[42]

The run of copies of *Time* magazine in 1974 provides a vivid sense of the epoch regarding itself as both dispiriting and bizarre. There are reports on: the oil crisis; the emergence of a black underclass; weekly updates on Watergate; and undisguised astonishment at the turn of events in the Bay Area. In March that year, newspaper heiress, Patty Hearst, a student at University of California Berkeley, was kidnapped by the Symbionese Liberation Army. She showed up a few weeks later as an SLA guerrilla, having assumed the nom-de-guerre, Tania, and having participated in the robbery of the Hibernia Bank in San Francisco.[43] The magazine carried a photograph of a poster proclaiming 'we love you Tania' on the Berkeley campus bulletin board.[44] Overseas, there were accounts of terrorist outrages in the Middle East, famine in Africa and the Khmer Rouge's ominous advance on Phnom Penh. The magazine's British correspondent reported on winter strikes, resulting in a three-day working week and power cuts. The journalist conveys the Blitz spirit of ordinary Britons enduring everyday privations, but his descriptions are also reminiscent of Orwell's drab vision of a totalitarian England in *Nineteen Eighty-Four* (1949).

A *Time* article, well attuned to this prevailing gloomy spirit, is 'The Ghost Town of Gantries'. David Lee reports in this piece on the dilapidated state of Cape Canaveral in Florida, the launch site for the Apollo Space Programme. The programme had been recently wound up due to excessive expense, waning public interest and political expediency.[45] Lee declares that the pad with its Saturn rockets and gleaming equipment were once a symbol of American confidence and ambition. Now, all he sees are weeds and rust. He reports how the 'launch towers and other equipment at the complex that cost $68 million were sold as scrap.'[46] The sense of lost illusion since Armstrong and

---

[42] Hal K. Rothman, *The Greening of a Nation? Environmentalism in the United States since 1945* (Belmont CA: Wadsworth, 1998), p. 169.
[43] See William Graebner, *Patty's Got a Gun: Patricia Hearst in 1970s America* (Chicago: Chicago University Press, 2008), p. 24.
[44] 'The Hearst Nightmare', *Time*, 29 April 1974, 27–33 (29).
[45] See John M. Logson, *After Apollo? Richard Nixon and the American Space Program* (New York: Palgrave Macmillan, 2015), pp. 117–24.
[46] David Lee, 'The Ghost Town of Gantries', *Time*, 15 April 1974, 33.

Aldrin stepped onto the Moon in 1969 is palpable. Lee quotes the director of the Johnson Space Center: 'the space program furnished a spiritual drive that brought this country together in a way we have not experienced in peacetime since the early exploration of the land we live in'.[47] Post-utopian ennui is rendered explicit in one of the article's subheadings, with the space programme and launch site now described as 'corridors to nowhere'.[48]

There is little evident charisma in the account of space travel at the beginning of Ursula K. Le Guin's *The Dispossessed*, published in the year of Watergate, Patty Hearst, Cambodia, slumpflation and the scrapped space programme. Le Guin's protagonist, the dissident scientist, Shevek, attempts to leave Anarres for her propertarian sister planet, Urras. He makes his way through a rioting mob, some bent on killing the 'traitor', and he then climbs aboard the gargantuan Urrasti freighter, *Mindful*.[49] The narrator describes the ship preparing to launch, supported by 'its huge skeletal gantries', 'its lack of human scale', and the engines' ominous appearance with their 'vast black tunnels' (p. 8). When the rockets fire the crowd scatters; the hulk lifts off, leaving an ashen patch. Le Guin belongs to the first generation of writers for whom space travel is a historical actuality, rather than being exclusively a matter of imaginative projection; and at this juncture, she is one of the first authors to be writing about space travel and other worlds when the actual pursuit of manned space exploration has lost its allure.

The *Dispossessed* initially had a subtitle of 'an ambiguous Utopia', and Le Guin's fiction from the late 1960s onwards has a prominent strain of examining the perplexing contrariness which imagining the ideal state often entails. *Left Hand of Darkness* (1969) is an amalgamation of Woolf's shifting sense of gender in *Orlando* (1928) with the fantastical frozen vision of C.S. Lewis's Narnia chronicles. The uninhibited fluency of sexual being in Le Guin's hermaphrodite Eskimo-like tribe is contrasted with its rigid beliefs and destructive paranoia over external influences. Her short story 'The Ones who Walk away from Omelas' (1973) is a speculative arcadia, which while ostensibly taking its cue from William James, replays a dilemma ironically contemplated by More in his account of Utopian bondsmen – that the price of happiness for the many must be the misery of the few (in this case a single child). *The Word for World is Forest* (1972) is a militant parable of the Vietnam War where the jungles' defoliation by Agent Orange becomes a master metaphor for American moral turpitude. The novel takes place on a densely wooded planet, which is being aggressively logged by alien colonists. The timber is then shipped back to polluted treeless Earth in vast inter-planetary haulers. The colonists oppress and exploit the pigmy indigenous forest-dwellers, the Athseans, who accord cultural significance to their dreams (as an extension of concrete reality); and who, left to their own devices, would enjoy a pacific existence among their arboreal glades. Dreams are also central to *The Lathe of Heaven* (1971), a Sartrean foray with an imaginative existential examination of good and bad faith. An oneirologist, William Haber, discovers that one of his patients, George Orr, can alter reality through his dreams. Haber develops a technique to direct Orr's reconstructive dreaming; and

---

[47] Lee, 'The Ghost Town of Gantries', 33.
[48] Lee, 'The Ghost Town of Gantries', 33.
[49] Ursula K. Le Guin, *The Dispossessed* (London: Gollancz, 2002), p. 7. Further in-text citations are to this edition of the novel.

having exhausted the possibilities for his own professional advancement, he turns his attention to perfecting the planet and humankind, with ambiguous results. The elimination of pollution, war, racism, poverty, inequality and disease comes at the price of creating a drab society in which no-one can be distinguished from anybody else. A disheartened Orr surveys this perfect homogenous world and asks of his physician, 'why is everything so shoddy, why is everybody so joyless'?[50]

In the *Dispossessed*, the theoretical physicist, Shevek, feels compelled to leave his native Anarres, because he finds himself effectively disbarred from academic work by an influential scientist, who has passed off Shevek's innovative research as his own. Shevek goes into exile, believing he will enjoy academic freedom on Urras, and that his original if unorthodox investigations will be supported for their contribution to scientific knowledge. He becomes increasingly disillusioned as he realises that Urras's material allure and wealth disguises its extreme social inequality; that all dissent is ruthlessly suppressed; and that he has been under surveillance since he arrived on the planet. His research on a unifying theory for instant transportation and communication, 'a theory of the General Field in temporal physics' (explicitly compared to Einstein's general theory of relativity) was never regarded by his hosts as a noble intellectual pursuit in itself, but exclusively valued for its potential military applications, and as a means to secure a political and commercial advantage over competitor planets. As Shevek exclaims at the height of his disaffection with Urras, 'you cannot say good morning without knowing which of you is "superior" to the other, or trying to prove it [...]. There is no freedom' (p. 286). The book's central structural feature is its alternating chapters on Shevek's experience on Urras with those recounting his childhood, adolescence, and young adulthood on Anarres, including the difficulties he experiences in his career and in maintaining his relationship with his partner, Takver, and their daughter, Pilun. The novel concludes with the two strands dovetailing, as Shevek returns to his home planet on the *Davenant*, an interstellar craft from a third planet, Hain. He only leaves once he has made his potentially transformative equations on space and time available to all peoples. In the closing scene, Shevek envisages his reunion with Takver and Pilun. He wishes that he had brought back a picture of a lamb for his daughter to see (as a symbol of childhood, innocence and arcadia). 'But he had not brought anything', the narrator observes, 'his hands were empty, as they had always been' (p. 319).

Utopian ambiguity is split across the novel's sister planets in the solar system of Tau Ceti: between the rich and abundant Urras and the arid and egalitarian Anarres (the latter is sometimes described as the former's moon). Anarres's colony was founded by a visionary, the female Urrasti seer, Odo. She had led her followers from Urras, some 200 years before the novel's central events (with an oblique allusion to the early tradition of American utopian religious communities, such as Shakers, Rappites and Zoarites). Daniel Jaeckle notes a key influence on Le Guin for the imagining of Annaresti social principles is the nineteenth-century Russian anarchist, Peter Kropotkin, in its earnest anti-materialist co-operative spirit.[51] Yet, the text also resonates with the social idealism

---

[50] Ursula K. Le Guin, *The Lathe of Heaven* (London: Gollancz, 2001), p. 147.
[51] See Daniel P. Jaekle, 'Interpersonal Ethics in Ursula K. Le Guin's *The Dispossessed*', *Anarchist Studies* 20 (2012), 61–77.

of More, Morris, Plato and Wells. Anarres's anarchism is explicit, as the narrator explains, 'there was to be no controlling centre, no capital, no establishment for the self-perpetuating machinery of bureaucracy and the dominance-drive of individuals seeking to become captains, bosses, Chiefs of State' (p. 81). While the egalitarian principles of Odonians are consonant with Morris's social principles, they still eschew the anarchic pastoralism of *News from Nowhere* (1890). Odo, the narrator reveals, 'had no intention of trying to de-urbanise civilisation' (p. 81). The planet's arid terrain, however, means the demographic distribution resembles More's *Utopia* (1516). Cities are sparse, practical and minimal in design, and like those of Utopia, they have few private spaces; all conurbations have to be surrounded by a sufficient expanse of land to be able to support their populations (a large territory out of necessity on Anarres, because of the soil's poor quality).

Individual desires and wishes on Anarres have to be subordinated to the community's greater good, both in terms of the allocation of employment, and one's personal relationships. There is a strong sense of collectivism. Like More's Utopia in the sixteenth century and the People's Republic of China in the middle and later part of the twentieth century, almost the entire population is required to undertake social duties in addition to their usual employment. In Utopia, this was regular periods of agriculture work, and the Annaresti perform community service every ten days. Technology is ubiquitous, though not for the purposes of providing material comfort for its citizenry, but as a means to survive in a forbidding environment where crop failure is a frequent occurrence. And while Ono originally condemned bureaucracy, contemporary Anarres is similar to Wells' Modern Utopia in the central storage of information for the global state's effective administration, a 'human/computer network of files' with an 'enormous, continual input and outgo of information concerning every job to be done, every position wanted, every workman needed, and the priorities of each in the general economy of the worldwide society' (p. 222).

Aspects of Anarres are also reminiscent of the *Republic*, even if these associations entail some intriguing inversions. There is widespread nursery provision and dormitory-style accommodation for much of the adult population. The state's rationalism is encapsulated in the Annaresti language, described late in the novel by the Terran ambassador, as she attempts to flatter Shevek, as 'the only rationally invented language that has become the tongue of a great people' (p. 280). There may be no formal governance; but there is still a clear sense of hierarchy in its various committees, social organisations and syndicates, in which the intellectual elite assumes a leading role. Anarres has almost no visual culture; and ironically, from a Platonic perspective, the one art form which endures on the planet is theatre, known as 'the Art', 'a thing complete in itself' (p. 131). Travelling companies are described as being as 'welcome as the rain in the lonely desert towns', and their productions 'rising out of and embodying the isolation and communality of the Annaresti spirit' (p. 131). Yet the only playwright specifically discussed in the *Dispossessed* stages a disastrous satire, and ends up suffering a form of internal banishment – confined to an asylum.

Shevek's destination on Urras is A-IO, clearly intended as an imaginative recreation of contemporary North America. There are also mentions, in passing, of an authoritarian centralised state with a command economy, the cadre of Thu (for which read the

USSR), and an ongoing war in a third-world country (for which read Vietnam). A-IO is initially presented as a nation of extraordinary wealth, opulence, grandeur and sensuousness, with its Manhattan-like skylines, impressive houses and apartments, and chic restaurants. In an early encounter with Iotic design, Shevek is taken aback by its sensual sigmoidal forms in contrast to the brutal functionalism of Anarresti architecture. He is struck by 'the smooth curves' of an Iotic interior, 'into which stubborn wood and steel had been forced; the smoothness and delicacy of surfaces' (p. 19). Yet, the visual, tactile and olfactory sumptuousness of A-IO is always on the cusp of excess. When visiting a confectioners in the New York-like Nio Esseia, Shevek is overwhelmed by ambrosial odours wafting through the store, 'the air was sweet and warm, as if all the perfumes of the spring were crowded into it' (p. 173). In the midst of an animated discussion on the benefits of state socialism and the fact that daily struggles on Anarres for survival have worn down the animating idealism of Odo's foundational pronouncements, Shevek casually rests his hand 'against the ornate, gold in-laid mantelpiece' of his Urrasti apartment (p. 144).

The planetary division of the *Dispossessed* suggests an allegory of contemporary geopolitics combined with some pertinent reflections on both the promise and limitations of canonical utopian projection. And the central conceit is self-evidently to establish a dynamic between opposing ideas of the good society. Both projections are, to a lesser or greater extent, compromised by their own internal contradictions. The novel is not a straightforward manifesto for dynamic Odonian anarchism as it is sometimes read from a political-science perspective.[52] At its most fundamental, this was a matter of contrasting the principal goods of both planets – the pleasures of living in a comfortable and affluent society which is constructed on the basis of instrumental relationships versus a society of refreshing equality and communal spirit, but at the price of comfort and the likelihood of any stability in one's personal relationships. The text plays out these oppositions in a number of ways, and does so in a noteworthy fashion through its aesthetic considerations. As Shevek comments, beauty is all-pervasive in the smarter Iotic districts, except, that is, in the anxious expressions on the inhabitants' faces. The converse is also true, as Shevek asserts, 'on Annares, nothing is beautiful, nothing but the faces' (p. 190).

The novel's opposition of anarchic and propertarian visions has attracted some criticism, or at least significantly qualified praise. For Fredric Jameson, writing in the mid-1970s, the *Dispossessed* was a beguiling exercise in utopian reductionism. The novel committed a 'positive omission' in its portrait of Ononian anarchism on barren Urras; there is the significant absence 'of the Darwinian life-cycle itself, with its predators and victims alike the sign that human beings have surmounted historical determinism, and have been left alone with themselves to invent their own destinies'.[53] And Jameson subsequently swung this critical perspective around in the early years of this century to consider the shortcomings of the portrayal of the possessive Iotic

---

[52] See contributions to *The New Utopian Politics of Ursula K. Le Guin's* The Dispossessed, ed. by Laurence Davis and Peter Stillman (Lanham: Lexington Books, 2005).
[53] Fredric Jameson, 'World Reduction in Le Guin' (1975), reprinted in his *Archaeologies of the Future: The Desire Called Utopia and Other Science Fictions* (London: Verso, 2007), pp. 267–80 (p. 272).

society, such that the reader never gains a clear insight into its system of governance. Le Guin's narrative bravura goes hand-in-hand with an emphasis of Urras's excessive consumption, but without he says, 'a complementary critique of the political and social drawbacks of capitalism'.[54]

Tom Moylan struck a similar note of detraction in his influential account of 1970s American science fiction, *Demand the Impossible* (1984). Moylan coined the term 'critical utopias' to describe the novels of Piercy, Joanna Russ and Samuel R. Delany, in addition to those of Le Guin. The critical utopia was supposed to be a literary means of advancing a radical political and social agenda. This type of writing harnessed concrete reformatory possibilities of conventional utopias, while dispensing with the didactic blueprints characteristic of earlier utopian fiction. These were authors ready to exploit all the liberating imaginative possibilities of the utopian genre. 'Inspired by the movements of the 1960s and finding new imagery in the alternatives being explored in the 1970s', Moylan writes, 'the critical utopia is part of the political practice and visions shared by a variety of autonomous oppositional movements that reject the domination of the emerging system of transnational corporations and post-industrial production and ideological structures'.[55]

Moylan went on to provide what still remains the most stimulating single-chapter account of the *Dispossessed*. However, Le Guin's novel also proved to be a considerable disappointment for him – failing to live up to the radical utopian agenda which he had envisaged for it. He thought Le Guin had stumbled in her best-known work. She had eschewed experimentalism for a standard realist style. Where was the feminist manifesto? Homosexuality was banished to the margins. Le Guin had chosen that staid figure of a Caucasian man for her protagonist, and charted his progress through a tired device, the 'bourgeois *Bildungsroman*'.[56] The author, furthermore, had gone out of her way to celebrate social orthodoxy in Shevek's wish for a settled life with his nuclear family; and she had structured the book as a series of static binary oppositions, thereby enshrining the dominion of one term over another. Chris Ferns subsequently addressed a number of these criticisms. Ferns pointed out that there are plenty of commanding female figures in the *Dispossessed*; a gay character plays a significant role in the narrative; if the central relationship is one in which the nuclear family is prominent, then the text does not lack for depictions of alternative social arrangements; Le Guin uses a wide range of figures across her writing, and her choice of a conventional protagonist should be understood in the context of such narrative diversity; the novel's binary oppositions are constantly shifting, undermined by their internal contradictions (and Moylan anyway works within his own master binary of 'critical utopia' and 'transnational corporation'). If Le Guin's text is realist, then at least it offers a sustained examination of utopian possibilities in this era; and in this respect, her novel differs significantly from two of the books Moylan champions for their refreshing radicalism, Joanna Russ's *The Female Man* (1975),

---

[54] Jameson, *Archaeologies of the Future*, p. 156.
[55] Tom Moylan, *Demand the Impossible: Science Fiction and the Utopian Imagination* (London: Methuen, 1986), p. 11.
[56] Moylan, *Demand the Impossible*, p. 109.

and Samuel R. Delany's *Trouble on Triton* (1976). Russ and Delany's novels certainly provide multifaceted, polyvalent forms of literary expression, but the utopian is presented as only one scenario among many, and the ideal social form becomes incidental to the main thrust of the works as imaginative explorations of contemporary sexual mores.[57]

One might suggest, furthermore, that the main difficulty with the notion of the critical utopia is that it also tends to reduce literature to proselytising in the cause of a particular ideology without any means of sustaining an interpretative distance from the events or phenomena being described. Another way of approaching Le Guin's book would be to regard it as an exemplification of its period, without limiting that representation to a single perspective. This could be generally summarised as the novel's success in encapsulating and inflecting the prevailing national mood, with its compromised utopianism to be set alongside President Jimmy Carter's diagnosis of an America malaise in the 1970s, a lack of confidence across the political spectrum.[58] Jameson suggested that in spite of the *Dispossessed*'s realist credentials, one can still detect various other narrative types in the book, such as travel narrative, Orwellian dystopia, and the adventure story. So, like all good modern science fiction writing, Le Guin's book exhibits what he terms 'generic discontinuities', stylistic fissures, reminiscent of the expressive capabilities of the older forms, a collage which operates, he says, as 'a kind of foregrounding of the older generic models themselves, a kind of estrangement effect practiced on our generic receptivity'.[59]

Yet for all the generic variety one might wish to discern in the *Dispossessed*, the book still remains a striking work of determined realism, with its omniscient narrator, explicit establishing frameworks, coherent and consistent temporal and spatial relations, clear demarcation between internal and external experience, privileged access to the psychological states of a main character, a figure who substantially focalises the novel's action; and whose thoughts, calculations and impulses are revealed through a mixture of dialogue, narration and free indirect discourse. And one might argue, moreover, that it is not so much generic discontinuities which are pertinent in this context, but the kind of 'necessary anachronisms' which Georg Lukács proposed as the hallmarks of the realist genre in the first half of the nineteenth century, the means by which European novels could step outside their historical confines (such as in Scott's Waverley fiction), and capture something akin to the totalising spirit of their own age.[60] Whereas historical distancing was a central consideration for Lukács; in Le Guin's text, it is the tension between the fantastical settings of the work and the persuasive concrete documentary descriptions through which its various episodes are realised. This was a case both of finding appropriate geo-political parallels to the inter-connected histories

---

[57] See Chris Ferns, *Narrating Utopia: Ideology, Gender, Form in Utopian Literature* (Liverpool: Liverpool University Press, 1999), pp. 218–29.

[58] Jimmy Carter, transcript of television address, 15 July 1979 [read at http://www.pbs.org/wgbh/americanexperience/features/primary-resources/carter-crisis/, accessed 23 October 2015].

[59] Jameson, 'Generic Discontinuities in SF; Bran Aldiss' *Starship* (1973), reprinted in his *Archaeologies of the Future*, pp. 254–66 (p. 263).

[60] See Georg Lukács, *The Historical Novel*, trans. by Hannah and Stanley Mitchell (London: Merlin Press, 1962), especially pp. 34–55.

of Anarres and Urras, and of working through the material and psychological implications of living in a long-standing anarchic community.

The mutually suspicious and distant relationship of the planets can, of course, be interpreted as an imaginative reworking of Cold War rivalries of the USA and the USSR. The book certainly keys into the concerns expressed in the Western press on the treatment of dissidents in the Soviet Union. From the middle of 1973 until early the following year, there were weekly reports in the American media on the persecution of the novelist Alexander Solzhenitsyn. In February 1974, Solzhenitsyn was stripped of his USSR citizenship and deported from Moscow to Frankfurt (making the cover of *Time*). And in the mid-1970s, the Russian nuclear scientist Andrei Sakharov began to attract interest in the West by taking a public stance on human-rights abuses in the Soviet Union. While a contemporary concern with Soviet dissidents is an aspect of the novel, the main prototype for Shevek seems to have been a central figure in twentieth-century American history, an internal dissident. Shevek's experience corresponds in some respects with that of J. Robert Oppenheimer, the leading American theoretical physicist of the 1930s and 1940s, and director of the Manhattan Project developing the atomic bomb during the Second World War. Le Guin knew Oppenheimer. Her father, the cultural anthropologist, Alfred Kroeber, was a colleague of Oppenheimer's at UC Berkeley in the 1930s, and the physicist visited the family home on a number of occasions.[61] Shevek possesses a number of Oppenheimer's traits – brilliance at conceptual physics, a facility with languages, attractiveness, unworldliness, social gaucheness, an unwillingness to discuss science with anyone outside of his discipline, and sympathy for radical politics.

One can also detect parallels in the respective narratives. Shevek works for the government of A-Io without being fully aware of the implications of his undertaking. Oppenheimer was shocked by the dropping of the second bomb on Nagasaki in 1945, described in an FBI report as a 'nervous wreck' on hearing of the effects of the attack.[62] He was kept under intensive surveillance by the FBI from before, during, and after his directorship of the Manhattan Project. Shevek's pursuit by Iotic security services in the novel's later stages had its real-world equivalent in Oppenheimer's appearance before the House Un-American Activities Committee in the 1940s and 1950s. And Shevek's attempts to make his discovery of a temporal-spatial simultaneity universally available have a correspondence with Oppenheimer's various post-war initiatives to use atomic science, 'as a real instrument in the establishment of peace', as he wrote.[63] Yet, for all of these instructive similarities, one cannot quite discern an exact analogy between the physicist and Le Guin's protagonist. It was rather the author attempted to produce an impressionistic sense of contemporary American parable, an exemplification of how Oppenheimer's friend, Isidor Rabi, once attempted to summarise the scientist as being a constellation of 'many bright, shining splinters'.[64] Shevek took on the guise of the

---

[61] See Charlotte Spivack, *Ursula K. Le Guin* (Boston: Twayne, 1984), p. 2.
[62] Report quoted in Ray Monk, *Inside the Centre: The Life of J. Robert Oppenheimer* (London: Vintage Digital, 2012), p. 456.
[63] Oppenheimer to Marcelle Bier, 31 August 1945; quoted in Monk, *Inside the Centre*, p. 461.
[64] Quoted in Monk, *Inside the Centre*, p. 3.

modern mythologised American inventor; a figure whose own experience includes a radical alternative vision of social organisation and a confrontation with the state.

The *Dispossessed* seems especially adept at mapping a sense of complex interiority onto external reality, and then naturalising that sense in a concrete world. The result is an intriguing chiastic dynamic. From a contemporary American perspective, the anarchic society of Anarres is rendered, if not familiar, then at least approachable though the habituated perceptions of the indigenous Shevek; while the ostensibly familiar consumerist world of Urras is rendered strange, as Shevek attempts to decipher its perplexing social and economic codes. The novel's realism also operates by providing persuasive accounts both of the degeneration of the utopian state and the implications of a society which puts the collective before any notion of personal happiness. One significant thread is the shift from the kinetic circumstances of the anarchic state when it was founded on Anarres to exhausted stasis by the time Shevek is an adult. The political machinations on Anarres, which lead in part to Shevek's decision to leave for affluent Urras, are reminiscent of the kinds of conflicts and faculty manoeuvrings in academic life (as, say, described by Alison Lurie in her campus fiction from the same period).

The personal difficulties of Anarres's directed collectivism, even under optimal circumstances, are made compellingly clear; especially in the requirements made of women. In an early scene, Shevek is hospitalised after an accident. He is visited by his mother, with whom he has had almost no contact since he was a young child (she is a successful engineer). He understands the obligations that the state places on its ablest citizens, but he is still resentful; unable to overcome the nagging sense of having been abandoned. When they meet, he refuses to acknowledge any bond between them. When his mother departs, both having exchanged courteous if cool farewells, he thinks he sees, but cannot quite be sure, his mother's face momentarily contort in anguish. However much one might be tempted to criticise such episodes, despite their psychological precision and narrative subtlety, as being little more than demonstrations of an emotional essentialism, the contemporary referent remains pertinent as to the choices many women were obliged to make in the 1970s, especially those employed in such notionally idealistic fields as academia, between competing demands of career and family.

The aesthetic aspects of Shevek's experience once more come to the fore in the book's conclusion. The altruistic Hainish provide an interstellar ship, the *Davenant*, to take the physicist back to his home planet. As if to emphasise the story's circularity, the narrator compares the appearance of this craft to the one in which Shevek left Anarres for Urras in the opening chapter. The *Davenant* 'was about as different as it could be from the freighter *Mindful*' (p. 313). The Hainish vessel, the narrator goes on, 'was as bizarre and fragile as a sculpture in glass and wire; it had no look of a ship at all' (p. 313). There is even a garden aboard, 'where the lighting had the quality of sunlight, and the air was sweet with the smell of earth and leaves' (p. 313). The synthetic space-borne Eden suggests an alternative to the ways of both Urras and Anarres. The ship seems to touch upon a kind of Kantian conception of beauty, a perfect fit of one's perceptual capacities to the phenomenal experience of the world, a satisfying sense of convergence and balance which eschews both Iotic aesthetic excessiveness and Onian asceticism.

Yet the ship as a delicate confection of glass and wire also seems to be on the point of vanishing just as one apprehends its image. Hope in Bloch's sense of anticipatory transformation cannot be said to be entirely absent from Le Guin's fiction, but rather like the image of this spaceship, it still seems ephemeral. In the closing chapter, Shevek glimpses the possibility of confronting Anarres's social ossification, and Ono's idealistic writings still have sufficient utopian attraction for one of the *Davenant*'s crew members to request that he accompanies Shevek on his return. However, the narrative's circularity, and the closing emphasis on emptiness, Shevek's hands being empty 'as they had always been', that common sense of dispossession in the societies surveyed, suggests that Le Guin's novel is perhaps best understood as a meditation on stifled utopian aspiration, in keeping with the spirit of the mid-1970s.

Tom Wolfe, chronicler of Ken Kesey as leading light of 1960s counterculture, published one of his best-known works, *The Right Stuff*, in 1979. Wolfe documented in this book the development of the Mercury space programme, with the purpose of conceiving the early astronauts as the embodiment of a rugged pioneering Americanism. Old-fashioned notions of heroism and patriotism could be rendered simultaneously admirable and risible through a sustained form of ironic investigation and description. By doing so, he offered a wry means of recovering the notion of manned space exploration from the doldrums. Wolfe often attempted to distil what he considered the defining characteristics of a particular era, a kind of self-conscious historical narrative without temporal detachment from the events being documented. In 1976, the bicentenary of the founding of the republic, he claimed to have detected the Geist of that decade in an essay for the *New York* magazine, entitled 'The "Me" Decade and the Third Great Awakening'. The piece begins with an account of a young executive, attending a group-therapy session at the Ambassador Hotel in Los Angeles. The trainer enjoins two hundred attendees lying on the carpet in the hotel's banqueting suite to 'take your finger off the repress button'.[65] Then the trainer encourages the attendees to concentrate on 'the one thing that you would most like to eliminate from your life'; and the young executive shouts 'haemorrhoids'. Wolfe recounts her attempts to cope with this 'morbid presence'. She reveals that she has a fabulous career as a Hollywood distributor; she characterises herself as a 'seductive physical presence'. In the boardroom, she is, Wolfe reports, the 'sexual princess, the Circe, taking a meeting and clouding men's minds'; but at the same time, she wants 'nothing more in this world than to go down the corridor to the ladies' room and get some Vaseline and then push the peanut back up her intestines with her finger'. Pain and humiliation merge on the hotel carpet. She moans, everyone else joins in, and the collective wail soars toward a crescendo. It is both a communal and personal catharsis as each participant concentrates on their own sense of incompleteness. Wolfe then suggests that the episode is the key to the current era, 'the explanation of certain grand puzzles of the 1970s', he declares, 'a period that will come to be known as the Me Decade'.

---

[65] Tom Wolfe, 'The "Me" Decade and the Third Great Awakening', *New York Magazine*, 23 August 1976 [Read online at http://nymag.com/news/features/45938/, accessed 24 July 2019].

Wolfe's thesis in this essay was that the trend of modern America is toward emotive individualism. And this movement has been buoyed by a great economic swell, an extraordinary increase in personal wealth since the 1940s. He gives his piece an idealistic twist by claiming that American workers had defied the expectations 'of the old utopian socialists such as Saint-Simon, Owen, Fourier and Marx'. It was not industrial socialism which had supplied the self-evident goods of discretionary income, political freedom and relief from grinding toil, but industrial capitalism and market forces. The result had not been workers' communities, but the sprawl of middle-American suburbia, with its 'barbecue pits and fish ponds, with concrete cherubs urinating into them on the lawn out back'. Yet, such gaudy materialism had not extinguished spiritualism as a defining aspect of American life; even if that sense of faith had become focussed on the overriding importance of the self as a composite of reverence and anxiety. The first Christian awakening in the eighteenth century, Wolfe suggests, challenged the authority of colonist's church, and paved the way for the American Revolution; the second in the nineteenth century created a sense of 'Christian asceticism', the necessary psychological bedrock for building self-sufficient communities in a harsh and forbidding environment. And the third great awakening of the modern age, he contends, had taken myriad forms, but all led back to one source, a personal compulsion, expressed in the injunction, '*Let's talk about me!*'

Wolfe's social-historical analysis was certainly questionable. Marx was not a utopian socialist. The post-war economic boom was over by the time of writing (never to recover fully), and with the benefit of hindsight, individualism as a defining characteristic is more plausibly associated with the 1980s than the 1970s. Wolfe's account is socially exclusive, seemingly focussed on preponderantly white middle-class experience, and if his depiction of the unnamed female film executive can evade censure for being misogynistic, then it certainly remains less than complimentary. The essay is an attempt to define its historical moment, and what seems to be a gratuitous metaphor in referring to a protruding haemorrhoid as a 'peanut' has a contemporary political resonance. President Jimmy Carter had been a Georgian peanut farmer before entering politics (and was known as such). Another work, published in the same year as Wolfe's article, and indeed, ostensibly proceeding from a diametrically opposite position, also has a sense of evangelical zeal. Marge Piercy's best-selling *Woman on the Edge of Time* is animated by feminist outrage; yet it operates in the dynamic articulated by Wolfe in the 'Me Decade'. Utopianism is invested with overwhelming subjective passion in Piercy's novel, evangelism with a therapeutic purpose, '*Let's talk about me*', as a means of addressing social grievance.

Woman on the Edge of Time is sometimes discussed as though it were a work of social realism, certainly in its contemporary American episodes; yet it is perhaps best approached as a feminist melodrama in its sensational display of domestic cruelties.[66] These qualities are apparent from the opening pages. Thirty-seven-year-old Chicana, Consuelo (Connie) Ramos, opens the door of her New York apartment to her pregnant niece, Dolly, who has just been attacked by her pimp and partner, Geraldo. The abusive boyfriend turns up and renews the assault. Fearing that he will kill her niece and the

---

[66] See Moylan, *Demand the Impossible*, p. 149.

unborn baby, Connie assails him: 'she smashed the wine jug into his face. His nose flattened like a squashed bug on a windshield [...]. She raised the jug to hit him again, but her arms were caught behind her. She twisted. Someone caught her hard in the nape. And she went out'.[67] Geraldo takes the unconscious Connie to a psychiatric hospital. He is aware of her history of disturbed behaviour and violence; and he knows that with her record incarceration will be a formality. The opening episode sets in train the narrative's twin strands: Connie's attempt to escape from the asylum, and her sustaining vision of a holistic and compassionate society.

By exploring female experience in a popular narrative form, Piercy seems to be aligned with those other fluent chroniclers of 1970s American feminism, most notably the picaresque of Erica Jong and Rita Mae Brown, even if Piercy's psychiatric odyssey is considerably bleaker than their respective accounts of modern heterosexual and lesbian self-discovery. Piercy's protagonist, Connie, is impoverished, with faded looks (on which she mournfully reflects); a patchy education; she has a history of violence, and mental illness; and her young daughter, Angelina, has been taken from her for adoption under questionable circumstances. Piercy's choice of a marginal figure for her protagonist, whom she then imbues with a rich inner life is a repudiation of the notion that sophistication and a capacity for sustained intricate imaginative reflection are the preserve of the higher social echelons. She succeeds in constructing a vital and sympathetic portrait of someone whom, one suspects, most of her readers would have crossed the street to avoid.

As Kerstin Shands points out, Piercy often depends in her fiction on emotional profusion and lyrical conviction rather than rational analysis and measured observation.[68] And it can be difficult to discern much higher-order symbolic reflection in her oeuvre. Piercy's two autobiographical novels *Small Changes* (1973) and *Braided Lives* (1982) explore the immediacy of particular events, rather than extrapolating to more general observations on the circumstances of middle-class educated women in the 1950s and 1960s. Nevertheless, it is still possible to detect a Foucauldian aspect to *Woman on the Edge of Time*, in the notion that enforced confinement provides an examination of what Foucault termed the 'micro-physics of authority'.[69] It is within an institution or a state apparatus of this type that one can detect the power relations which determine social interactions within the wider society. Piercy's novel at least implies that one should view the psychiatric hospital as being indicative of the oppressive forces which still shape America in the later part of the twentieth century.

After she is confined, Connie begins to receive visits from a future being, Luciente, a 'sender' who is capable of contacting other beings from different times and places with telepathic propensities, 'a catcher', of which Connie is a notable exponent. Connie, alongside her various contemporary incarcerations and betrayals by friends and family, is periodically transported to the perfect state of Mattapoisett in the twenty-second

---

[67] Marge Piercy, *Woman on the Edge of Time* (London: Women's Press, 1979), p. 16. All further in-text references are to this edition of the novel.
[68] Kerstin W. Shands, *The Repair of the World: The Works of Marge Piercy* (Westport, CT: Greenwood Press, 1994), p. 17.
[69] Michel Foucault, *Discipline and Punish: The Birth of the Prison*, trans. by Alan Sheridan (London: Allen Lane, 1977), p. 26.

century. This is a rural community in what was once Massachusetts. Connie is supposed to have been selected for this projection in order to secure the pre-history of the revolution which resulted in the establishment of this agrarian anarchic community. The forces which have scarred humanity, such as industrial conglomerates and the military have now been almost entirely banished in the future state. Piercy's commonwealth operates as a kind of sustained and imaginative pastiche of canonical utopias. Like More's *Utopia*, all tasks are shared out amongst the members of the community, such that no-one has to work more than a limited number of hours each day. Like Morris's *News from Nowhere*, the society has an absolute commitment to personal freedom, informal principles of education and collective discussion to reach communal decisions. As Connie notes, Mattapoisett has the appearance of the past, rather than the future. Yet like Wells' *Men like Gods*, there are predictions of widespread, non-intrusive technology, such as 'kenners', small devices for communication, connected wirelessly to central servers, which the Mattapoisettians wear on their wrists (anticipating twenty-first-century smart watches), and 'spinners', which are unicellular organisms, grown into long strings and then woven into responsive fences and barriers.

However, there are also some intriguing revisions of scientific romance. The egalitarian society of the twenty-second century has produced a benign variant of Dr Moreau's chimeras, such that human beings have now achieved inter-species communication (with higher mammals such as chimpanzees and dolphins mastering human speech). Piercy also follows the example of Scogan in Huxley's *Crome Yellow* (1921) by suggesting that there would be a liberation for woman from the obligations of childbirth through an extra-uterine means of reproduction. Embryos are fertilised and gestated in a giant 'Brooder', a bio-mechanical device for maximising genetic diversity; and as in Huxley's *Island* (1962), the 'phone-booth' constraints of the nuclear family have been superseded by more pliant notions of kinship, whereby three friends in Mattapoisett agree to raise the child (with no continuation of the parental relationship once the child reaches adulthood). Accordingly, parenting is elective, communal and does not come with lifetime obligations.

The community has many features one might associate with a hippy commune. Hair is worn long; clothes are practical, colourful, made from natural durable fabrics, embellished with bangles and beads. Everyone chooses their own name, and can change their appellation according to their shifting sense of selfhood. The names the Mattapoisettians choose are reminiscent of the monikers adopted by Kesey's Merry Pranksters. As in Le Guin's *Left Hand of Darkness*, there is fluency in gender and sexual roles, with no formal prescription on these so long as they are not deemed to be personally coercive or intrusive. Connie originally thinks Luciente is a man, only subsequently to discover that she is, in fact, a woman; and Connie is initially disconcerted when she sees the squat, hirsute, piratical Barbarossa acting as wet nurse to the community's sucking infants. Language usage reflects this liberation from gendered prescriptions, with the neutral term 'per' substituting for English third-person pronouns, 'he' and 'she'. In keeping with the therapeutic expressiveness of Wolfe's Me-Generation, uninhibited emoting is encouraged by the Mattapoisettians. At one point, the narrator describes a communal meal as a 'madhouse, with people sat naked, with their emotions pouring out' (pp. 74–75). An older member of the community openly wails over his supper. Piercy's Mattapoisett was described admiringly by Moylan from his critical-utopian perspective as 'democratic, anarchist, communist, environmentalist, feminist, non-racist – where freedom and responsibility are balanced in a steady-state economy and non-repressive value system'.[70]

The abstracted attributes of utopian projection are contrasted in a short episode in which Connie, after an intrusive procedure in the Rockhampton Psychiatric Hospital, envisages an alternative dystopian future for twenty-second-century Mattapoisett (and Piercy is unusual in this period in presenting the utopian and the dystopian as parallel possibilities). Connie briefly meets Gildina, a young woman living in a windowless high-rise apartment; she is barely able to walk because of the cartoon-like enhancement of her secondary sexual characteristics. She works one short-term contract after another to a 'flak' [man]. Gildina subsists on flavourless microwavable convenience food, disposing of the plastic packaging as soon as the contents are consumed. Every aspect of her life is determined by property relations; and while there is little prospect of the microwavable packaging being recycled; there is every prospect Gildina will be before she reaches middle age. Her organs will be used as replacement parts for affluent masters of the universe, living in pampered luxury on off-world platforms. This instrumentalist and disposable depiction of women has a prominent antecedent in the sexualised vision of Lenina in *Brave New World* (1932), but Piercy's despotic patriarchy seems so extreme as to almost stray into parody. When Connie awakens in her hospital bed after her operation, she interprets this dystopian encounter as a call to arms: 'so that was the other world that might come to be. That was Luciente's war, and she was enlisted in it.' (p. 301)

Critics have commented on the similarity of *Woman on the Edge of Time* to Ken Kesey's *One Flew over the Cuckoo's Nest* (1962).[71] Indeed, one could even regard Piercy's novel as a kind of 1970s feminist palimpsest of Kesey's seminal work of 1960s anti-authoritarianism. Both books suggest determinations of insanity are a consequence of the standard psychiatric practice of labelling, which treats delusional behaviour as having an analogous cause to physical ailments.[72] Both writers indicate the difficulties of escaping the consequences of a diagnosis of mental illness. Being labelled schizophrenic meant certain kinds of constraint and interventionist treatments inevitably ensued. Both books suggest some patients are incarcerated merely for their reluctance to conform to social norms. Kesey's protagonist, McMurphy, is a rebellious petty criminal, who ends up hospitalised; and Piercy's Connie Ramos is committed, partly because of Geraldo's deviousness, and partly because of her own erratic behaviour, a consequence of the depredations and violence to which she has been routinely subjected. Both novels have episodes of unsuccessful escape; the suicide of a young, vulnerable patient; the use of obligatory invasive procedures to modify what is deemed unacceptable behaviour. McMurphy is given electroshock therapy, and eventually lobotomised. Connie is scheduled for an operation on her cortex. Both

---

[70] Moylan, *Demand the Impossible*, p. 134
[71] See, for example, Frances Bartkowski, *Feminist Utopias* (Lincoln, NA: University of Nebraska Press, 1989), pp. 85–86, Moylan, *Demand the Impossible*, p. 123, and Shands, *Repair of the World*, p. 62.
[72] On the significance of labelling and deviance in post-World War Two psychiatric practice, see Thomas J. Scheff, *Being Mentally Ill: A Sociological Theory* (Chicago: Aldine, 1966), especially pp. 32–33, and pp. 80–83.

dénouements feature vengeful acts by their central characters, directed at oppressive institutional authority. Two significant innovations in Piercy's novel are the overturning of Kesey's masculine perspective, such that the principal instrument of medical authority in *One Flew over the Cuckoo's Nest* is the manipulative and controlling female Nurse Ratchet; whereas Connie has to contend with an array of condescending male psychiatrists and relatives. The second innovation, with no exact correlative in Kesey's book, is Connie's imaginative transit to the utopian community of Mattapoisett.

Piercy's utopianism seemingly combines two traditions of idealistic fiction – the imaginative leap sometimes employed by Wells as a mean of moving from one space to another; and Morris's dream vision of the coming social paradise. It is not apparent in the novel's early stages that the author is entirely sure which of these routes she should be following. However, there are subsequently clear parallels between the contemporary American narrative and the prospective utopia and dystopia. Connie's future transportation occurs at those points when she is in a state of distress. The prospective inhabitants of Mattapoisett have a number of similarities with Connie's friends and fellow patients. One of them, Bee, of whom she is particularly fond, bears a striking resemblance to her former lover, Claude; and the death of one young patient in the hospital is followed by the death of a young Mattapoisettian. The ubiquitous violence of Connie's modern America has an equivalence in Mattapoisett, which is also reminiscent of the draconian aspects of More's original utopians. Luciente argues because there will always be malign forces, one must be prepared to fight and defend the principles in which one believes. Within her own anarchic community, those guilty of repeated crimes of violence are dealt with harshly. For the first offence, a perpetrator may receive some form of community service. For any further offence, he or she can expect to be executed on the paradoxical grounds, as Luciente explains, that 'we aren't willing to live with people who use violence' (p. 209).

We are presumably meant to interpret Luciente's contrary endorsement of lethal force as a necessary adjunct to the revolutionary properties of utopian projection, and as a legitimation of Connie's action in poisoning her physicians toward the end of the novel, as a kind of one-woman guerrilla campaign. Yet even within the book's ethical schema, these are questionable actions. It is difficult, for example, to see how assassinating one's doctors will lead to a better society. Connie's actions turn out to be as futile as they are dubious, with no sense of impending transformation of psychiatric care. The book finishes with an extract from Connie's medical record, which confirms her open-ended incarceration. The reader is left with an interpretation of utopia which the novel both tacitly accepts and ostensibly rejects, that the dream of radical paradise has become a symptom of clinical psychosis. It is either as a means of promoting actions which have calamitous consequences, or it is a salvific myth, which does not encourage pragmatic and incremental forms of social reform.

If one were to consider the implications of Siegel's film with which we began, and of Piercy's novel with which we are to conclude, it can be difficult to detect much difference in the formal status of the actions they depict. Both works finish with visions of psychosis as a social phenomenon; and both suggest that eliminating one's opponents is a legitimate course of action, alongside the acceptance that such actions will not necessarily resolve the difficulties identified. Piercy's heroine, moreover, seems to offer a final sardonic variant on Wolfe's Me-Generation in which the expressive community has become predominantly a matter of subjective projection. But in the end, all-consuming self-reflection did not provide Wolfe's promised 'explanation of certain grand puzzles of the 1970s'. It rather supplied another instance of the defining quandary of the age – where once there had been the possibility of creating the good society, there was now no way back, and no easy road ahead.

In 1985, Ursula K. Le Guin published what she described as her 'archaeology of the future', *Always Coming Home*. She explained that her intention in this book was to expand the anarchic aspects of the *Dispossessed* into 'an even more open utopia'.[73] This would be to extend the sense of utopian diffusion in the earlier work, such that the idealistic blueprint would now be dispensed with entirely. Like Morris and Piercy's visions, this version of the future looks like the past; and in this instance the society, or rather series of inter-connected communities, were to be established in a northern Californian valley. In keeping with its declared principles, the book had no centre. It was assembled as a sensitively curated anthropological collection of poems, short stories, legends and fragmented memoirs in which the utopian was supposed to be divined rather than explicitly rendered – to be assembled from the reader's own reflections and active construction of possible associations in this anatomy. Yet, this was such an impressionistic kind of utopia that it seemed to have withdrawn entirely into the realm of arcadia; and so far as *Always Coming Home* could be treated as being utopian, it seemed out of step with its own moment, presenting an idealistic vision in keeping with the cultural preoccupations of the previous decade rather than with the current one. Le Guin implicitly acknowledged *Always Coming Home*'s anachronistic sensibilities when she commented on the limited fictional possibilities of ideal communities in an age in which 'we seem only to write dystopias'.[74] But she also noted the interdependency of the opposing positions, that 'every eutopia contains a dystopia, every dystopia contains a eutopia'.[75] This may not have been a new idea; but it was still a striking chiasmus which would develop into the central aesthetic principle for the pre-eminent author to combine the real with the fantastic from the late twentieth century onwards; and she is Margaret Atwood.

---

[73] Ursula K. Le Guin, 'A Non-Euclidian View of California as a Cold Place to Be', in Thomas More, *Utopia* (London: Verso, 2016), pp. 163–94 (p. 163), originally published 1989.
[74] Ursula K. Le Guin, 'Utopiyin, Utopiyang', in More, *Utopia* (2016), pp. 195–98 (p. 195).
[75] Le Guin, 'Utopiyin, Utopiyang', p. 197.

7

Atwood's Scar; or, the Origins of Ustopia

Near the end of Margaret Atwood's *The Handmaid's Tale* (1985), the first-person narrator, Offred (known throughout by her assigned patronym) considers how she and her sister handmaids appear to the uninitiated. 'We must look good from a distance', she muses, 'picturesque, like Dutch milkmaids on a wallpaper frieze, like a shelf full of period-costume ceramic salt and pepper shakers'.[1] The reader is well aware by this point that there is a significant difference between the predicament of the handmaids in the Republic of Gilead and their smart appearance. Gilead's evangelical archconservative society has been successful in expunging all obvious signs of decadent Western liberalism from modern America. The young women in pastoral guise are compelled to be surrogates, with the exclusive social and biological function of becoming progenitors of children for the unfertile wives of senior government officials and military officers. The repetition of their image as Dutch milkmaids in the decorative pattern and in the faintly comic suggestion of period-costumed condiment sets are in accordance with the book's dramatic circumstances. The novel is about domestic incarceration, of returning women to their 'rightful' place of hearth and home, as though they were to be regimented back into a wallpaper pattern, and rendered useful insofar as they can dispense salt and pepper at the dinner table.

Offred's use of 'picturesque' to describe the handmaids seems straightforward. The abstract adjective is employed in the familiar sense of looking like a picture, and the mental image conjured up is supposed to possess a certain charm. However, 'picturesque' also has a more technical sense in eighteenth-century aesthetic theory as the bridging category between the sublime and beautiful. In the most influential account of English aesthetics from that period, Edmund Burke argued we associate the sublime with objects and experiences which we find terrifying, but from which we are sufficiently removed so as not to feel any imminent danger. The sublime makes an enduring impression on our minds, producing a particular type of pleasure in displaced pain, 'delight', he terms it.[2] By way of contrast to the grandness and sustained impression of the sublime, the beautiful is associated with such trivialities as smoothness, regularity and smallness. Burke suggests an encounter with a beautiful object will undoubtedly

---

[1] Margaret Atwood, *The Handmaid's Tale* (London: Vintage, 2010), p. 224. All further in-text references are to this edition
[2] Edmund Burke, *A Philosophical Enquiry into the Origins of Our Ideas of the Sublime and Beautiful*, ed. by James T. Bolton (Oxford: Blackwell, 1987), pp. 35–37.

produce pleasure, but the sensation will not have any intensity, and will pass as soon as the external stimulus has been removed. For Burke, aesthetic encounters can only be of two kinds, either the sublime, as a powerful expression of removed if exquisite pain, or the beautiful which is a source of unalloyed pleasure, but only of a thin and transient kind. The aesthetic theories subsequently developed by William Gilpin, Uvedale Price and Richard Payne Knight introduced the 'picturesque' as an intermediary category between sublimity and beauty, especially as it might be applied to design and landscape.[3] We might experience the moderating sensation of the picturesque if we were to contemplate the roughened surface of a lake as the wind whisks across it; or cast our eye over undulating hills; or take in the prospect of clusters of trees, where there is no obvious symmetry to their arrangement, but in which one can still detect a satisfying proportionality between each arboreal group.

Like Offred, Atwood possesses a keen sense for the pictorial possibilities of a given episode. The author was in the early to middle stage of her career when she wrote the *Handmaid's Tale*, an imagistic writer, with an eye for colour and form. The effect of many of her more memorable scenes is dependent on the precise rendering of such impressions, often with an explicit use of the sublime. In the early part of the *Handmaid's Tale*, for example, Offred describes the spectre of executed criminals; their bodies displayed on the town's redbrick wall. There are six new corpses suspended near the main gateway, with 'their hands tied in front of them, their heads in white bags tipped sideways on their shoulders'. Offred reflects that the bags obscuring the faces 'are the worst, worse than the faces themselves would be. It makes the men look like dolls on which faces have not yet been painted' (p. 42). She then entertains the idea that they look like snowmen, 'with the coal eyes and carrots having fallen out' (p. 42); and this childhood association of snowmen leads to a descriptive simile for a further detail she has just noticed. As the blood seeps through the white cloth, where the mouth should have been, 'it makes an alternative mouth, a small red one, like the mouths painted by thick brushes by kindergarten children' (p. 42). After revealing that the executed men were doctors accused of carrying out abortions before the Great Change, she turns her attention back to the stain on the bag:

> The red of the smile is the same as the red of the tulips in Serena Joy's garden, towards the base of the flowers where they are beginning to heal. The red is the same, but there is no connection. The tulips are not tulips of blood the red smiles are not flowers, neither things make a comment on the other. The tulip is not a reason for disbelief in the hanged man or vice versa. Each thing is valid and really there. It is through a field of valid objects that I must pick my way [...]. I put a lot of effort into making such distinctions.
>
> p. 43

---

[3] See, for example, William Gilpin, *Three Essays on Picturesque Beauties; on Picturesque Travel; and, on Sketching Landscape*, 3rd edn (London: Cadell and Davies, 1808), pp. 8–23; Uvedale Price, *An Essay on the Picturesque, as Compared with the Sublime and Beautiful; and, on the Use of Studying Pictures, for the Purpose of Improving Real Landscape* (London: Robson, 1796), p. vii–viii, p. 26, p. 33, and pp. 40–41; and Richard Payne Knight, *An Analytical Inquiry into the Principles of Taste*, 2nd edn (London: Payne and White, 1805), pp. 146–52.

Offred, then, endeavours to maintain the difference between the classes of objects with which she is presented: tulips in the garden of her Commander's wife, Serena Joy, on the one side, and the smudged bag over the head of an executed physician on the other. The fact that she expends a considerable amount of intellectual effort in preserving these distinctions can be interpreted as a necessary ploy to maintain one's sanity in a society committed to dispensing with conventional taxonomies. The beauty of cut flowers (irrespective of the standing of the garden in which the flowers grow) is contrasted with the sublime spectacle of white-coated bodies; the sight of which seems to have the effect of throwing understanding and imagination out of kilter. These perceptions are conceived as aesthetic judgements which are discrete and opposed to one another. Yet the narrative is contrary in this respect, as the colour red provides a connective strand between each phenomena: the red of the flowers as a floral stigmata to be associated with the grim spectacle of the corpses; placing the two images side-by-side, just as Offred struggles to preserve a distinction between them. One might consider that the tensions in this passage are indicative of the aesthetic and thematic principles of the text as a whole. Indeed, one might regard this episode as providing an uncompromising commitment to the notion that the beautiful and the sublime *should* possess an equal and complementary force; and to find an expressive means of holding such ideas together. And one might even be tempted to term this constellating of sublime and beautiful images in Atwood's prose as a kind of new-form narrative picturesque, which does not so much attempt to insert a mediating category between the extremes of aesthetic perception as supply an innovative means of representing them within the same conceptual field.

In an essay collection on Atwood which appeared prior to the publication of the *Handmaid's Tale*'s, the volume's editors suggest that her fiction's hallmarks are stylistic and thematic variety; 'she is not one of those authors', they observe, 'who rewrites, attempting to a refine the process, the same basic book'.[4] This position is borne out by the range of novels she produced in the early part of her career, with every work seemingly providing a new experimental departure. *Surfacing* (1972) is a quest narrative in which an emotionally disconnected protagonist searches for her missing father in the northern Quebecois wilderness; *Lady Oracle* (1976) is a comic *Künstlerroman* in which the central figure is an accidental author incapable of settling upon a fixed persona, and who ends up faking her own death; and *Life Before Man* (1978) is a finely modulated exercise in lyrical realism. The novel charts the lives and relationships of a group of middle-class Torontonians in their thirties, set against the backdrop of the Royal Ontario Museum (and its extensive palaeontological collection). Indeed, the *Handmaid's Tale* could also be seen to conform to this programme of narrative and formal diversification, as it represented her first attempt at an ominous speculative tale set in the near future.

Nevertheless, it is still possible to detect some common elements to all of Atwood's early novels; and these trends and preoccupations, if anything, became more pronounced as her career progressed. There is an imaginative compulsion, such that any idea should

---

[4] Arnold E. Davidson and Cathy N. Davidson, 'Introduction', in *The Art of Margaret Atwood: Essays in Criticism*, ed. by Arnold E. Davidson and Cathy N. Davidson (Toronto: Anansi, 1981), pp. 9–14 (p. 9).

be pressed toward its most extreme form. There is the studied artfulness of narratives with the slow and often almost incidental revelation of significant plot point; and the striking use of temporal dislocation. Atwood is self-evidently interested in modern female experience. Nearly all her protagonists are women, often confronted by formidable circumstances, where the prevailing social standards have been established by men. She has utilised an array of narrational styles, but prefers the first-person narrator of qualified reliability. The typical Atwoodian inner voice is idiosyncratic, wry, acerbic, sometimes bitter, occasionally exuberant, shifting between the self-deprecatory and opinionated; and often in tension with the events depicted in a given episode. And then there is the poetic strain to her fiction, a striving for symbolic density, distillation of experience; and the lyricism is often heightened toward the end of a chapter or section, with main verbs omitted to produce a sense of imagistic compactness.

An intriguing example of the difficulties of interpreting the *Handmaid's Tale* in a concise fashion is provided by the film adaptation made in 1990, from a screenplay by Harold Pinter. The film was not a success, described by David Thomson as an exercise in 'thin-blooded and mean-spirited artiness'.[5] Its relative failure was not exclusively down to Pinter's adaptation, which had been extensively revised by the time the film was shot (with some textual input from Atwood).[6] The production also suffered from a change of director, a limited budget and some odd casting.[7] Yet, the central problem remained Pinter's inability to find a suitable cinematic equivalent to Atwood's elliptical style. From the first draft, Pinter had a climactic interview between Offred and the Commander which had no clear correlation to any of the exchanges between these characters in the novel. The episode, which remained in place through all versions of the script to the final film, despite Atwood's protestations, has Offred assassinating the Commander as though she were a combination of Judith of the Apocrypha and Charlotte Corday.[8] The Commander is characterised in the screenplay as a brutal and manipulative instrument of an authoritarian regime instead of the nuanced portrait of uncertain masculinity which Offred supplies. The Commander's probable punishment in Atwood's tale is disgrace. When last glimpsed in the novel, he holds his head in his hands, having rowed with his wife, and wonders what his handmaid/mistress has disclosed about his conduct, and to whom. Pinter substituted one pessimistic construction for another. His abiding political interest in this period was American interventionist policy in Latin America; and Gilead stood for him as a kind of homecoming of the right-wing militarised regimes of Somoza and Pinochet.[9] Outraged

---

[5] David Thomson, *The New Biographical Dictionary of Film* (New York: Knopf, 2004), p. 701.

[6] See Margaret Atwood Collection of Papers, Thomas Fisher Rare Book Library, University of Toronto, Ms Coll.200 Box 212, especially folders 7, 14, 20 and 25, correspondents, notes, and annotated screenplays for the *Handmaid's Tale*.

[7] On the film's difficulties, see Christopher C. Hudgins, 'Three Unpublished Harold Pinter Film Scripts: *The Handmaid's Tale*, *The Remains of the Day*, *Lolita*', *Pinter Review*, no vol. number (2005–08), 132–39.

[8] See Harold Pinter, 'Handmaid's Tale, Draft; 17 November 1986', Pinter Archive, British Library, Add Mss 88880/2/51, f. 150ʳ. Atwood's objections to the climactic scene can be found in the Atwood Archive, Ms Coll. 200 Box 212 f. 25.

[9] Pinter makes his anti-American views clear in an interview with Brian Appleyard, see Appleyard 'The New light that Burns within Harold Pinter', *Times*, 16 March 1984, 12. See also Michael Billington, *Harold Pinter*, rev. edn (London: Faber and Faber, 2007), p. 286 passim.

at what he saw as ongoing American neo-colonialism and subterfuge, he suggested in this script that such injustice and mendaciousness needed to be met with violence. Similarly art in the late twentieth century had to be earnest, decisive, linear and exemplary; and not merely as Atwood's enigmatic prose suggested, lyrical, reflective and, on occasion, wryly humorous.

Pinter's interpretative problems were a manifestation of a central difficulty in divining what Atwood's book was actually about. Early reviewers variously hazarded that it was 'a politic Canterbury Tale', a form of creative psychological biography, a social commentary animated 'by a grotesque satire of theocracy', but one which still invited serious contemplation of scripture.[10] Its sexual politics could be feminist or post-feminist, or perhaps not even feminist at all. Lorna Sage read it as a riposte 'to the tendency of present-day feminists toward a kind of separate purity'.[11] And Mary McCarthy's frequently cited disparagement of the book seems to have been provoked by a sense of the women's movement having being let down. It was just too fantastical, she thought, that a modern democratic state could so rapidly regress to medieval religiosity and cruelty. Feminism and the doctrines of human rights were not going to be deposed by such a numbskull theocracy.[12] The subsequent academic discussion has been more confident of the work's feminist credentials, but still undecided as to exactly what type of feminism was being expounded. There are general proclamations, such as the book 'disrupts conventional boundaries as a way of exploring the means by which male-centred cultures ensure their own hegemony'; or it is a matter of forging practical political opposition, as the novel serves as 'a double witness to the patriarchal society that occurred, and still occurs internationally'; or, it is a novel of fluid choric expressiveness, rather than a call for direct action, a text in which 'images of desire deriving from the human body and natural world constitute a "feminine" alternative language'.[13]

There is extensive evidence in Atwood's own documentation of the novel's background and the immediate topics and concerns which it addresses in elliptical fashion (both by way of research and affirming the novel's topicality). Atwood collected press clippings, as one might expect, on such matters as the rise of fundamentalist belief in America and the emergence of an explicit religious component in conservative politics. There are reports in her archive of a mid-Western mother going to court 'to confront the forces of evil, as represented by the spread of "secular humanism" through the textbooks and texts in American schools'; another describes the prominent evangelist Pat Robinson mulling over a run for president.[14] One reveals how an Ohio construction worker had been held in connection with a series of explosions at abortion clinics; with his fiancée's mother insisting that 'he was an exceptionally fine

---

[10] See Janet Karsten Larsen, 'Margaret Atwood's Testaments: Resisting the Gilead Within', *The Christian Century*, 20–27 May 1987, 496–98.
[11] Lorna Sage, 'Projections from a Messy Present', *TLS*, 21 March 1986, 307.
[12] See Mary McCarthy, 'Breeders, Wives and Unwomen', *The New York Times*, 9 February 1986, 1, 35.
[13] See respectively Magali Cornier Michael, *Feminism and the Postmodern Impulse: Post World War II Fiction* (Albany: State University of New York, 1996), p. 138; Marion Wynne-Davies, *Margaret Atwood* (Tavistock: Northcote House, 2010), p. 40; and Coral Anne Howells, *Margaret Atwood*, 2nd edn (Basingstoke: Palgrave Macmillan, 2005), p. 105.
[14] Alex Brummer, 'Battle of the Bible Belt', *Guardian*, 19 July 1986, 17; William Johnson, 'Evangelist Mulls over Running for US President', *Globe and Mail*, 21 October 1985, A9.

Christian boy'.¹⁵ And Robert Fear has a piece in the *New York Times* which asks, 'what causes the high U.S. rate of infant deaths'.¹⁶

Mary McCarthy might have been sceptical as to the possibility of a sudden lurch toward a repressive theocracy, but that, of course was exactly what had happened in Iran after the 1978 revolution. A piece in the *Guardian* by Colin Smith recounts how many middle-class urban women who had enjoyed Western-style freedoms of dress and expression under the Shah, found these liberties swiftly curtailed after his fall (Professor Piexioto draws an explicit comparison between Gilead and the Iranian republic in his concluding historical notes).¹⁷ Smith also describes the brutal conditions in the women's jail in Tehran, including the beating of the soles of feet as standard punishment (the fate of Monica, Offred's rebellious friend). Concerns over surrogacy and demographic decline are covered in articles from the *New York Times* and the *Toronto Star*. The former describes a trial in New Jersey where the surrogate refused to surrender her child. And the latter has a jocular piece 'Making a Baby for Christmas' where the correspondent reports on an initiative to correct the nation's demographic shortfall, reporting that a progressive Conservative MP has extolled Canadians to '"start with renewed vigour" over the holidays to increase the country's population'.¹⁸

The *Handmaid's Tale* is standardly classified as a dystopia; and in this respect, one might fruitfully compare it to another popular work released in the same month as the novel's publication, Peter Weir's film *Witness* (1985), precisely because it seems to address a similar set of concerns, but from an opposing point of view. Weir's thriller begins with gently swaying grass and an extended family dressed like early American pilgrims. The unspecified pre-twentieth-century period is further suggested by the appearance of horse-drawn carriages. It is only when the group walks toward a farmhouse that a superimposed title reveals the setting to be modern-day Pennsylvania. The family is not a group of pilgrims, but the Amish of Lancaster County, an insular Christian sect of German and Swiss origin. *Witness* draws on familiar assumptions about the Amish – strong community ethos, pacifism, the pursuit of a self-reliant rural life; stoical acceptance of the Almighty's will; rejection of all vanity and egotism, as well as labour-saving technology.¹⁹ The story has a recently widowed Amish woman, Rachel Lapp (Kelly McGillis) travelling to a visit her family in Ohio with her eight-year-old son, Samuel (Lukas Haas). Their train is cancelled, and they have a long wait at Philadelphia Thirtieth Street Station. During this delay, Samuel inadvertently witnesses a murder in the station washroom, committed by two corrupt policemen. The case is investigated by a detective, John Book (Harrison Ford). Samuel eventually identifies one

---

[15] Associated Press Report, 'US Abortion Clinic Rocked by Explosion', 2 January 1985.
[16] Robert Fear, 'What Causes the High U.S. Rate of Infant Deaths?', *New York Times*, 20 March 1985, 19.
[17] Colin Smith, 'Inside Khomeini's Slaughterhouse', *Observer*, 6 May 1984, 9.
[18] Carol Lawson, 'Surrogate Mothers Grow in Number Despite Questions', *New York Times*, 1 October 1986, C 1, C 18 (C 1); Canadian Press Report, 'Make a Baby for Christmas', *Toronto Star*, 22 December 1984.
[19] See, for example, John A. Hostetler, *Amish Society* (Baltimore: John Hopkins University Press, 1970); and Linda Egenes, *Visits with the Amish: Impressions of the Plain Life* (Iowa City: University of Iowa Press, 2009). See also Donald B. Kraybill on gender relations and shifting attitudes to technology in the Amish community in his *Riddle of Amish Culture*, rev. edn (Baltimore: John Hopkins Press, 2001), pp. 80–110.

of the murderers from a photograph. Through various machinations, Book is injured in an exchange of gunfire, and realising that Rachel and Samuel are in danger, drives them back to their farm in Lancaster County, at which point he collapses from his wound.

The narrative's main purpose is to bring together Rachel and Book in this conservative society, and then to chart their developing relationship. Book adopts traditional Amish dress so as not to draw attention to himself. Once he has sufficiently recovered, he contributes to running the farm, getting up in the middle of the night to milk the cows. He proves to be an able carpenter, constructing wooden toys for Samuel; and in one set piece, participates in the day-long communal raising of a barn for a newly married couple. There is some comic interplay over the storage of his gun and its ammunition (a symbol of his previous combative urban existence). The central characters indulge in longing looks at one another as their unconsummated affair progresses. In a memorable scene, Book manages to get the radio to work in his defunct car; he whirls Rachel around the hayloft to the strains of Sam Cook's 'What a Wonderful World'. *Witness* concludes with a predictable shootout, but by this stage it is evident that the cultural divide is too wide for the would-be lovers to cross. Book's departure for the city is imminent when he is glimpsed in the background of a late episode, smoking a cigarette and chatting with the local police. The final scene is a long shot of him driving away from the farm through the fields of grass, while a neighbouring Amish farmer, a rival for Rachel's affections, strolls in the opposite direction.

Pauline Kael was not impressed by the film's reworking of those familiar topoi of virtuous countryside and venal city. She observed the Amish seemed to represent a 'quaint dreamland, a Brigadoon of tall golden wheat and shiny-clean faces'; and the corresponding depiction of urban modernity was just as extreme, 'a squalid, hyped-up view of life in Philadelphia [produced] from prolonged exposure to TV cop shows'.[20] Nevertheless, she was prepared to concede *Witness*'s popular utopian appeal, such that one might well regard the film in its entirety as a '"Lost Horizon" for the mid-eighties'.[21] Weir was careful to temper the film's sense of American idyll, intimating that such a conservative and insular society could not be without its tensions, jealousies and rivalries. It is gossipy and censorious, and any infraction of its customs and codes invites censure (Rachel is warned that her fondness for Book may result in her being 'shunned'). Weir's film, it seems, is equally committed as the *Handmaid's Tale* to providing a vision of an orthodox religious community, but reaches toward a utopian rather than a dystopian conclusion.

Both Weir's film and Atwood's novel are interested in examining the implications of living in orthodox societies, rather than exploring their theological implications. *Witness* offers an account of foundational American mythology (there are allusions throughout to classical westerns, *High Noon*, *Seven Brides for Seven Brothers* and *The Searchers*), but it is a mythology refracted through modern liberal sensibilities, so that one can regard the Amish as exemplifying those virtues of a pioneering spirt and self-

---

[20] Pauline Kael, 'Plain and Simple', *The New Yorker*, 25 February 1985, [read online at http://www.newyorker.com/magazine/1985/02/25/plain-and-simple, accessed 5 March 2019]. See also John P. McGowan's observations on the More-like strictures of Amish society as portrayed in *Witness* in his 'Looking at the (Alter)natives: Peter Weir's *Witness*', *Chicago Review*, 35 (1986), 36–47.

[21] Kael, 'Plain and Simple'.

reliance, but at the same time, rejecting individualism, commercial enterprise and the right to self-defence through bearing arms. Weir's lead character is named 'Rachel', after the favourite of Jacob's two wives and a biblical matriarch in Genesis. Atwood uses a passage from Genesis 30 as an epigraph for the *Handmaid's Tale*, in which Rachel is cast in a different light. Having lamented her barrenness, Rachel instructs Jacob to 'behold my maid Bilhah, go in unto her, and she shall bear upon my knees, that I may also have children by her'. However, the clearest thematic parallel between the works concerns Offred's observation, with which we began, that Gilead's handmaids have the picturesque appearance of Dutch milkmaids. The simile becomes a literal device in *Witness*, an emblem and a means of visually configuring the ideal society. The director constructed the view of the Lapps' farmhouse as though it were a seventeenth-century Dutch interior with sparse wooden furnishings; and he then lit it with a precise chiaroscuro. And Weir's central means for conceiving how Rachel should appear in *Witness*, and the explicit prototype for the film's central episode *was* a Dutch picture, Johannes Vermeer's well-known genre painting, *The Milkmaid* (see Figs. 7.1 and 7.2).[22]

Perhaps, then, one might approach the *Handmaid's Tale* and *Witness* as though they were pendant portraits for the mid-1980s, respectively providing dystopian and utopian visions: one as an unnerving expression of liberal feminist anxieties over conservative trends in North American society and politics; the other as a soothing balm, offering a pre-modern religious community as an American ideal which can paradoxically be seen through its pacifism and its uncommercial communal ethos as being consonant with liberal rather than libertarian principles. Yet one might also wish to qualify such a position by suggesting that Atwood in the *Handmaid's Tale* was already endeavouring to incorporate such idealistic alternatives into her own text with a kind of uncanny conflation of opposing views, paralleling the novel's blurring of the aesthetic categories of the sublime and beautiful. Atwood retrospectively traced her own interest in the interplay of the utopian and dystopian to her review of Piercy's *Woman on the Edge of Time* on its publication in 1976.[23] She focussed in that piece on the novel's depiction of the future utopian community of Mattapoisett, while upbraiding other reviewers for concentrating on the book's contemporary episodes. She read the novel's modern-day American component as being akin to a dystopian romance, acting as a counterweight to its vision of radical idealism.[24]

In a conference address in Rennes in 1998, Atwood wondered out loud whether her best-known novel was a feminist dystopia, and unsurprisingly, reached no clear-cut conclusion on this matter. However, she did suggest that 'all dystopia begins in utopia. Utopia and dystopia are the obverse and reverse of the same thing'.[25] And then writing

---

[22] On *Witness*' visual style and Weir's use of Vermeer, see Serena Formica, *Peter Weir: A Creative Journey from Australia to Hollywood* (Bristol: Intellect, 2012), pp. 123–35.

[23] See Margaret Atwood, *In Other Worlds: SF and the Human Imagination* (London: Virago, 2011), p. 66.

[24] Margaret Atwood 'An Unfashionable Sensibility', review of Piercy's *Women on the Edge of Time*, originally published in *The Nation*, 4 December 1976, reprinted as ' Marge Piercy: *Women on the Edge of Time, Living in the Open*', in Margaret Atwood, *Second Words: Selected Critical Prose, 1960–1982* (Toronto: Anansi, 1982), pp. 272–78 (p. 273).

[25] Margaret Atwood, '*The Handmaid's Tale*: A Feminist Dystopia?', in *Lire Margaret Atwood: The Handmaid's Tale*, ed. by Marta Dvorak (Rennes: Presses universitaires de Rennes, 1999), pp. 17–30 (p. 24).

Figure 7.1 Johannes Vermeer, *The Milkmaid*, c. 1660, oil on canvas, 45.5 cm × 41 cm, Rijksmuseum, Amsterdam.

more than two decades after the *Handmaid's Tale*'s appearance, and shortly after the publication of *The Year of the Flood* (2009) the second instalment of her speculative post-apocalyptic MaddAddam trilogy, Atwood came to the view that there was a need for a term which could encapsulate this intertwining of utopian and dystopian perspectives. Her coinage was 'Ustopia', the amalgamation of 'the imagined perfect society and its opposite', such that the notion of each contained 'a latent version of the other'.[26]

Of course, Atwood is far from being unique or original in making such observations on the negative implications of utopian projection. In Samuel Johnson's romance, *Rasselas, The History of the Prince of Abissinia* (1759), the prince confesses to his tutor, Imlac, that he has day-dreamed about establishing an ideal republic before being shocked at his own complacency in effortlessly assuming the destruction required to

[26] Margaret Atwood, *In Other Worlds*, p. 66.

Figure 7.2 Kelly McGillis as Rachel Haas, *Witness*, 1985, film still, film directed by Peter Weir, © Paramount Pictures, All Rights Reserved.

put such plans into practice (including the murder of his own family). Many works from the late nineteenth century speculating on the negative effects of idealistic schemes, such as the proliferation of responses to Bellamy's *Looking Backward* (1888), all bent on demonstrating that oppression and catastrophe will be the inevitable consequences of founding a society on such an eccentric socialist manifesto. And, as we saw in the last chapter, Ursula K. Le Guin made an almost identical authorial pronouncement to Atwood on generic interplay, that 'every eutopia contains a dystopia, every dystopia contains an eutopia'.[27] There are, however, some difficulties in the historical contingencies of these apparently straightforward oppositions. As Gregory Claeys reveals in his 'natural history' of such dark imaginings, the term 'dystopia' probably has an eighteenth-century origin (earlier than its usual first citation in a parliamentary speech by John Stuart Mill in 1868); and while it is entirely possible to apply the term retrospectively, it does not come into standard usage until the later part of the twentieth century (used principally as a medical term in the early part of the last century).[28] Hence, Bertrand Russell described Huxley's *Brave New World* (1932) as one of those utopias 'written to make us still more unhappy', in contradistinction to that abundance of late-Victorian utopias intended to have precisely the opposite effect; and Orwell's friend, George Woodcock, described in the 1950s those depictions of planned

---

[27] Ursula K. Le Guin, 'Utopiyin, Utopiyang', in Thomas More, *Utopia* (London: Verso, 2016), pp. 195–98 (p. 197).
[28] Gregory Claeys, *Dystopia: A Natural History* (Oxford: Oxford University Press, 2018), p. 273.

societies which express the fears of modern men as 'Utopias in the negative'.[29] As Claeys points out, no critical examination of the dystopian literary genre appeared until the early 1960s. The most notable of these early discussions was Chad Walsh's *From Utopia to Nightmare* (1962), which established the juxtaposition of the utopian and dystopian as a critical axiom.[30]

So, we might question the readiness with which dystopia can be either counterpoised or integrated into the utopian in a straightforward fashion, given that it is not a term which can be said to have a distinctive existence until the second half of the last century; and we might also wonder precisely what definition of dystopia is being applied in these circumstances. As Claeys observes, there are nearly as many ways of defining dystopia (and whether or not the term can be synonymously used with anti-utopia) as there are for utopia; and then there is the question of the slippage in Atwood's usage. The blending of 'Ustopia' implies the presence of mutually active components, but the further use of 'latent', misleadingly I think, implies either the utopian or dystopian is dormant in the obverse state. Nevertheless, there is both insight and a sense of development in Atwood's coinage. It is a commonplace that the dystopian has become the dominant mode since the late twentieth century. And no coincidence that Tom Moylan, who had attempted to align what he termed critical utopias of the 1970s, a species of science fiction, with the radical politics of that era, felt compelled to produce a millennial revision of his own terminology. In what was effectively a sequel to his first study, Moylan describes the development of the more pessimistic critical dystopia, as a response to what he decries as the wholesale rejection of a socialist vision in Western states. Speculative writing had taken a darker turn, and what remained of that reformatory utopian project was given lyrical expression in the book's title, *Scraps of the Untainted Sky* (2000).[31] One could only now find utopian remnants in dystopian ubiquity, a set of circumstances which was the only reasonable response to the dismal condition of late modernity. Moylan found such moments of utopian illumination in the late twentieth-century works of Octavia Butler and Kim Stanley Robinson. He makes almost no mention of Atwood; and, of course, what she was proposing in the strong form of ustopianism was not so much a theory of remnant, but rather a more sustained interaction of utopian and dystopian impulses.

My contention, then, is that the ustopian for Atwood has come to stand for more than the simultaneous presence of utopian and dystopian elements in her fiction. And for that matter it goes beyond the blurring of conceptual boundaries we encounter in the elliptical and symbolic style in the *Handmaid's Tale*. The more extensive notion as a matter of aesthetic practice is that in certain circumstances the utopian and the dystopian should be understood as *being the same thing*. If we can detect the ustopian impulse in her first speculative work, than we can also see this being worked through as a conscious principle in her MaddAddam trilogy. As an author, Atwood is often at

---

[29] Bertrand Russell, 'Review of '*Brave New World*', *New Leader*, 11 March 1932, 9, reprinted in *Aldous Huxley: The Critical Heritage*, ed. by Donald Watt (London: Routledge and Kegan Paul, 1975), pp. 210–12 (p. 210); George Woodcock, 'Utopias in the Negative', *Sewanee Review*, 64 (1956), 81–97, quoted in Claeys, *Dystopia*, p. 274.

[30] Claeys, *Dystopia*, p. 275.

[31] Moylan's title is taken from the closing sentence of E.M. Forster's 'The Machine Stops' (1909).

her most intriguing when she writes at the intersection of the speculative and the real, and this chapter will conclude with a consideration of ustopianism in her finest novel, *The Blind Assassin* (2000).

It seems a typical piece of Atwoodian contrariness to conceive of her first male protagonist as being the last man on earth. The early novel *Life before Man* highlighted the palaeontological enthusiasms of one of her characters; and we now have a novel on life nearly after Man. In the idea of the last representative of the human race, there is an allusion to that nineteenth-century speculative romance on the end of things from a female perspective, Mary Shelley's *The Last Man* (1826). Shelley's Lionel Verney finds himself wandering alone in the ruins of Rome after a plague has exterminated humankind in the year 2100 ACE. Atwood's *Oryx & Crake* (2003), the first part of the MaddAddam trilogy, starts with a simple statement of fact, which perhaps indicates a certain necessity for the third-person narrator to preserve some distance from this curiously depopulated world, so as not to engender too much incredulity in the reader; or perhaps, this initial narrative flatness is intended as a feature of a new perspicacious style, a tempering of the author's usual instinct for lyrical allusion when the story is to be developed at considerable length. 'Snowman wakes before dawn' is its first sentence, as the central character blinks into consciousness.[32] Maybe we are supposed to detect a faint echo of the *Handmaid's Tale* in the character's name: 'Snowman', reminiscent of Offred's impression of the bodies of doctors hanging from the town wall, with their 'heads of snowmen, with the coal eyes and the carrot noses fallen out'. We might already wonder given *Oryx & Crake*'s length whether the epic is supposed to be a generic influence; and that suspicion is encouraged by the initial account of early-morning light. 'On the eastern horizon there's a greyish haze', the narrator observes, 'lit now with a rosy deadly glow' (p. 3). The description looks like a variant on the standard Homeric compound epithet of a rosy-fingered dawn, negatively connoted in this instance with its 'greyish haze', a grim association of iridescence.

We soon discover that we are on the archetypal location of the beach, as the narrative voice moves closer to Snowman's perspective in free-indirect style. Snowman stands on the shore. He listens to 'the shriek of birds that nest out there and the distant ocean grinding the ersatz reefs of rusted car parts and jumbled bricks and assorted rubble sound[ing] almost like holiday traffic' (p. 3). Initially, this looks like a rather odd figurative evocation of reefs and rocks with the tidal swell rolling over them. And then there is Snowman's broken wristwatch, a 'talisman', where its lack of function equals 'zero hour'. Snowman is a twenty-first-century addition to the long line of literary figures who find themselves washed up on the beach, including Odysseus, Crusoe (Snowman stumbles across his own footprints in the style of Defoe's eponymous hero), Gulliver and, more recently, Will Farnaby in Huxley's *Island* (1962). None of these figures, however, face such a challenging set of circumstances as Atwood's protagonist. It transpires that nearly all of humankind has been exterminated by a synthetic virus. The new corals are indeed constructed from rusted automobiles and rubble; and the irony of the observation on the similarity to the sound of the sea to holiday traffic is

---

[32] Margaret Atwood, *Oryx & Crake* (London: Virago, 2013), p. 3. All further in-text references are to this edition.

that there are no more holidays, just as there is no more traffic. The talismanic stopped-watch accurately records a reset of all time to zero hour. Katherine Snyder plausibly conceives of Snowman as a case study in post-traumatic stress, with his misfiring memory and unexpected flashbacks, a portrayal, she suggests, 'of the shock or wound that disrupts the integrity of the subject'.[33] Yet, this interpretation does not quite acknowledge the character's comic aspects. He is dishevelled and eccentric: his bent sunglasses have a lens missing; he is swaddled in a 'dirty bedsheet' (p. 3); and he has an 'authentic-replica Red Sox baseball cap' plopped on his head (p. 3).

Oryx & Crake has two diachronic narratives related synchronously (similar to Le Guin's *The Dispossessed* (1974)). One half of the novel describes Snowman's experience of being the last man; and the other is an extended *Bildungsroman*, charting Snowman's development from childhood to early middle age, and his coincidental role in humanity's downfall. Atwood has claimed that all the science she considers in this work already exists; and that the various catastrophic and fantastical events described could with a sufficient ill-wind come to pass.[34] However, she is not a futurologist in the mould of H.G. Wells, Isaac Asimov, Arthur C. Clark and William Gibson. In her 1970s review of Piercy's *Women on the Edge of Time*, she dismissed the compact wireless devices all Mattapoisettians wear on their wrists to communicate with one another as preposterous, 'uncomfortably reminiscent of silliness such as Dick Tracy's two-way wristwatch radios'.[35] Her vision of the near future in *Oryx & Crake* is technologically conservative. Pre-apocalyptic modernity is still a world in which people travel to work by train, play games on PCs, and communicate with one another by email and telephone calls. The novel's speculative narrative seems intended to be an imaginative amplification of current social and cultural trends, rather than an attempt to furnish a convincing technological future state. Governance in pre-apocalyptic America is the exclusive concern of multi-national conglomerates, and the economic pressures of growing inequality have divided society into two main groups: a corporate world of plush, gated communities (with all the necessary facilities for work and relaxation provided in these compounds); and the impoverished conditions of the majority of the population, many of whom inhabit dilapidated inner-city precincts, known as the 'Pleeblands' (an adjusted amalgamation of 'plebs', Latin: 'common people', and land).

The pre-apocalyptic narrative follows the friendship of two middle-class boys growing up in a corporate-scientific community, Jimmy, who will become 'Snowman' after the apocalypse, and Glenn, who is named after the brilliant if eccentric Toronto pianist, Glenn Gould; but is referred to as Crake throughout the novel. He adopts 'Crake' as the username for a Darwinian online computer game, Extinctathon, in which imaginary species are created and perish under shifting environmental pressures. Crake eventually attends a prestigious East Coast research centre to pursue undergraduate and postgraduate studies in biotechnology. The less academically-astute

---

[33] Katherine V. Snyder, '"Time to go": The Post-apocalyptic and the Post-traumatic in Margaret Atwood's *Oryx and Crake*', *Studies in the Novel*, 43 (2011), 470–89 (p. 479).

[34] See, for example, Margaret Atwood, '*The Handmaid's Tale* and *Oryx and Crake* in Context', *PMLA*, 119 (2004), 513–17 (p. 513).

[35] Margaret Atwood, 'An Unfashionable Sensibility', review of Piercy's *Women on the Edge of Time*, p. 274.

Jimmy only manages to secure a place to study media at the insalubrious and cash-strapped Martha Graeme liberal arts college, named in honour of the distinguished modern American dancer and choreographer. The third main figure is Oryx, an exotic and enigmatic presence. A type of African antelope, 'Oryx' suggests that her defining characteristics are gracefulness and prey. Atwood leaves Oryx's origins obscure. Born into an impoverished peasant community in south-east Asia (Oryx does not say where, but probably Northern Thailand), she is sold by her desperate parents to a Fagan-like impresario. He takes her to a large bustling city. From a young age she appears in pornographic films; Jimmy first sees her face as an erotic still displayed on a virtual gateway to the extinction game. She is eventually trafficked and held captive, presumably for the purposes of sexual gratification, in a suburban American home. Jimmy recognises her when network news covers her escape from modern bondage. After college, Jimmy embarks on a career in marketing, and is eventually recruited by his friend, Crake, to devise the promotional campaign for a potent synthetic aphrodisiac he has developed, the BlyssPluss pill.

Through some creative plotting, a love triangle develops between the three main figures. While Jimmy promotes the BlyssPluss pill, Oryx is charged with its international distribution. As Jimmy subsequently learns, Crake has also genetically engineered a race of neo-humans, the Crakers, in a sealed cell, dubbed the Paradice [sic] Dome. Crake is eventually revealed to be a demented genius, with aspects of Victor Frankenstein, Rotwang and Dr Strangelove, but he is mainly a millennial version of Dr Moreau. Disgusted by the selfishness and viciousness of Man, Crake decides that the creation of the ideal society requires a real-life round of Extinctathon. The globally dispensed BlyssPluss pill has a delayed-release fast-acting airborne lethal virus. Crake's maniacal scheme is to eradicate humankind and repopulate the earth with the Crakers, conceived as a kind of second coming of the originating African tribe. These creatures are designed to live harmoniously with themselves and not to cause any environmental damage. Pacific, beautiful, supplied in a range of alluring skin tones, they are herbivorous ruminants with insect repellent incorporated in their skin. They do not suffer from sexual jealousy; they lack, initially at least, a higher consciousness, and all the destructive tendencies Crake believed came with such a capacity for self-reflection and insight. They may not be as slow-witted and as passive as Wells' Eloi, but they are still destined for a picturesque arcadian existence, to be blended into the *locus amoenus* of the once-again bountiful earth. By the post-apocalyptic zero hour, Oryx and Crake are both dead; and Snowman (whom unbeknown to himself was inoculated against the virus) is left behind to enact the last part of his erstwhile friend's master plan, leading the Crakers out of the Paradice Dome and into the new land.

One can straightforwardly view *Oryx & Crake* as being indicative of a general interest in apocalypse at the turn of the twenty-first century; in those prophesies of the world's end, with their origins in the last book of the New Testament, 'The Revelation of St John' ('apokalypsis' means revelation in ancient Greek), and presaged in the books of Ezekiel and Daniel in the Old Testament. Of course, as Frank Kermode reminds us, impending cataclysm has been a persistent idea of the Christian era, with biblical forecast combined with Sibylline oracles to produce *saecula*, those points of raised anxiety with a sense of imminent termination. There have been significant and enduring figures in the promotion of such awful endings, such as Joachim of Flora whose thirteenth-century tripartite historical schema influenced the writings of Dante and Hegel, and whose predictions could even still be detected in the National Socialist coinage of 'Third Reich'.[36] Kermode famously argued that a hallmark of modernist literature was its turning away from depictions of an explicit termination to the embrace of a diffuse eschatology. In the works of Yeats, Eliot, Pound and Joyce, the End is 'no longer imminent, the End is immanent'.[37] Yet, one might also suggest there is an explicit reversal of that tendency in the 1990s and the 2000s with the second millennial expectation of the last days. Catastrophe was a staple of Hollywood cinema in this period, with such films as *Twister* (1996), *Independence Day* (1996), *Volcano* (1997), *Deep Impact* (1998), *Armageddon* (1998), *The Core* (2003) and *Day After Tomorrow* (2004).[38]

The sense of imminent destruction received added symbolic impetus with the terrorist assault of 9/11 in 2001. Yet, we should also acknowledge the strength of the opposing case – that the turn of the twenty-first century was one of the least likely periods to face global calamity. The notion of apocalypse was incongruous when compared to the immediate level of threat. Worldwide instability was much more apparent before and after this epoch. The possibility of nuclear conflagration diminished with improved relations between Russia and the USA from the late 1980s onwards. There were certainly dreadful episodes in the 1990s, such as the Rwandan genocide and the Balkan civil war, but these events never had the potential to develop into all-consuming global conflicts. Aids threatened to be a pandemic in the early 1980s; but it was apparent by the late 1990s that while its mortality rate was tragically high, it was controllable with antiretroviral medication; the total number of deaths from Aids since its outbreak in 1981 is almost certainly still less than that from Spanish Flu in a single year, 1918.[39]

An optimistic account of the epoch was provided by the *Economist* in its millennium issue in December 1999, with articles on wealth, population, work, cities and rights. The issue's premise was the lot of global population had improved dramatically over the last century, and would continue to do so. The triumph of Western modernity had been the extension and consolidation of democratic societies; and one could be reasonably confident that the sense of contentment produced by these form of political organisations would endure. The essay on wealth equivocates on the question of unending growth, but still concludes by suggesting that technological advance will continue to improve human lives.[40] Economic circumstances seemed propitious in

---

[36] See Frank Kermode, *The Sense of an Ending: Studies in the Theory of Fiction with a New Epilogue* (Oxford: Oxford University Press, 2000), first published 1966, pp. 11–14.

[37] Kermode, *The Sense of an Ending*, p. 25.

[38] Kirsten M. Thompson points out that there were twice as many apocalyptic films produced in the 1990s than the previous decade in her *Apocalyptic Dread: American Film at the Turn of the Millennium* (Albany: State University of New York Press, 2007), p. 12.

[39] WHO states 34 million people have died worldwide of Aids, see http://www.who.int/gho/hiv/en/, accessed 11 April 2019. John M. Barry proposes a conservative estimate of 50 million deaths from influenza in the outbreak of 1918. The great majority of Aids deaths have occurred in Africa. Deaths from Spanish Flu were globally distributed; see Barry, *The Great Influenza: The Story of the Deadliest Pandemic in History* (London: Penguin, 2005), pp. 396–98.

[40] 'The Road to Riches', *Economist*, 23 December 1999 [https://www.economist.com/special/1999/12/23/the-road-to-riches, accessed 3 March 2018].

America and Europe at the turn of the century with strong market performance, high rates of employment and low rates of inflation. The advent of an economic and currency union in Europe was not intended merely as a pragmatic fiscal measure, but as an affirmation of shared Enlightenment values across the whole continent of security, freedom and justice. The era's principal ecological anxiety of the depleted ozone layer and global warming offered the prospect of environmental catastrophe, though the predicted dire effects of rising temperatures still seemed distant.

It might be too glib to characterise the turn of the century as the golden age of liberal democracy, but global prospects certainly appeared that much bleaker in the 2010s. The banking crisis in 2008 resulted in the worst economic depression since the 1930s, followed by a sovereign debt debacle which reduced some European states to the verge of default. In the same era, there were questionable military interventions by Western powers in the Middle East. There was repression of democratic movements and protracted civil wars in the same region. There was the prospect of nuclear proliferation to erratic and unstable states, the emergence of bellicose and nihilist forms of radical Islam, the spread of disruptive populism in various manifestations across Europe and North America, the implementation of isolationist policies, and the ever-shortening horizon of irreversible climate change. Yet, perhaps that *is* the point – the apocalyptic zeitgeist favours the anticipation of a global crisis, rather than being in the midst of one; and it was, perhaps, a paradoxical combination of the associations of decisive millennial revelation with a less-threatening set of circumstances which created a sense of imminent global calamity.

As with the *Handmaid's Tale*, Atwood's background investigations for *Oryx & Crake* consist of newspaper cuttings and magazine articles, referred to, in this instance, as 'the brown box'. The box's contents suggest that the factors which are supposed to bring the world to its chaotic terminus are standard features of modern advanced societies, rather than emanating from some malign external threat, committed as a matter of either ideological or theological conviction to the eradication of Western modernity.[41] Atwood's reflections on the contributory factors to societal disintegration are numerous and varied in her novel; these include: the callous indifference to individuals of American corporatism, junk food, the perils of genetic engineering and stem-cell research, industrial farming and the use of pesticides, the questionable motives of pharmaceutical conglomerates, the general promotion of science and technology as a means to truth and understanding over the alternative insightful claims of the arts, the corrosive effects of online pornography and the playing of violent computer

---

[41] The contents of the brown box are now in the Atwood Archive Ms. Coll.355, Box 111. Notable items include an issue of *GQ*, May 2002 on the male species with articles entitled 'Living Forever' and 'Cloning Elvis'; a special issue of *Scientific American*, September 2001, on nanotechnology; Stuart Laidlaw's *Secret Ingredients: The Brave New World of Industrial Farming* (Toronto: McClelland and Stewart, 2004); Carolyn Abraham's consideration of high-functioning autism in 'Is there a Geek Syndrome?', *Globe and Mail*, 19, October 2002; Duncan Campbell's article on the Earth Liberation Front, 'US Eco-Arsonists Put Heat on FBI', *Guardian Weekly*, 15–21 March 2001, 7; Stuart Millar's report on teenage computer culture and hacking in 'Teenage Clicks' *Guardian*, 5 June 2001, G2, 2–3; and Andrew Perrin's exposé of the Thai sex industry, 'In Bangkok Men Order Girls like Pizza', *Globe and Mail*, 15 December 2001, A 17.

games (especially by teenage boys), sex trafficking (especially in south-east Asia), the emergence of twenty-something West Coast technologists as the new Masters of the Universe, middle-class America's withdrawal into gated communities, the dilapidated state of inner cities (Detroit, in particular), and the dysfunctional nature of the modern nuclear family. Fredric Jameson persuasively suggests that Atwood presents in *Oryx &Crake* a lurid vision of entropic Americana, where all the colours 'have a loathsome pastel quality'.[42] The apocalypse has become aligned with the dystopian, a matter of viewing the present state of the early twenty-first century through a fish-eye lens, conceiving of the millennial epoch as though it were already in a state of terminal decay.

Of course, Atwood has a long-standing commitment to liberal and environmental interests. There are many documents in her archive which testify to her campaigning from the 1970s onwards for such causes as protecting the wilderness of Northern Ontario from commercial logging, addressing the abuse of human rights in her work for Amnesty International and PEN, and in her support for numerous local initiatives.[43] However, as already suggested, there is an incorporating impetus to her fiction, such that any idea which is included in the work necessarily entails its opposite; and the notion, moreover, that the form of the aesthetic cannot be straightforwardly determined by its apparent ethical and social precepts. The sense of moral equivocation is sharply realised in this work in the account of Oryx's induction into the Asian sex industry as a child, and her subsequent transportation to America. The events are related from Oryx's point of view. She reports on the facts of her experience (as she recalls them) with a mixture of sanguine acceptance and tedium. She bears no ill-will toward either the child trader, who purchased her from her parents, or indeed, the American man, who imprisoned her in his Texan home. It would seem that the artistic challenge in this segment of the novel is to write about a topic which mainstream liberal opinion regards as being morally repugnant, without then providing any straightforward evaluation. It may well be that Oryx's story is intended as an account of a kind of contextual deficiency, an inert irony, such that the victim does not even realise that he or she has been abused, because he or she does not possess the social and psychological co-ordinates to make proper sense of their experience; or Oryx's tale may be intended as a testament to the durability of some children, capable of withstanding all manner of horrors without exhibiting obvious signs of trauma.[44]

Such a departure from received ethical opinion perhaps indicates a desire on the author's part to adopt a totalising perspective on the world and its cruelties; if not to

---

[42] Fredric Jameson, 'Then you are Them', *London Review of Books*, 10 September 2009, [https://www.lrb.co.uk/v31/n17/fredric-jameson/then-you-are-them, accessed 3 March 2019].
[43] Atwood Archive Ms.Coll.520 Box 13, f. 1–9.
[44] The standard work on childhood resilience is Emily Werner and Ruth S. Smith, *Vulnerable, but Invincible: A Longitudinal Study of Resilient Children and Youth* (New York: McGraw Hill, 1982). Werner and Smith suggest that a third of the children they studied since 1955 remained unaffected by their adverse circumstances. See also recent studies on the resilience of children in war: A.S. Masten and A.J. Narayan, 'Child Development in the Context of Disaster, War, and Terrorism: Pathways of Risk and Resilience', *Annual Review of Psychology*, 63 (2012), 227–57; and Marwan Diab and others, 'Effectiveness of Psycho-Social Intervention: Enhancing Resilience among War-Affected Children and the Moderating Role of Family Factors', *Child Abuse and Neglect*, 40 (2015), 24–35.

distil all phenomena into a single historical viewpoint, then at least to try to grasp the central elements which shape modern experience. Atwood admires Jonathan Swift (there are epigraphs from the satirist for both the *Handmaid's Tale* and *Oryx & Crake*) and, in this work she applies something akin to universal Swiftian scepticism to the world as it is encountered. The fault-line in Swift is often taken to be that the satirical and imaginative force of the representation compromises the moral observation being made. Part of the unnerving quality of *A Modest Proposal* (1729) is that it seems to advocate gentrified cannibalism as a public service, a means of alleviating Irish poverty with as much remorseless logic and relish as its desire to expose the dire economic and social consequences of absentee landlordism and British indifference to her western territory. *Oryx & Crake* similarly seems to accept the apocalyptic prospect it ostensibly wishes to caution against. One can see that as an exercise in speculative fiction, Atwood is interested in the imaginative and dramatic possibilities of constructing a post-apocalyptic terrain. The general sanguine acceptance of this new dispensation and the matter-of-fact way in which the calamity is reported (in this book and the trilogy as a whole) do not entirely dispel the impression of momentary alignment, if not actual agreement, with Crake's messianic utopianism.

Atwood's overall approach in the MaddAddam trilogy is perhaps too ebullient, associative, and scabrous to match the psychological particularity and the objective causative relations of classic realism with a sense of spiritual revelation. The suggestion in the palindrome of 'MaddAddam' of completion and sealed tidiness is misleading in this respect. Atwood does not attempt, for example, to emulate Patrick White in imbuing the modern landscape with a sense of Blakean vision, or of systematically working out biblical narrative in symbolic form in the Australian outback (in White's *Riders of the Chariot* (1961), for instance, four marginalised figures are drawn together in the interior by a shared apocalyptic vision). Even if Atwood is not consistent in her use of scripture, there is still a conspicuous attempt in *Oryx & Crake* to devise an imaginative means of conceptualising modern experience within the terms of such archetypes. There are many scriptural allusions in Atwood's account of the apocalypse and afterwards. Snowman eventually plays Cain to Crake's Abel. He assumes Moses' mantle when leading the Crakers out of the dome into the new land. One might even regard him as a kind of embodiment of Miltonic providence in the expulsion of Adam and Eve, as the progenitors of *all* humankind, take their first steps beyond Eden in *Paradise Lost*'s final book. Snowman, more generally, takes on the responsibilities of a prophet in his attempt to fashion a rudimentary cosmogony for his charges by recounting the apotheosised lives of Oryx and Crake (even if, as Françoise and Jeff Storey note, there is a slippage in his mythologising, 'more reminiscent of Zeus and Hera than of the Judeo-Christian tradition').[45] Scriptural allusion, however, is at its clearest in the trilogy's second instalment, *The Year of the Flood* (2009), where the biblical association of plague with the airborne BlyssPluss virus is overlaid with the narrative of Noah's deluge.

---

[45] Françoise Storey and Jeff Storey, 'History and Allegory in Margaret Atwood's *Oryx and Crake*', *Cycnos* 22 (2006), [read online at http://revel.unice.fr/cycnos/index.html?id=607, accessed 11 April 2019].

As Snowman discovers toward the end of *Oryx & Crake*, he is not, after all, the last human left alive; and we subsequently learn that a select group have providentially survived the cataclysm, as though preserved in the ark while the synthetic plague, the 'waterless flood' swept away the evils of late capitalism. *The Year of the Flood* covers the same twenty-five-year period prior to the apocalypse as *Oryx & Crake*, but is now mainly viewed from the perspective of a female character, Toby, who in Atwood's coincidental text-world was at school with Jimmy and Glenn (the former's first girlfriend). The novel's central section recounts Toby's experience of the Gardeners. This is a 1960s-style commune with strong religious-environmental convictions (the book's original title was *God's Gardeners*).[46] The Gardeners conceive of themselves as an eco-anarchic movement, vehemently opposed to the corporate governance of modern urban society, prepared to undertake the occasional act of sabotage. Yet the construction of their green community is, in practice, hierarchical and conservative; and its liturgy and hymnody could be modelled on that of the Anglican Communion. Each of the novel's sections is named after a saint or feast day in the Gardener's calendar, such as 'Creation Day', 'The Feast of Adam and All Primates', 'Mole Day', 'Saint Rachel Day' (after the early environmentalist Rachel Carson), and 'April Fish'. The start of each section has a sermon from the community's founder, its de facto archbishop, an accidental Noah, the self-styled Adam One, who explains in his sermons the significance of the feasts and saints' days.

Adam One considers, for instance, the origin of 'Poisson d'Avril' or April Fool's Day. He implies in the sermon at the beginning of Year Fourteen (eleven years before the flood) that there is a salient comparison to be made between this modern order and its early adherents. 'April Fish', he claims, 'was surely first a Christian festival, as a Fish image was used by the early Christians as secret signals of their faith in times of oppression'.[47] Adam One correctly follows St Augustine's explanation of this image's cryptic acrostic significance, but then comically over-extends his exegesis. 'The Fish was an apt symbol', Adam One explains, 'for Jesus first called as his Apostles two fishermen surely chosen by him to help conserve the Fish population. They were told to be fishers of men instead of being fishers of Fish, thus neutralizing two destroyers of Fish!'[48] These twenty-first-century Ecotopians press scripture into the service of whatever cause happens to be uppermost in their minds. Hence the conversion of Christ's disciples is improbably interpreted as an ecological strategy for conserving Galilean fish stocks.

There is evidently an ustopian tension in the depiction of a small self-contained organic community, and the desolate and violent inner-city circumstances of the Pleeblands where the Gardeners are situated for most of the *Year of the Flood* (tending their plants and bees on slum rooftops). And indeed, one might extend that notion to the conceptual opposition to the MaddAddams, a bio-terrorist organisation which

---

[46] Title on various early plans and drafts, see for example Atwood Archive Ms. Coll.595 Box 5, f. 3-20. See also Emma Brockes interview, 'Margaret Atwood: '"I have a big following among the biogeeks". "Finally! Someone understands us!"', *Guardian*, 24 August 2013, [http://www.theguardian.com/books/2013/aug/24/margaret-atwood-interview, accessed 11 April 2019].
[47] Margaret Atwood, *The Year of the Flood* (London: Virago, 2013), p. 234.
[48] Atwood, *Year of the Flood*, p. 234.

engineers flora and fauna to assault the dominant corporate structures in this vision of decaying America. However, one could also propose that there are inherently ustopian aspects of the notion of the eco-religious sect itself; and indeed, such communities have self-evident apocalyptic tendencies. One suspects that God's Gardeners are intentionally reminiscent of the American People's Temple. The Temple had been founded in Indianapolis in the late 1950s before moving to Mendocino County, California to create a 'socialist Eden', and thence to San Francisco, where it grew in strength under the Reverend Jim Jones' charismatic leadership. Faced with objections as to how the Temple was run, it then relocated to Guyana to establish an agricultural community, 'Jonestown'. In 1978, the Temple was visited by a Californian congressman investigating charges of authoritarianism and human-rights abuses. The politician's party was ambushed on the airstrip as it was about to leave. That night and the following morning the Temple enacted a pre-arranged suicide plan, resulting in the deaths of 912 members, including 276 children.[49] This would have been a dark turn in the God's Gardeners storyline which Atwood manifestly refused to take; but at the same time, the authoritarian and manipulative traits of Adam One do not entirely dispel the possibility of such a paranoid and self-destructive outcome. As it happens, the Gardeners turn out to be subject to a Job-like cosmic irony – a religious sect with apocalyptic tendencies, which does not fully foresee the coming cataclysm.

Atwood configures the world, then, in terms of binaries, of considering how any positive entails its negative; and a central purpose of her fiction is to explore such polarities, of finding images which can draw together such oppositions, to be seen as a singular event (of which her ustopianism is a part). And if one is going to write about the end of things, then one might as well consider their beginnings as well; and one might also reflect on the provenance and significance of writing and storytelling. We can detect intentions of this kind throughout this speculative trilogy, but they are particularly prominent in the final instalment, *MaddAddam* (2013). This process, it seems, necessitates some identification and disaggregation of the fundamental narrative modes from which the trilogy is composed. And we might approach the question as to how Atwood utilises such typologies through Erich Auerbach's consideration of the oppositions of early expressiveness in *Mimesis* (1946), his landmark trans-historical study of European realism. Auerbach began his study with a late episode from the *Odyssey* in which Odysseus has just arrived home to Ithaca. His wife, Penelope, does not recognise him, and she instructs the housekeeper and Odysseus' former nurse, Eurycleia, to wash his feet as is customarily required by Greek hospitality. The nurse notices a scar on the traveller's left thigh. As soon as she touches it, she realises the man she is tending is her master. Eurycleia drops his foot into the basin, and is about to exclaim with joy, when Odysseus grabs her by the throat.

Auerbach concedes that he omitted in his excursus the episode's lengthy middle section situated between Eurycleia's noticing the scar and the foot striking the basin. This passage describes how Odysseus sustained his injury, gouged by a boar while hunting at his grandfather's house, along with accounts of his grandfather's stalwart

---

[49] See John R. Hall, *Gone from the Promised Land: Jonestown in American Cultural History* (New Brunswick, NJ: Transaction, 1987), p. 288.

character, and the members of his extended family. Auerbach thinks the modern instinct to treat this digression as a means of generating suspense is mistaken. For him, the interpolation is rather indicative of a key aspect of primary epic, that for all its running back and forth through time in discrete and precisely realised planes of existence, the *Odyssey* still constructs meaningful experience as a compelling present. In Homer, he says, all things 'are brought to light in perfect fullness; so that a continuous rhythmic procession of phenomena passes by, and never is there a form left fragmentary or half-illuminated, never a lacuna, never a gap'.[50] It is entirely different from that other 'equally ancient and equally epic style from a different world of forms', that of ancient scripture.[51] Auerbach claims the Old Testament's most significant aspects are its occlusions and omissions. In the story of Abraham and Isaac, he suggests, the narrative of sorrowful duty in impending filial sacrifice only reveals as much as is necessary to allow one moment to succeed another. 'All else is left in obscurity', he says, 'the decisive points of narrative alone are emphasised, what lies between is non-existent, time and place are undefined and call for interpretation'.[52]

These observations on the formal properties and psychological effects of Homeric and scriptural style are then extended into a consideration of their different intentions. The Homeric world-view is grand, patrician, fashioned into a unifying trajectory (rage and war in the *Iliad*, guile and travelling in the *Odyssey*). In contrast, there is little ostensible connection between the episodes which comprise the Old Testament. Scripture's principal figures are remarkable only for their ordinariness, only exceptional insofar as Jehovah compels them to endure many humiliations in his service. Yet as diverse as these biblical tales may be, there is still a 'vertical connection' in their providential selection; and this means the claims of scripture are more profound than those of its Hellenic counterpart. The Old Testament 'presents universal history; it begins with the beginning of time, with the creation of the world, and will end in the Last Days, the fulfilling of the Covenant, with which the world will come to an end'.[53] And it is in terms of the tension between the unified foregrounded present of epic style on the one side and the partial, occluded, multi-layered biblical style on the other that Auerbach examines the development of literary realism from antiquity to the twentieth century.

An overall intention of Atwood's trilogy would seem ostensibly to be to draw together epic and scriptural modes, as simultaneous means of interpretation, as a kind of restatement of these fundamental opposing forms in an expression of their likely terminus. As we have already seen, the trilogy's biblical aspects are apparent, from the structuring of individual episodes to the overarching form of the *Year of the Flood* as a reworking of scriptural style. Atwood's main characters, Snowman, Adam One and Toby, are all ordinary figures whom in keeping with scriptural expectations must suffer humiliations and reversals through their various tales, and to find themselves by

---

[50] Erich Auerbach, *Mimesis: The Representation of Reality in Western Literature*, trans. by Willard R. Trask (Princeton NJ: Princeton University Press, 1953), pp. 6–7.
[51] Auerbach, *Mimesis*, p. 7.
[52] Auerbach, *Mimesis*, p. 11.
[53] Auerbach, *Mimesis*, p. 16.

circuitous and improbable routes as prophets for the new *saecula*. One should acknowledge there are no claims in this schema to divine truth; and no sense of faith in an omniscient being whose will is manifested in these figures' storylines. This trilogy offers a speculative version of biblical universal history; and it has the apocalypse of last days as its central motif; but it does not by its conclusion regard the global cataclysm as the end of time, but rather conceives of this event as a terminus to a particular phase, then extended into a form of post-apocalyptic idealism. We can also identify some formal elements of primary epic in her speculative trilogy. There is the central focus on the figure of Jimmy, Odysseus-like, in the opening of *Oryx & Crake*; there is the movement back and forth across discrete temporal planes; and there is the sense in this opening novel that all episodes are being realised in the present. Any suspense that is created is subordinated to the principle that we are already aware of what is going to transpire. As Snowman indicates in the novel's opening chapter, the time is zero hour, and there is now *only* a present for him in which all experience is to be presented, with no concrete sense of future or past; and as if to emphasise whimsically the Attic aspect of the post-apocalyptic world, human characters after the mass extermination abandon modern clothing, winding bed sheets around themselves in imitation of chitons.

MaddAddam, the final part of the trilogy, mainly takes place after the great change, and traces the interactions between four main groups: a set of middle-aged humans, associated with the Gardeners before the plague, the MaddAddams the twenty-something set of scientists who worked for Crake, a small number of sociopaths who have survived the mass extermination because they were incarcerated (eliminated in the narrative's course), the Crakers, and the Pigoons, a genetically modified breed of pigs with human-like powers of reflection (reminiscent of Odysseus' crew on Circe's bewitching island, transformed into swine). The final novel's most noteworthy strand is its reflexive account of storytelling. In *MaddAddam*, Snowman has slipped into a coma, and Toby has assumed the role of story maker to the Crakers. Toby endeavours to make intelligible to her charges the events leading up to the Great Change and the reasons for collective survival into this new epoch. *MaddAddam* also recounts how one of the Crake children, Blackbeard, is particularly taken with Toby. He displays a lively intelligence and a creative imagination (an unintended aptitude from his creator's perspective). He learns from Toby how to write. 'I am Blackbeard', he says as well as writes near the novel's conclusion, 'and this is my voice that I am writing down to help Toby. If you look at this writing I have made you can hear me (I am Blackbord) talking to you inside your head'.[54] *MaddAddam* concludes with Blackbeard assuming Toby's mantle as imaginative chronicler and custodian of post-chaos literature, with the transformation of utterance into grapheme, with its capacity for both a narrative of full presence and the suggestion of a telling absence, the marker for both a new type of world and a return to ancient forms of expression and record. Blackbeard misspells his name at one point to reveal inadvertently his central social and cultural purpose in this new society as 'Blackbard'.[55]

---

[54] Margaret Atwood, *MaddAddam* (London: Virago, 2014), p. 457.
[55] Atwood, *MaddAddam*, p. 460.

One might also be tempted to consider the MaddAddam trilogy in terms of the paradigmatic account of postmodernism supplied by Jean-François Lyotard.[56] The condition of postmodernity in this thesis is indicated by the collapse of the grand narratives of the Enlightenment. The consequence of such overarching modes of thought and progress had been to assimilate or exclude all other identities, histories and temporalities. For Lyotard, the positive postmodern alternative after the fragmentation of such a totalising vision is, in itself, a form of utopianism in which a world is imagined of consisting of multiple, small-scale collectives, none of which has the capacity or the will to subordinate the others. *MaddAddam*'s conclusion looks to the kind of small-scale agrarianism communitarianism one can find in the works of Morris, Kropotkin, Piercy and Le Guin. The trilogy ends with the surviving humans, Crakers and Pigoons living harmoniously. There has been some fantastical interbreeding between the Crakers and the young MaddAddam women. The latter give birth to human-Crake hybrids, whose qualities and future remain undetermined; but the novel's close has a sense of a fantastical improvisation on a Lyotardian conspectus in which the collapse of grand narratives ends up with these variously associated post-human communities living side-by-side. One might be tempted to interpret the trilogy's conclusion as a celebration of the possibility of personal and gender fluency once conventional and arbitrary forms of social constraint have been abandoned. Yet, the ustopian dynamic of the trilogy as a whole makes it difficult to accept such a proposition at face value. The postmodern world of MaddAddam remains extremely close to a narrative of grim survival. Atwoodian ustopianism cannot resolve the tensions entailed in producing a cautionary epic on the destructive capacities of biotechnology and corporate excess, while at the same time producing a vision of post-human idealism, premised on the virtual eradication of the human race.

There is an indicative moment of patriarchal violence in the *Odyssey*, when Odysseus, having returned to his palace in Ithaca, takes hold of Eurycleia by the throat to prevent his erstwhile nurse from exposing him. He whispers in her ear that should she give him away, 'I will not spare you when I kill the rest of the serving maids in my palace'.[57] He will spare her, but having slain all of Penelope's suitors, he then acts on the second part of his threat, instructing his son, Telemachus, to dispense with those maids who consorted with the suitors. The young women are shut in a pen, and a ship's cable wound around each of their necks. The nooses are then collectively tightened until the women are lifted into the air, struggling and flapping like thrushes or pigeons 'with their feet, not for very long'.[58] This episode made a marked impression on Atwood. She adapted it for an image of the Gilead's religious authoritarianism, when Offred witnesses a group of women prisoners being collectively strangled for their sexual malefactions. And later in her *The Penelopiad* (2005), Atwood retold the *Odyssey* from

---

[56] See Jean-François Lyotard, *The Postmodern Condition: A Report on Knowledge*, trans. by Geoff Bennington and Brian Massumi (Manchester: Manchester University Press, 1984). See also Gary Browning, *Lyotard and the End of Grand Narratives* (Cardiff: University of Wales Press, 2000), pp. 21–39.
[57] Homer, *Odyssey*, trans. by Richard Lattimore (New York: HarperCollins, 1991), p. 295.
[58] Homer, *Odyssey*, p. 333.

Penelope's perspective, in which Odysseus' wife is infuriated by the serving women's summary executions. She believes her maids had little choice about entering into these liaisons; and they had served as her informants on the suitors' plans and actions. There is also a sense of a national patriarchal epic being related from a feminine perspective, and one which also features fantastical and actual violence committed against young women in Atwood's *fin de siècle* novel, *The Blind Assassin*.

I might have concluded this account of Atwood by examining her exploration of ustopian permutations through the second decade of the twenty-first century, such as in *The Heart Goes Last* (2015), a light-hearted novel, a game-playing cross-over of utopian and dystopian predicaments, in which the central characters, a dispirited blue-collar American couple, are given the opportunity to live in a safe and secure mid-Western community on condition they serve as inmates in the local penitentiary in alternate months (there is a final fanciful act with Elvis Presley impersonators in Las Vegas, looking like an homage to Demian Lichtenstein's 2001 movie, *3000 Miles from Graceland*). And I might also have considered one of the most recent of the *Handmaid's Tale*'s afterlives in the MGM television series, a beguiling adaptation of the novel, a production which is strikingly attuned to the era of #MeToo, insurgent political populism and the ISIS Caliphate. The series seems to be both faithful to and an elaboration of its literary source. The series' distinctive look has high tones added to a fundamentally desaturated palette. The extensive use of short focal lengths in extreme close up produces a sharp contrast between a hyperreal foreground and hazy background. The visual style provides an effective corollary to the novel's aesthetic in which colours and concepts seem to seep into one another, such as in Offred's observation of hanged doctors, with blood diffusing through the white cloth bags covering their heads. Yet, perhaps the more interesting ustopian questions are raised when the utopian and dystopian are treated in Atwood's oeuvre as a matter of concrete historical phenomenon, as well as speculative and fantastical projection. And those ideas are examined in their most incisive form, with a self-conscious dramatic conclusion, in her *Blind Assassin*.

The *Blind Assassin*'s central event is disclosed in the opening sentence when octogenarian former Toronto socialite, Iris Chase, announces 'ten days after the war ended, my sister Laura drove a car off a bridge'.[59] The two styles which Auerbach characterises as the fundamental expressive modes of Western fiction, of the narrative of full presence, and the enigmatic, multi-layered mode are both apparent as distinct relational types in this work. Iris's memoir is the novel's main component. The memoir recounts her childhood, her young adult life up to her sister's suicide, a summary of what happened afterwards, and a commentary on her current circumstances. Iris's narrative is complemented by other kinds of writing: pre-war social columns from Canadian newspapers (a pastiche of period cuttings); and substantial extracts from Laura Chase's short decontextualised and sparsely-punctuated modernist masterpiece, posthumously published in 1947, the titular *Blind Assassin*. Nested within this fragmented novella are two other tales: an oriental romance in the style of William

---

[59] Margaret Atwood, *The Blind Assassin* (London: Virago, 2001), p. 3. Further in-text references are to this edition.

Beckford with a literal appearance of a blind assassin; and an instalment of a pulp science-fiction story from the 1940s. Of course, the overall purpose of this exercise from Iris's perspective is to bring a complicated and fraught family saga into full illumination; and her ostensible reason for doing so is to effect an improbable reconciliation with her estranged granddaughter, currently undertaking charitable works overseas. Iris portrays herself in a faintly comic late-Gothic confinement in the style of Miss Havisham, 'an older woman, living alone in a fossilised cottage, with hair like a spider's web' (p. 636). And we learn in the novel's penultimate section that she dies pretty much with the century. Her obituary notice in the *Port Ticonderoga Herald and Banner* is dated 29 May 1999. While moving back and forth across distinct temporal planes, a hallmark of the novel, the final word belongs to Iris, with the last instalment of her memoir serving as the book's conclusion, ironically entitled 'The Threshold'.

It is also apt, given the popularity of the device of the first-person narration to explore the reliability of perception, and the unstable relationship of fleeting consciousness to the external world, of mind to matter (and as Atwood's favoured form), that it should have a geriatric exponent in this novel as a means of constructing a retrospective view of the twentieth century. Iris is a striking literary creation, with a crotchety means of chronicling her life; a curmudgeon who sweeps away lilies strewn over her sister's grave, probably left there, she hazards, by some lachrymose postgraduate student. She crankily presents the annual Laura Chase memorial prize to a youthful recipient, who bends down from her great willowy height to bestow a benevolent kiss on the withered custodian of the lost Plath-like literary talent; and Iris delights in penning acerbic obstructive missives to academics who approach her for information and assistance in developing their ground-breaking readings of her late sister's proto-feminist masterpiece.

A real-world critic has suggested that the *Blind Assassin* should be understood as an exploration of guilt and grief, and its dominant literary register is that of the Gothic.[60] Both observations stand in need of qualification. If the novel is about grief, then it is a reflection on that emotion at some psychological remove, not an account of the overwhelming blaze of immediate distress. The book's original title, though referring to a different narrative was 'The Angel of Bad Judgment', and that remains, at least in part, Iris's view on her wilful sibling.[61] The novel is certainly full of standard Gothic tropes: doubles, lunacy, a sanatorium, a large gloomy Victorian house, yet, as with Iris' self-characterisation as Dickens's withered bride, there is a knowing self-detachment in the use of these devices. If one were to propose a single type of writing as an overarching definition of the work then it would be the period romantic historical fiction, such as Margaret Mitchell's *Gone with the Wind* (1934) with the popular sweep of romance recuperated for a grander literary purpose.

There are certainly a good number of direct and indirect references to ideal circumstances throughout the *Blind Assassin*. The girls are the grandchildren of the

---

[60] Howells, *Atwood*, pp. 155–69.
[61] There is an ur-text in the Atwood archive entitled 'The Angel of Bad Judgment' from which both *Alias Grace* (1996) and the *Blind Assassin* developed (Atwood Ms. Coll. 335, Box 60, f. 1). Atwood makes clear her view on the intended relationship of the sisters in the *Blind Assassin* in a fax to her Canadian publisher, 11 January 1999 (Atwood Ms. Coll. 335 Box 65 f. 23).

founder of a button factory in the fictitious provincial Canadian town of Ticonderoga (with the factory still being run for much of the novel by their father). They are raised in a provincial mansion, Avilion, which is Tennyson's name for the Isle of Avalon in his *Idylls of the King* (1859–85). Avalon is the Isle of the Blest in Arthurian legend, the place where Excalibur was forged, and where the king's body was taken after his death. The house's central hallway has decorative stained-glass windows in the pre-Raphaelite style of William Morris, illustrating episodes from the medieval romance 'Tristram and Isoud'. After Avilion has been sold, it is converted into a retirement home and renamed 'Valhalla', much to Iris's amusement, as she observes the Nordic 'hall of the slain' is supposed to be the destination of warrior souls after glorious demise in combat, rather than a resting place for pacific souls lingering on the threshold. Toronto high society of the 1930s is viewed through the perfecting prism of the social columns of period newspapers, a procession of ivory-silk ball gowns and debutante silver-service tea parties – a globe of manicured perfection.[62] The Toronto hotel in which much of the period action takes place is called the Arcadian Court (Iris first spies her future sister-in-law, Winifred, making her icy regal progress through its lobby, 'as if gliding, with little nods and tiny calibrated waves of the hands' (p.287)); and later, Winifred organises, as an unintentionally surreal homage to Coleridge's dreamland, the Xanadu charitable ball, which Iris graces as the Abyssinian Maiden.

As the *Blind Assassin*'s early reviewers observed, the sister's central relationship with the elder sibling trying to restrain the headstrong behaviour of the younger one has a number of fictional prototypes, such as the Dashwoods in Austen's *Sense and Sensibility* (1811) and the Schlegels in Forster's *Howard's End* (1910).[63] The younger sister's name, Laura, also suggests Christina Rossetti's *Goblin Market* (1862) as a significant source. Rossetti's poem begins with the idyll of the close childhood relationship between Lizzie and Laura, before the younger sister suffers from a wasting sickness, having succumbed to the temptations of the Goblin men, and having fed voraciously on their fruit-wares (standardly interpreted as a beguiling symbolic confluence of consumerism and sublimated female sexuality).[64] Lizzie refuses to taste the fruit, and saves her sister by restoring the juices to the goblins. The poem concludes with both sisters attaining a state of middle-class contentment and responsible parenthood. That is a heart-warming prospect which eludes both sisters in the *Blind Assassin*. Iris contracts a disastrous marriage with the predatory businessman and financier Richard Griffen; and Laura's short ill-starred life ends with the reckless plunge off the bridge at the Ticonderoga Ridge. Yet, there is a moment in which the spirit of the idyll is seemingly preserved. All the main characters are glimpsed in a single moment of easy and unaffected gaiety at a works picnic for the button factory in the early 1930s, before the Depression begins to bite. The episode is captured in a photograph with the sisters standing either side of Alex Thomas, a socialist labour organiser, and adopted son of a non-conformist

---

[62] Atwood Ms. Coll. 335, Box 79 contains photocopies of clippings from the social columns of the *Globe* and *Mayfair* magazine from the mid-1930s.

[63] See, representatively, Allison Pearson, 'Review of *The Blind Assassin*', *Daily Telegraph*, 16 September 2000, Supplement, 03.

[64] See Isobel Armstrong, *Victorian Poetry: Poetry, Poetics, and Politics* (London: Routledge, 1993), pp. 347–52.

minister. On contemplating the image toward the novel's end, Iris surmises that 'the picture is of happiness, the story not. Happiness is a garden walled with glass; there's no way in or out' (p. 632).

The clearest account of the utopian and its obverse, however, occurs in the modernist novel within the novel. The story is about two unnamed lovers who engage in a furtive relationship, meeting in cheap hotel rooms and borrowed apartments in Toronto in the late 1930s and early 1940s. The unnamed female narrator recounts how her lover concocts fantastic tales for her amusement, as a kind of post-coital inverted Scheherazade (he is a socialist fugitive with aspirations of being a science-fiction writer; and she is urbane, moneyed and dissatisfied). His story is an oriental romance. He tells of the planet Zycron, and its capital city, Sakiel-Norn. The city has the appearance of exotic grandeur, with palaces, fountains and brightly-coloured birds. Yet, it is also a place of extreme if fanciful cruelty. The tale may be other-worldly, but as the narrator explains, it has echoes of the ancient history of Hittites, and the Babylonian code of Hammurabi. There are two classes in Sakiel-Norn: the aristocratic Snifards, and the serf-class of Ygnirods. Sakiel-Norn is renowned for its exquisitely patterned carpets, woven by young Ygnirod children. Intricate work on the looms in darkness results in the children going blind before their tenth birthdays; thereafter, they have to eke out an existence as prostitutes, pickpockets or assassins. The last groups are adept at executing their commissions in the pitch dark. The principal story in this strange Manichean world concerns one of these blind assassins, dispatched to cut out the tongue of a Snifard princess who has been chosen to be sacrificed by the king in his role as high priest (her predecessors had taken to protesting loudly when the priest was about to carry out his religious duty). On encountering the maiden in her chamber, the assassin falls in love with her and abandons his mission. The couple make their escape from the fabulous city, only to be captured by a barbarian race, which calls itself the 'People of Joy', but is known to their foes as the 'People of Desolation' (p. 144).

Later, the man tells his lover the story of the 'Peachwomen of A'aA'. It starts out as fantastic masculine utopia, a reworking of a portion of a pulp science-fiction story which Atwood recalls from her own Toronto childhood as the 'Spider Queen' story.[65] In the *Blind Assassin* version, two space-fighter pilots, Will and Boyd, are engaged in combat with the Lizard Men of Xenor. Their craft having been damaged in a dogfight is pulled into the gravitational field of an unknown planet in a parallel dimension. The spaceship goes into an uncontrolled spin causing the aviators to pass out. When they recover consciousness, they discover they have crashed on A'aA. To their delight, they find the planet is entirely populated by young women, just 'the peachiest dames' (p. 432) they have ever seen. These women gratify every carnal desire (telepathically anticipating the men's wishes). Afterwards, Will and Boyd 'have a delicious meal of nectar, which the men are told, would stave off age and death' (p. 433). They wander through a fabulous garden, and are then 'taken to a large room full of pipes from which they could select any pipe they wanted'. 'Pipes?', the female lover asks incredulously; 'to go with the slippers, which were issued to them next' (p. 433), he dryly responds. The prototypical

---

[65] See Atwood, '*The Handmaid's Tale*: A Feminist Dystopia?' p. 22. The description of the story as the 'Spider Queen' is from her MS notes for this address, Atwood Ms. Col. 335 Box 136, f. 4.

'Spider Queen', as Atwood recalls it, is coyer in its account of the interaction between alien pulchritude and heroic earthmen. The men's satiation is limited to the consumption of a large amount of food.

The 'Spider Queen' also has a fantastical ustopian ending. The earthmen are eventually chased by the women. The females assume an arachnid character. When they catch the men, they paralyse them, and then insert eggs into their bodies. So, the 'Spider Queen' turns out to be a gender-crossed version of Wells' *Time Machine*, with the men as the Eloi and the women as the Morlocks (and indeed one could even read it as a perverse variant of Charlotte Perkin Gilman's *Herland*). 'The Peachwomen of A'aA' has a more prosaic conclusion. The pilots eventually weary, Rasselas-like, of having their every wish gratified; and they discover they are trapped in a giant transparent globe. Will despondently observes, 'it's paradise, but we can't get out of it. And anything you can't get out of is Hell'. To which a peachwoman retorts 'A'aA *is* happiness: there's nowhere else to go from here', she says, 'relax. Enjoy yourselves. You'll get used to it.' (p. 436)

The orientalist and science-fiction strands of the *Blind Assassin* initially look as though they are anomalous components in this historical novel, not adding much to its thematic richness. However, as John Updike argued, the passages should be understood as a symbolic diffusion throughout the text. 'This extra-terrestrial fantasy parodies the lover's social situation', he observed, 'and, double nested in the novel radiates outward through the book's realistic levels, making them glow'.[66] We might not want to follow Updike to his conclusion, not immediately at any rate, that it is 'history which is the ultimate blind assassin, a vast repository of cruelties and annihilations'.[67] However, we can see immediately how the passages provide an oblique perspective on the events recounted in Iris's memoir. The relationship of the lovers in 'The Blind Assassin' mirrors that of the affluent socialite and the threadbare revolutionary. The class difference is reflected in the social demarcations of Zycron, where she is the daughter of the aristocratic Snifards and he a scion of the Ygnirod serf-class. Iris is required by her father to marry Richard Griffen out of personal obligation to save the family firm, so, the Snifard princess is expected to submit to the priesthood's sacrificial will (for which read capitalism); and just as the maiden's tongue is to be sliced out to preclude any possibility of complaint, so there is the expectation of dutiful reticence in young society women. When describing her father's suggestion she should marry Richard, the garrulous octogenarian Iris recalls her youthful muteness, repeating three times in her account of this life-defining interview that 'I said nothing' (p. 277). The suspension between the 'People of Joy' and the 'People of Desolation' is an apt metaphor for the fluctuating state in which the affair leaves the female narrator of the novel within the novel. The pulp ustopia of the 'Peachwomen of A'aA', where Will and Boyd find themselves trapped in a 'globe of happiness', has its corollary in the late episode when Iris contemplates the picture of a young woman alongside Alex, remarking that 'the picture is of happiness, the story not. Happiness is a garden walled with glass; there's no way in or out'.

---

[66] John Updike, 'Love and Loss on Zycron', *New Yorker*, 18 September 2000, 142–45 (p. 142).
[67] Updike, 'Love and Loss', p. 143.

When Updike proposed that it is 'history which is the ultimate blind assassin, a vast repository of cruelties and annihilations' he seemed to be transforming Atwood's Angel of Bad Judgment into Walter Benjamin's apocalyptic Angel of History, blown forward, facing backwards, surveying the steady accumulation of global cataclysms.[68] However, a more appropriate comparison might be Hegel's Owl of Minerva, taking flight at dusk, at the century's end for sombre reflection and comprehension.[69] If the novel possesses a universal historical aspect, then it also seems to be concerned with history in a more restricted sense. It is generally assumed that the *Blind Assassin* was Atwood's attempt to write the great Canadian novel. One might go further than this to suggest that the novel draws on a particular perception of modern Canada in terms of the ideal and its opposite: as a nation with a small population in an abundant land (33 million citizens in a territory the size of continental Europe); of a place of great natural beauty and wildness, but also a place of isolation and despair (the theme of Atwood's early *Surfacing*); as a nation which sees itself as being unified; but has also experienced periodic convulsions, in danger of splitting into anglophone and francophone constituencies; as a nation which successfully stands up to its powerful southern neighbour, and acquiesces to it; as a state which successfully combines European-style social welfare with American-style entrepreneurship; or as a state which provides ample evidence of the impossibility of reconciling the two. The tragedy of the Chase sisters unfolds under the competing attentions of the socially idealistic, Europeanised, Alex Thomas and the duplicitous North American financier, Richard Griffen.[70] And there is, perhaps, the wider suggestion that it is Canadians themselves, who possess an ustopian tendency, to see themselves both as the People of Joy *and* the People of Desolation.

One might also consider the *Blind Assassin*'s self-reflexive characteristics; and especially those of its protagonist, Iris Chase, the button heiress, who spends half the novel being pursued and the other half in pursuit. 'Buttons' seem especially apt as a generic means of attachment, given the work's overall intent to fasten together its various different narrative types; although one might be tempted, in the end, to reduce all its narrative diversity to those two fundamental modes identified by Auerbach: the Homeric, with its absolute and immediate disclosure; and Old Testament scripture with its emphasis on absence, concealment and multi-layeredness. For, of course, the declared intention of the text is to expose, to illuminate. While some critics have complained that the lengthy descriptions of period garments and interiors do nothing to increase the novel's suspense, such details can be understood to have an analogous function as the digression which precedes Eurycleia's discovery of Odysseus' scar, bringing the details of all experience into a full present.[71] Revelation may be the novel's

---

[68] See Walter Benjamin, 'Theses on the Philosophy of History', in *Illuminations*, ed. by Hannah Arendt, trans. by Harry Zohn (London: Jonathan Cape, 1970), pp. 255–66 (pp. 259–60).

[69] See G.W.F. Hegel, *Philosophy of Right*, trans. by T.M. Knox (Oxford: Clarendon Press, 1967), p. 13.

[70] Twentieth-century Canadian contrariness is described by Robert Bothwell in 'Affluence and its Discontents, 1960–1980', in his *The Penguin History of Canada* (Toronto: Penguin Canada, 2007), pp. 403–31, and by Margaret Conrad, in 'Liberalism Triumphant, 1945–1984', in her *A Concise History of Canada* (Cambridge: Cambridge University Press, 2012), pp. 226–57.

[71] See, for example, Allison Pearson's review of the *Blind Assassin*; Thomas Mallon, 'Wheels within Wheels', *New York Times*, 3 September 2000 [https://www.nytimes.com/2000/09/03/books/wheels-within-wheels.html]; and Adam Mars Jones 'Where Women Grow on Trees', *The Observer*, 17 September 2000, review section, p. 13.

watchword, but part of the tale still remains occluded. As the elderly Iris observes, 'I look back over what I've written and I know it's wrong, not because of what I've set down, but because of what I've omitted. What isn't there has presence, like the absence of light' (p. 484). But that again does not quite cover it. For if we were to consider the text in such fundamental literary modes, then by the end it is clear that Atwood wants to shape the piece as though it were cast in a third form, as Attic tragedy, that mode of representation disbarred from Plato's *Republic*, and understood by Aristotle in terms of property and effect.

The novel's climax is the interview between Iris and Laura in a café in Port Ticonderoga. In the course of this scene, there are significant revelations for both characters (anagnorisis), but especially in Iris's disclosure to Laura that Alex Thomas was killed in action and that she had been his lover. The revelation eventually leads to another one, which most readers, I suspect, will have foreseen, that it is Iris, not Laura, who is the author of the 'Blind Assassin' (published with her sister's name on it as an instrument of vengeance against her husband). In the fateful conversation in the café, Iris becomes the angel of bad judgment, an inadvertent agent of destruction, *the* blind assassin. Her disclosure results in a double peripeteia, a reversal of state and fortune. For Aristotle, we may recall, the effect is especially pronounced when the moments of anagnorisis and peripeteia converge. The revelation that Alex Thomas's affections lay with the older sister, rather than the younger, is the catalyst for Laura's suicide, as she picks up her sister's car keys and storms to her doom. For Iris, it is the moment of the fateful utterance which cannot be unsaid, the self-inflicted wound: Iris's scar. This final interview, however, also marks the transformation of Iris from passivity to action, and from reticence to prolixity. The episode adds a further layer of symbolic allusion around the central classical opposition of blindness and insight, and this, in turn, finds expression in the principal character's name: 'Iris' can refer to a genus of flowering plants (hence indicative of her early decorative social function), and to the coloured ring in the eye, which controls the amount of light reaching the retina.

The Blind Assassin should then perhaps be understood as an attempt at the original genre of ustopian tragedy; and that might be said to be a fitting undertaking for the start of the twenty-first century; as an exploration of the ideal and its opposite in the art form which Plato banished from the ideal state on the grounds of its misleading incompetence. For Aristotle, the desired effect of tragedy, of course, was to generate a moment of katharsis, the expiation of pity and fear in the audience. His wider intention, it seems, was to suggest that tragedy directs the spectators toward an emotional mean, and allows them to gain an appreciation, an insight into the fundamental parlous and unknowable nature of one's existence. In the final analysis, Atwood can be seen to be exemplary of an era in which the utopian has become a literary category which it is difficult to identify exclusively and discretely, just at the same time as it becomes significantly present in the dystopian.

Atwood finished her 1998 Rennes address on whether the *Handmaid's Tale* should be interpreted as a feminist dystopia with a line from the American poet, Wallace Stevens: 'The imperfect is our paradise'.[72] That, of course, can be read as a straightforward

---

[72] Quoted in Atwood '*The Handmaid's Tale*: A Feminist Dystopia?', p. 30.

denial of the utopian. The line comes from 'The Poems of our Climate'; and this poem begins with a description of a pristine floral display: 'Clear water in a brilliant bowl,/ Pink and white carnations. The light/In the room more like a snowy air,/Reflecting snow'.[73] Stevens rejects lucid perfection for the amalgamated, the alloyed, 'The evilly compounded, vital I,/And made it fresh in the world of white'.[74] Amia Srinivasan thinks the poem offers a contrast between 'two ways of being in the world: a mode whose *telos* is perfection and completeness, and a mode that rejects the sufficiency of perfection and the possibility of final completeness'.[75] That remains the struggle for utopian projection in art; and it remains the notable achievement of the *Blind Assassin* that the ideal is presented in such an alloyed form, 'The evilly compounded, vital I,/And made it fresh in a world of white', as the richness and complexity of experience, already there before the mind's eye, if only we can bring ourselves to see it.

---

[73] Wallace Stevens, 'The Poems of our Climate', *The Collected Poems of Wallace Stevens* (London: Faber and Faber, 1955), pp. 193–94 (p. 193).
[74] Stevens, 'The Poems of our Climate', p. 194.
[75] Amia Srinivasan, 'The Imperfect is our Paradise: Wallace Stevens, Kitsch, Philosophy', transcript of paper delivered in the Schmilosophy Seminar, 2013, All Souls College, Oxford, read online at http://users.ox.ac.uk/~corp1468/Schmilosophy_files/Schmilosophy.pdf., accessed on 19 April 2019.

Conclusion: The Utopian Prospect

How does utopia end? We can consider various imaginative possibilities. We might, say, entertain the idea that More's Utopians are eventually overrun by the rapacious Zapoletes assisted by disgruntled bondsmen; or Swift's Houyhnhnms are decimated by a lethal strain of equine flu leading to the rise of the Yahoos; or that Le Guin's Odonians eventually succumb to the inducements of an extraordinarily wealthy planet which promises to transform their infrastructure as part of a belt and road initiative, but such an investment comes at the price of increasing economic interest and the steady erosion of communal principles. Some ideal projections, of course, already have putative endings embedded in their discussions. Plato's *Republic* has a late consideration of the main political systems in the fourth century BCE as an implicit acknowledgement that all phenomenal considerations are subject to mutability and decay. That the ideal state would be subject to the same inexorable forces as anything else with material existence. For Wells in *A Modern Utopia*, the projection's flimsiness is expressed in the image of a film inflating into a bubble. When the bubble bursts, the Voice and his irritable travelling companion return to the noise and bustle of contemporary London in the first decade of the twentieth century. And a notable feature of Huxley's *Island* is that the concrete projection of an ideal society with its amalgamation of Buddhism and crop science ends with the state being overthrown in a *coup d'état*.

One might reformulate the question to consider how commentators on utopianism and especially those on its various literary or aesthetic formulations bring their own studies to a close. The answer is that they often do so despondently. Frank and Fritzie Manuel have a final section in *Utopian Thought in the Western World* entitled 'Epilogue: The Utopian Prospect' (from which this chapter's title derives). They envisaged from their late 1970s perspective a kind of ongoing Wellsian entropic dissipation. They ask 'have we been discussing a propensity that had a beginning more than three thousand years ago, experienced glorious moments, is now virtually exhausted or, what amounts to the same thing, is leading a treadmill existence, living on past performances repeated with only trivial variations'.[1] At first, the reader may think the Manuels are about to challenge this maudlin conspectus; but the conclusion does indeed confirm this is their view. They may wish as intellectual historians 'for a fresh utopian vision to order the conflicting needs and desires of civilization'.[2] However, as they make clear in their

---

[1] Frank E. Manuel and Fritzie P. Manuel, *Utopian Thought in the Western World* (Cambridge, MA: Belknap Press, 1979), p. 801.
[2] Manuel and Manuel, *Utopian Thought*, p. 814.

closing sentence 'this is more a utopian wish than a great expectation'.³ Krishan Kumar was hardly more encouraging when he suggested nearly a decade later that the idea of 'utopia as a form of social imagination has clearly weakened – whether fatally we cannot say'.⁴ There is a deliberate decision not to spell out the fate of idealism in Gregory Claeys' utopian survey. '*Our* ideal world must be very much our own creation', he declares at the end of *Searching for Utopia* (2011), 'and a series reckoning with the fate we face if we fail to create it'.⁵ And when Claeys returned to this topic from the opposing perspective in his recent study of dystopia, he affirmed that sense of utopian exhaustion. For the twenty-first century, the dystopian, he says, 'increasingly defines the spirit of our times'.⁶ He quotes Slavoj Žižek's prophesy that we are 'approaching an "apocalyptic zero-point"', and Martin Rees's equally grim prediction that humankind has entered its terminal century.⁷

Of course, it was possible early in the twentieth century to write about the transformative possibilities of utopianism with more confidence. Writing against the background of the collapse of the Weimar Republic, Karl Mannheim concluded his investigation by equating utopianism with a Hegelian transcendent consciousness. The striving for a higher state of awareness has been not merely dialectical in its progress, but an epical struggle, 'a long tortuous, but heroic development'; and just as modern people have the possibility not to be dictated to by blind fate, they must preserve the utopian impulse as it is that capability of progressive imaginative idealism which will enable human beings to grasp the opportunity to both shape and comprehend their own destiny.⁸ And as we might expect, given the wide-ranging optimistic diffusion of anticipatory transformative consciousness to be detected in a myriad of aesthetic and cultural phenomena, Bloch finishes the last chapter of his *Principle of Hope*, entitled 'Wishful Images of the Fulfilled Moment', with a resounding declaration of the desire of the exile to return, the hope for 'real democracy', a political and artistic settlement which 'shines into the childhood of all, and to which no one has yet been: homeland'.⁹

Ruth Levitas, exploring the concept of utopia from a sociological perspective in the 1980s, is distinctively Blochian in her closing observations on the unresolved problematic of utopianism. Hope, for her, needs to be embedded in concrete agency, and only when such a practical amalgamation is achieved 'will we see our dreams come true'.¹⁰ Bloch reappears in the final paragraph of her 2010 examination of utopian method for progressive sociological conceptualisation. She observes that 'we must build into the blue, and build, ourselves into the blue' (she has an earlier chapter on the

---

³ Manuel and Manuel, *Utopian Thought*, p. 814.
⁴ Krishan Kumar, *Utopia and Anti-Utopia in Modern Times* (Oxford: Blackwell, 1987), p. 423.
⁵ Gregory Claeys, *Searching for Utopia: The History of an Idea* (London: Thames & Hudson, 2011), p. 213.
⁶ Gregory Claeys, *Dystopia: A Natural History* (Oxford: Oxford University Press, 2018), p. 498
⁷ Slavoj Žižek, *Living in the End Times* (London: Verso, 2010), p. x, quoted in Claeys, *Dystopia*, p. 501.
⁸ Karl Mannheim, *Ideology and Utopia: An Introduction to the Sociology of Knowledge*, trans. by Louis Wirth and Edward Shils (New York: Harvest, [c. 1965]), p. 263.
⁹ Ernst Bloch, *The Principle of Hope*, trans. by Neville Plaice, Stephen Plaice and Paul Knight, 3 vols (Cambridge, MA: MIT Press, 1986), III, p. 1376.
¹⁰ Ruth Levitas, *The Concept of Utopia* (New York: Philip Allan, 1990), p. 200.

importance of the colour for both Bloch and for an array of painters).[11] Levitas finishes with a set of injunctions to her reader to: 'Mourn. Hope. Love. Imagine. Organise.'[12] Tom Moylan has moments of utopian reflection in the conclusions to both of his studies. At the end of the first in the mid-1980s, critical utopianism is at the vanguard of impending radical transformation, 'a seditious expression of social change and popular sovereignty'.[13] And in his millennial revision of his thesis, *Scraps of the Untainted Sky*, the significantly reduced means of utopian are celebrated in the success of anti-globalisation demonstrators who prevent President Bill Clinton giving a speech to WTO delegates in Seattle in 1999 (a president whose relative achievements and governance have improved from the perspective of the second decade of the twenty-first century).[14] In a lecture on the possibility of an American utopia in 2014, Fredric Jameson provided a weary analysis of its prospects on the basis of either reformation or revolution in the era of late capitalism. He offered a latter-day version of Bellamy's industrial army as the cornerstone for a new America. It was an improbable suggestion, delivered in such deadpan style that it was difficult to discern whether the measure was being advanced in earnest, or merely as an exasperated thought experiment, an ironic suggestion in the absence of any utopian policy which at that historical juncture made any sense.[15]

In the course of this study, I have attempted to explore the relationship of the aesthetic to the utopian, and have done so by examining the ways in which formal aspects have shaped the significance of what is ostensibly being proposed. This undertaking has involved endeavouring to define the utopian or the social and personal ideal in the terms of that particular work or body of work. The principal focus has been on the literary, and insofar as this has been possible, to treat texts with demonstrable aesthetic attributes as though they were literary artefacts. The overall approach has been to analyse such works within their synchronic and diachronic moments; that is, the extent to which they both respond to the particular concerns of their own epoch and revise, refute, or even overgo earlier imaginings of ideal states. It has also been my intention to think about utopianism in terms of the wider oeuvre of the authors under view, such that one might contemplate the influence of such idealism in those works which are not explicitly concerned with utopian themes, and indeed, consider how such projections intersect with literary depictions of the self. We began with Plato's *Republic* as a dialogue which contrasts the ideal state with notions of truth and social organisation as expressed in Attic tragedy. The claims of the ideal hierarchical society in the *Republic* and the *Laws*, were set alongside the creative social vision of the *Symposium* (with its account of Eros). Thomas More's *Utopia* established a tradition of

---

[11] Ruth Levitas, *Utopia as Method: The Imaginary Reconstitution of Society* (Basingstoke: Palgrave Macmillan, 2013), p. 220.
[12] Levitas, *Utopia as Method*, p. 220.
[13] Tom Moylan, *Demand The Impossible: Science Fiction and the Utopian Imagination* (New York: Methuen, 1986), p. 213.
[14] See Tom Moylan, *Scraps of the Untainted Sky: Science Fiction, Utopia, Dystopia* (Boulder, CO: Westview Press, 2000), pp. 282–84.
[15] Fredric Jameson, *An American Utopia: Fredric Jameson in Conversation with Stanley Aronowitz* (2014), [https://www.youtube.com/watch?v=MNVKoX40ZAo&t=1206s, accessed 8 January 2019].

proposing an idealistic blueprint in conjunction with a diagnosis of contemporary social and political malaise; and that work possessed meta-utopian components which allowed for a radical configuration of the very ideals that it seems to advance. *Utopia*, in this respect, could be regarded as an anticipatory commentary on its author's subsequent writings and actions.

Recent scholarship on Jonathan Swift identified the extent to which Swift was influenced by classical and modern projections of the ideal state (and especially More's *Utopia*). Swift, it was suggested, provided an anatomy of utopia in the eighteenth century. The influence of his satirical refraction of social idealism can be identified in works of many prominent utopian and anti-utopian writers (including Carlyle, Butler, Orwell and Atwood); and as I argued, it is worth considering the development of Swift's utopianism alongside that other significant eighteenth-century discourse of social idealism, universal rights, as articulated by Kant. Swift's consideration of the bleaker implications of a perfected settlement has a forceful nexus with rights discourse in the middle of the last century. The critical consensus remains that the nineteenth century represents the high watermark of utopian projection (in terms of number of works produced), and we saw in this section how Thomas Carlyle was a central figure for understanding Victorian idealism. Other prominent English idealistic projections, such as those of William Morris, were indebted to his social analysis.

Wells, Orwell and Huxley were configured as a triptych of utopian and anti-utopian writers. I endeavoured to demonstrate the web of connections between them; the ways in which their various idealistic projections could not be wholly detached from their wider literary perspectives, and all of their works were inflected with prominent autobiographical strands. I proposed in the penultimate chapter that American literary idealism in the 1970s should be seen in the context of a post-utopian mood; the assumption across the political spectrum that the utopian had been within reach in the previous era, but that opportunity had been comprehensively squandered. In the last chapter, I suggested Margaret Atwood's 'Ustopian' coinage served not so much as an indication of the latency of the utopian within the dystopian and vice versa, or indeed, as a narrow shaft of hopeful illumination on an overwhelmingly desolate landscape; but rather, it was indicative of a modern tendency for such terms to merge, to occupy the same conceptual field; and that, furthermore, the aesthetic effect of such a conflation is at its most striking and even poignant when it is conceptualised and presented in a narrative where the speculative elements have been kept to a minimum.

It is possible to discern such distinct ustopian impulses from at least the later part of the twentieth century. In addition to the works already discussed, one can detect such an ambiguous conflation in, for example, J.G. Ballard's *Crash* (1973). Ballard's novel conjoins Sadean hallucinatory eroticism within a vision of contemporary London, of cars, flyovers, airports, carparks, photographs and an obsession with celebrity. The unrelenting focus on sexual gratification, death and assorted automotive collisions could only be judged externally to be dystopian. Ballard was convinced that he had made a profound insight into the way in which cars and traffic constituted human beings as erotic entities in the modern world, and as such, and for all its stark luridness, the novel made an implicit claim for psycho-sexual veracity. *Crash*'s first-person narrative persona, called 'James Ballard', shuts off any possibility of ethical valuation from within the book itself; that the sense of subjective desire and satiation is given full and extreme expression. Ballard, the author rather than the character, stated he had envisaged *Crash* as a 'psychopathic hymn'; and it was a matter of artistic commitment not to deviate from the phenomenological directedness of the book's libidinous vision.[16]

Perhaps more in tune with the spirit of subjective ustopianism I am describing here, and certainly indicative of the possibilities of the intertwining of such perspectives in the early twenty-first century is Kazuo Ishiguro's *Never Let Me Go* (2004), with its conjectural historical narrative running from the early 1970s until the late 1990s. The novel, of course, has a standard dystopian conceit. In this parallel version of England, clones are produced for the purpose of supplying spare organs; and after their fourth donation almost all of these young adults are euphemistically termed to have 'completed'. As with a number of such minimally speculative ustopian works, *Never Let Me Go* has a first-person narrator, a thirty-one-year-old carer (and prospective donor), Kathy H. She recounts in everyday prose her childhood in what appears to be an idyllic boarding school, and her relationship with two schoolmates into adulthood (both of whom have 'completed' by the story's close). Ishiguro avoids in this curious and affecting *Bildungsroman* any mention of intricate medical procedures. He does not provide any Huxley-like detail of the process of cloning. There is no demonstrable sense of horror or melodrama in the predestination of the narrator and her friends. The tale's Gothicism is limited to a faintly comic episode in a gentile if decrepit Victorian house in an English seaside town.

One can speculate as to what elements of contemporary experience are being refracted through the twin lens of the utopian and dystopian in *Never Let Me Go*: the demographic circumstances of an aging population which will consume an increasing portion of common resources and demand more indulgence from the younger generation; the unselfish dedication of those who work in the caring professions; the passivity and assent of many people to operate within the terms of the world as it is presented to them (as a matter of sanguine acceptance rather than philosophical stoicism); and the inclination of former pupils of small independent schools to recall their institutions (especially if they have since closed) as if they constituted if not quite the perfect society, then at least a period of enduring stability and contentedness, with the formation of relationships never to be bettered. No accident, I suppose, that we can pick out the origins of this exercise when we note that the school's teachers are known as Guardians (in distant homage to the *Republic*'s rulers), and the protagonist's given name with only the initial capital of her surname provided is reminiscent of 'Joseph K', the central persecuted figure in Kafka's *The Trial* (1925). Ishiguro's novel does not ultimately deny either of its generic polarities; and the book concludes with a luminescent if melancholy affirmation of the richness of human experience, in spite of the cruel requirements by which these lives have been framed.

I am proposing, then, by way of conclusion that the notion of the utopian in literary terms in the early part of the twenty-first century is not to be the abandoned form of

---

[16] Quoted in Travis Elborough 'The Road to Crash' in J.G. Ballard, *Crash* (London: Fourth Estate, 2011), P.S. Section, pp. 8–11 (p. 11).

representation which the more pessimistic accounts of dystopian hegemony would have us believe. It all depends on how one conceptualises the ideal in the literary and judges its purpose. And for further evidence of this one might look to Caroline Edwards' recent tracing of a Blochian anticipatory consciousness, as an oblique configuration of hopefulness (though detached from Bloch's idiosyncratic Marxism) in British fiction of the first two decades of this century. The central impetus of her project is to tease out in the works of such authors as Joanna Kavenna, Grace McCleen, Jon McGregor and Claire Fuller what she regards as revelatory moments of 'temporal alterity'.[17] Given I have committed to providing a prospect of literary utopianism in the twenty-first century as a matter of restricted prophesy I will aver that fictional works will continue to examine the ustopian formulations already outlined. Such works will have to respond directly and indirectly to the rise of political populism, the shifting standards of sexual and social mores, a Western society which has become more open and accepting of the idea of gender fluency. One might say that it will be virtually impossible to escape the personally constitutive aspect of social media. One might also look to what is sometimes termed the New Sincerity, that is, as an affirmation of authentic feeling in cultural expression in opposition to the characteristic neutralising irony of some postmodernist expression; and we might note that while the ironic suffuses Atwood's fiction, the ustopianism of Ballard and Ishiguro depends on the unimpeachable sincerity of their first-person narrators. It is certainly not impossible as the environmental calamities of the Anthropocene become more imminent that ustopianism will as a counter-measure assume a more demonstrable utopian character.

As I mentioned at the beginning of this study, there is evidence that utopianism has a continuing influence in political discourse with such works as Rutger Bregman's *Utopia for Realists* (2014, 2017). Bregman's book operates rhetorically by adopting the popular sense of utopianism as a hopelessly impractical even fantastical measure; and then inverting this view to show how the study's signature policy of universal basic income is then eminently practical on a cost-benefit basis. However, we also noted that such a measure requires a firm foundation on which to build, a secure constitutional settlement and relatively propitious economic circumstances. At the other end of the spectrum is David Bell's *Rethinking Utopia: Place, Power, Affect* (2017), an energetic exercise in political speculation. Bell's study follows Levitas in declaring as a matter of sociological conviction that the utopian should not be abandoned as a conceptual basis for critiquing current political models and generating viable alternatives. The book's ostensible difficulty, as a self-declared contribution to political theory, is that it never advocates a concrete action or policy. Its key terms (never exactly defined) of utopianism, post-utopianism, dystopianism and anti-utopianism are subject to a kind of conceptual version of Brownian motion, randomly colliding with one another.

In *Rethinking Utopia*, the author identifies a number of works of cultural production to be considered throughout the study. These are: Zamyatin's *We*, a conceptual installation by the Russian artist, Ilya Kabalov; 'The Man who Flew into Space from His

---

[17] Caroline Edwards, *Utopia and the Contemporary British Novel* (Cambridge: Cambridge University Press, 2019), p. 4.

Apartment' exhibited in New York in 1988, a semi-humorous Icarian account of the Soviet space programme; *Code 46* (2007) a somewhat obscure science-fiction film directed by Michael Winterbottom; and Le Guin's *The Dispossessed*. There is not much indication as to why these works have been chosen. They are not considered within their historical circumstances. The texts illuminate localised points, and these sit uneasily between a specific instance and universal observation: hence *Code 46* is said 'to present the viewer with an opposition between "authentic" utopian place and "inauthentic" dystopian placelessness'; but it remains uncertain as to whether this is only a restricted interpretation of this particular film, or a generalised proposition on the interrelation of these two opposing positions.[18] The chapters have no clear beginnings, middles or ends, and the connections between the discussion's various segments are not readily apparent. Conceptually, the study makes considerable play of the array of theories, but the application of these to utopian circumstances is oblique. Yet, for all these shortcomings there is still an appealing and resonant quality to this work; and, this, to some extent, is a consequence of what I have suggested is the value attributed to candid subjectivity; the sense that the ideal is to be closely aligned with personal experience.

There is a noticeable increase in the use of the first-person pronoun as *Rethinking Utopia* progresses, and various autobiographical details are successively disclosed. The study's central purpose and underlying principles are eventually announced as being not so much a matter of judicious examination, as intuitive and improvised expressiveness. The reader is treated to an account of the author, as a seventeen-year-old, encountering free jazz. Listening to this music, Bell reveals, was initially a disorientating experience, nauseating even 'this was noise! Chaos! This music didn't take me to a place but to meaningless, formless space', he recalls.[19] But he persevered. He cannot quite recall which album he was 'listening to when it finally clicked' though he thinks it was probably by Cecil Taylor or Archie Shepp. He describes his epiphany: 'I no longer observed it from afar but joined with it. Finding that the chaos was in fact a "multi- dominant" form of self-organisation'.[20] This, then, would seem to explain the style of Bell's utopian reformulation, not so much a lineal cognitive exercise as a post-leftist structure of feeling, operating in terms of the improvisational principles of free jazz; hence swirling ideas; hence the quick-fire selection of a small set of artefacts as though they were melodies, momentarily articulated before merging back into a wall of sound; and hence the ending of the book's last chapter, which draws together jazz and utopia in a speculative propinquity: 'might an album like The Ornette Coleman's Double Quartet's *Free Jazz: A Collective*, improvisation which remains impenetrable to me to this day', Bell wonders, 'be all the more utopian for the fact I still cannot make any sense of it? Utopian(ism) begins in this world, but opens up worlds we cannot even dream of'.[21]

---

[18] David M. Bell, *Rethinking Utopia: Place, Power, Affect* (London: Routledge, 2017), p. 64.
[19] Bell, *Rethinking Utopia*, p. 157.
[20] Bell, *Rethinking Utopia*, p. 157.
[21] Bell, *Rethinking Utopia*, p. 158.

That, of course, is to finish with an interrogative and hanging preposition. Even if I follow in part Bell's associative method, I intend to bring proceedings to a close in a more definitive fashion, with an account of what one might consider a distillation of the utopian spirit, and to set this example at an instructive tangent to this study's predominantly literary considerations, as a matter of symbolic distillation. One can detect, I think, in the work of the Russian filmmaker Andrei Tarkovsky, a constant striving for the visionary, the subjective and reflective, as an expression of the utopian in art. Tarkovsky's reputation rests on a small body of work: seven full-length films made between 1962 and 1986. The first five were made in the Soviet Union, and the last two in self-imposed exiled in Italy and Denmark (he died of cancer in Paris in 1986, aged 54). His first full-length film *Ivan's Childhood* (1962) was a revisionist war film recounting the short life of a young scout at the front; *Andrei Rublev* (1964) portrays the life of the monk and icon painter, the eponymous Rublev; *Solaris* is a science-fiction film about spiritual journeying and homecoming; *Mirror* (1974–75) is an autobiographical account of a middle-aged poet, who might be dying, as he reflects on his childhood in the countryside and Moscow in the 1940s (with poetry by Tarkovsky's father). *Stalker* (1979), notionally a return to science fiction, can be understood as a romance quest set in a post-industrial landscape. *Nostalgia* (1983), the term in Russian has a suggestion of affliction as well as overly fond reflection, examines the homesickness of a Russian musicologist in Italy researching the life of his eighteenth-century compatriot, the musician Pavel Sosnovsky. And in *Sacrifice* (1986) Tarkovsky attempts a Chekhovian tragi-comedy, as a suicidal theatre critic contemplates what meagre measures he might undertake to prevent a nuclear conflagration.

The ideal for Tarkovsky was clearly in one sense a matter of compositional precision. He preferred to film in the rectangular 4:3 aspect ratio, where the square frame allowed for the play of symmetrical and asymmetrical elements. In the colour films (*Mirror* onwards), there is a careful control of palette, often with pastel shades, and coding for thematic and symbolic purposes. There are recurrent motifs: childhood, memory, return, sacrifice and dreams. There are elemental components: water – torrential rain and standing and rippling pools in *Stalker*; fire – the all-consuming blaze of the home at the end of *Sacrifice*; earth – extensive tracts of glutinous mud in *Ivan's Childhood*; and air – made visible in the wisps of mist hanging above shots of water, and as an animating presence, in the sudden gusts of wind which unexpectedly disturb a landscape, such as in *Mirror*'s opening scene. After a short comic exchange between a lost doctor and the poet's mother in the Russian countryside, the doctor departs (never to be seen again). He turns one last time to look back at her, a breeze ruffles the wheat surrounding him, and the moment has a remarkable sense of sharply recalled unrealised potential, such as one might compare to Wordsworth's spots of time, Ibsen's symbols and Joyce's epiphanies.

The Tarkovsky film where the notion of the utopian in art, a striving for a revelatory experience, is at its clearest is *Andrei Rublev*. If this film can be considered a suitable conclusion to this study then it is because it offers a sustained if oblique discussion on the necessary conditions of its own fabrication. *Andrei Rublev* is set in the late Middle Ages. It examines a period in which the sense of Russian nationalism and reunification is stirring (though Tarkovsky's bleak account of the period provoked suspicion and dissatisfaction from the Soviet authorities). In its final form, the film consists of seven episodes spanning twenty years of Rublev's life from 1400 onwards. Not much was known about Rublev in the 1960s, and Tarkovsky invented most episodes in the film. The director certainly was not interested in portraying historical events in their correct order, or even placing them within their correct period. Rublev's life is set against the rivalry of Grand Duke Vassili and his younger brother, Yuri, for control of the territories north-east of Moscow. The central dramatic event is the fall of the city of Vladimir to the younger duke aided by an army of Tartars. The film's final episode depicts the casting of a bell for Vladimir's cathedral, an act of celebration and thanksgiving for the patriot, Vassili, having vanquished his treasonous sibling and driven the Tartars from Russian territories. Educated Russians regarded the Middle Ages as a bloody era, but also a period of national resurgence. In this context, as Mark Le Fanu observes, 'Rublev's paintings can be seen as the cultural symbol of this renaissance. In Tarkovsky's project, there were, as it were, opportunities for both optimism and pessimism.'[22]

Andrei Rublev offers a strikingly different account of medieval life to Carlyle and Morris's pacific communities. Indeed, the portrayal is now reminiscent of the familiar imagery of the wasted landscape of the Anthropocene. The film opens with a peasant attempting to fly in a balloon constructed from animal skins. Having launched his primitive dirigible from a bell tower, the peasant travels a short distance, before being killed when he crashes. As Rublev walks toward the monastery, a man is being strapped to a wheel to be broken while protesting his innocence; a mummer is arrested for blasphemy and insubordination by the duke's men while cavorting with peasants, and has his head thumped on a tree (we later learn he survives a long imprisonment, but has his tongue sliced out). As Rublev and his assistants and apprentices prepare the cathedral in Vladimir for its decoration, he recalls the fate of itinerant stonemasons who left the city to undertake a commission for a palace for the younger brother at Zvenigorod. As they walk, through a wood, filled with birdsong, they are intercepted by the elder duke's secretary and blinded for their impertinence – left scrambling around in sightless terror. In the city's sacking by Yuri and his Tartar allies, there is carnage in the cathedral. In the melee, Rublev kills a Tartar soldier with an axe. The cathedral's treasurer is then interrogated for the location of the church's gold and jewels. He refuses to disclose their whereabouts while delivering quips at his captors' expense. The Tartars patiently bind his body and face with bandages until only his mouth remains uncovered. They bring his jovial insults to an end by laying him flat on his back and pouring boiling pitch into the exposed orifice, resulting in silence at the point one would expect to hear his screams.

Tarkovsky's approach to violence is to avoid any sensationalism, as though to emphasise the quotidian nature of such events. These scenes are complemented by other episodes that point to extreme hardship: a winter famine where the monks at Rublev's monastery are reduced to eating roots; and the son of a master bell forger casually reveals that his father and the rest of his family recently perished in the plague. At the film's centre is the dilemma about how it is possible to produce beauty,

---

[22] Mark Le Fanu, *The Cinema of Andrei Tarkovsky* (London: British Film Institute, 1987), p. 37.

representations of the ideal in a rich iconography in a world characterised by violence and the arbitrary exercise of power. And we see in the film much of that violence is directed toward artists. The film is as much about the creative process as practice. We never actually see Rublev at work; the only time we see him using paint is when he hurls it across the prepared surface of the cathedral walls, more in the abstract style of Jackson Pollock than a medieval icon painter, an angry gesture at the recollection of the fate of the blinded artisans. Indeed, Rublev takes a vow of silence after killing the Tartar soldier, and does not practise his trade for many years. It is only in the closing shots that the film shows examples of the real Rublev's work. And there is a startling transfiguration of black and white to colour in these final images, a testament to the exquisiteness and precision of vision which arises from the grey and frequently chaotic conditions of their composition – a glimpse of the ideal arising from apparently dystopian circumstance.

In his writings, Tarkovsky complained about the leaden historical symbolism and elongated allegorical devices which had to be employed by the previous generation of Soviet directors; an expedient for making films in an oppressive political climate, where official displeasure could easily result in personal disaster.[23] Yet Tarkovsky's disdain for such figuration does seem slightly anomalous given the evident symbolic and allegorical components in his own work. These are particularly prominently displayed in *Andrei Rublev*'s final section, which, as Maya Turovskaya points out, 'bears the almost symbolic title: "The Bell".[24] The episode takes place in 1423, and begins with the archduke's men looking for the bell-founder, and finding only his son, Boriska, idling in his decimated village. Boriska is puckish, slim, evidently a precocious and somewhat irritating adolescent. He eventually persuades the sceptical troops that his father had entrusted him (and only him) with the secrets of casting; and by badgering, he eventually secures the commission to produce the bell to celebrate Vladimir's liberation. He has to command a team of experienced and frequently uncooperative assistants (who had worked for his father). In a sequence of cameos, he is shown choosing a spot high above the city for the furnace. His assistants stand on their professional pride, and refuse to help. Boriska and his friend have to dig the substantial pit themselves. There is the extensive quest for just the right grain of clay for the mould's construction. Eventually, the perfect blend is identified by Boriska as he scrambles in the snow and mud on the side of the steep bank. In another scene, Boriska demands silver and gold plates from the city to be added to the amalgam of tin and bronze. There are arguments with his team about the construction of the foundry and the timing of the casting. Boriska gets his way through a combination of visionary certitude, teenage tantrum and ruthless calculation. At one point, he orders his only friend from his village to be flogged to encourage the founders to obey his commands. The bell is cast at night as an image of an inferno. After the metal has cooled, the mould and scaffolding are broken away to reveal its massive curvilinear form, embossed with the duke's coat of arms. The bell is hoisted onto a temporary derrick in preparation for its inaugural ringing.

---

[23] See for example, Andrey Tarkovsky, *Sculpting in Time: Reflections in Cinema*, trans. by Kitty Hunter Blair (Austin: University of Texas Press, 1987), pp. 68–69.

[24] Maya Turovskaya, *Tarkovsky: Cinema as Poetry*, ed. by Ian Christie and trans. by Natasha Ward (London: Faber and Faber, 1989), p. 45.

Turovskaya suggests Boriska is recognisable as a mythical Soviet archetype endeavouring to construct the utopian society, the dynamic and transformative comrades 'from the beginning of the thirties, during the first days of industrialisation and the early Five Year Plans'.[25] Boriska embodies, she says, 'the same frenzied and selfless approach, risking their own lives and those of others, expecting neither privileges, nor recompense for their efforts'.[26] Bells also occupy a significant place within Russian culture (the gargantuan cracked Tsar Bell, damaged by fire in 1737, is displayed in the Kremlin's grounds). And as Karl Schlögel points out, a feature of the rapid redesign of the capital at the time of the Great Purge was that 'not only belfries disappeared, but also the sound of bells, without which old Moscow could not be imagined'.[27] The nature of absolute power, relevant to both the medieval and the modern era is also on display in this episode in *Andrei Rublev* as the archduke, his entourage and visiting diplomats ride out of the city. They are viewed from a high shot, and as they make their way toward the bell, serfs prostate themselves along the roadside. The dignitaries stare impassively at Boriska when he is presented to them. The moment of truth arrives as his assistants slowly swing the clapper until it eventually comes into contact with the rim of the resonator. The bell chimes clear and true. These events have been viewed by Rublev, who later that evening encounters the teenager, sobbing alone in a muddy ditch. Boriska confesses to him that his father never revealed to him the 'secret' of bell founding; and his success, we can infer, is a consequence of blind faith, cussedness, a measure of innate ability, some technical understanding inherited from his father, and a great deal of good fortune.

This episode's purpose would seem to be to provide an epiphany for Rublev, as the success of the bell casting and Boriska's confession persuades him to end his vow of silence and resume painting; and so initiates the final shots of ravishing icons. If the episode of the bell offers a parable of artistic dedication, and that it encapsulates the plight of the artist in authoritarian circumstances, then it also more narrowly seems to offer an allegory on the process of filmmaking from the director's perspective, as an act of collective endeavour, of the necessity of having a sense of vision, of giving the impression of understanding, of direction, and control, the requirement to overcome a whole set of obstacles; and that one cannot be exactly sure how everything will turn out, just as the bell may crack in its moulding, or fail to ring when hoisted and struck. One of the sources of Soviet scepticism as to the merits of this film was the apparent centrality of the Orthodox Church and faith to a historical narrative on the Russian state. The religious imagery is explicit, not just in the biblical subject matter of the icons which Rublev paints, but also in specific scenes, such as a hallucinatory transposition of Christ at Calvary to a snowy ridge in the Russian landscape. Yet *Andrei Rublev* is devoid of formal theological content; and religion itself seems to be constructed as an analogous undertaking to aesthetic expressiveness. The appeal of Rublev as an icon painter for Tarkovsky is that that the icon is not conceived as a mimetic milieu, and that spirt and matter are supposed to be embodied within its image. The sense of imminence

---

[25] Turovskaya, *Tarkovsky*, p. 45.
[26] Turovskaya, *Tarkovsky*, p. 45.
[27] Karl Schlögel, *Moscow, 1937*, trans. by Rodney Livingston (Cambridge: Polity, 2014), p. 46.

of being is not subject to any notion of deferral and latent transformative capacity, but is evident in the here and now of its immediate realisation. This must be so of icon painting, and of film, and of all great and enduring artistic expressions in the search for the utopian, just as the bell eventually rings out, clear and true, making the world and all that's in it resound.

Bibliography

Collections and Manuscript Items

Atwood, Margaret, Papers, Thomas Fisher Rare Book Library, University of Toronto, MS Coll. 200 onwards
Cockerell, Sydney, Ms Diary, British Library, Add Ms 52633
Pinter, Harold, Archive, British Library, Add Mss 88880 onwards

Printed and Digital Items

Ackland, Michael, 'Modern Biographies of Sir Thomas More', in *A Companion to Thomas More*, ed. by A.D. Cousins and Damian Grace (Madison: Farleigh Dickenson University Press, 2009), pp. 39–52
Ackroyd, Peter, *The Life of Thomas More* (London: Vintage, 1999)
Adams, Robert P., *The Better Part of Valor: More, Erasmus, Colet, and Vives, on Humanism, War, and Peace, 1496–1535* (Seattle: University of Washington Press, 1962)
Aeschylus, *Oresteia*, trans. by Christopher Collard (Oxford: Oxford University Press, 2002)
Alighieri, Dante, *The Divine Comedy: Inferno*, trans. by Charles S. Singleton (Princeton: Princeton University Press, 1980)
Anon., 'Exhibition of National Portraits at South Kensington', *The Times*, 19 April 1866
Anon., 'The Road to Riches', *Economist*, 23 December 1999 [https://www.economist.com/special/1999/12/23/the-road-to-riches]
Anon., 'Big Data, Big Brother: China Invents the Digital Totalitarian State: The Worrying Implications of its Social-Credit System', *The Economist*, 17 December 2016 [https://www.economist.com/briefing/2016/12/17/china-invents-the-digital-totalitarian-state]
Anthony, P.D., *John Ruskin's Labour: A Study of Social Theory* (Cambridge: Cambridge University Press, 1983)
Appleyard, Brian, 'The New Light that Burns within Harold Pinter', *Times*, 16 March 1984, 12
Aristophanes, *The Birds and Other Plays*, trans. by David Barrett and Alan Sommerstein (London: Penguin, 1978)
Aristotle, *The Politics and the Constitution of Athens*, ed. by Stephen Everson (Cambridge: Cambridge University Press, 1996)
Armstrong, Isobel, *Victorian Poetry: Poetry, Poetics and Politics* (London: Routledge, 1996)
Arnott, Peter D., *Public and Performance in the Greek Theatre* (London: Routledge, 1991)
Associated Press, 'Khmer Rouge Survivor Tells of Horrific Conditions at Torture Centre', *Guardian*, 29 July 2009 [https://www.theguardian.com/world/2009/jun/29/cambodia]
Atwood, Margaret, *Surfacing* (London: Virago, 1979)
Atwood, Margaret, *Second Words: Selected Critical Prose, 1960–1982* (Toronto: Anansi, 1982)
Atwood, Margaret, *Lady Oracle* (London: Virago, 1982)
Atwood, Margaret, *Life Before Man* (London: Vintage, 1996)

Atwood Margaret, 'The Handmaid's Tale: A Feminist Dystopia?', in *Lire Margaret Atwood: The Handmaid's Tale*, ed. by Marta Dvorak (Rennes: Presses universitaires de Rennes, 1999), pp. 17–30

Atwood, Margaret, *The Blind Assassin* (London: Virago, 2001)

Atwood, Margaret, 'The Handmaid's Tale and Oryx and Crake in Context', *PMLA*, 119 (2004), 513–17

Atwood, Margaret, *The Penelopiad: The Myth of Penelope and Odysseus* (Edinburgh: Canongate, 2005)

Atwood, Margaret, *The Handmaid's Tale* (London: Vintage, 2010)

Atwood, Margaret, *In Other Worlds: SF and the Human Imagination* (London: Virago, 2011)

Atwood, Margaret, *Oryx & Crake* (London: Virago, 2013)

Atwood, Margaret, *The Year of the Flood* (London: Virago, 2013)

Atwood, Margaret, *MaddAddam* (London: Virago, 2014)

Atwood, Margaret, *The Heart Goes Last* (London: Bloomsbury, 2015)

Auerbach, Erich, *Mimesis: The Representation of Reality in Western Literature*, trans. by Willard R. Trask (Princeton, NJ: Princeton University Press, 1953)

Augustine, *The City of God Against the Pagans*, ed. and trans. by R.W. Dyson (Cambridge: Cambridge University Press, 1998)

Bacon, Francis, *New Atlantis*, in *Three Early Utopias*, ed. by Susan Bruce (Oxford: Oxford University Press, 2008), pp. 149–86

Busch, Justin E.A., *The Utopian Vision of H.G. Wells* (Jefferson: McFarland, 2009)

Baker-Smith, Dominic, *More's Utopia* (London: HarperCollins, 1991)

Ballard, J.G., *Crash* (London: Fourth Estate, 2011)

Barry, John M., *The Great Influenza: The Story of the Deadliest Pandemic in History* (London: Penguin, 2005)

Bartkowski, Frances, *Feminist Utopias* (Lincoln, NE: University of Nebraska Press, 1989)

Batchelor, John, *H.G. Wells* (Cambridge: Cambridge University Press, 1985)

Bates, A.W.H., *Anti-Vivisection and the Profession of Medicine: A Social History* (Basingstoke: Palgrave Macmillan, 2017)

Bätschmann, Oskar and Pascal Griener, *Hans Holbein* (London: Reaktion, 1997)

Baynes, Kenneth, 'Toward a Political Conception of Human Rights', *Philosophy and Social Criticism*, 35 (2009), 371–90

Beaumont, Matthew, *Utopia, Ltd.: Ideologies of Social Dreaming in England 1870–1900* (London: Haymarket, 2009)

Beecher, Jonathan, 'Women's Rights and Women's Liberation in Charles Fourier's Early Writings', in *Utopian Moments: Reading Utopian Texts*, ed. by Miguel A. Ramiro Avilés and J.C. Davis (London: Bloomsbury Academic, 2012), pp. 92–98

Bell, David M., *Rethinking Utopia: Place, Power, Affect* (London: Routledge, 2017)

Bellamy, Edward, *Looking Backward: 2000–1887*, ed. by Matthew Beaumont (Oxford: Oxford University Press, 2009)

Benjamin, Walter, *Illuminations*, ed. by Hannah Arendt, trans. by Harry Zohn (London: Jonathan Cape, 1970)

Bernier, Marie Louise, *Journey Through Utopia* (London: Routledge & Kegan Paul, 1950)

Billington, Michael, *Harold Pinter*, rev. edn (London: Faber and Faber, 2007)

Bingham, Dennis, *Acting Male: Masculinities in the Films of James Stewart, Jack Nicholson and Clint Eastwood* (New Brunswick, NJ: Rutgers University Press, 1994)

Bloch, Ernst, *Natural Law and Human Dignity*, trans. by Dennis J. Schmidt (Cambridge, MA: MIT Press, 1984)

Bloch, Ernst, *The Principle of Hope*, trans. by Neville Plaice, Stephen Plaice and Paul Knight, 3 vols (Cambridge, MA: MIT Press, 1986)

Bloch, Ernst, *The Utopian Function of Art and Literature: Selected Essays*, trans. by Jack Zipes and Frank Mecklenburg (Cambridge, MA: MIT Press, 1988)

Booker, M. Keith, *The Post-Utopian Imagination: American Culture in the Long 1950s* (Westport, CT: Greenwood Press, 2002)

Bothwell, Robert, *The Penguin History of Canada* (Toronto: Penguin Canada, 2007)

Bowker, Margaret, 'Roper [More], Margaret (1505-1544)', *Oxford Dictionary of National Biography* (Oxford: Oxford University Press, 2004) online edn [http://www.oxforddnb.com/view/article/2407]

Bowman, Silvia E., *The Year 2000: A Critical Biography of Edward Bellamy* (New York: Bookman Associates, 1958)

Boyle, John, Fifth Earl of Cork and Orrery, *Remarks on the Life and Writings of Dr Jonathan Swift*, ed. by João Fróes (Newark, DE: University of Delaware Press, 1998)

Bradbury, Ray, *Fahrenheit 451* (New York: Simon & Schuster, 2013)

Bregman, Rutger, *Utopia for Realists: And How We Can Get There*, trans. by Elizabeth Manton (London: Bloomsbury, 2017)

Breuer, Hans-Peter, and Roger Parsell, *Samuel Butler: An Annotated Bibliography of Writings about Him* (New York: Garland, 1990)

Brockes, Emma, 'Margaret Atwood: "'I have a big following among the biogeeks". "Finally! Someone understands us!"', *Guardian*, 24 August 2013 [http://www.theguardian.com/books/2013/aug/24/margaret-atwood-interview]

Browne, Sir Thomas, *Pseudoxia Epidemica*, ed. by Robin Robbins, 2 vols (Oxford: Clarendon Press, 1981)

[Browning, Elizabeth Barrett], 'Thomas Carlyle', in *A New Spirit of the Age*, ed. by R.H. Horne, 2 vols (London: Smith, Elder, 1844), II, pp. 253-80

Browning, Gary, *Lyotard and the End of Grand Narratives* (Cardiff: University of Wales Press, 2000)

Bryan, Steven, *The Gold Standard at the Turn of the Twentieth Century: Rising Powers, Global Money, and the Age of Empire* (New York: Columbia University Press, 2010)

Bugliosi, Vincent, *Helter Skelter: The Shocking Story of the Manson Murders* (London: Arrow, 1992)

Burdekin, Katharine, *Swastika Night* (New York: Feminist Press, 1985)

Burke, Edmund, *A Philosophical Enquiry into the Origins of Our Ideas of the Sublime and Beautiful*, ed. by James T. Bolton (Oxford: Blackwell, 1987)

Burnyeat, M.F., 'Utopia and Fantasy: The Practicability of Plato's Ideally Just City', in *Psychoanalysis, Mind and Art: Perspectives on Richard Wollheim*, ed. by Jim Hopkins and Anthony Savile (Oxford: Blackwell, 1992), pp. 175-87

Busch, Justin E.A., *The Utopian Vision of H.G. Wells* (Jefferson: McFarland, 2009)

Butler, Samuel, *Erewhon; or, Over the Range*, ed. by Peter Mudford (London: Penguin, 1985)

Callenbach, Ernest, *Living Poor with Style* (New York: Bantam, 1972)

Callenbach, Ernest, *Ecotopia Emerging* (Berkeley, CA: Banyan Tree, 1981)

Callenbach, Ernest, *Ecotopia* (Berkeley, CA: Heyday, 2014)

Campanella, Tommaso, *City of the Sun: A Poetical Dialogue*, trans. by Daniel J. Donno (Berkeley, CA: University of California Press, 1981)

Carlsson, Chris, ed., *Ten Years that Shook the City: San Francisco, 1968-1978* (San Francisco: City Lights Books, 2011)

Carlyle, Thomas, *Critical and Miscellaneous Essays*, 5 vols (London: Chapman and Hall, 1899)

Carlyle, Thomas and Jane Welsh Carlyle, *Carlyle Letters Online* [http://carlyleletters.dukeupress.edu/clo/]
Carlyle, Thomas, *Works,* 30 vols (London: Chapman and Hall, 1896–1899)
Cave, Terence, ed., *Thomas More's* Utopia: *Early Modern Europe: Paratexts and Contexts,* (Manchester: Manchester University Press, 2008)
Cavendish, Margaret, *The Blazing World and Other Writings*, ed. by Kate Lilley (Harmondsworth: Penguin, 1994)
Chambers, R.W., *Thomas More* (London: Cape, 1935)
Cioffi, Frank, *Wittgenstein on Freud and Frazer* (Cambridge: Cambridge University Press, 1998)
Claeys, Gregory, ed., *Utopias of the British Enlightenment* (Cambridge: Cambridge University Press, 1994)
Claeys Gregory, ed., *Modern British Utopias, 1700–1850*, 8 vols (London: Pickering & Chatto, 1997)
Claeys, Gregory, ed., *Late Victorian Utopias: A Prospectus*, 6 vols (London: Pickering & Chatto, 2009)
Claeys, Gregory, *Searching for Utopia: The History of an Idea* (London: Thames & Hudson, 2011)
Claeys, Gregory, *Dystopia: A Natural History* (Oxford: Oxford University Press, 2018)
Clark, Ronald W., *The Life of Bertrand Russell* (London: Jonathan Cape and Weidenfeld & Nicholson, 1975)
Clayton, Tim, and Sheila O'Connell, *Bonaparte and the British: Prints and Propaganda in the Age of Napoleon* (London: British Museum, 2015)
Connor, Steven, *The English Novel in History 1950–1995* (London: Routledge, 1996)
Conrad, Margaret, *A Concise History of Canada* (Cambridge: Cambridge University Press, 2012)
Crane, R.S., 'The Houyhnhnms, the Yahoos, and the History of Ideas', in *Reason and Imagination: Studies in the History of Ideas*, ed. by J.A. Mazzeo (London: Routledge & Kegan Paul, 1962), pp. 231–53
Daly, Herman E., *Steady-state Economics*, 2nd edn (London: Earthscan, 1992)
Davidson, Arnold E. and Cathy N. Davidson, eds., *The Art of Margaret Atwood: Essays in Criticism* (Toronto: Anansi, 1981)
Davis, David Brion, *Slavery and Human Progress* (Oxford: Oxford University Press, 1984)
Davis, David Brion, *The Problem of Slavery in Western Culture* (Oxford: Oxford University Press, 1988)
Davis, J.C., *Utopia and the Ideal Society: A Study of English Utopian Writing, 1516–1700* (Cambridge: Cambridge University Press, 1981)
Davis, Laurence, and Peter Stillman, eds., *The New Utopian Politics of Ursula K. Le Guin's* The Dispossessed (Lanham: Lexington Books, 2005)
Delaney, Samuel R., *Trouble on Triton: An Ambiguous Heterotopia* (Middletown, CT: Wesleyan University Press, 1976)
Diab, Marwan and others, 'Effectiveness of Psycho-Social Intervention: Enhancing Resilience among War-Affected Children and the Moderating Role of Family Factors', *Child Abuse and Neglect*, 40 (2015), 24–35
Dickson, Keith A., *Towards Utopia: A Study of Brecht* (Oxford: Clarendon Press, 1974)
Dinshaw, Minoo, *Outlandish Knight: The Byzantine Life of Steven Runciman* (London: Allen Lane, 2016)
Donnelly, Jack, *Universal Human Rights in Theory and Practice*, 2nd edn (Ithaca, NY: Cornell University Press, 2003)

Dover, K.J., *Aristophanic Comedy* (London: Batsford, 1972)
Dunaway, David King, *Huxley in Hollywood* (London: Bloomsbury, 1989)
Duquesne, M., *A New Voyage to the East-Indies in the years 1690 and 1691* (London: Droig, 1696)
Dyck, Erika, *Psychedelic Psychiatry: LSD from Clinic to Campus* (Baltimore: Johns Hopkins University Press, 2008)
Dyer, Christopher, *Making a Living in the Middle Ages: The People of Britain 850–1520* (New Haven: Yale University Press, 2002)
Eagleton, Terry, *Heathcliff and the Great Hunger: Studies in Irish Culture* (London: Verso, 1996)
Edwards, Caroline, *Utopia and the Contemporary British Novel* (Cambridge: Cambridge University Press, 2019)
Egenes, Linda, *Visits with the Amish: Impressions of the Plain Life* (Iowa City: University of Iowa Press, 2009)
Ehrenpreis, Irwin, *Swift: The Man, His Works, and the Age*, 3 vols (London: Methuen, 1962–1983)
Erasmus, Desiderius, *The Praise of Folly*, trans. by Clarence H. Miller, 2nd edn (New Haven: Yale University Press, 2003)
Erasmus, Desiderius, *The Education of a Christian Prince*, ed. by Lisa Jardine, trans. by Neil M. Cheshire and Michael J. Heath (Cambridge: Cambridge University Press, 1997)
Ferns, Chris, *Narrating Utopia: Ideology, Gender, Form in Utopian Literature* (Liverpool: Liverpool University Press, 1999)
Fite, Warner, *The Platonic Legend* (New York: Scribner's Sons, 1934)
Foister, Susan, *Holbein in England* (London: Tate, 2006)
Formica, Serena, *Peter Weir: A Creative Journey from Australia to Hollywood* (Bristol: Intellect, 2012)
Foucault, Michel, *Discipline and Punish: The Birth of the Prison*, trans. by Alan Sheridan (London: Allen Lane, 1977)
Fourier, Charles, *The Utopian Vision of Charles Fourier: Selected Texts on Work, Love, and Passionate Attraction*, trans. and ed. by Jonathan Beecher and Richard Bienvenu (Columbia, MO: University of Missouri Press, 1971)
Fourier, Charles, *The Theory of Four Movements*, ed. by Gareth Stedman Jones and Ian Patterson, trans. by Ian Patterson (Cambridge: Cambridge University Press, 1996)
Foxe, John, *Foxe's Book of Martyrs: Select Narratives*, ed. by John N. King (Oxford: Oxford University Press, 2009)
Storey, Françoise and Jeff Storey, 'History and Allegory in Margaret Atwood's *Oryx and Crake*', *Cycnos* 22 (2006) [read online at http://revel.unice.fr/cycnos/index.html?id=607]
Freud, Sigmund, *Civilisation and Its Discontents*, trans. by David McLintock (London: Penguin, 2002)
Fromm, Erich, *The Anatomy of Human Destructiveness* (London: Pimlico, 1997)
Fry, Roger, *Vision and Design* (London: Chatto and Windus, 1920)
Frye, Richard, 'The Economics of Utopia', *Alternative Futures: The Journal of Utopian Studies*, 3 (1980), 71–81
Gilbert, Martin, *A History of the Twentieth Century: Volume 1, 1900–1933* (London: HarperCollins, 1997)
Gilman, Charlotte Perkins, *The Yellow Wall-Paper, Herland, and Selected Writings*, ed. by Denise D. Knight (London: Penguin, 2009)
Gilpin, William, *Three Essays on Picturesque Beauties; on Picturesque Travel; and on Sketching Landscape*, 3rd edn (London: Cadell and Davies, 1808)

Godwin, William, *Enquiry Concerning Political Justice: and its Influence on Modern Morals and Happiness*, ed. by Isaac Kramnick (Harmondsworth: Penguin, 1985)

Graeber, Wilhelm, 'Swift's First Voyages to Europe: His Impact on Eighteenth-Century France', in *The Reception of Jonathan Swift in Europe*, ed. by Hermann J. Real (London: Thoemmes Continuum, 2005), pp. 5–16

Graebner, William, *Patty's Got a Gun: Patricia Hearst in 1970s America* (Chicago: Chicago University Press, 2008)

Green, J.R., *Theatre in Ancient Greek Society* (London: Routledge, 1994)

Greenblatt, Stephen, *Renaissance Self-Fashioning: From More to Shakespeare* (Chicago: University of Chicago Press, 1980)

Groys, Boris, *Art Power* (Cambridge, MA: MIT Press, 2013)

Guin, Jeff, *Manson: The Life and Times of Charles Manson* (London: Simon & Schuster, 2014)

Guthrie, W.K.C., *A History of Greek Philosophy: IV Plato: The Man and his Dialogues: Earlier Period* (Cambridge: Cambridge University Press, 1975)

Guy, John, *Thomas More* (London: Edward Arnold, 2000)

Habermas, Jürgen, 'The Concept of Human Dignity and the Realistic Utopia of Human Rights', *Metaphilosophy*, 41 (2010), 464–80

Hall, John R., *Gone from the Promised Land: Jonestown in American Cultural History* (New Brunswick, NJ: Transaction, 1987)

Harrington, James, *The Commonwealth of Oceana* and *A System of Politics*, ed. by J.G.A. Pocock (Cambridge: Cambridge University Press, 1992)

Harvey, David, 'Neoliberalism as Creative Destruction', *The Annals of the American Academy of Political and Social Science*, 610 (2007), 22–44

Hawkesworth, Jonathan, 'An Account of the Life of the Reverend Jonathan Swift, D.D.', in *The Works of Dr Jonathan Swift*, 12 vols (London: Bowyer and others, 1768), I, pp. 1–76

Hayek, F.A., *The Road to Serfdom* (London: Routledge, 2000)

Hegel, G.W.F., *Philosophy of Right*, trans. by T.M. Knox (Oxford: Clarendon Press, 1967)

Higgins, Ian, *Jonathan Swift* (Tavistock: Northcote House, 2004)

Hilton, James, *Lost Horizon* (London: Pan, 1947)

Hitchens, Christopher, *Arguably: Essays* (New York: Twelve, 2011)

Hölderlin, Friedrich, *Hyperion; or, The Hermit in Greece*, trans. by Howard Gaskill (Cambridge: Open Book, 2019)

Homer, *Odyssey*, trans. by Richard Lattimore (New York: HarperCollins, 1991)

Hostetler, John A., *Amish Society* (Baltimore: Johns Hopkins University Press, 1970)

Howells, Coral Anne, *Margaret Atwood*, 2nd edn (Basingstoke: Palgrave Macmillan, 2005)

Hudgins, Christopher C., 'Three Unpublished Harold Pinter Film Scripts: *The Handmaid's Tale, The Remains of the Day, Lolita*', *Pinter Review*, no vol. number (2005–08), 132–39

Hume, David, *History of England*, 6 vols (Indianapolis: Liberty Classics, 1983)

Hume, David, *Essays: Moral, Political and Literary*, ed. by Eugene F. Miller, revised edn (Indianapolis: Liberty Classics, 1987)

Huntington, John, 'H.G. Wells: Problems of an Amorous Utopian', in *H.G. Wells under Revision*, ed. by Patrick Parrinder and Christopher Rolfe (Selinsgrove: Susquehanna University Press, 1990), pp. 168–80

Huxley, Aldous 'The Outlook for American Culture: Some Reflections in a Machine Age', *Harper's Magazine*, 155 (August, 1927), 265–72

Huxley, Aldous, *Jesting Pilate: The Diary of a Journey* (London: Chatto & Windus, 1948)

Huxley, Aldous *Letters*, ed. by Grover Smith (London: Chatto & Windus, 1969)

Huxley, Aldous, *The Hidden Huxley: Contempt and Compassion for the Masses*, ed. by David Bradshaw (London; Faber & Faber, 1994)
Huxley, Aldous, *Brave New World* (London: Flamingo, 1994)
Huxley, Aldous, *Brave New World Revisited* (London: Vintage, 2004)
Huxley, Aldous, *Crome Yellow* (London: Vintage, 2004)
Huxley, Aldous, *The Doors of Perception* and *Heaven and Hell* (London: Vintage, 2004)
Huxley, Aldous, *Island* (London: Vintage, 2005)
International Criminal Court, 'Darfur, Sudan, Situation in Darfur, Sudan, ICC-02/05' [https://www.icc-cpi.int/darfur].
Ishiguro, Kazuo, *Never Let Me Go* (London: Faber & Faber, 2005)
Jacobs, Naomi, 'Failures of the Imagination in Ecotopia', *Extrapolation*, 38 (1997), 318–26
Jaekle, Daniel P., 'Interpersonal Ethics in Ursula K. Le Guin's *The Dispossessed*', *Anarchist Studies* 20 (2012), 61–77
Jameson, Fredric, *Postmodernism; or, The Cultural Logic of Late Capitalism* (London: Verso, 1991)
Jameson, Fredric, *Archaeologies of the Future: The Desire Called Utopia and Other Science Fictions* (London: Verso, 2007)
Jameson, Fredric, 'Then you are Them', *London Review of Books*, 10 September 2009, [https://www.lrb.co.uk/v31/n17/fredric-jameson/then-you-are-them]
Jameson, Fredric, *An American Utopia: Fredric Jameson in Conversation with Stanley Aronowitz* (2014), [https://www.youtube.com/watch?v=MNVKoX40ZAo&t=1206s]
Janaway, Christopher, *Images of Excellence: Plato's Critique of the Arts* (Oxford: Oxford University Press, 1995)
Janis, Mark W., Richard S. Kay and Anthony W. Bradley, *European Human Rights Law: Text and Materials*, 3rd edn (Oxford: Oxford University Press, 2008)
Johns, Alessa, *Women's Utopias of the Eighteenth Century* (Urbana: University of Illinois Press, 2003)
Johnson, Samuel, *The History of Rasselas, Prince of Abissinia*, ed. by D.J. Enright (London: Penguin, 1985)
Johnson, Samuel, *The Poems*, ed. by David Nichol Smith and Edward L. McAdam, 2nd edn (Oxford: Clarendon Press, 1974)
Joyce, James, *Selected Letters*, ed. by Richard Ellmann (London: Faber & Faber, 1975)
Kael, Pauline, 'Plain and Simple', *The New Yorker*, 25 February 1985 [http://www.newyorker.com/magazine/1985/02/25/plain-and-simple accessed 5 March 2019]
Kael, Pauline, *Deeper into the Movies: The Essential Kael Collection, from '69-'72* (London: Marion Boyars, 1996)
Kahn, Charles H., 'Myles Burnyeat and Michael Freder, The Pseudo-Platonic Seventh Letter', *Notre Dame Philosophical Reviews*, 9 November 2015 [https://ndpr.nd.edu/news/the-pseudo-platonic-seventh-letter/]
Kant, Immanuel, *Anthropology from a Pragmatic Point of View*, trans. by Victor Lyle Dowdell, rev. edn (Carbondale: University of Southern Illinois Press, 1978)
Kant, Immanuel, *Political Writings*, ed. by Hans Reiss, trans. by H.B. Nisbet, 2nd edn (Cambridge: Cambridge University Press, 1991)
Kant, Immanuel, *Critique of Judgement*, ed. by Nicholas Walker, trans. by James Creed Meredith (Oxford: Oxford University Press, 2007)
Kaplan, Fred, *Thomas Carlyle: A Biography* (Cambridge: Cambridge University Press, 1983)
Karyotis, Georgios, and Roman Gerodimos, eds., *The Politics of Extreme Austerity: Greece in the Eurozone Crisis* (Basingstoke: Palgrave Macmillan, 2015)

Kemp, Peter, *H.G. Wells and the Culminating Ape: Biological Imperatives and Imaginative Obsessions* (Basingstoke: Macmillan, 1996)
Kermode, Frank, *The Sense of an Ending: Studies in the Theory of Fiction with a New Epilogue* (Oxford: Oxford University Press, 2000)
Kesey, Ken, *One Flew Over the Cuckoo's Nest* (London: Penguin, 2005)
Knight, Richard Payne, *An Analytical Inquiry into the Principles of Taste*, 2nd edn (London: Payne and White, 1805)
Kraut, Richard, ed., *The Cambridge Companion to Plato* (Cambridge: Cambridge University Press, 1992)
Kraybill, Donald B., *Riddle of Amish Culture*, rev. edn (Baltimore: Johns Hopkins University Press, 2001)
Kristeller, P.O., 'Thomas More as a Renaissance Humanist', *Moreana; Thomas More and Renaissance Studies*, 65–66 (1980), 5–22
Kraynak, Robert, 'A Revolution in Plato Scholarship', *Perspectives on Political Science*, 40 (2011), 188–91
Kumar, Krishan, *Utopia and Anti-Utopia in Modern Times* (Oxford: Blackwell, 1987)
Kumar, Krishan, *Utopianism* (Milton Keynes: Open University Press, 1991)
Larsen, Janet Karsten, 'Margaret Atwood's Testaments: Resisting the Gilead Within', *The Christian Century*, 20–27 May 1987, 496–98
Lee, David, 'The Ghost Town of Gantries', *Time*, 15 April 1974, 33
Le Fanu, Mark, *The Cinema of Andrei Tarkovsky* (London: British Film Institute, 1987)
Le Guin, Ursula K., *The Left Hand of Darkness* (London: Orbit 1992)
Le Guin, Ursula K., *The Lathe of Heaven* (London: Gollancz, 2001)
Le Guin, Ursula K, *The Dispossessed* (London: Gollancz, 2002)
Le Guin, Ursula K., *The Word for World is Forest* (London: Gollancz, 2015)
Le Guin, Ursula K., *Always Coming Home* (London: Gollancz, 2016)
Le Guin, Ursula K., 'A Non-Euclidian View of California as a Cold Place to Be', in Thomas More, *Utopia* (London: Verso, 2016), pp. 163–94
Le Guin, Ursula K., 'Utopiyin, Utopiyang', in Thomas More, *Utopia* (London: Verso, 2016), pp. 195–98
Le Guin, Ursula K., 'The Ones who Walk away from Omelas', in *The Unreal and the Real: Selected Stories*, 2 vols (New York: Simon & Schuster, 2016), II, *Outer Space, Inner Lands*, pp. 1–8
Leibniz, G.W., *Theodicy: Essays on the Goodness of God the Freedom of Man and the Origin of Evil*, ed. by Austen Farrer, trans. by E.M. Huggard (Chicago: Open Court, 1990)
Leranbaum, Miriam, *Alexander Pope's 'Opus Magnum', 1729–1744* (Oxford: Clarendon Press, 1977)
Levin, Susan B., *The Ancient Quarrel between Philosophy and Poetry Revisited: Plato and the Greek Literary Tradition* (Oxford: Oxford University Press, 2001)
Levitas, Ruth, *The Concept of Utopia* (New York: Philip Allan, 1990)
Levitas, Ruth, *Utopia as Method: The Imaginary Reconstitution of Society* (Basingstoke: Palgrave Macmillan, 2013)
Liddell, H.G. and R. Scott, *Greek-English Lexicon*, 7th edn (Oxford: Clarendon Press, 1883)
Lipow, Arthur, *Authoritarian Socialism in America: Edward Bellamy & the Nationalist Movement* (Berkeley: University of California Press, 1982)
Livi-Bacci, Massimo, *A Concise History of World Population*, trans. by Carl Ipsen, 2nd edn (Oxford: Blackwell, 1997)
Logan, George M., *The Meaning of More's 'Utopia'* (Princeton: Princeton University Press, 1983)

Logson, John M., *After Apollo? Richard Nixon and the American Space Program* (New York: Palgrave Macmillan, 2015)

Lukács, Georg, *The Historical Novel*, trans. by Hannah and Stanley Mitchell (London: Merlin, 1989)

Lyotard, Jean-François, *The Postmodern Condition: A Report on Knowledge*, trans. by Geoff Bennington and Brian Massumi (Manchester: Manchester University Press, 1984)

MacCarthy, Fiona, 'Morris, William (1834–1896), designer, author, and visionary socialist' *Oxford Dictionary of National Biography* [http://www.oxforddnb.com/view/10.1093/ref:odnb/9780198614128.001.0001/odnb-9780198614128-e-19322]

MacCarthy, Fiona, *William Morris: A Life for our Time* (London: Faber & Faber, 1994)

MacCarthy, Fiona, *Anarchy and Beauty: William Morris and his Legacy, 1860–1960* (London: National Portrait Gallery, 2014).

McGowan, John P., 'Looking at the (Alter)natives: Peter Weir's *Witness*', *Chicago Review*, 35 (1986), 36–47

MacIntyre, Alasdair, *After Virtue: A Study in Moral Theory*, 2nd edn (London: Duckworth, 1985)

MacIntyre, Alasdair, *Whose Justice? Which Rationality?* (London: Duckworth, 1988)

Mackenzie, Norman, and Jeanne Mackenzie, *The Time Traveller: The Life of H.G. Wells* (London: Weidenfeld and Nicholson, 1973)

Mandeville, Bernard, *The Fable of the Bees; or, Private Vices, Publick Benefits*, commentary by F.B. Kaye, 2 vols (Indianapolis: Liberty Fund, 1988)

Manley, Delarivier, *The New Atlantis*, ed. by Ros Ballaster (London: Penguin, 1992)

Mannheim, Karl, *Ideology and Utopia: An Introduction to the Sociology of Knowledge*, trans. by Louis Wirth and Edward Shils (New York: Harvest, [c. 1965])

Mantel, Hilary, *Wolf Hall* (London: Fourth Estate, 2010)

Manuel, Frank E., *The Prophets of Paris* (Cambridge, MA: Harvard University Press, 1962)

Manuel, Frank E., and Fritzie P. Manuel, *Utopian Thought in the Western World* (Cambridge, MA: Belknap Press, 1979)

Marcuse, Herbert, *Eros and Civilisation: A Philosophical Inquiry into Freud* (London: Ark, 1987)

Marcuse, Herbert, *One-Dimensional Man*, 2nd edn (London: Beacon Press, 1991)

Marius, Richard, *Thomas More* (London: Collins, 1985)

Mars Jones, Adam, 'Where Women Grow on Trees', *The Observer*, 17 September 2000, review section

Marshall, Jim, *The Haight: Love, Rock, and Revolution* (San Rafael, CA: Insight Editions, 2014)

Martin, Rex, and David A. Reidy, eds., *Rawls's Laws of Peoples: A Realistic Utopia?* (Malden, MA: Blackwell, 2006)

Marx, Karl, *Later Political Writings*, ed. and trans. by Terrell Carver (Cambridge: Cambridge University Press, 1996)

Masten, A.S., and A.J. Narayan, 'Child Development in the Context of Disaster, War, and Terrorism: Pathways of Risk and Resilience', *Annual Review of Psychology*, 63 (2012), 227–57

McCarthy, Mary, 'Breeders, Wives and Unwomen', *The New York Times*, 9 February 1986, 1, 35

McCrudden, Christopher, 'Human Dignity and Judicial Interpretation of Human Rights', *European Journal of International Law* 19 (2008), 655–724

McCutcheon, Elizabeth, *My Dear Peter: The Ars Poetica and Hermeneutics for More's Utopia* (Angers: Moreana, 1983)

McGilligan, Patrick, *Clint: The Life and Legend* (London: HarperCollins, 1999)
Mellor, Anne K., *English Romantic Irony* (Cambridge, MA: Harvard University Press, 1980)
Mezciems, Jenny, 'The Unity of Swift's "Voyage to Laputa": Structure as Meaning in Utopian Fiction', *MLR*, 72 (1977), 1–21
Michael, Magali Cornier, *Feminism and the Postmodern Impulse: Post World War II Fiction* (Albany: State University of New York Press, 1996)
Mill, John Stuart, *On Liberty* and *Considerations of Representative Government*, ed. by R.B. McCallum (Oxford: Blackwell, 1945)
Milton, John, *Areopagitica and Other Writings*, ed. by Edward Poole (London: Penguin, 2014)
Milton, John, *Paradise Lost*, ed. by Alastair Fowler, rev. 2nd edn (Harlow: Pearson Education, 2007)
Monk, Ray, *Inside the Centre: The Life of J. Robert Oppenheimer* (London: Vintage Digital, 2012)
More, Thomas, *Latin Poems*, ed. and trans. by Clarence H. Miller and others, *The Complete Works of St. Thomas More* (New Haven: Yale University Press, 1984)
More, Thomas, *The Tower Works: Devotional Writings*, ed. by Garry E. Haupt (New Haven: Yale University Press, 1980)
More, Thomas, *Utopia*, ed. by Edward Surtz, S.J. and J.H. Hexter, *The Complete Works of St. Thomas More* (New Haven: Yale University Press, 1965)
More, Thomas, *Utopia: Latin Text and English Translation*, ed. by George Logan, Robert M. Adams, and Clarence H. Miller, trans. by Robert M. Adams (Cambridge: Cambridge University Press, 1995)
More, Thomas, *The Confutation of Tyndale's Answer*, ed. by Louis A. Schuster and others, 3 vols, *The Complete Works of Sir Thomas More* (Yale: Yale University Press, 1973)
Morris William, *Collected Letters*, ed. by Norman Kelvin, 4 vols (Princeton: Princeton University Press, 1984–96)
Morris, William *Collected Works*, ed. by May Morris, 24 volumes (London: Longmans Green, 1910–1915)
Morris, William, *News from Nowhere and Other Writings*, ed. by Clive Wilmer (London: Penguin, 1993)
Morton, A.L., *The English Utopia* (London: Lawrence & Wishart, 1969)
Moylan, Tom, *Demand the Impossible: Science Fiction and the Utopian Imagination* (London: Methuen, 1986)
Moylan, Tom, *Scraps of the Untainted Sky: Science Fiction, Utopia, Dystopia* (Boulder, CO: Westview Press, 2000)
Moyn, Samuel, *The Last Utopia: Human Rights in History* (Cambridge, MA: Belknap Press, 2012)
Muir, John, *Journeys in the Wilderness: A John Muir Reader* (Edinburgh: Birlinn, 2009)
Muižnieks Nils, 'Addressing the Needs of the Victims of the Srebrenica Genocide must be the Priority', Commissioner for Human Rights, Council of Europe, 7 July 2015 [https://www.coe.int/en/web/commissioner/-/addressing-the-needs-of-the-victims-of-the-srebrenica-genocide-must-be-the-priority]
Murdoch, Iris, *The Fire and the Sun: Why Plato Banished the Artists* (Oxford: Oxford University Press, 1977)
Murray, Nicholas, *Aldous Huxley: An English Intellectual* (London Abacus, 2009)
Narborough, Sir John, and others, *An Account of Several Late Voyages & Discoveries* [...] (London: Smith and Walford, 1694)

Nelson, Eric, *The Greek Tradition in Republican Thought* (Cambridge: Cambridge University Press, 2004)
Nietzsche, Friedrich, *The Birth of Tragedy and Other Writings*, ed. by Raymond Geuss, trans. by Ronald Speirs (Cambridge: Cambridge University Press, 1999)
Nietzsche, Friedrich, *Thus Spoke Zarathustra*, trans. by R. J. Hollingdale (London: Penguin, 1974)
Novotný, František, *The Posthumous Life of Plato* (The Hague: Martinus Nijhoff, 1977)
Nozick, Robert, *Anarchy, State, and Utopia* (Oxford: Blackwell, 1974)
O'Neill, William L., *Coming Apart: An Informal History of America in the 1960's* (Chicago: Ivan R. Dee, 2005)
Ogle, Thomas, 'George-Monck Berkeley's *Literary Relics*', *The Monthly Review*, 2nd series, 3 (1790), 242
Orrieux, Claude, and Pauline Schmitt Pantel, *A History of Ancient Greece*, trans. by Janet Lloyd (Oxford: Blackwell, 1999)
Orwell, George, *The Collected Essays, Journalism and Letters: Volume 4, In Front of Your Nose*, ed. by Sonia Orwell and Ian Angus (Harmondsworth: Penguin, 1971)
Orwell, George, *Nineteen Eighty-Four* (London: Penguin, 1989)
Orwell, George, *Coming Up for Air* (London: Penguin, 2000)
Orwell, George, *Essays* (London: Penguin, 2000)
Orwell, George, *Homage to Catalonia* (London: Penguin, 2000)
Orwell, George, *Keep the Aspidistra Flying* (London: Penguin, 2000)
Orwell, George, *Animal Farm: A Fairy Story* (London: Penguin, 2013)
Orwell, George, *Seeing Things as They Are: Selected Journalism and Other Writings*, ed. by Peter Davison (London: Harvill Secker, 2014)
Owen, Robert, *A New View on Society and Other Writings*, ed. by Gregory Claeys (London: Penguin, 1991)
Parrinder, Patrick, 'Imagining the Future: Zamyatin and Wells', *Science Fiction Studies*, 1 (1973) [https://www.depauw.edu/sfs/backissues/1/parrinder1art.htm]
Parrinder, Patrick, ed., *H.G. Wells: The Critical Heritage* (London: Routledge & Kegan Paul, 1972)
Passmann, Dirk F. and Heinz J. Vienken, *The Library and Reading of Jonathan Swift: A Bio-Bibliographical Handbook*, 4 vols (Frankfurt am Main: Peter Lang, 2003)
Pater, Walter, *Plato and Platonism* (London: Macmillan, 1893)
Patterson, James, *America in the Twentieth Century: A History*, 5th edn (Belmont, CA: Thomson Wadsworth, 2000)
Pearl, Jason H., *Utopian Geographies and the Early English Novel* (Charlottesville: University of Virginia Press, 2014)
Pearson, Allison, 'Review of *The Blind Assassin*', *Daily Telegraph*, 16 September 2000, Supplement, 03
Pearson, Roger, *Voltaire Almighty: A Life in Pursuit of Freedom* (London: Bloomsbury, 2005)
Perry, Charles, *The Haight-Ashbury: A History* (New York: Wenner Books, 2005)
Peterson, William, *Malthus* (London: Heinemann, 1979)
Piercy, Marge, *Small Changes* (Greenwich, CT: Fawcett, 1973)
Piercy, Marge, *Vida* (New York: Summit, 1979)
Piercy, Marge, *Woman on the Edge of Time* (London: Women's Press, 1979)
Piercy, Marge, *Braided Lives* (Harmondsworth: Penguin, 1982)
Piketty, Thomas, *Capital in the Twenty-First Century* trans. by Arthur Goldman (Cambridge, MA: Belknap Press, 2014)

Plato, *Laws*, ed. and trans. by Trevor J. Saunders (Harmondsworth: Penguin, 1975)
Plato: Complete Works, ed. by John M. Cooper (Indianapolis: Hackett, 1997)
Plimtpon, George, ed., *Writers at Work: The Paris Review Interviews*, 2nd series (New York: Viking, 1963)
Pohl, Nicole, *Women, Space and Utopia, 1600–1800* (Aldershot: Ashgate, 2006)
Pohl, Nicole, 'The Quest for Utopia in the Eighteenth Century', *Literature Compass*, 5 (2008), 685–706
Pohl, Nicole, 'Utopianism after More: The Renaissance and Enlightenment', in *The Cambridge Companion to Utopian Literature* ed. by Gregory Claeys (Cambridge: Cambridge University Press, 2010), pp. 51–78
Pope, Alexander, *An Essay on Man*, ed. by Maynard Mack, Twickenham Edition of the Works of Alexander Pope (London: Methuen, 1950)
Pope, Alexander, *An Essay on Man*, ed. by Tom Jones (Princeton: Princeton University Press, 2016)
Popper, Karl, *The Open Society and its Enemies*, 8th edn (London: Routledge, 2002)
Price, Uvedale, *An Essay on the Picturesque, as Compared with the Sublime and Beautiful; and, on the Use of Studying Pictures, for the Purpose of Improving Real Landscape* (London: Robson, 1796)
Rawls, John, *A Theory of Justice*, rev. edn (Cambridge, MA: Belknap Press, 1999)
Rawson, Claude, ed., *The Character of Swift's Satire: A Revised Focus* (Newark, NJ: University of Delaware Press, 1983)
Rawson, Claude, *God, Gulliver, and Genocide: Barbarism and the European Imagination, 1492–1945* (Oxford: Oxford University Press, 2001)
Rees, Christine, *Utopian Imagination and Eighteenth-Century Fiction* (Harlow: Longman, 1996)
Richardson, Peter, *No Simple Highway: A Cultural History of the Grateful Dead* (New York: St Martin's Press, 2015)
Roper, William, *The Life of Sir Thomas More*, in *Two Early Tudor Lives*, ed. by Richard S. Sylvester and Davis P. Harding (New Haven: Yale University Press, 1962), pp. 195–254
Rothman, Hal K., *The Greening of a Nation? Environmentalism in the United States since 1945* (Belmont CA: Wadsworth, 1998)
Rowlands, John, *Holbein: The Paintings of Hans Holbein the Younger* (Boston: Godine, 1985)
Ruskin, John, *Fors Clavigera: Letters to the Workmen and Labourers of Great Britain*, ed. by Dinah Birch (Edinburgh: Edinburgh University Press, 2000)
Ruskin, John, *'A new and noble school': Ruskin and the Pre-Raphaelites*, ed. by Steven Wildman (London: Pallas Athene, 2012).
Russ, Joanna, *The Female Man* (London: Gollancz, c. 2011)
Ryskamp, Charles, and others, *Paintings from the Frick Collection* (New York: Frick Collection, 1990)
Sage, Lorna, 'Projections from a Messy Present', *TLS*, 21 March 1986, 307
Saint-Simon, Henri, *Selected Writings on Science, Industry and Social Organisation*, ed. and trans. by Keith Taylor (London: Croom Helm, 1975)
Salmon, Nicholas, 'The Political Activist', in *William Morris*, ed. by Linda Parry (London: Philip Wilson, 1996), pp. 58–65
Sargent, Lyman Tower, *Utopianism: A Very Short Introduction* (Oxford: Oxford University Press, 2010)
Sargent, Lyman Tower, *Utopian Literature in English: An Annotated Bibliography from 1516 to the Present* (University Park, PA: Penn State Libraries Open Publishing, 2016) [https://openpublishing.psu.edu/utopia/]

Sarris, Andrew, 'Don Siegel: The Pro among the Pod People', *Film Comment*, September-October 1991, 34–38
Scheff, Thomas J., *Being Mentally Ill: A Sociological Theory* (Chicago: Aldine, 1966)
Schimmel, Noam, 'A Safe Place to Call Home: Securing the Right of Rwandan Genocide Survivors to Resettlement outside Rwanda', *The Journal of Humanitarian Assistance*, 4 April 2010 [https://sites.tufts.edu/jha/archives/688]
Schlögel, Karl, *Moscow, 1937*, trans. by Rodney Livingston (Cambridge: Polity, 2014)
Schofield, Malcolm, 'The Noble Lie', in *The Cambridge Companion to Plato's Republic*, ed. by G.R.F. Ferrari (Cambridge: Cambridge University Press, 2007), pp. 138–64
Schopenhauer, Arthur, *Pararega and Paralipomena*, trans. by E.F.J. Payne, 2 vols (Oxford: Clarendon Press, 1974)
Scott, Sir Walter, 'Memoirs of Jonathan Swift D.D.', in *Works of Jonathan Swift*, ed. by Sir Walter Scott, 2nd edn, 19 vols (London: Bickers & Son, 1883), I, pp. 1–464
Searle, G. R., 'Socialism and Malthusianism in Late Victorian and Edwardian Britain', in *Malthus: Past and Present*, ed. by Jacques Dupâquier, Antoinette Fauve-Chamoux and Eugene Grebenik (London: Academic Press, 1983), pp. 341–56
Shaffer, Elinor S., *Erewhons of the Eye: Samuel Butler as Painter, Photographer and Art Critic* (London: Reaktion, 1988)
Shands, Kerstin W., *The Repair of the World: The Works of Marge Piercy* (Westport, CT: Greenwood Press, 1994)
Sharpe, J.A., 'Economy and Society' in *The Sixteenth Century*, ed. by Patrick Collinson, Short Oxford History of the British Isles (Oxford: Oxford University Press, 2002), pp. 17–44
Shelley, Percy Bysshe, *Shelley's Prose; or, The Trumpet of a Prophecy*, ed. by David Lee Clark (London: Fourth Estate, 1988)
Segal, Howard P., *Utopias: A Brief History from Ancient Writings to Virtual Communities* (Chichester: Wiley-Blackwell, 2012)
Skinner, B.F., *Walden Two* (New York: Macmillan, 1960)
Skinner, Quentin, 'Sir Thomas More's *Utopia* and the Language of Renaissance Humanism', in *The Language of Political Theory in Early Modern Europe*, ed. by Anthony Pagden (Cambridge: Cambridge University Press, 1987), pp. 123–58
Skinner, Quentin, *The Foundations of Modern Political Thought*, 2 vols (Cambridge: Cambridge University Press, 1998)
[Smedley Jonathan], *Gulliveriana: or, a Fourth Volume of Miscellanies* (London: Roberts, 1728)
Smith, Adam, *The Wealth of Nations, Books I–III* (London: Penguin, 1986)
[Smith, William Henry], 'Past and Present by Carlyle', *Blackwood's Edinburgh Magazine*, 54 (1843), 121–38
Snyder, Katherine V., '"Time to go": The Post-apocalyptic and the Post-traumatic in Margaret Atwood's *Oryx and Crake*', *Studies in the Novel*, 43 (2011), 470–89
Sorenson, David R., 'Swift, Jonathan', in the *Carlyle Encyclopedia*, ed. by Mark Cumming (Madison: Fairleigh Dickinson University Press, 2004), pp. 456–57.
Spinoza, Baruch, *Collected Works*, ed. and trans. by Edwin Curley, 2 vols (Princeton, NJ: University of Princeton Press, 2016)
Spivack, Charlotte, *Ursula K. Le Guin* (Boston: Twayne, 1984)
Srinivasan, Amia, 'The Imperfect is our Paradise: Wallace Stevens, Kitsch, Philosophy', transcript of paper delivered in the Schmilosophy Seminar, 2013, All Souls College, Oxford, [http://users.ox.ac.uk/~corp1468/Schmilosophy_files/Schmilosophy.pdf]
St Clair, William, *The Reading Nation in the Romantic Period* (Cambridge: Cambridge University Press, 2004)

Stevens, Wallace, *Collected Poems* (London: Faber & Faber, 1955)
Stevens, Wallace, *The Collected Poems*, ed. by John N. Serio and Chris Beyers, corrected edn (New York: Penguin Random House, 2015)
Stange, G. Robert, 'Refractions of *Past and Present*' (1976), in *The Critical Response to Thomas Carlyle's Major Works*, ed. by D.J. Trela and Rodger L. Tarr (Westport, CT: Greenwood, 1997), pp. 169–80
Strauss, Leo, *The City and Man* (Chicago: University of Chicago Press, 1978)
Street, Joe, 'Dirty Harry's San Francisco', *The Sixties: A Journal of History, Politics, and Culture*, 5 (2012), 1–21
Swift, Jonathan, *Voyages de Capitaine Lemuel Gulliver*, trans. by Abbé Desfontaines (Paris, Amsterdam, 1787)
Swift, Jonathan, *Prose Works*, ed. by Herbert Davis, 14 vols (Oxford: Basil Blackwell, 1939–1968)
Swift, Jonathan, *The Poems of Jonathan Swift*, ed. by Harold Williams, 2nd edn, 3 vols (Oxford: Clarendon Press, 1958)
Swift, Jonathan, *The Correspondence of Jonathan Swift*, ed. by Harold Williams, 5 vols (Oxford: Clarendon Press, 1963–1965, reissued 2012)
Swift, Jonathan, *Correspondence*, ed. by David Woolley, 4 vols (Frankfurt am Main: Peter Lang, 1997–2007)
Swift, Jonathan, *A Tale of a Tub and Other Works*, ed. by Marcus Walsh, The Cambridge Edition of the Works of Jonathan Swift (Cambridge: Cambridge University Press, 2010)
Swift, Jonathan, *Gulliver's Travels*, ed. by David Womersley, The Cambridge Edition of the Works of Jonathan Swift (Cambridge: Cambridge University Press, 2012)
Swift, Jonathan, *Parodies, Hoaxes, Mock Treatises*, ed. by Valerie Rumbold, The Cambridge Edition of the Works of Jonathan Swift (Cambridge: Cambridge University Press, 2013)
Swift, Jonathan, *Irish Political Writings after 1725: A Modest Proposal and Other Works*, ed. by David Hayton and Adam Rounce, The Cambridge Edition of the Works of Jonathan Swift (Cambridge: Cambridge University Press, 2018)
Tanitch, Robert, *Eastwood* (London: Cassell, 2005)
Tarkovsky, Andrey, *Sculpting in Time: Reflections in Cinema*, trans. by Kitty Hunter Blair (Austin: University of Texas Press, 1987)
Temple Bart, Sir William, *Works*, 4 vols (London: Clarke and others, 1757)
Thompson, E.P., *William Morris: Romantic to Revolutionary*, rev. edn (London: Merlin Press, 1976)
Thompson, Kirsten M., *Apocalyptic Dread: American Film at the Turn of the Millennium* (Albany: State University of New York Press, 2007)
Thomson, David, *The New Biographical Dictionary of Film* (New York: Knopf, 2004)
Thoreau, Henry David, *Walden*, ed. by Stephen Fender (Oxford: Oxford University Press, 1997)
Tittler Robert and Norman Jones, eds, *A Companion to Tudor Britain*, (Oxford: Blackwell, 2004)
Treadwell, Michael, 'Swift's Relations with the London Book Trade to 1714', in *Author/Publisher Relations During the Eighteenth and Nineteenth Centuries*, ed. by Robin Myers and Michael Harris (Oxford: Oxford Polytechnic Press, 1983), pp. 1–36
Tschachler, Heinz, 'Despotic Reason in Arcadia? Ernest Callenbach's Ecological Utopias', *Science Fiction Studies*, 11 (1984), 304–17
Turovskaya, Maya, *Tarkovsky: Cinema as Poetry*, ed. by Ian Christie and trans. by Natasha Ward (London: Faber and Faber, 1989)

United Nations, *Universal Declaration of Human Rights* [http://www.un.org/en/universal-declaration-human-rights/]
Updike, John, 'Love and Loss on Zycron', *New Yorker*, 18 September 2000, 142–45
Vanden Bossche, Chris R., *Carlyle and the Search for Authority* (Columbus: Ohio State University Press, 1991)
Vatter, Harold G. and John F. Walker, eds., *History of the U.S. Economy since World War II*, (Armonk, NY: Sharpe, 1996)
Voltaire, *Candide and Other Stories*, trans. by Roger Pearson (Oxford: Oxford University Press, 2006)
Waddell, Nathan, *Modernist Nowheres: Politics and Utopia in Early Modernist Writing, 1900–1920* (Basingstoke: Palgrave Macmillan, 2012)
Wark, McKenzie, *Molecular Red: Theory for the Anthropocene* (London: Verso, 2016)
Watson, Gary M. and Hugh Rockoff, *History of the American Economy*, 10th edn (Mason, OH: South Western Thomson, 2005)
Watt, Donald, ed., *Aldous Huxley: The Critical Heritage* (London: Routledge & Kegan Paul, 1975)
Wells, H.G., *New Worlds for Old* (London: Constable, 1908)
Wells, H.G., *The Research Magnificent* (London: Macmillan, 1915)
Wells, H.G., *The Sleeper Awakes* and *Men like Gods* (London: Odhams Press, [c. 1921])
Wells, H.G., *The Shape of Things to Come* (London: Hutchinson, 1933)
Wells, H.G., *A Modern Utopia*, ed. by Gregory Claeys (London: Penguin, 2005)
Wells, H.G., *The History of Mr Polly*, ed. by Simon J. James (London: Penguin, 2005)
Wells, H.G., *The Invisible Man*, ed. by Andy Sawyer (London: Penguin, 2005)
Wells, H.G., *The Time Machine*, ed. by Patrick Parrinder (London: Penguin, 2005)
Wells, H.G., *Tono-Bungay*, ed. by Patrick Parrinder (London: Penguin, 2005)
Wells, H.G., *The Island of Dr Moreau*, ed. by Patrick Parrinder (London: Penguin, 2012)
Wells, H.G., *War of the Worlds*, ed. by Patrick Parrinder (London: Penguin, 2012)
Wells, H.G., *The Rights of Man; or, What Are We Fighting for?* (London: Penguin, 2016)
Werner, Emily, and Ruth S. Smith, *Vulnerable, but Invincible: A Longitudinal Study of Resilient Children and Youth* (New York: McGraw Hill, 1982)
White, Patrick, *Riders in the Chariot* (London: Vintage, 1996)
Williams, Kathleen, ed., *Swift: The Critical Heritage* (London: Routledge & Kegan Paul, 1970)
Wilson, Ted, *Battles for the Standard: Bimetallism and the Spread of the Gold Standard in the Nineteenth Century* (Aldershot: Ashgate, 2000)
Winter, Jay, *Dreams of Peace and Freedom: Utopian Movements in the Twentieth Century* (New Haven: Yale University Press, 2006)
Wittgenstein, Ludwig, *Lectures and Conversations on Aesthetics, Psychology and Religious Belief*, ed. by Cyril Barrett (Oxford: Blackwell, 1970)
Wolfe, Tom, 'The "Me" Decade and the Third Great Awakening', *New York Magazine*, 23 August 1976. [Read online at http://nymag.com/news/features/45938/]
Wolfe, Tom, *The Electric Kool-Aid Acid Test* (London: Black Swan, 1995)
Wolfe, Tom, *The Right Stuff* (London: Vintage, 2005)
Woolf, Virginia, *Letters*, ed. by Nigel Nicholson, 6 vols (London: Hogarth, 1975–1980)
Woolf, Virginia, *A Moment's Liberty: The Shorter Diary*, ed. by Anne Olivier Bell (London: Hogarth, 1990)
Woolf, Virginia, *Essays*, 6 vols, ed. by Andrew McNeillie and Stuart N. Clarke (London: Hogarth, 1989–1996)
Wright, Erik Olin, *Envisioning Real Utopias* (London: Verso, 2010)

Wynne-Davies, Marion, *Margaret Atwood* (Tavistock: Northcote House, 2010)
Yared, Aida, 'Eating and Digesting "Lestrygonians": A Physiological Model of Reading', *James Joyce Quarterly*, 46 (2009), 469–79
Youings, Joyce, *Sixteenth-Century England* (London: Allen Lane, 1984)
Zamyatin, Yevgeny, *A Soviet Heretic: Essays*, ed. and trans. by Mirra Ginsburg (Chicago: University of Chicago Press, 1970)
Zamyatin, Yevgeny, *We*, trans. by Clarence Brown (London: Penguin, 1993)
Zuckert, Catherine H., *Plato's Philosophers: The Coherence of the Dialogues* (Chicago: University of Chicago Press, 2009)

Index

Page numbers in *italics* refer to figures.
Italics are used in headings for names of films, television programmes and publications.

Achilles 20, 32
Ackroyd, Peter 41
Adams, Robert P. 57
advisers of princes 48
Aeschylus, *Oresteia* 26–7
aesthetic theory and practice
    in the eighteenth century 99, 108, 110, 185–6
    of Huxley 142
    and the ideal state 20, 22, 27
    of modernity 124
    oppositions of 173, 177
    summary 219
    and the transformative spirit 5
    and work 118, 121–2, 159
agriculture 46, 50, 81
America *see* United States of America
Amish people, representations of 190–2
anarchy
    of communes 159, 162
    in *The Dispossessed* 172, 173, 177
    in *News from Nowhere* 117, 118
Andrei Rublev (film) 224–8
anti-vivisection 126
apocalyptic works 198–9, 201, 202
Apollo Space Programme 169–70
apples 95
architecture
    in *The Birds* 26
    in *The Dispossessed* 173
    Morris on 112
    in *News from Nowhere* 117–18
    in *Utopia* 53
    Wells on 131, 136
Aristophanes
    in *Symposium* (Plato) 31, 33
    Acharnians 25
    Birds 25–6
    Clouds 24–5

Aristotle 19–20, 214
Armstrong, Isobel 104
art
    Carlyle on 102
    in counterculture America 159
    in *The Dispossessed* 172
    in *Island* 147
    More on 60–1
    Morris on 113, 116, 118, 121–2
    in *Nineteen Eighty-four* 153
    Plato's influence on 30
    in *Republic* 7, 21, 22, 23, 24, 27
Athens 13–14, 21
Atwood, Margaret 185–93, 195–8, 200–14
    binaries of 204
    early novels 187–8
    moral equivocation of 201
    scriptural allusions 202–3, 205–6
    Swift, influence of 88
    ustopias of 192–3, 195–6, 220
    WORKS
    Blind Assassin 208–14
    The Handmaid's Tale 185–93, 195, 207, 208
    The Heart Goes Last 208
    Life Before Man 187, 196
    MaddAddam 204, 206, 207
    Oryx & Crake 196–8, 200–3, 206
    The Penelopiad 207–8
    The Year of the Flood 203, 205–6
Auerbach, Erich, *Mimesis* 204–5
Augustine, Saint 18, 29
authoritarian regimes 11–12
Aviation Security Act, Germany 64–5

Bacon, Francis 70–1, 96
Baker-Smith, Dominic 55

Ballard, J.G., *Crash* 220–1
Bates, Alan 126
Bätschmann, Oskar 40
beaches, characters washed up on 196
Beaumont, Mathew 120
beauty
   aesthetics of 185, 186–7
   in artworks 23, 24
   Erewhon 114
Bell, David M., *Rethinking Utopia* 3, 222–3
Bellamy, Edward, *Looking Backward 2000-1887* 113, 115–16
Bertillon, Alphonse 133
biological engineering 126, 198
Blind Assassin (Atwood) 208–14
Bloch, Ernst
   influence of 5
   on *Men like Gods* 137
   on *Republic* 11–12, 20, 34
   on *Utopia* 59
   WORK
   The Principle of Hope 4–5, 218
Bolt, Robert, *A Man for All Seasons* 41, 42
Booth, Wayne 148
Boswell, James 103
Boyle, John 85
Bradshaw, David 144
Bregman, Rutger, *Utopia for Realists* 3, 222
Browning, Elizabeth Barrett 108
Budé, Guillaume 37–8
Burke, Edmund 185–6
Burns, Robert 100
Burnyeat, M.F. 22
Butler, Samuel, *Erewhon* 88, 113–15

Callenbach, Eric
   Ecotopia 164–9
   Living Poor with Style 167
Canada 213
cannibalism 84, 89, 94
Cape Canaveral, Florida 169
capitalism
   alternatives to 115–16, 166–7
   of America 4
   collapse of 120
   destructive nature of 107–8
   Morris on 110
   Wells on 128

Carlyle, Thomas 93–111
   on America 96
   Fact, notion of 106
   German works, articles on 98–9
   heroes, ideas on 100–1, 103, 105, 109
   historiography, views on 99–100, 101
   industrialisation 94–5, 107, 109–10
   justice, nature of 106
   literature 110
   monasteries 104–5
   Saint-Simonists, intrigued by 97
   social writing of 97–8, 101–2
   Swift, use of 93–4
   utopia, references to 96
   workhouses 105–6
   writing style of 107–8
   WORKS
   Battle of the Books 93
   The French Revolution 100
   On Heroes and Hero-worship and the Heroic in History 100–1
   Latter-Day Pamphlets 93
   Past and Present 93, 94, 102–10
   Reminiscences 111
   Sartor Resartus 93
   Signs of the Times 101–2
   The State of German Literature 98, 99
Chamber, R.W. 41
China 18
Christianity
   in America 179
   missionary work 126
   and Plato 28–9
   religious communities 104–5, 191–2
   scriptural allusions of Atwood 202–3, 205–6
   and *Utopia* 50, 54, 56
Cicero 28–9
cinema *see* films
cities
   Aristotle on 19
   in *The Birds* 26
   in *Ecotopia* 165
   in *Gulliver's Travels* 77
   London 117–18, 135
   in *Looking Backward* 115
   Los Angeles 161–2
   planning of 26
   San Francisco 157, 158–60, 161

Socrates on 15, 61
   in *Utopia* 50-1, 52, 53, 54, 57
   Wells on 129, 133-4, 136
Claeys, Gregory 122, 194, 195, 218
classes
   in *Brave New World* 140-1
   in *A Modern Utopia* 133-4, 136
   in *Nineteen Eighty-four* 153
   in *Republic* 15, 16, 18, 55
   slaves 55, 56-7
   in *Time Machine* 125
   see also women
clothing 52, 53, 93, 159, 181, 206
Cockerell, Sydney 121
Cold War 176
collectivism 117, 140, 146, 172, 177
colonialism 125
comedies, role of 21, 22, 24, 25-6
commoners, dispossessed 47
communes 159-60, 162, 181, 203-4
communism 2, 18, 29, 48
communitarianism 118, 122, 207
Concerning the Best State of a Commonwealth and the New Island of Utopia (More) *see Utopia* (More)
Connor, Steven 152
Conrad, Joseph 133
coprophilia 82
counterculture, American 158-63
critical utopias 174-5
Cromwell, Thomas 42, 44, 62, 96
currency *see* money

Daly, Herman 166, 167
Davis, David Brion 56
Davis, J.C. 46
deception for social control 18-19
defecation 82
Defoe, Daniel, *Robinson Crusoe* 67
Delany, Samuel R., *Trouble on Triton* 174-5
deluded principles and progressive circumstances 81-2
democracy 14, 18, 96, 200
Desfontaines, Abbé Pierre 74
dignity 64-5, 89-91
Dirty Harry (film) 157-8, 162-3
The Dispossessed (Le Guin) 170, 171-8
   anarchic and propertarian visions 173

   circularity of the story 177-8
   collectivism of 172, 177
   criticism of 173-5
   dynamics of 177
   hierarchy of 172
   influences on 171-2
   parallels to 175-6
   realism of 175, 177
dispossessed people 47
dissidents 176
domesticity of More 52
doppelgängers 135
Dover, Kenneth 25
dress and uniform 52, 53, 93, 159, 181, 206
drugs 18, 142, 145, 146, 160
Dunaway, David 144
dung 82
dystopias
   in *Island* 146
   in *Nineteen Eighty-four* 154
   and utopias 184, 192-5
   of Wells 128
   in *Woman on the Edge of Time* 182
   see also ustopias

Eagleton, Terry 86
ecological ideas 165-6, 168-9
economics
   of America 163, 178-9
   and *Ecotopia* 166-7
   and *Fable of the Bees* 74
   and *Gulliver's Travels* 77, 79, 84, 87
   and *Looking Backward 2000-1887* 116
   and *A Modern Utopia* 131-2
   and *Past and Present* 104
   twenty-first century 3-4, 199-200
   and *Utopia* 47-8, 53
Ecotopia (Callenbach) 164-9
education 15-16, 23, 54, 55, 85
Edwards, Caroline 5, 222
egalitarianism
   in *Animal Farm* 150
   in *The Dispossessed* 171-2
   in *Utopia* 52, 54
   in *Woman on the Edge of Time* 181
Eichthal, Gustave d' 97
eighteenth-century utopias 66-70
   see also Gulliver's Travels (Swift); Swift, Jonathan

enclosure, of land in England 46–7
end of utopia 217–18
Englishness 120, 150–1
Enlightenment project 66
environmental policies *see* ecological ideas
Erasmus, Desiderius 29, 42, 45
   Education of a Christian Prince 56
Eros 31, 32, 33–4, 159–60
eugenicism 18, 129, 133, 141
   see also genetic engineering
evil, permitted by God 68–70
excreta 82
extermination 77, 78, 86–7, 89–90

Fact, Carlyle's notion of 106
families
   in *Brave New World* 140
   of Britain 151
   in *Gulliver's Travels* 85
   in *Island* 145–6
   in *Looking Backward* 115
   of More 42, 43, 44
   in *Nineteen Eighty-four* 153
   poor 94
   in *Republic* 16, 19–20
   in *Utopia* 52, 54
   in *Woman on the Edge of Time* 181
farces, role of 21
feminism 167, 189
Ferns, Chris 174
film, in works of Wells 130
films
   Andrei Rublev 224–8
   Dirty Harry 157–8, 162–3
   The Handmaid's Tale 188–9
   Witness 190–2, *194*
financial systems 104
   see also economics; money
flying island in *Gulliver's Travels* 80–1
food, in *Gulliver's Travels* 80–1
Ford, Henry, *My Life and Work* 141
foreign policy 57–8, 77, 78, 87
forests 165, 166
Foucault, Michel 180
foundation myths 18
Fourier, Charles 95, 119
   Theory of the Four Movements 95
French Revolution, Carlyle on 100

Frye, Richard 166
Furbank, P.N. 147–8

Galton, Francis 133
Garcia, Jerry 160
gender 167–8, 170, 181
genetic engineering 198
   see also eugenicism
genocide 89–90
   see also extermination
German literature, Carlyle on 98–9
Germany 64–5
Giles, Peter 45, 49
Godwin, William 85, 86
   The Adventures of Caleb Williams 88
gold 131–2
Goodman, Paul 165
governance
   in *The Dispossessed* 172
   in *Gulliver's Travels* 80
   in *A Modern Utopia* 134–5
   in *Republic* 14, 15–16, 24
   in *Utopia* 50–1
Greenblatt, Stephen 41
Gregory of Nazianzus 29
grief 137, 209
Griener, Pascal 40
Groys, Boris 22
Guinn, Geoff 161
Gulliver's Travels (Swift) 73–89
   allusions to *Utopia* 76–8
   Britain depicted in 78–9
   contemporary views of 85–6
   defecation and dung 82
   deluded principles and progressive circumstances 81–2
   economics 77, 79, 84, 87
   education 85
   extermination 77, 78, 86–7, 89
   family and social organisation 85
   flying island 80–1
   food 80–1
   governance 80
   Houyhnhnms, roles of 84–5, 86–7, 89
   influence of 88
   introductory letters of 75–6
   irony in 80
   legal profession 77
   literary allusion in 74–5, 76

modernity, described in 84
More venerated in 71
More's influence on 75, 87–8
satirical writing, importance of 76
science satirised in 80
significance of 88
social idealism 78–80
travel narratives 73–4
as utopian text 66, 88
Yahoos, roles of 83–4, 86, 89
Guthrie, W.K.C. 22
Guy, John 41

Habermas, Jürgen 3, 64, 65–6, 88
Hamilton, Mary, *Munster Village* 68
The Handmaid's Tale (Atwood) 185–93
aesthetics of 185, 186–7
compared to *Witness* 191–2
Odyssey, use of 207
religious community of 192
sources for 189–90
subject of 189
ustopia of 192–3, 195
The Handmaid's Tale (film) 188–9
The Handmaid's Tale (television) 208
happiness
in *Brave New World* 142–3
in *Past and Present* 106
in *Republic* 17–18, 19
in *Utopia* 54, 55
Harrington, James, *The Commonwealth of Oceana* 67, 96
Harvey, David 2
Hayek, F.A., *The Road to Serfdom* 2
Henry VIII, king 71
Herbert, Edward, *Life and Reigne of Henry VIII* 71
heroes, Carlyle on 100–1, 103, 105, 109
Hexter, J.H. 45
Higgins, Ian 83
history, Carlyle on 99–100
Hitchens, Christopher 42
Hodgson, William, *The Commonwealth of Reason* 67
Holbein, Ambrosius 38
Holbein, Hans, the Younger
Portrait of Sir Thomas More 38, 39, 40–1

Preparatory Drawing for the Family Portrait of Thomas More, 42, 43, 44
Holocaust, anticipation of 89
Homer, *Odyssey* 204–5, 206, 207
Horn, Frantz 98
horses 87, 93
see also Houyhnhnms
Houyhnhnms 77, 80, 84–5, 86–7, 89
human rights 3, 63–6, 88, 138
Hume, David 67
Huntington, John 135
Huxley, Aldous 138–48
America, use of 141–2
drugs 146
influences on 88, 139, 141, 144
Plato, influence of 138
on Wells 129, 139
WORKS
Brave New World 139–43, 154, 194
Crome Yellow 138–9
Doors of Perception 146
Island 138, 144–8, 217
Jesting Pilate 139

idealism of Utopia 1–5
individualism 118, 134, 142, 178–9
industrialisation 94–5, 107, 109–10
interbreeding 207
invisibility 125
Irish people, satires of 81, 83–4, 86, 88, 94
irony
in *Gulliver's Travels* 80
in *Meno* 27–8
in *A Project for the Advancement of Religion* ... 80
in *Republic* 12–13, 22–3
of Swift's life 90, 91
in *Utopia* 28, 61–2
in *Wolf Hall* 44
Ishiguro, Kazuo, *Never Let Me Go* 221
Island (Huxley) 138, 144–8, 217

Jacobs, Naomi 167
Jaeckle, Daniel 171
Jameson, Fredric 22, 173, 175, 201, 219
Janaway, Christopher 24
Janis, Mark 63
Jocelyn of Brakelond 103

Johnson, Samuel 90, 103
  The History of Rasselas, Prince of Abissinia 2, 193
Jones, Jim 204
Joyce, James, *Ulysses* 82
justice, nature of
  in *Erewhon* 113
  in *Gulliver's Travels* 77, 79
  in *News from Nowhere* 118
  in *Past and Present* 106
  in *Republic* 14, 15, 17, 24
  in *Utopia* 46–7, 48, 51, 54
  in *Woman on the Edge of Time* 183
Justin Martyr 29

Kael, Pauline 158, 191
Kant, Immanuel 64, 67, 88
  The Metaphysics of Morals 65
Kermode, Frank 148, 198, 199
Kesey, Ken 160–1
  One Flew over the Cuckoo's Nest 182–3
Kristeller, Paul 45
Kumar, Krishan 128, 218

labour shortages 47–8
languages 85, 172, 181
last man on earth, stories of 196
Le Fanu, Mark 225
Le Guin, Ursula K. 170–8
  criticism of 173–5
  influences on 171–2
  WORKS
  Always Coming Home 184
  The Dispossessed 170, 171–8
  The Lathe of Heaven 170
  Left Hand of Darkness 170, 181
  The Ones who Walk away from Omelas 170
  The Word for World is Forest 170
leadership, in *Republic* 15
Leary, Timothy, *Doors of Perception* 160
Lee, David 169–70
Leibniz, Gottfried Wilhelm 96
  Theodicy 69–70, 104
Levin, Susan 23
Levitas, Ruth 5, 136, 218–19
liberated society 159–60
Lipow, Arthur 115
Lipset, Thomas 37

literary context 4, 5–6
Logan, George 44, 45, 54
London 117–18, 135
Los Angeles, California 161–2
love *see* Eros
LSD 160
Lukács, Georg 41, 175
Lyotard, Jean-François 207

MacCarthy, Fiona 110–11
MacIntyre, Alasdair 26
MaddAddam (Atwood) 204, 206, 207
Magnesia 24
Mandeville, Bernard, *Fable of the Bees* 74–5, 76
Manley, Delariviére, *New Atlantis* 68
Mannheim, Karl 58–9, 218
Manson, Charles 161–2
Mantel, Hilary 41
  Wolf Hall 42, 44, 62
Manuel, Frank and Fritzie P.
  on eighteenth century writers 66, 70
  Utopian Thought in the Western World 11, 28, 59–60, 217
Marcuse, Herbert, *Eros and Civilization* 159
Marius, Richard 41
Marx, Karl 29, 95
McCarthy, Mary 189
McCutcheon, Elizabeth 44–5
mechanisation 101–2, 114–15, 119, 122
medievalism 104, 112–13, 117
mental illness 182–3
Mescaline 146
Mezciems, Jenny 77
micro-utopias, women's 68
Mill, John Stuart 95–6
  Considerations of Representative Government 96
millennium, turn of 199–200
Milton, John, *Areopagitica* 29–30
missionary work 126
mobility of citizens 52–3, 54, 131, 132
A Modern Utopia (Wells) 130–6
  canon of utopian writing 130–1
  classes 133–4
  doppelgängers 135
  ending of utopia 217
  eugenicism 133
  individualism 134

mobility of citizens 132
narrative voice 130
population 132–3
socialism 134
sociological ideas 136
surveillance 132–3
travel to 130
world state 131–2
modernist literature 199, 211
monasteries 104–5
Mond, Sir Alfred 143
money
   in *Ecotopia* 167
   in *Gulliver's Travels* 77
   in *Looking Backward* 115
   in *A Modern Utopia* 131–2
   universal basic income 3
   in *Utopia* 48, 53
moral philosophy of *Utopia* 50, 54–5
morality in *Republic* 26
More, Thomas 37–62
   on art 60–1
   biographies of 41
   coinage of Utopia 1
   fictional representation of 41–2
   as Humanist scholar 45–6
   likenesses of 38, *39*, 40–1, 42, *43*, 44
   literary devices used by 44
   philosophy of 54
   on pride 40
   psychological state of 59–60
   Utopia see Utopia (More)
Morris, William 110–22
   Bellamy, influence of 115–16
   Butler, influence of 113–15
   Carlyle, influence of 97–8, 110–12, 122
   death of 121
   medievalism 112–13
   News from Nowhere 112, 113, 116–22
Morton, A.L. 66
Moylan, Tom 174, 182, 219
   Scraps of the Untainted Sky 195, 219
Muižnieks, Nils 90
murders, Manson 162
Murdoch, Iris 22, 27
Murray, Nicholas 148
music 159

National Socialism 2, 18
negative sense of Utopia 1–2
Nelson, Eric 58
News from Nowhere (Morris) 116–22
   art, role of 121–2
   communitarianism 118, 122
   individualism 118
   influence of 121
   justice, nature of 118
   London in 117–18
   machines 122
   medievalism 112, 113, 117
   revolution 120
   sexual relations 119
   wish-fulfilment 120
   women 119–20
   work, aestheticisation of 118
Nietzsche, Friedrich, *Birth of Tragedy* 30
nineteenth century utopianism 94–122
'nothingness' of Utopia 58
Nozick, Robert, *Anarchy, State, and Utopia* 3
Nuremburg trials 63

Ogle, Thomas 85–6
O'Neill, William 160, 162
Oppenheimer, J. Robert 176
optimism
   for the future 218–19
   of the twentieth century 199–200
   of Wells 128–9
Orwell, George 148–55
   dystopianism 154
   on *Gulliver's Travels* 88, 89
   on Swift 88, 89
   Wells, influence of 129, 149
   WORKS
   Animal Farm 150, 151–2
   Coming Up for Air 149, 150, 151
   Homage to Catalonia 150, 151
   Keep the Aspidistra Flying 149, 152
   The Lion and the Unicorn 150–1
   Nineteen Eighty-Four 88, 149, 151, 152, 153
   Wells, Hitler and the World State 148–9
Oryx & Crake (Atwood) 196–8, 200–3, 206
overpopulation, threat of 132

Paine, Thomas, *The Rights of Man* 63
Parrinder, Patrick 127
Past and Present (Carlyle) 102–10
   Boswell 103
   children, eating of 94
   Fact, notion of 106
   happiness 106
   industrialisation 107, 109–10
   Jocelyn of Brakelond 103
   justice, nature of 106
   medievalism 104
   monasteries 104–5
   work 93
   workhouses 105–6
   writing of 102
   writing style of 107–8
Pater, Walter 30
Patlock, Robert, *The Life and Adventures of Peter Watkins* 67
patriotism 18, 148, 161
Peloponnesian War 13
People's Temple 204
performance, prohibition of 21, 27
Perry, Charles 159
pessimism of the twenty-first century 200
philosophers 16, 25, 29, 50, 135
picturesque, meaning of 185–6
Piercy, Marge
   autobiographical novels 180
   Woman on the Edge of Time 179–84, 192, 197
Piketty, Thomas, *Capital in the Twenty-First Century* 3
Pinter, Harold 188–9
Plato 11–36
   readings of 28–30
   in *Utopia* 49–50
   WORKS
   Apology 24–5
   Crito 28
   Laws 23–4
   Letters 14, 23
   Meno 27–8
   Philebus 21
   Politics 19
   Republic see *Republic* (Plato)
   Symposium 30–5
poetry, educational purpose 15–16, 20–1
poetry, eighteenth century 68–9

Pohl, Nicole 68
political systems, Hellenic 14
Pope, Alexander, *An Essay on Man* 68–9
Popper, Karl 2
   Open Society and its Enemies 11, 12
population
   in *A Modern Utopia* 132
   in *Republic* 19
   in *Utopia* 47–8, 52–3
positive sense of Utopia 1–3
postmodernism 22, 207
poverty 48–9, 84, 94, 95
pride 40, 78
privacy 53, 132–3
private property 48, 53
proletariat, role of 95, 151
Promethean projects 126
prospects for utopia 217–19, 221–2
psychiatric practices 182–3

race relations
   in *Ecotopia* 168
   in *Gulliver's Travels* 77, 79–80
   in *A Modern Utopia* 133
   see also genocide
rationalism 29
Rawls, John, *Theory of Justice* 2–3
Rawson, Claude 89
Reid, Thomas 101–2
religious communities 104–5, 191–2
representative art see art
reproduction
   in *Brave New World* 141
   in *Crome Yellow* 139
   in *Erewhon*, of machines 114
   in *Republic* 33, 34
   in *Utopia* 52
   in *Woman on the Edge of Time* 181
   see also eugenicism; interbreeding; sexual relations
Republic (Plato) 15–24
   class structure 15–17
   deception for social control 18–19
   education 15–16, 23
   ending of utopia 217
   family and social organisation 16, 19–20
   governance 14, 15–16, 24
   justice 14, 17, 24

performance, prohibition of 21, 27
poetry, purpose of 15–16, 20–1
political systems 15
readings of 29–30
representative art 21, 22, 23, 24
status of the text 22–4
summary 219
and technocratic administrations 18
virtues 15, 16, 17
women 16
republicanism of Utopia 50, 51
revolution, potential for 95, 120, 151
road trips 160–1
Robinsonades 67
Roper, William 41
Rossetti, Christina, *Goblin Market* 210
Rothman, Hal 169
Rousseau, Jean-Jacques 70
Rumbold, Valerie 72
Runciman, Steven 153
Ruskin, John 111
Russ, Joanna, *The Female Man* 174–5
Russell, Bertrand 194

Sade, Marquis de 70
Sage, Lorna 189
Saint-Simon, Henri de
    Nouveau Christianisme 97
    Reorganisation of European Society 95
Saint-Simonists 97, 102, 115
Sakharov, Andrei 176
Samson, Abbot 103, 105
San Francisco, California 157, 158–60, 161
Saunders, Trevor 22
savagery, instinctual 83, 168
Schimmel, Noam 90
Schlögel, Karl 227
Schofield, Malcolm 18
Schopenhauer, Friedrich 2
science
    Atwood, use of 197
    Huxley, use of 143
    satirised by Swift 80
    Wells, use of 124, 125–6, 128, 131, 137, 148
Scott, Sarah, *Millennium Hall* 68
Scott, Sir Walter 41–2, 86, 98–9
    Minstrelsy of the Scottish Border 96
serio ludere [serious play] 37

sexual relations
    in *Brave New World* 141–2
    in counterculture America 159–60
    in *Ecotopia* 167
    in *News from Nowhere* 119
    in *Nineteen Eighty-four* 153–4
    in *Republic* 18
    in *Symposium* 33
    in *Utopia* 54
    in *Woman on the Edge of Time* 181
Shakespeare, William, in works of Huxley 142–3
Shands, Kerstin 180
sheep farming 46
Shelley, Mary, *The Last Man* 196
Shelley, Percy 30
Sidney, Sir Philip, *Defence of Poesy* 30
slaves 55, 56–7
Smedley, Jonathan 85
Smith, Colin 190
Smith, William Henry 109
Snyder, Katherine 197
social divisions *see* classes; women
social reform 95–6
socialism 2–3
    of Bellamy 115
    of Morris 113, 116, 117
    of Wells 134
socialists, utopian 95
Socrates
    on Achilles, misrepresentation of 20
    on comedy 24–5
    on ideal states 15
    on individuals 17–18
    on justice 14
    on love 33–4
    on performance, prohibition of 21
    on poetry 16
    prosecution of 14, 28
    on representative art 21, 23
    in *Republic* (Plato) 12
    rhetoric of 25
    on social control 18
    in *Symposium* (Plato) 31, 34–5
    on women 16
Solzhenitsyn, Alexander 176
Sophocles
    Antigone 26
    Oedipus 147

sovereignty of kings 48–9
Soviet Union dissidents 176
space programmes 169–70, 178
Spinoza, Baruch 29
Srinivasan, Amia 215
St Edmund's Abbey 103
Steele, Richard 90
Stevens, Wallace, *The Poems of our Climate* 214–15
Strauss, Leo 22–3
sublime, aesthetics of 185, 186–7
Surtz, Edward 45, 46
surveillance 53, 132–3
Swift, Jonathan 70–91
   dignity and 90–1
   Irish people, satires of 81, 83–4, 86, 88
   irony of his life 90, 91
   and Kant 67
   misanthropy of 86
   More, influence of 66
   significance of 87
   summary 220
   WORKS
      Gulliver's Travels see *Gulliver's Travels* (Swift)
      Hints Towards an Essay on Conversation 91
      A Modest Proposal for Preventing the Children . . . 84, 86, 88, 94, 202
      A Project for the Advancement of Religion . . . 80
      A Proposal for Giving Badges to the Beggars . . . 84, 88
      The Publick Spirit of the Whigs 90
      Some Few Thoughts Concerning the Repeal of the Test 75
      A Tale of a Tub 71, 80
      A Tritical Essay upon the Faculties of the Mind 72

Tarkovsky, Andrei, *Andrei Rublev* 224–8
technocratic administrations 18
technology, uses of 125
Temple, Sir William 71, 72
theatre festivals, banning of 21
theatrical performances 159, 172
theodicy 68–70
Thompson, E.P. 110

Thomson, David 188
Thrasymachus 14
totalitarianism 11, 128, 151, 152
tragedy 20, 21, 26–7, 214
transformative spirit 5
traveller tales 67, 73, 87
Tschachler, Heinz 168
Turovskaya, Maya 226, 227
twentieth century, optimism of 199–200
twenty-first century, pessimism of 200

United States of America
   capitalism 4
   Carlyle on 96
   counterculture of 1960s 158–64
   as future of the world 139–40
   used by Huxley 141–2
   utopian fiction of 1970s 164–84
   utopian vision of 115
Universal Declaration of Human Rights 64, 138
Updike, John 212, 213
urban conurbations *see* cities
ustopias
   of Atwood 192–3, 195–6, 220
   of others 220–1
   prospects for 222–3
   see also dystopias
utilitarianism 30
utopia, meanings of 1–2
Utopia (More) 44–62
   agricultural labour 50, 172
   architecture of 53
   Budé's letter to Lipset 37–8
   cultural activities 61
   demographic change 52–3
   domestic arrangements of 52
   dress and uniform of 52
   education 54, 55
   egalitarianism 52
   enclosure, of land in England 46–7
   England, depicted in 28
   exchange mechanisms 53
   foreign policy 57–8
   genesis of 45
   governance of 50–1
   happiness 55
   interpretations of 44–5, 46, 58–60
   irony of 61–2

justice, nature of 46, 47, 48, 51, 54
kings, sovereignty of 48–9
moral philosophy of 54–5
movement, restrictions on 54
'nothingness' of 58
origin of 'utopia' 11
philosophers, role of 50
Plato in 49–50
privacy and surveillance 53
property and ownership 48, 53
republicanism of 51
sexual relations 54
slaves 55, 56–7
society, vision of 50
summary 219–20
women 55
utopian socialists 95
Utopianism 1–5, 11

Vann Nath 89–90
vermin, use of term 80
violence 168, 183, 207, 225–6
vivisection 126
Voltaire 69, 74, 100

Walsh, Chad, *From Utopia to Nightmare* 195
war games 168
Weir, Peter 190–1
Wells, H.G. 123–49
  alternative utopias 136–7
  eugenicism 133
  human rights 138
  individual transformations 127
  influence of 129
  influences on 123, 131
  modernity of 123–4, 127
  Orwell, attacked by 148–9
  Orwell, response to 149
  overpopulation, threat of 132
  science and technology, use of 124, 125–6, 128, 131, 137, 148
  socialism 134
  utopianism of 127–8, 128–9, 138
  WORKS
  Anticipations 129
  History of Mr Polly 127
  The Invisible Man 125
  The Island of Dr Moreau 126–7, 127–8
  Men like Gods 137
  A Modern Utopia 130–6
  New Worlds for Old 133, 134, 136
  The Research Magnificent 123, 136
  The Rights of Man 138
  The Shape of Things to Come 129, 144
  The Time Machine 88, 125
  Tono-Bungay 123, 127, 136
  The War of the Worlds 125, 128
  When the Sleeper Awakes 128
wilderness 165
Wilmer, Clive 113
Witness (film) 190–2, *194*
Wolfe, Tom
  The Electric Kool-Aid Acid Test 160
  The "Me" Decade and the Third Great Awakening 178
  The Right Stuff 178
Wollstonecraft, Mary, *Vindication of the Rights of Women* 63
Woman on the Edge of Time (Piercy) 179–84, 192, 197
women
  in *The Dispossessed* 174, 177
  in *Ecotopia* 167–8
  in *The Handmaid's Tale* 185
  in *Men like Gods* 137
  micro-utopias of 68
  in *A Modern Utopia* 133
  in *News from Nowhere* 119–20
  in *Republic* 16
  rights of 63
  in *Utopia* 55
  in *Woman on the Edge of Time* 179–80
Womersley, David 74, 75, 76, 80
Woodcock, George 194–5
wool trade 46
Woolf, Virginia 123–4
work, aestheticisation of 118, 159
workhouses, Carlyle on 105–6
world states 131
Wright, Erik Olin, *Envisioning Real Utopias* 3

The Year of the Flood (Atwood) 203, 205–6

Zamyatin, Yevgeny 127